How to Do *Everything* with Your

Palm™ Handheld

Third Edition

Dave Johnson
Rick Broida

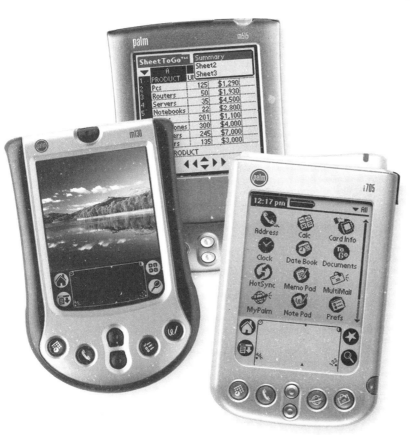

McGraw-Hill/Osborne

New York Chicago San Francisco
Lisbon London Madrid Mexico City
Milan New Delhi San Juan
Seoul Singapore Sydney Toronto

McGraw-Hill/Osborne
2600 Tenth Street
Berkeley, California 94710
U.S.A.

To arrange bulk purchase discounts for sales promotions, premiums, or fund-raisers, please contact **McGraw-Hill**/Osborne at the above address. For information on translations or book distributors outside the U.S.A., please see the International Contact Information page immediately following the index of this book.

How to Do Everything with Your Palm™ Handheld, Third Edition

Palm OS, Palm Computing, HandFAX, HandSTAMP, HandWEB, Graffiti, HotSync, iMessenger, MultiMail, Palm.Net, PalmConnect, PalmGlove, PalmModem, PalmPoint, PalmPrint, PalmSource and the Palm Platform Compatible Logo are registered trademarks of Palm, Inc. Palm, the Palm logo, MyPalm, PalmGear, PalmPix, PalmPower, AnyDay, EventClub, HandMAIL, the HotSync Logo, PalmGlove, Palm Powered, the Palm trade dress, Smartcode, Simply Palm, WeSync and Wireless Refresh are trademarks of Palm, Inc.

234567890 FGR FGR 0198765432

ISBN 0-07-222528-9

Publisher:	Brandon A. Nordin
Vice President	
& Associate Publisher:	Scott Rogers
Senior Acquisitions Editor:	Jane Brownlow
Project Editor:	Patty Mon
Acquisitions Coordinators:	Emma Acker, Tana Allen
Technical Editor:	Denny Atkin
Copy Editors:	Marcia Baker, Dennis Weaver
Proofreader:	Pam Vevea
Indexer:	Valerie Perry
Composition:	Carie Abrew, Apollo Publishing Services
Illustrators:	Michael Mueller, Lyssa Wald
Series Design:	Mickey Galicia
Cover Series Design:	Dodie Shoemaker
Palm Photos:	Courtesy of Palm, Inc.

This book was composed with Corel VENTURA™ Publisher.

Dedication

For Barbara, who's finally getting some well-deserved happiness.
—Dave

For James Stewart, a good and generous friend who reminds me that there's hope yet for humanity.
—Rick

About the Authors

Dave Johnson is the editor of *Handheld Computing Enterprise & Wireless* magazine and writes a weekly e-mail newsletter on digital photography for *PC World* magazine. In addition, he's the author of two dozen books that include *How to Do Everything with Your Digital Camera*, *How to Do Everything with MP3 and Digital Music* (written with Rick Broida), and *How to Use Digital Video*. His short story for early readers, *The Wild Cookie*, has been transformed into an interactive storybook on CD-ROM. He's also busy writing a book of family-style robot construction projects. In his spare time, Dave is a scuba instructor and wildlife photographer.

Rick Broida has written about computers and technology for over 12 years. A regular contributor to CNET and *Computer Shopper*, he specializes in mobile technology. In 1997, recognizing the Palm's unparalleled popularity and the need for a printed resource covering the platform, Rick founded *Handheld Computing* (formerly *Tap Magazine*). He currently serves as editor of that magazine, which recently expanded to include all handheld platforms and devices. Rick has conducted Palm training seminars across the Midwest. He lives in Michigan with his wife and two children.

About the Technical Editor

Denny Atkin has been writing about technology since 1987, and about handheld computers since the Newton's release in 1993. After working with such pioneering technology magazines as *Compute!* and *Omni*, he's now Editorial Director of *Handheld Computing Magazine*. Atkin lives with his wife, son, and giant Maine Coon cat in Vermont, a state where PDAs are nearly as popular as maple syrup.

Contents at a Glance

Contents

Acknowledgments

This book was great fun to write—actually, to rewrite—because of the great team at Osborne. Our thanks to Jane Brownlow, Emma Acker, Tana Allen, Patty Mon, Marcia Baker, and Dennis Weaver. We'd especially like to thank tech editor Denny Atkin, who corrected the wildly inaccurate things we wrote.

Dave: Despite the fact that Rick lies constantly about his inability to beat me at Jedi Knight II, I must thank him for being a great friend and wonderful co-author. Thanks, also, to Kris and the kids for continuing to put up with me through insane book chapter deadlines.

Rick: As much as it pains me to do so, I must once again extend my thanks to Dave, a terrific co-author, great friend and, thankfully, mediocre Jedi Knight II player. I'd also like to thank Parker, who asks "how's the book doing?" every single time we meet. Finally, thanks as always to my endlessly supportive wife, Shawna, who may one day read past the acknowledgements page.

Introduction

The Palm is such a great little device that any book about it runs the risk of reading like a promotional brochure. Dave and Rick have written thousands of pages about the Windows platform, and half of it always seems to be apologetic. "If you don't see the File menu, you need to reboot and send $94 in cash to Microsoft…." Books about computers are often more about getting it to work in the first place or explaining why it doesn't work right than about telling you what you can actually accomplish.

Not the Palm, though. It's one of the most forgiving, user-friendly, and non-crashable computers ever devised. And because it suffers from so few technical glitches, this book is mostly about doing things with your Palm—accomplishing stuff and making your life more fun and more efficient. In that sense, this is the most enjoyable writing experience we've ever had.

And what do we mean by Palm? We mean any device that runs the Palm operating system. That includes not only Palm-branded models, but also those from companies like Handspring, Kyocera, and Sony. No matter what kind of Palm device you have, this book can help.

This book starts at the beginning. If you haven't yet chosen a Palm, Part I discusses the various models and which ones best suit your needs. From there, you get a guided tour of your Palm and the desktop software. We teach you things you never knew about getting around in your Palm's apps, as well as how to share data with your PC, Mac, and other Palm devices. Having trouble with Graffiti? Be sure to check out Chapter 4, which features tons of Graffiti hints, tips, and shortcuts.

Part II of the book, "Get Things Done," focuses on accomplishing the most important kinds of tasks you need to do every day with your Palm. We show you the Palm's core applications and then tell you stuff you'd never think of—like how to get the most out of your Palm when you go on a business trip.

Part III goes "Beyond the Box," and that's where things get really interesting. Read those chapters and you will learn how to connect to the Internet, use your PDA on a long trip, and use your Palm as a complete replacement for a laptop. You will see how to manage your finances, track your stocks, and balance your checkbook. We also delve into the arts, with chapters on painting pictures and making music. You might not think there's a lot to say about playing games, but a whole world of entertainment awaits you—and we show you how to tap into it (pun intended). In fact, you might throw away your Game Boy after reading Chapter 17. And, yes, we said people rarely have trouble with their Palms, but it does happen occasionally. We have that covered as well.

We wrote this book so you could sit down and read it through like a novel. But if you're looking for specific information, we made it easy to find. Plus, you can find special elements to help you get the most out of the book:

- **How to...** These special boxes explain, in a nutshell, how to accomplish key tasks. Read them to discover key points covered in each chapter.

- **Notes** These provide extra information that's often very important to gain understanding of a particular topic.

- **Tips** These tell you how to do something smarter or faster.

- **Shortcuts** Is there a faster way to get the job done? Probably—and if there is, we'll flag it for you with a shortcut symbol.

- **Sidebars** Here we address related—and, sometimes, unrelated—topics. Sidebars can be pretty interesting, if only to see us bicker like an old married couple.

Within the text, you also find words in special formatting. New terms are in italics, while specific phrases you see on the Palm screen or need to type yourself appear in boldface.

Can't get enough of Dave and Rick? See the back page of *Handheld Computing Magazine*, where we continue our lively "Head2Head" column. You can also send questions and comments to us at **dave@bydavejohnson.com** and **rick@broida.com**. Thanks, and enjoy reading the book!

Part I

Get Started

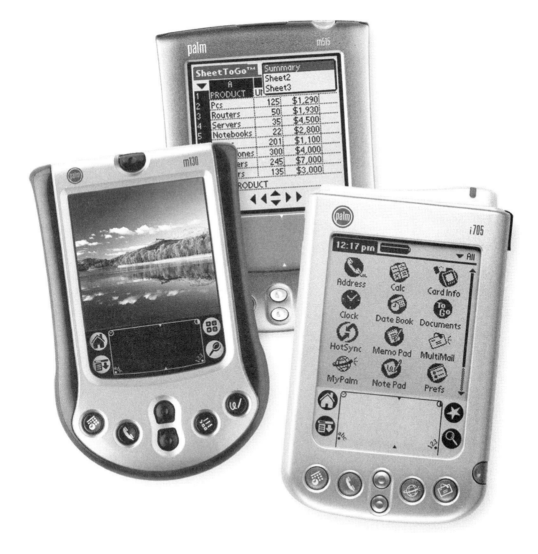

Chapter 1

Welcome to Palm

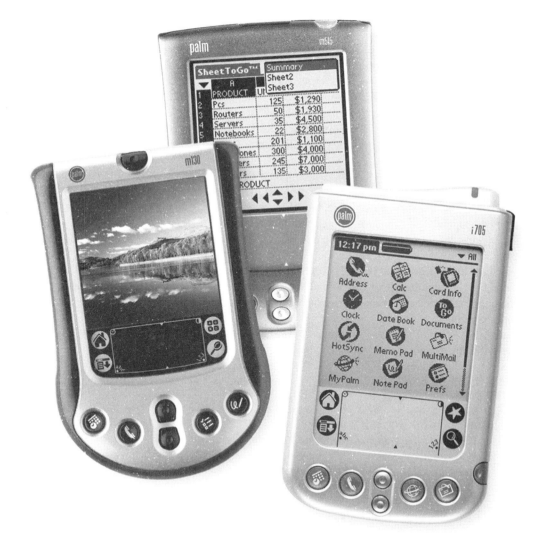

It all started with a block of wood. In 1994, Jeff Hawkins, founder of a little-known company called Palm Computing, envisioned a pocket-size computer that would organize calendars and contacts, and maybe let travelers retrieve their e-mail from the road. This idea of a "personal digital assistant," or PDA, was by no means new, but previous attempts—like Apple's highly publicized Newton MessagePad—had failed to catch on with consumers.

Hawkins knew he'd have a tough time selling the concept, so he decided to convince himself before trying to convince investors. His device would be roughly the size of a deck of cards—much smaller and lighter than the Newton—and would therefore fit in a shirt pocket. But would it be practical even at that size? Would it be comfortable to carry around? Hawkins decided to find out. Before a single piece of plastic was molded, before a single circuit board was designed, the Palm Computing Pilot (the original name of the device we're here to extol) existed solely as a block of wood.

Hawkins cut a piece of balsa wood to the size he'd envisioned for his handheld device, put it in his shirt pocket, and left it there—for several months. He even took it out from time to time and pretended to take notes, just to see if the size and shape felt right. Though he quickly came to realize that such a form factor made perfect sense, doors slammed whenever he showed the "product" to potential investors. "The handheld market is dead," was the mantra at the time.

Fortunately, modem maker U.S. Robotics didn't think so, and liked the idea of the Pilot so much that it bought Palm Computing outright. In March 1996, the company unveiled the Pilot 1000, and the rest is history.

Flash forward six years. The Pilot—which would eventually be renamed PalmPilot and then just Palm—had become the fastest-growing computer platform in history, reaching the million-sold mark faster than the IBM PC or Apple Macintosh. In the interim, U.S. Robotics had been assimilated into networking giant 3Com, and Palm Computing along with it. The Palm line had grown to include a variety of models, and companies like IBM, Sony, and Symbol Technologies had adopted the Palm operating system for their own handheld devices.

Hawkins himself departed Palm Computing in 1998—not to take up golf, not to find a new career, but to reinvent the wheel he'd already invented. In September 1999, his new company, Handspring, introduced the Visor—a licensed Palm clone that in many ways surpassed the devices that preceded it.

Today, the *Palm platform* (an umbrella term used to describe not only the actual hardware, but the operating system that drives it) is dominant in the burgeoning handheld market. Even Microsoft's Pocket PC operating system, a slimmed-down version of Windows that runs on competing handheld devices, has failed to make much headway against the Palm juggernaut.

NOTE *In this book, we discuss handhelds made by Palm, Handspring, Sony, and other companies. However, we mostly refer to them as "Palms" or "Palm devices." That's just our way of referring to all handhelds that utilize the Palm Operating System—including those from Handspring, Sony, and so forth. Thus, regardless of whether you own a Palm i705, Visor Prism, Sony CLIÉ PEG-N760C or whatever, the information in this book applies to you!*

What's the Difference Between "Palm" and "a Palm"?

It's easy to get confused between "Palm," "Palm Computing," "Palm OS," and other terms we use frequently in this book. Therefore, here's a lexicon to help you understand the basic terminology.

- ■ **Handheld PC**   A portable, pocket-size computer like the Palm m505, Handspring Visor, and Sony CLIÉ.
- ■ **Handspring**   Makers of the Visor and Treo series of handheld PCs.
- ■ **Operating System**   The core software that makes a handheld PC function.
- ■ **Palm, Inc.**   The company that makes handheld PCs that run the Palm Operating System (OS).
- ■ **Palm OS**   The operating system used in Palm, Handspring, HandEra, Sony, and many other handheld PCs.
- ■ **Palm Powered**   Denotes a handheld PC that runs the Palm OS. "Palm Powered" is a registered trademark of Palm, Inc.
- ■ **PalmSource**   The division of Palm, Inc., responsible for developing the Palm OS.
- ■ **PDA**   Short for personal digital assistant, a generic term used to describe any handheld PC.
- ■ **Pocket PC**   Microsoft's Windows-like operating system for handheld PCs. Found in devices from Casio, Compaq, Hewlett-Packard, and other vendors.
- ■ **Sony**   Makers of the CLIÉ series of handheld PCs.

What Makes Palm So Unique?

Why all the fuss? What makes a Palm OS device so special? Why has it succeeded where so many others have failed? To answer these questions, we'll first need to look at what a Palm device actually is. Put simply, it's a pocket-size electronic organizer that enables you to manage addresses, appointments, expenses, tasks, and memos. If you've ever used a Franklin Planner or similar kind of paper-bound organizer, you get the idea.

However, because a Palm is electronic, there's no paper or ink involved. Instead, you write directly on the device's screen, using a small plastic stylus that takes the place of a pen. A key advantage here, of course, is that you're able to store all of your important personal and business information on a device that's much smaller and lighter than a paper planner.

What's more, you can easily share that information with your Windows-based or Macintosh computer. Palm devices are not self-contained: they can *synchronize* with a desktop computer and keep information current on both sides. This is an important advantage, as it effectively turns your

Palm device into an extension of the computer you use every day. Changes and additions made to your desktop data are reflected in the Palm, and vice versa (see Figure 1-1).

Saying that a Palm is an extension of your PC is only a half-truth: in reality, it has evolved into a computer in its own right. That's because it is capable of running software written by parties other than Palm Computing, and those parties (known as software developers) now number in the tens of thousands. There are literally thousands of programs and databases that extend your Palm's capabilities, from spreadsheet managers and expense trackers to electronic-book readers and Web browsers. Got five minutes to kill? You can play a quick game of Bejeweled. Need to check your e-mail while traveling? Snap on a modem and dial your Internet service provider.

NOTE *While the first several chapters of this book are devoted to the Palm's core capabilities—the things it can do right out of the box—the majority of it focuses on these "extended" capabilities—the things that have elevated the Palm from a basic electronic organizer to a full-fledged handheld PC.*

Above all else, simplicity is a major key to the Palm platform's success. The devices are amazingly easy to use, requiring no more than a few taps of the stylus to access your data and a little memorization to master the handwriting-recognition software. Most users, even those who have little or no computer experience (like Dave), find themselves tapping and writing productively within 20 minutes of opening the box.

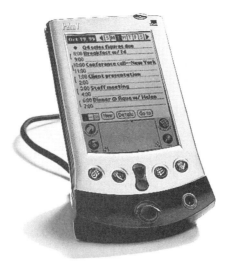

FIGURE 1-1   A Palm device connects to a PC via a HotSync cradle (or cable, in the case of the m100), which allows data to be synchronized on both devices.

An Overview of the Hardware

Whether you're still shopping for a Palm OS device or you've been fiddling with one for a month, it's good to have an understanding of the different models that exist. Originally, only Palm Computing manufactured Palm devices, but it wasn't long before other companies adopted the *operating system* for similar or slightly modified devices of their own.

What's an Operating System?

Windows is an operating system. Mac OS X is an operating system. The core software that drives any computer is an operating system. Hence, when we refer to the Palm OS, we're talking about the software that's built right into the device—the brains behind the brawn. The Palm OS itself not only controls the Palm's fundamental operations, such as what happens when you press a button or tap the screen, but also supplies the built-in applications (the address book, memo pad, date book, and so on—all of which we'll discuss in detail in later chapters).

The Palm OS is the key ingredient that links the various Palm devices, whether they're manufactured by Palm Computing, Handspring, Sony, or one of the other companies licensed to use the Palm OS.

NOTE   *These licensees have been granted permission by Palm Computing to use the Palm OS in hardware of their own design. It's kind of like the way you can get PCs from a hundred different companies, yet they all run Windows.*

You'll see that a Palm Computing m100 looks quite a bit different from, say, a Sony CLIÉ (see Figure 1-2), but on the inside they're fundamentally the same. They both use the Palm Operating System, and therefore operate in similar fashion and are capable of running all the same software.

When we refer to a "Palm OS device," then, we're talking about *any* of the various handheld devices that run the Palm Operating System. And now we're going to look at the different makes and models, because while the underlying software may be the same, the hardware often varies dramatically.

The Palm Computing Models

In the relatively brief history of the Palm line, Palm Computing has produced nearly two dozen different models, with more sure to follow. During their evolution, the devices have grown smaller and thinner, gained a few extra capabilities, and enjoyed some minor but appreciable improvements to their screens. Here's a brief history of the series, from past to present.

The Pilot 1000 and 5000

The duo that started it all, the Pilot 1000 and 5000 (see Figure 1-3) arrived on the scene in the early spring of 1996. Physically, the two were identical, the only difference between them being the amount of memory they contained.

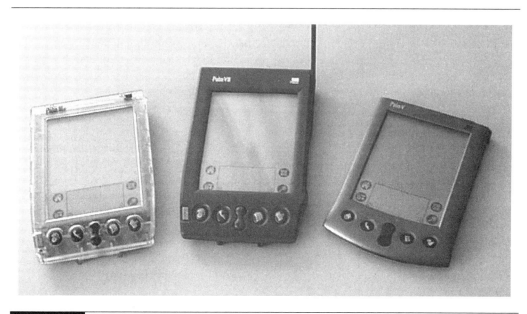

FIGURE 1-2   Palm OS devices don't all look the same, and in fact can look quite different, but they all use the same core operating system.

FIGURE 1-3   The Pilot 1000, patriarch of a large and successful family.

NOTE *The amount of RAM, or memory, in a Palm device is directly related to how much software and data it can store. More is always better, especially when you start loading up on electronic books, corporate databases, third-party software, and such.*

The Pilot 1000 came with 128K of RAM—a seemingly paltry amount, especially relative to the hundreds of megabytes found in today's computers. But that was enough to store hundreds of contact listings, appointments, tasks, and memos. The Pilot 5000 sported four times the memory: 512K, enough for thousands of entries.

In these early days, there was very little third-party software, so few users had to worry about running out of memory. But that changed in a hurry, and it wouldn't be long before the baseline standard for Palm RAM became 8MB—64 times that of the original Pilot 1000.

The PalmPilot Personal and Professional

Roughly a year after the first Pilots debuted, Palm Computing supplanted them with the PalmPilot line (see Figure 1-4). Why the name change? The Pilot Pen Corporation was understandably displeased with Palm's choice of moniker, and took their gripe to court. The result: "Pilot" was out the window, at least for Palm Computing. After the PalmPilot generation, the courts ruled, Palm would have to avoid using the word altogether.

NOTE *It is a true testament to the device that consumers have weathered two name changes. In the often-confusing computer marketplace, such alterations would spell death for many products.*

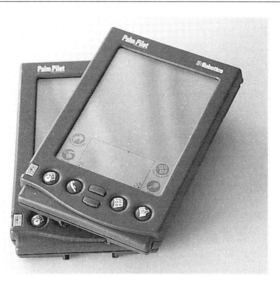

FIGURE 1-4 With their backlit screens and capacious storage, the PalmPilot Personal and Professional proved even more popular than their predecessors.

Like the Pilot 5000, the PalmPilot Personal included 512K of RAM. Unlike the Pilot 5000, it featured a backlit screen. Hold the power button down for a couple seconds, and the screen would glow green, making it visible in low-light situations. This was a major improvement, something early adopters of the Pilot line had vigorously requested. Most importantly, it meant that Dave's beloved Apple Newton MessagePad no longer had the upper hand in screen visibility, which he used to crow about every five minutes.

The real news was the PalmPilot Professional, which served up a whopping megabyte (or 1,024K) of memory, the same backlit screen, and a new addition to the operating system: Mail. This program made it possible for you to bring along copies of the e-mail messages received on your PC, and even to reply to those messages and compose new ones right on your Palm.

Around the same time, Palm Computing introduced a modem (see Figure 1-5) that could clip onto the bottom of the PalmPilot Professional. This allowed you to dial into your computer from a remote location, with the sole purpose being to synchronize Palm and PC.

NOTE   *Eventually, third-party software would be written that let you dial directly into your Internet service provider, and to send and receive e-mail using your existing accounts— no PC required. We'll tell you all about these capabilities in Chapter 13.*

The Palm III

With the proven popularity of the PalmPilots, legions of devoted users were expecting some revolutionary changes in the next model. What they got was decidedly evolutionary: the Palm III

FIGURE 1-5   The PalmPilot Modem, which is still in use today (and is now called the PalmModem), adds communications capabilities to a Palm device.

(see Figure 1-6) boasted a sleeker design, more RAM and an infrared communications port, but no built-in modem, voice recorder, or any of the other goodies that were rumored to be in the works.

Wary of feature overload, Palm Computing had decided to keep things simple. Adding a built-in modem would have compromised the Palm's prized compactness, reasonable price, and amazing battery life (up to two months on a single pair of triple-A cells). Obviously, Palm had made the right move: Despite mixed reactions from existing users and the media, the Palm III became a smash hit.

With a then-amazing 2MB of RAM, this model had room to accommodate a lot more third-party software (which was proliferating at an incredible rate). And the *infrared* (IR) transceiver seemed like an interesting idea: By pointing one Palm III at another, users could wirelessly swap virtual business cards, appointment information, even memos.

NOTE *While it sounded great on paper, this implementation of IR was risky. For starters, it assumed that the people you'd meet would also have IR-equipped Palms. What's more, it didn't conform to the computer-industry standards for infrared communication, so you couldn't, say, synchronize wirelessly with your IR-equipped notebook. But the story has a happy ending. With over 20 million Palms out there, finding "beam buddies" is not a problem. And the most current versions of the Palm OS include support for IR synchronization.*

Finally, for the *Star Trek* crowd, the Palm III came with a flip-up plastic screen shield that made it look remarkably similar to Captain Kirk's communicator. When he thinks people aren't looking, Dave likes to lean into his and murmur, "Beam me up, Scotty."

FIGURE 1-6   The slim, curvaceous Palm III brought 2MB of RAM and IR "beaming" to the table.

The Palm VII

Breaking with a long-standing tradition of not pre-announcing new products, Palm Computing announced the Palm VII (see Figure 1-7) in December 1998—about 10 months before it actually shipped. Part of the reason was to give software developers a head start in creating applications for this unique model—which would afford a wireless connection to the Internet.

Barely half an inch longer than the Palm III—but virtually identical otherwise—the Palm VII hides a two-way radio transceiver that enables it to send and receive e-mail and pull information from the Internet—all without wires. If there was one way to make the Palm significantly better, this was it.

The Palm IIIe, Palm IIIx, and Palm V

In between the December 1998 announcement of the Palm VII and its October 1999 debut, Palm Computing introduced three more new models (see Figure 1-8). Targeted at so-called "power users," the Palm IIIx served up 4MB of RAM, an internal slot that promised exciting expansion options, and a higher-contrast screen that offered much-improved visibility.

Business as usual, or so it seemed. (Save for the Palm VII, Palm Computing seemed content to keep making small, incremental improvements to the device line.) But then came the Palm V, which still ranks as one the sexiest, coolest, most lust-worthy handheld PCs ever created. Matchbook-

FIGURE 1-7   Flip up the Palm VII's antenna, and you have near-instantaneous access to e-mail and the Internet.

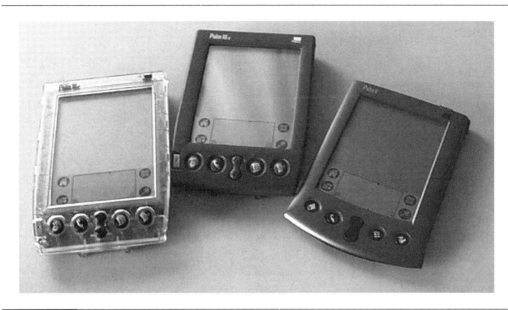

FIGURE 1-8   With the Palm IIIe, Palm IIIx, and Palm V, Palm Computing answered the call of bargain hunters, power users, and executives, respectively.

thin and sheathed in striking anodized aluminum, the designed-from-scratch Palm V dismissed all notions of geekiness and thus emerged as the "Palm for executives."

Despite having "only" 2MB of memory, the Palm V sold like hotcakes, as did the Palm IIIx. And in October 1999, with the holiday season approaching, Palm Computing unveiled the cream of the crop: the Palm Vx, loaded with a whopping 8MB of RAM.

In the interim, the Palm III was phased out and replaced with the Palm IIIe, an entry-level model priced below $200. It lacked a few bells and whistles, but had the distinction of being the most affordable model ever offered by Palm Computing. (It has subsequently been replaced with the Palm m100 series.)

The Palm IIIc

In March 2000, Palm took the next major step in the evolution of handheld computing: color. The Palm IIIc (see Figure 1-9), the first Palm OS device with a color screen, opened the door to color games, color maps, and color photographs, thus expanding the handheld's capabilities even further. It includes 8MB of RAM and a rechargeable battery, making it a compelling choice for power users. Plus, its extremely bright screen offers definite relief for those who find the other models' grayscale screens hard on the eyes.

FIGURE 1-9   The Palm IIIc can display up to 256 colors and comes with a rechargeable battery.

The Palm IIIxe

Successor to the Palm IIIx (see Figure 1-8), the Palm IIIxe was virtually identical. It had 8MB of RAM instead of 4MB, used a newer version of the OS (3.5), and came in black instead of charcoal gray. Like all members of the Palm III family, it has been discontinued.

The Palm m100, m105, and m125

Unveiled in September 2000, the Palm m100 (as seen in Figure 1-10) brought a new name, a new face, and a new price to the Palm line. At $149, it was notable for being the most affordable Palm yet introduced, and gained instant popularity among students and other cost-conscious buyers. The m100 looks like a thicker, curvier cousin of the Palm V, with a shell that's plastic instead of metal and a screen shield that flips a full 360 degrees. If you tire of the m100's color (basic black), you can swap its faceplate for a more colorful alternative (such as purple, gold, even wood).

Another nifty feature offered by the m100 series (and no other Palm device to date) is a small see-through window in the screen cover. When the unit is off and you press the Scroll-up button, the date and time appear on the screen, visible through the window. Not too earth-shattering, but a nice perk.

In March 2001, Palm unveiled a souped-up m100, the m105. It has 8MB of RAM to the m100's 2MB, and comes with Palm's Mobile Internet Kit (discussed in Chapter 13) and a HotSync cradle. Then came the virtually identical m125, which added an expansion slot to the feature set (more on that in Chapter 12).

FIGURE 1-10   The Palm m100 series features swappable faceplates that can dramatically change the look of the device.

The m100 series does have one shortcoming: their screens are about 25 percent smaller than other Palm-branded models. They're still plenty sharp, but if you have less-than-stellar eyesight, you may want to consider a different model.

The Palm m500, m505, and m515

Taking a cue from Handspring and Sony, Palm finally created handhelds with serious expansion capabilities. Introduced in March 2001 the m500 and m505 (see Figure 1-11) look like Palm V doppelgangers, but have one particularly important new asset: a small slot that can accommodate memory cards and other expansion options.

What's the difference between the m500 and m505? In a word, color. The latter sports a 16-bit color screen, a major improvement over the Palm IIIc's 4-bit screen. In early 2002, Palm addressed complaints about the m505's dim screen by introducing the m515, which offers a brighter display and 16MB of internal memory. The m505 was summarily discontinued.

The Palm m130 and i705

Whew—that's a lot of models already. At the time of this writing, Palm had recently introduced yet another pair of handhelds, each compelling in its own way. The m130 is basically an m125 (swappable faceplates, expansion slot, and so forth) with a color screen and rechargeable battery.

FIGURE 1-11   The m500 and m505 look like the Palm V, but add expansion capabilities (and, in the case of the m505, color) to the mix.

The i705 (covered in detail in Chapter 13) is Palm's next-generation wireless model, with its built-in modem and robust support for e-mail and Web access.

What Is the Universal Connector?

All current Palm models—including the m125, m130, m500 series and i705—have a feature that should please users and hardware developers alike. It's called the Universal Connector—the serial port on the bottom of the handhelds. This standardized connector helps to insure compatibility with other models, synchronization cradles, and expansion devices—something previous product lines couldn't deliver. (For example, Palm III accessories weren't compatible with the Palm V, and vice versa.) Alas, the Universal Connector is found only on Palm-branded handhelds—but we're secretly hoping it'll be adopted by Handspring, Sony, and other device makers.

The Handspring Models

Remember Jeff Hawkins, the guy who invented the Palm, then left the company to start again? He took with him a license to use the Palm OS, the intent being to build newer and better hardware around it. The result: the Handspring Visor line (see Figure 1-12).

Introduced in September 1999, the Visor closely resembled the Palm III. It was almost exactly the same size and weight—a "clone" in the truest sense—and it ran a virtually identical version of the Palm OS. (Handspring took the liberty of enhancing the appointment calendar and calculator.)

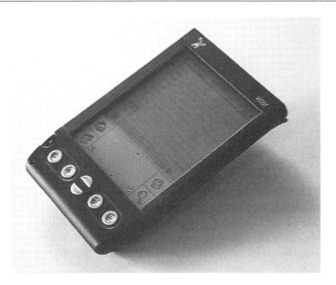

| FIGURE 1-12 | Though the Handspring Visor may look like a plain old Palm, it's different in one very important way. |

If the Visor was just a Palm III clone, why bother with it? Because it was a clone with one very important addition: a cartridge-based expansion slot (very similar to the design of Nintendo's Game Boy) that could accommodate a wide and growing variety of nifty hardware. This seemingly tiny modification, dubbed *Springboard,* allowed the Visor to double as an MP3 music player, a digital camera, a cellular phone, and much more. Thus, the Visor was akin to a Palm III on steroids, able to stretch way beyond its core functionality.

While this is a very useful book for Visor owners, there's another one that's even better: *How to Do Everything with Your Visor,* written by the same authors (McGraw-Hill/Osborne, 2001). In it you'll find more detailed information about the Visor's unique features and Springboard modules.

In early 2002, Handspring innovated yet again with the Treo, a handheld PC/phone hybrid. Find out more about it in Chapter 13.

The Sony Models

Sony's first stab at a Palm OS handheld—the CLIÉ PEG-S300—was as dull as its name. But the company rebounded big time with a series of models packed with innovative and exciting features. Among the highlights: high-resolution color screens, a Memory Stick expansion slot, MP3 playback, a "jog dial" for one-handed operation, and enhanced audio (see Figure 1-13). If you're thinking of upgrading to one of Sony's models or you already own one, we'd like to humbly suggest a little book called *How to Do Everything with Your Sony CLIÉ.* It's due in bookstores before the end of 2002.

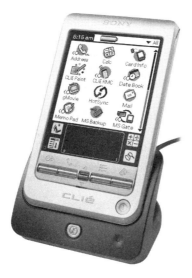

FIGURE 1-13   The Sony CLIÉ series offers features not found in any other
Palm OS handhelds

The Rest of the Models

Just as Microsoft licenses the Windows operating system to computer manufacturers, so has Palm
Computing licensed the Palm OS to other companies. That makes it possible for companies like
Kyocera Wireless and Samsung to produce devices that combine the Palm OS with a cell phone,
or for HandEra to create a Palm III-like handheld that has a CompactFlash slot (for use in enterprise
business environments).

IBM and Franklin Covey

IBM was among the first companies to adopt the Palm OS, the result being exact replicas of two
Palm Computing-manufactured models, but with the IBM logo. These business-minded models
have been discontinued.

Franklin Covey, a retail operation best known for its Franklin Planner products, took a similar
tack, offering Palm-built handhelds in different packaging and with slightly modified software
bundles. From a hardware and OS standpoint, Franklin Covey models are identical to their Palm
counterparts. However, they come with Franklin's own desktop software in place of Palm Desktop
(see Chapter 3). If you own one of Franklin Covey's models, most of the material in this book is
still applicable (and downright useful).

The Symbol Technologies Line

Another early adopter of the Palm OS, Symbol Technologies is a developer of mobile data solutions. In creating a Palm device that could scan bar codes, Symbol started with the Palm III design and effectively grafted a barcode reader onto it. The result, the SPT 1500, looked like a slightly elongated Palm III. In 1999, Symbol took the idea a giant leap farther with the SPT 1700, a radically redesigned and decidedly futuristic-looking Palm OS device. In 2000, the SPT 1733 added wireless connectivity to the mix.

Because of their scanning (and, in some models, wireless networking) capabilities, the Symbol models are suited for use in hospitals, warehouses, large offices, and anywhere else that barcodes might be in use.

The HandEra 330

HandEra (formerly TRG Products) originally entered the Palm market with memory-expansion hardware and software. In late 1999, however, the company introduced its very own Palm OS device: the TRGpro. Identical to the Palm IIIx on the outside but somewhat different within, the TRGpro had a rear socket for use with industry-standard CompactFlash cards.

NOTE   *While the Handspring Visor has a somewhat similar design, its expansion slot is proprietary, meaning it works only with devices that have been designed for the Visor. This is not a bad thing; it's just two different implementations of a similar idea. Meanwhile, the m500 series uses a third kind of technology for expansion, which is also incompatible with the other two. Welcome to the wonderful world of computers, folks.*

Next came the HandEra 330, which still ranks as one of the most advanced Palm OS handhelds to date. It includes a high-resolution grayscale screen, enhanced audio capabilities (including voice recording), a pair of expansion slots, a jog wheel, and a "virtual" handwriting-recognition area that disappears when you don't need it. Though designed with corporate deployment in mind, the HandEra 330 is a great consumer model and one of our favorite Palm Powered handhelds.

The Kyocera Wireless and Samsung Smartphones

It seemed like a natural marriage: take two devices that live in your pocket and combine them into a single, integrated piece of hardware. And so the Kyocera Wireless (formerly Qualcomm) QCP 6035 (see Figure 1-14) and Samsung SPH-I300 were born, two radically different unions of cell phone and Palm handheld.

The QCP and I300 look and operate much like regular cell phones, but with all the advantages of the Palm OS mixed in. Among them:

- You can quickly look up a phone number in your contact list, then dial that number with a tap on the screen.
- You can view a detailed history of your incoming and outgoing calls.
- You can send and receive e-mail using an included mail program.
- You can surf the Internet using an included Web browser.

FIGURE 1-14   The QCP 6035 is a cell phone with a Palm inside—or is it the other way around?

Plus, you've still got all the power of the Palm OS, so your phone doubles as your appointment calendar, to-do list, and so on. At press time, Kyocera had just introduced the 7135—a color version of the popular 6035. Samsung, meanwhile, was prepping an updated version of the I300. Look for both models if you're interested in a Palm-based smartphone, as they offer a wealth of great features.

In the meantime, see Chapter 13 for more information on choosing and operating a Palm/phone hybrid.

Where to Find the Best Prices

Everyone likes to save a buck, and with a little smart shopping you can do exactly that. Even if you're just looking for accessories like modems and spare HotSync cradles, it pays to do some research. Below you'll find a few notes regarding where and how to shop, and where to find the best deals.

NOTE *Some models are not as widely available as others. The Kyocera and Samsung smartphones, for instance, must be purchased from the cellular companies that offer service for them.*

- If you're comfortable shopping online, you can find some of the best deals on the Web. We recommend starting with a site called PriceGrabber (**www.pricegrabber.com**), which provides up-to-date price comparisons for most Palm devices and many accessories, drawn from a large number of Web merchants. It even gives you shipping costs, so you know your out-the-door total before heading to the merchant's site.

- Another worthwhile online destination: Web auctions. eBay (**www.ebay.com**) is a treasure trove of new, used, and refurbished Palm devices. Just remember to use common sense: sometimes people get caught in a bidding frenzy and wind up paying as much for a used model as they would for a new one.

- Check the Web sites for Palm, Handspring, and Sony for package deals. They often offer bundles (like a handheld with a case and keyboard) that you won't find anywhere else, and at discounted prices. Handspring sometimes sells refurbished inventory as well, and those deals can be hard to pass up.

- Another great source for inexpensive refurbished handhelds is ReturnBuy (**store.returnbuy.com**). We found a Palm V (a discontinued model, but still a sweet one) selling for $59.99 and an m505 for just $199 (a $200 savings). Just be sure to investigate the warranty policy for any refurbished item you buy. While ReturnBuy guarantees the reconditioned units to be in perfect working order, you may have to pay extra if you want a warranty—or you may not be able to get one at all.

Our Favorite Models

Rick: Well, obviously I'm partial to Charlize Theron, who's an actress now but did start out as a model, and…oh, sorry, wrong sidebar. At the moment, I'm in love with two handhelds: the Kyocera QCP 6035 smartphone and the Sony CLIÉ NR70V. Sony is really kicking out the hot hardware these days, but I can't ignore the communications acumen of the Kyocera. Sometimes I just have to carry both. If we could recreate the transporter accident from the *Star Trek* episode "The Enemy Within," perhaps we could merge these two models into one. That's what I really want.

Dave: We're off to a bad start when Rick starts referencing specific *Star Trek* episodes in the very first chapter. See what I have to put up with on a routine basis? And while I'd much rather go to the cotillion with Sandra Bullock than hang with Charlize Theron, let's focus on the issue at hand. Day to day, my PDA of choice remains a Handspring Visor Prism, now several years old. I've upgraded it to 16MB of memory and I leave a Bluetooth module in the expansion slot so it can access the Internet via my Bluetooth mobile phone. Those upgrades continue to make it the best Palm device ever. When I buy a new PDA, though, it's going to have to have a high-resolution screen, like one of the very cool Sony CLIÉ models—perhaps the PEG-NR70.

How to ... Decide Which Model to Buy

Sorry, we can't help you with this one. So many great handhelds, so few hands. Virtually every model available today—whether it's from Palm, Sony, Handspring, or any other Palm OS licensee—has its merits. The key thing to remember is that right out of the box, every one offers the same great core capabilities: contact and calendar management, easy-to-learn handwriting recognition, seamless synchronization with your PC, and access to a wealth of third-party software. With that knowledge in mind, you can focus on other aspects that you might find important: price, expansion capabilities, screen quality (color or grayscale), wireless options, and so on. In the end, you may just have to flip a coin. That's what we do.

TIP   *Auctions can also be a great way to sell your old Palm device if you're moving up to a newer one. You can also try a service like SellYourPalm.net (**www.sellyourpalm.net**), which will buy your old handheld outright.*

Where to Find It

Web Site	Address
Palm Computing	**www.palm.com**
Handspring	**www.handspring.com**
Symbol	**www.symbol.com**
HandEra	**www.handera.com**
Sony	**www.sonystyle.com/micros/clie/**
Kyocera Wireless	**www.kyocera-wireless.com**
Samsung	**www.samsung.com**

Chapter 2

Get to Know Your Palm Device

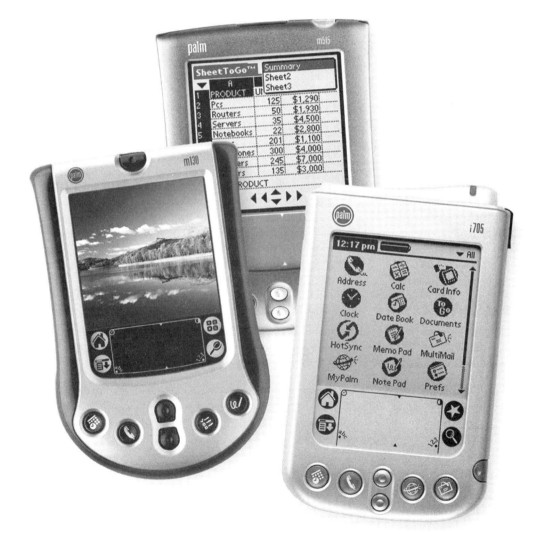

How to...

- Identify the buttons on a Palm device
- Identify the infrared transmitter
- Work with the screen and Graffiti area
- Install (or charge) the batteries
- Turn on a Palm device for the first time
- Use the Graffiti tutorial
- Reset a Palm device
- Configure a Palm device's preferences
- Reset the screen digitizer
- Work with the operating system
- Check how much memory is left
- Create and use shortcuts
- Work with Palm Desktop

Okay, enough history—it's time to dive in and start having fun. At the beginning of any lasting and meaningful relationship, you want to get to know the other person as well as possible—find out what makes them tick, what their boundaries are, and where they keep their batteries. With that in mind, we tailored this chapter as a kind of meet-and-greet, to help you overcome that bit of initial awkwardness. Let's turn this blind date into a blissful marriage with two kids, a dog, and a white picket fence!

A Guided Tour of the Hardware

By now, your Palm device is no doubt out of the box and getting the once-over. You're seeing buttons, a screen, some little pictures, and a rear compartment that looks just big enough to hold a pair of batteries. What is all this stuff? What does it do?

NOTE *Although fundamentally quite similar, some minor physical differences exist in the various Palm models. The Palm m515, for instance, has no battery compartment because it uses an internal rechargeable battery (as do most late-model Palms). We pop in as needed to alert you to such distinctions.*

The Screen

A Palm screen is capable of displaying roughly 15 lines of text, each about 32 characters across. Some models, like the m125, can display graphics with up to 16 shades of gray. Others, like the m515 and Visor Prism, add color to the mix (65,000 colors, to be exact). At press time, all

Handspring- and Palm-branded models have the same screen resolution—160 × 160 pixels—they've had since the original Pilot 1000.

 *One reason we're sweet on Sony's CLIÉ line is that many of them employ 320 × 320 pixel screens. That's actually four times the resolution of a standard Palm, which translates to sharper-looking text, clearer photos, more detailed maps, and so on. Better still, the latest CLIÉ—the NR70—has a 320 × 480 pixel screen, currently the highest resolution of any handheld!*

When you use a desktop computer, you use a mouse to navigate and a keyboard to enter data. With a Palm device, you use a plastic-tipped stylus for both navigation and data entry. That's because the screen is, technically speaking, a *touchscreen,* meaning you interact with it by tapping it and writing on it. If you want to access, say, the Expense program, you tap the Expense icon that appears on the screen. If you want to record the price of the dinner you just ate, you write the numbers on the screen.

NOTE *Many novice users think they have to double-tap the application icons, just like double-clicking with a mouse. Not true! A single tap is all you ever need when working with a Palm device.*

The Difference Between Tapping and Writing

Tapping the screen is the equivalent of clicking a mouse. You tap icons to launch programs, tap to access menus and select options in them, and tap to place your cursor in specific places. Writing on the screen is, of course, like putting a pen to paper. However, most writing you do on a Palm takes place in a specific area of the screen, which we discuss in the next section. But when you're working in, say, a sketchpad or paint program, you can scribble anywhere on the screen, just as though it were a blank sheet of paper.

TIP *Don't press too hard with the stylus. The screen is fairly sensitive, and light pressure is all it takes to register a tap or stylus-stroke. If you press too hard, you could wind up with a scratched screen—the bane of every Palm user.*

The Graffiti Area

As you've no doubt noticed, the bottom portion of the screen looks a bit different. That big rectangular box flanked by two pairs of icons is called the *Graffiti area,* referring to the handwriting-recognition software that's part of every Palm device. Graffiti makes it possible to enter information using the stylus, but you can do so only within the confines of the Graffiti area (as seen in Figure 2-1).

 We tell you more about Graffiti—how to use it and alternatives to it—in Chapters 4 and 18, respectively.

What about those icons on either side of the Graffiti area? They serve some important functions. Here's an overview:

The Applications Button   Represented by a picture of a house and located in the upper-left corner of the Graffiti area, the *Applications button* is the one you'll tap more often than any other. From whatever program you're currently running, the Applications button (see Figure 2-1) takes you back to the main screen—"home base," as it were (hence, the house picture).

NOTE *In older models, the Applications button was represented by a big curved arrow instead of a house.*

TIP *When you're using any program, tapping the Applications button returns you to the main screen. When you're viewing that screen, however, tapping the Applications button cycles through the application categories, which we discuss in the section "Why Use Categories?" later in this chapter.*

The Menu Button   Tapping the icon in the lower-left corner of the Graffiti area—aka the *Menu button* (see Figure 2-1)—gives you access to the drop-down menus that are part of the Palm Operating System (OS). These menus vary somewhat from program to program, insofar as the options they provide, but they're fairly consistent within the core Palm OS applications.

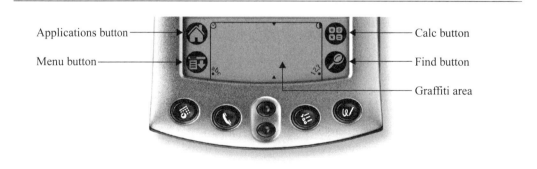

Applications button

Menu button

Calc button

Find button

Graffiti area

FIGURE 2-1   The Graffiti area is where you write data into your handheld and access various options like menus, the calculator, and "home base."

> TIP *The Menu button works like a toggle switch. If you accidentally tap it or simply want to make the drop-down menus go away, simply tap it again.*

The Calculator Button   Probably the most self-explanatory of all the buttons, *Calculator*—located in the upper-right corner of the Graffiti area (see Figure 2-1)—launches the built-in calculator. This functions like any other calculator you've ever used—but you can learn a bit more about it in Chapter 9.

> NOTE *The Palm i705 doesn't have a Calculator button in the Graffiti area—instead, it has a "star" button, which can be programmed to launch any "favorite" application you choose. Similarly, the Kyocera QCP 6035 has a "phone" button in place of Calculator, used to access the dial pad. On models such as these, you can access the Calculator simply by tapping its icon in the main Apps screen.*

The Find Button   Finally, we get to the little magnifying glass in the lower-right corner. Because a Palm can store such vast amounts of information, and because sifting through all that information to find what you're looking for can be tedious, there's a handy little search feature called the *Find button* (see Figure 2-1). We talk more about it in Chapter 9.

The Buttons

Below the Graffiti area on every Palm device, you can see a row of buttons. These serve some fairly obvious purposes: to turn the device on and off, to instantly launch the core applications (Date Book, Memo Pad, and so forth), and to scroll up and down in screens of data.

> NOTE *On some models, like the Palm m500 series, the power button is located at the top of the handheld.*

The Power Button

The *Power button* is fairly self-explanatory, but it serves another function on certain models. When you hold down the button for a couple seconds, one of two screen-related things may happen. First, you might see an onscreen slider tool used to adjust screen brightness. Second, the screen's backlight may turn on (or off, if it was on already). This varies from handheld to handheld, so experiment!

The Four Program Buttons

Say you want to look up a number in your address book. You could turn on your Palm device, tap the Applications button to get to the main screen, and then find and tap the Address button. There's a much faster way, though: simply press the Address button, which is represented by a picture of a phone handset. That serves the dual function of turning on the Palm device *and* loading the Address Book program.

The same holds true for the three other buttons (see Figure 2-2), which launch Date Book, To Do List, and Note Pad (or Memo Pad, in some models). You can use them at any time, whether the Palm is on or off, to quickly switch between the four core programs.

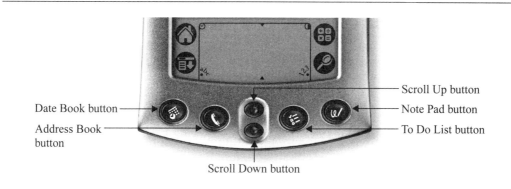

Date Book button —
Address Book button

Scroll Up button
Note Pad button
To Do List button

Scroll Down button

FIGURE 2-2   From the left to right: the Date Book, Address Book, Scroll Up/Down, To Do List, and Note Pad buttons (some models have a Memo Pad button in place of a Note Pad button)

The Scroll Buttons

Sandwiched between the two pairs of Program buttons, the *Scroll buttons* are used to cycle through multiple screens of data. If you're looking at a memo that's too long to fit on the screen in its entirety, you'd use the *Scroll-down button* to move down to the next section—not unlike turning pages in a book. The *Scroll-up button* simply moves you back a page.

NOTE   *In many programs, onscreen arrows serve the same function. Instead of having to press the Scroll buttons, you can simply tap the arrows with your stylus. This is largely a matter of personal preference: try both and decide which method you like better!*

The Back of the Palm

Flip your Palm device over. Yes, it's pretty boring back there (unless you happen to have a Palm IIIe or Visor Deluxe with the translucent shell), but you should know about one important area:

How to ... Reprogram Your Handheld's Buttons

Want the Memo Pad button to load your e-book viewer? Or the Calc button to load a sophisticated third-party number-cruncher instead of the built-in calculator? You can reprogram a Palm device's four hardware buttons and Calc button to run any installed program. Just tap the Prefs icon, and then select Buttons from the drop-down list in the top-right corner of the Preferences screen. Now, assign your desired applications to the various buttons.

Did you know?

Wireless HotSync

If you travel with a notebook PC, one that has an IR port of its own, you can HotSync your Palm device to it without the need for a cradle. This wasn't always possible, however—Palm added the IR HotSync capability to OS 3.3. Find out more about it in Chapter 4.

the Reset button. Every Palm has a little hole on the back that's used to reset the device. Hey, every computer crashes occasionally, and the Palm OS isn't entirely glitch-free. (We talk more about resetting in the troubleshooting section in Chapter 21.)

The Infrared Port

At the top (or on the side, in the case of the Visor) of every Palm device since the Palm III, there's a small, black-plastic window. This is the *infrared port,* also known as the *infrared transceiver* or *IR port.* It's used to wirelessly beam data from one Palm device to another, and has a range of about five feet. You learn more about beaming in Chapter 4.

SHORTCUT *By holding down the Address Book button for two seconds, you can automatically beam your "business card" to another handheld user. In Chapter 6, you learn how to designate an Address Book record as your card.*

The Stylus

Last, but definitely not least, we come to the *stylus.* Every Palm device has a small plastic or metal pen tucked away inside, usually accessible from the side or rear. As you discover in Chapter 20, dozens of third-party styluses are available—some are bigger, some are heavier, and some hide a ballpoint pen inside.

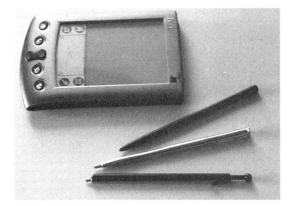

What all Palm styluses have in common is a plastic tip. Under no circumstances should you ever use any kind of ink pen or metal tip on a Palm device's screen. That's a sure way to create a scratch, and a scratched screen is a damaged screen.

There's one exception. In a pinch, or if you just don't feel like extracting the stylus, you can use your fingernail for light taps on the screen.

Using Your Palm Device for the First Time

Now that you're familiar with the Palm hardware, you're ready to start using it. This means installing the batteries (or charging the device, if it has a rechargeable battery), working your way through the startup screens, and checking out the Graffiti tutorial.

Installing the Batteries

Obviously there's nothing terribly complicated about this, but it's important that you install the batteries properly, following the directions outlined in the instruction manual. If you put them in backwards, your handheld won't work.

NOTE *If you purchased a handheld that has a rechargeable battery, obviously no batteries must be installed. Before you use the device for the first time, however, you must charge it completely using the HotSync cradle. We know you're eager to start using your handheld, but make sure you let it charge fully before going on to the next steps. This takes about four hours.*

The Great Battery Debate

Rick: As Palm handhelds get thinner and make the move to color screens, alkaline batteries are increasingly going bye-bye in favor of rechargeable cells. While the latter certainly have their advantages, let's not ignore the benefits of disposables. If your AAA batteries get low while you're traveling, you can buy new ones just about anywhere on the planet. A rechargeable Palm device, meanwhile, needs to return to its cradle. This could create some definite nightmares on the road. . . .

Dave: Sure, rechargeables need to be . . . recharged. But you needn't schlep around a HotSync cradle. I've long used the Tech Center Labs (**www.talestuff.com**) Emergency Charger for my Palm V—it tops off the Palm using a 9-volt battery—and I always carry Electric Fuel's Instant Power charger (**www.instant-power.com**) in my travel bag these days. It's a long-life fuel cell that can completely recharge your PDA three or four times—just the ticket for long trips away from the charging cradle. If you want to recharge your Palm on a long trip, there are lots of ways to do it. Read all about 'em in Chapter 20.

The Welcome Screens

Once the batteries are in and you turn your Palm device back over, you see a "welcome" screen that asks you to remove the stylus and tap anywhere to continue. You're about to undertake a one-time setup procedure that takes all of about 60 seconds. The two key tasks accomplished here are the calibration of the screen digitizer and the setting of the date and time.

What Is Digitizer Calibration?

Put simply, *digitizer calibration* is the process of teaching a Palm to accurately recognize taps on the screen. As you know, the screen responds to input from the stylus and this calibration process simply insures the precision of those responses. In a way, it's like fine-tuning a TV set.

NOTE   *Over time, you might discover your screen taps seem a little off. For example, you have to tap a bit to the left of an arrow for the screen to register the tap. At this point, it's time to recalibrate the digitizer, which you can do in the Prefs menu. We tell you how in the section, "Setting Palm Device Preferences."*

Setting the Date and Time

The last stage of the welcome process is setting the date and time (and choosing your country, if you live outside the United States). To set the time, you simply tap the box next to the words "Set Time," and then tap the up/down arrow keys to select the current time (don't forget to specify A.M. or P.M.). Tapping the box next to Set Date reveals a calendar. Again, a few strategic taps is all it takes to select today's date. (Be sure to choose the year first, then the month, and then the day.) When you've done so, tap the Today button.

```
┌─────────────────────────────┐
│ Setup   3 of 4              │
│ 1. Tap arrows and boxes to  │
│ change settings.            │
│                             │
│   Country:  ▼ United States │
│                             │
│   Set Time:  9:18 am        │
│                             │
│   Set Date:  11/7/99        │
│                             │
│ 2. Tap Next to continue.    │
│                             │
│ (Previous) (Next)           │
└─────────────────────────────┘
```

NOTE   *If you find yourself in a different time zone and need to change your Palm's clock, you needn't repeat the whole "welcome" process to do so. The date and time settings can be found in the Prefs menu, which we discuss in the upcoming section, "Setting Palm Device Preferences."*

The Graffiti Tutorial

On the last screen of the welcome wagon, you're given this option: To learn about entering text on your handheld now, tap Next. Doing so takes you to a brief but helpful tutorial on using *Graffiti,* the Palm's handwriting-recognition software. If you'd rather jump right into using your Palm and learn Graffiti later, tap Done instead of Next. You can revisit the Graffiti tutorial at any time by finding and tapping the Graffiti icon in the main Applications screen.

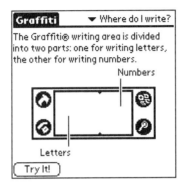

Why Use the Tutorial?

Mastering Graffiti is arguably the most difficult aspect of using a Palm device, because it requires you to learn and use a special character set. Thus, you should definitely spend some time with the tutorial. That said, most users can gain a working knowledge of Graffiti in about 20 minutes. And, after a few days' practice, you should be writing quickly, accurately, and effortlessly. We show you the ins and outs of Graffiti in Chapter 4.

TIP *You may have discovered a Graffiti cheat-sheet sticker among the materials that came with your handheld. However, the Palm OS has a built-in cheat sheet of its own. Just draw a line from anywhere in the Graffiti area all the way to the top of the screen. Presto—a diagram of all the Graffiti characters!*

Getting to Know the Operating System

We aren't exaggerating when we say working with Palm devices is roughly eight gazillion times easier than working with traditional computers. Although they're plenty powerful, Palm devices are a lot less complicated. There's no confusing menu system to wade through, no accidentally forgetting to save your document. Here we've highlighted some of the fundamental—but still important—differences between a Palm and a PC:

■ When you turn on a PC, you have to wait a few minutes for it to boot up. When you turn on a Palm device, it's ready to roll instantaneously. Same goes for shutting it off: just press the Power button and the screen goes dark. There's no lengthy shutdown procedure.

2

■ On a PC, when you're done working with a program (say, your word processor), you must save your data before exiting that program. On a Palm, this isn't necessary. Data is retained at all times, even if you, say, switch to your to-do list while in the middle of writing a memo. When you return to Memo Pad, you find your document exactly as you left it. This holds true even if you turn off the Palm!

■ In that same vein, you don't "exit" a Palm program so much as switch to another one. This is a hard concept for seasoned computer users to grasp, as we've all been taught to shut down our software when we're done with it. There's no exit procedure on a Palm device, and you'll never find that word in a drop-down menu. When you finish working in one program, simply tap the Applications button to return to home base or press one of the program buttons.

NOTE *We strongly encourage experimentation. Whereas wandering too far off the beaten track in Windows can lead to disaster, it's virtually impossible to get "lost" using a Palm. So tap here, explore there, and just have fun checking things out. Because there is no risk of losing data or running too many programs at once (impossible in the Palm OS), you should have no fear of fouling anything up. Play!*

The Icons

Icons are, of course, little pictures used to represent things. In the case of the Palm OS, they're used largely to represent the installed programs. Thus, on the Applications screen, you see icons labeled Address, Calc, Date Book, and so on—and all you do is tap one to access that particular program.

NOTE *Say, didn't you just learn that tapping a button in the Graffiti area is the way to load the calculator? And that you're supposed to press a button below the screen to load Date Book? In the Palm OS, there are often multiple ways to accomplish the same task. In this case, you can load certain programs either by tapping their onscreen icons or using their hardware-button equivalents.*

The Menus

As in most computers, *drop-down menus* are used to access program-specific options and settings. In most Palm programs, tapping the Menu button makes a small menu bar appear at the top of the screen. You navigate this bar using the stylus as you would a mouse, tapping each menu item to make its list of options drop down, and then tapping the option you want to access.

A New Way to Access Menus

With the introduction of OS 3.5, Palm added a new—and, some would say, more logical—way to access drop-down menus. Instead of tapping the Menu button (which you can still do), you merely have to tap the title bar at the top of the screen. In the Applications screen, for instance, you tap the clock in the top-left corner. In Address Book, you tap the word "Address." This isn't unlike working with a PC, where you click the mouse near the top of the screen to pull down menus.

How to ... Find Out How Much Memory Your Handheld Has Left

As you start to add records and install new software on your Palm, you may wonder how to check the amount of memory that's available. From the Applications screen, tap Menu | App | Info. The screen that appears shows the total amount of memory on your device and how much of it is free. Notice, too, the other options that appear when you tap Menu | App. There's Delete (used to delete third-party programs), Beam (used to beam third-party programs), and Copy (if you have a model with a memory expansion slot, which we discuss in Chapter 12).

TIP *If you use an older version of Palm OS, but still want this capability, a little program called MenuHack adds it. Download it from PalmGear (**www.palmgear.com**).*

The Applications Screen

On a Palm device, *home base* is the Applications screen, which displays the icons for all the installed programs. (It also shows you the time and a battery gauge, as the following illustrates.)

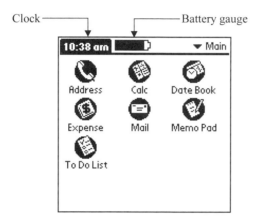

In the upper-right corner of the screen, you'll also notice a small arrow next to the word "All." What this means is the Applications screen is currently showing you all the installed programs. If you tap the arrow, you see a list of categories (see Figure 2-3) into which you can group your programs.

Why Use Categories?

The use of categories is entirely optional. They're intended solely to help you keep your applications organized. As you install more software, you wind up with more icons. Right out of the box, a Palm device has only about a dozen of them—a manageable number. But, suppose you install a few games and a mail program and an e-book reader. Now things are getting a little cluttered, icon-wise.

Categories offer you a way to minimize the clutter. As you saw in the drop-down list, the Palm comes with a number of categories already created. You can use them if you want or create your own.

How to Create and Modify Categories   Look again at the drop-down list in the upper-right corner of the Applications screen (see Figure 2-3). Notice the last option: Edit Categories…. Tapping this option takes you to a screen where you can add, rename, and delete categories. To rename or delete one, first select it by tapping it with the stylus (the category becomes highlighted). Then, tap the appropriate button.

To create a new category, tap the New button, and then write in the desired name. That's all there is to it!

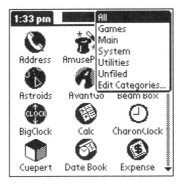

FIGURE 2-3 In the Applications screen, categories can be used to organize your programs.

How to Assign Programs to Categories   Once you tailor the categories to your liking, you must next assign your programs to them. This isn't difficult, but it could take you a few tedious minutes to complete. Here's how:

1. In the Applications screen, tap the Menu button, and then select Category....

2. Identify any one program you want to assign (you may have to scroll down the list, which you can do by using the onscreen arrows, the scroll bar, or the Scroll buttons), and then tap the little arrow next to it.

3. The list of categories appears. Pick one by tapping it.

4. Repeat the procedure for the other programs you want to assign.

5. Tap Done to return to the Applications screen.

Now, when you tap the category arrow in the corner and select one, you see all your reassigned icons have been placed in the respective screens.

One way to change the displayed category is to tap the aforementioned arrow, but there's a quicker way. If you tap the Applications button repeatedly, the Palm cycles through the categories that have programs assigned to them. Again, the Palm offers you two ways to accomplish the same goal.

Setting Palm Device Preferences

What would a computer be without a control panel where you can tweak the settings and customize the machine? The Palm OS has one, called *Prefs*. Find the Prefs icon in the Applications screen, tap it, and meet us at the next paragraph.

Divided into several different sections (all of them accessible by tapping the arrow in the upper-right corner of the screen), Prefs is the place to reset your Palm's digitizer, change the date and time, input any necessary modem settings, and more. In listed order, here's the scoop on each individual Pref.

Depending on which Palm model you have and which version of the OS it's running, the Prefs options may be a bit different than what we have listed here. Most of the options are self-explanatory, though, so not to worry. For what it's worth, we used a Palm m500 for this section of the chapter.

Buttons

As we explained earlier, the four physical buttons below the screen are used to quick-launch the four main Palm OS programs (Date Book, To Do List, and so forth). However, you can reassign these buttons to launch other programs instead. If you find you rarely use, say, To Do List, but you use Expense all the time, it could make sense to reassign the To Do List button accordingly.

After selecting Buttons from the drop-down menu in the Prefs screen, you see an icon that corresponds to each button. (You can also customize the Calc button.) All you do to change the function of any given button is tap the little arrow next to it, and then select the desired application. The buttons can launch any installed application—you're not limited to just the core Palm apps.

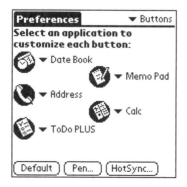

Notice, too, the three options at the bottom of the Buttons screen. *Default* restores the button assignments to their original settings. *Pen...* lets you choose what happens when you drag the tip of your stylus from the Graffiti area to the top of the screen. (This action can be made to load the built-in Graffiti help screens, invoke the onscreen keyboard, turn on backlighting, or one of several other options.) Finally, *HotSync...* enables you to reprogram the HotSync button on your docking cradle or optional modem—something we don't recommend doing.

Connection

The *Connection* screen lets you set up whatever modem you might be using with your Palm device or choose to HotSync via the unit's IR port (instead of using the cradle). You probably won't need to fiddle with the modem settings too much. The documentation included with any modem you buy notifies you if anything requires modification. As for IR HotSyncs, consult Chapter 14 for additional information.

NOTE *Your Palm device might not have the Connection option listed in Prefs. That's because in versions of the Palm OS prior to 3.3, this option was called Modem.*

Date & Time

Flying into another time zone? Hit this screen to change your handheld's internal clock (an important thing to remember so you don't miss your alarms!). You can also change the date if necessary, and set the Palm to automatically adjust for Daylight Savings.

Digitizer

Noticing a little "drift" in your stylus taps? You tap someplace, but it doesn't quite register, or it registers in the *wrong* place? It may be time to reset your screen's digitizer. You should do so the moment you notice a problem; the worse the drift gets, the harder it may be to get to this screen. All you do is select Digitizer from the menu and follow the instructions.

NOTE *Digitizer drift does occur over time, but if it becomes a frequent occurrence, it could point to a hardware problem. If your Palm device is still under warranty, contact customer service to see if a replacement is warranted. In the meantime, there are software utilities designed to compensate for digitizer drift. See Chapter 21 for more information.*

Formats

Few users need to spend much time in the Formats screen, where you can change the way dates, times, and numbers are displayed. You can also specify whether you want the calendar week to start on Sunday (the default) or Monday.

General

Probably the most frequently visited of the Prefs screens, *General* contains the following settings:

- **Auto-off After**   To help preserve battery life, your handheld will turn itself off after a designated period of inactivity. Here you can set the interval, from 30 seconds to 3 minutes. The lower you set it, the better your battery life will be.

- **Stay on in Cradle**   When this box is checked, your handheld will remain while it's in the HotSync cradle. This can be handy if you spend a lot of time at your desk and frequently need to consult your handheld for addresses, schedules, and so forth.

- **System Sound**   Adjust the volume for various system sounds (like beeps, HotSync tones, and so forth). If you want your handheld to be silent, set this to Off.

- **Alarm Sound**   Adjust the volume for alarms.

- **Alarm Vibrate**   This option appears only in models that have a vibrating-alarm feature. Set it to On if you want your handheld to vibrate when an alarm goes off. (And for totally silent alarms, set Alarm Sound to Off.)

- **Alarm LED**   On some models, the Power button doubles as an LED, which can be set to flash when an alarm goes off.

- **Game Sound**   Adjust the volume for games.

- **Beam Receive**   If this is off, you won't be able to receive programs and data beamed from other handhelds. However, keeping it off until you need it can help conserve power. Just *remember* it's off, so you don't pull your hair out trying to determine why you can't receive a beam.

Preferences	▼ General
Auto-off After:	▼ 2 minutes
Stay on in Cradle:	☐
System Sound:	▼ High
Alarm Sound:	▼ High
Alarm Vibrate:	▼ Off
Alarm LED:	▼ On
Game Sound:	▼ High
Beam Receive:	▼ On

In Palm handhelds with OS 3.5 and earlier (and in some non-Palm models), the General screen is also where you set the date and time.

Network

The slightly misnamed *Network* screen is where you enter the relevant information about your Internet service provider (ISP), if you're using a modem to dial into it. A handful of major ISPs are already listed in the Service menu, but you still need to provide your account username and password, plus the phone number for the ISP. The *Details...* button takes you to a screen with some advanced Internet settings, while the *Connect* button tells the modem to go ahead and dial in.

```
┌─────────────────────────────────┐
│ Preferences          ▼ Network  │
│                                 │
│    ▼ Service: Mindspring        │
│  User Name: ms564933            │
│   Password: [-Assigned-]        │
│ Connection: ▼ -Current-         │
│      Phone: [327-5940]          │
│                                 │
│                                 │
│                                 │
│  (Details...) ( Connect )       │
└─────────────────────────────────┘
```

Owner

In the tragic event that you lose your Palm device, you'd probably be very grateful to have it returned. The *Owner* screen is where you can put your name and contact information (address, phone number, e-mail address—whatever you're comfortable with). Then, if you use the Palm Operating System's security features (which we detail in Chapter 9) to "lock" the device every time you turn it off, the information on the Owner screen is displayed when the unit is turned on again. Then, if someone happens to find your handheld, they know how to return it to you, but won't have access to all your data. Smart!

```
┌─────────────────────────────────┐
│ Preferences            ▼ Owner  │
│ This handheld computer is owned by: │
│                                 │
│ Rick Broida                     │
│ If found, please call (212)867-5309. │
│ A reward will be paid           │
│                                 │
│                                 │
│                                 │
│                                 │
│                                 │
└─────────────────────────────────┘
```

Phone

If you plan to connect your handheld to a cell phone, which would enable you to send and receive e-mail and browse the Web, this is where you'd come to select the appropriate driver for your phone. However, by default, no such drivers are installed. See Chapter 13 for more information.

ShortCuts

Next, we come to *ShortCuts,* a tool designed to expedite the entry of often-used words and phrases. Let's say you're a Starfleet engineer and you use your Palm to keep track of your repair duties. The phrase "holodeck emitters" comes up quite a bit—but do you really have to write it out every time? What if you could just write "h-e" instead and have the words magically appear? That's the beauty of shortcuts.

As you see when you reach the ShortCuts screen, a handful of the little time-savers have already been created. There's one each for your daily meals, one for "meeting," and even a couple of date and time stamps (used to quickly insert the date and time, natch). Let's walk through the process of creating and using a new shortcut:

- Tap the New button.
- In the ShortCut Name field, write the abbreviation you want to use for this particular shortcut. As an example, let's use "bm" for "Buy milk."
- Tap the first line in the ShortCut Text field to move your cursor there. Now, enter the text you want to appear when you invoke the shortcut (in this case, "Buy milk").
- Tap OK. Now, let's invoke the new shortcut. Press the *To Do* button to launch the To Do List, and then tap New to create a new task.

■ To invoke this or any other shortcut (in any application, be it Date Book, Memo Pad or whatever), you must first write the shortcut stroke in the Graffiti area. This lets Graffiti know you're about to enter the abbreviation for a shortcut. The stroke looks like a cursive, lowercase letter *l* (see our Graffiti guide in Chapter 4). After you make the stroke, you see it appear next to your cursor. Now enter the letter *b,* and then the letter *m.* Presto! The words "Buy milk" magically appear.

Web Clipping

Few users will need to bother with this screen. Consult your handheld's documentation or the Palm, Inc., Web site if you need further information.

An Introduction to Palm Desktop

So far, we've talked mostly about the Palm itself: the hardware, the operating system, the basic setup procedures and considerations. One area is left to cover before you venture into real-world Palm use: the Palm Desktop.

What Is Palm Desktop?

Wondrous as a Palm device is in its own right, what makes it even more special is its capability to synchronize with your computer. This means all the data entered into your Palm is copied to your PC, and vice versa. The software that fields all this data on the computer side is Palm Desktop. (If you use Microsoft Outlook or another contact manager, you needn't use Palm Desktop at all. More on that in the next section.)

Viewed in a vacuum, *Palm Desktop* resembles traditional personal information manager (PIM) or contact-management software (see Figure 2-4). It effectively replicates all the core functionality of the Palm OS, providing you with a phone list, appointment calendar, to-do list, and memo pad. If you've never used such software before, you'll no doubt find Palm Desktop an invaluable addition, as it helps keep you organized at home or in the office (whereas a Palm device keeps you organized while traveling).

A Word About Synchronization

What happens when you synchronize your Palm device with your PC? In a nutshell, three things:

■ Any new entries made on your Palm device are added to Palm Desktop.

■ Any new entries made in Palm Desktop are added to your Palm device.

■ Any existing records modified in one place (the Palm, for example) are modified in the other (the desktop, same example), the newest changes taking precedence.

Therefore, synchronizing regularly assures your information is kept current, both in your Palm device and in Palm Desktop.

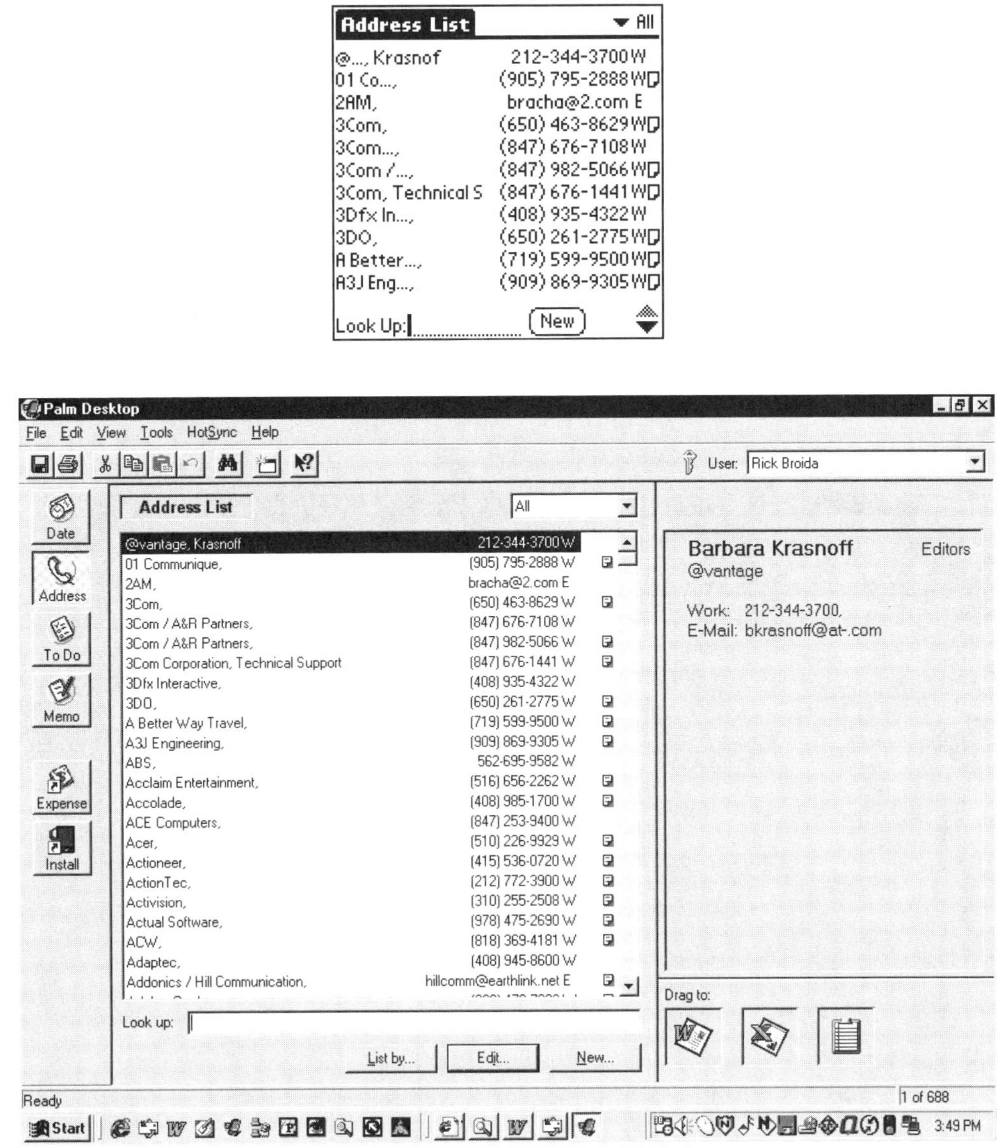

FIGURE 2-4   For those who don't use Microsoft Outlook, Palm Desktop provides a computer counterpart to the built-in handheld apps.

NOTE   *Already entrenched in Microsoft Office? All Palm devices come with software—usually Chapura's PocketMirror, but some have a special version of Puma Technologies' IntelliSync—that allows direct synchronization with Office (bypassing Palm Desktop). If you have a different contact manager (such as Lotus Organizer), you may need to upgrade to a different sync program, such as Puma's IntelliSync.*

The Differences Between the Windows and Macintosh Versions

While functionally similar, the Windows and Macintosh versions of Palm Desktop are different programs. Palm Desktop for Windows, shown in Figure 2-5, was built from scratch, while the Macintosh version, shown in Figure 2-6, is a modified version of *Claris Organizer,* a popular contact manager.

NOTE   *Older Palm models have serial—rather than USB—HotSync cradles, which means you may need to buy a PalmConnect Kit. This provides the hardware you need to make the connection to your Mac.*

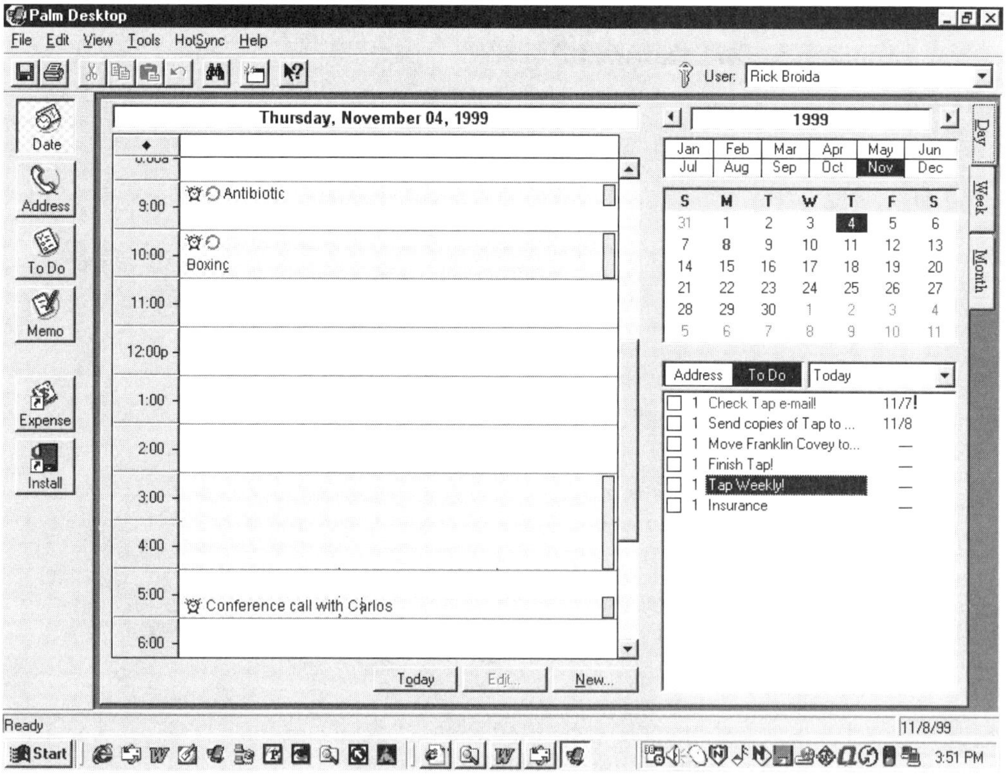

FIGURE 2-5   The Windows version of Palm Desktop

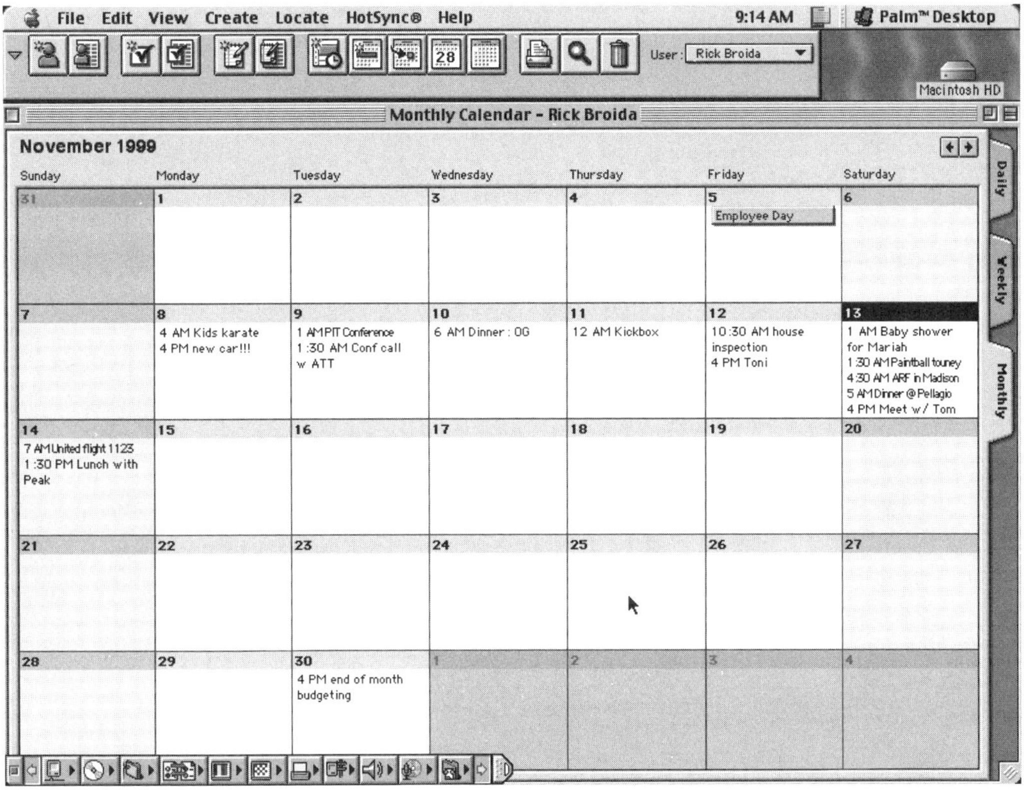

FIGURE 2-6   The Macintosh version of Palm Desktop looks and functions a bit differently from the Windows version, but both synchronize seamlessly with your handheld.

Where to Find It

Web Site	Address	What's There
Palm, Inc.	**www.palm.com/macintosh**	Mac-specific Palm information
Chapura	**www.chapura.com**	Outlook synchronization utility PocketMirror
DataViz	**www.dataviz.com**	Outlook synchronization utility Desktop To Go
Puma Technologies	**www.pumatech.com**	Contact manager synchronization utility IntelliSync

Chapter 3

Synchronizing with Your Desktop Computer

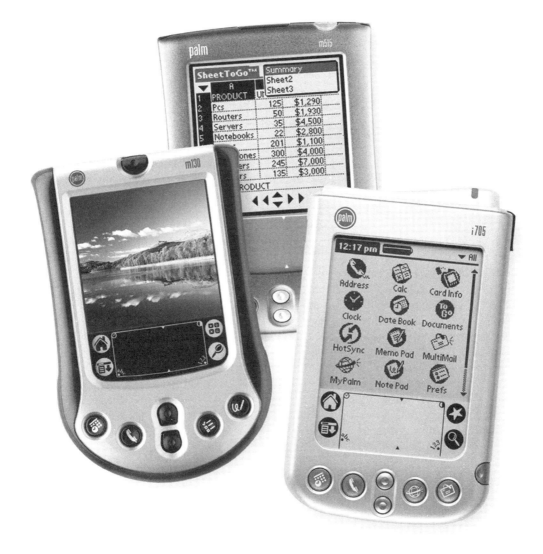

How to...

- Install the HotSync cradle
- Configure the HotSync cradle
- Identify serial ports in case of installation troubles
- Troubleshoot USB connection problems
- Install the Palm Desktop software
- Install the AvantGo software
- Set up the HotSync Manager
- Perform your first HotSync
- HotSync with a HotSync cable
- Interpret the HotSync log
- Keep your data synchronized just the way you like
- Perform HotSyncs on the go via IR or a modem

If you ask us, we'll tell you the coolest thing about the Palm is it was, perhaps, the first handheld PC to understand it isn't all about the little computer in your hand. It's just as much about the computer back on your desk. In other words, the Palm creators made sure the Palm fully integrated itself into your main computer system—the Windows or Mac desktop, depending on your preference—and all your data. No longer did using a handheld PC mean maintaining two different sets of contacts and appointments. No more did it mean laboriously transcribing tons of important data by hand. The Palm synchronizes with your desktop so elegantly, it's as if they were born to work together.

To be honest, the Palm wasn't the first handheld device that enabled you to share data with a desktop PC. Dave should know. He was an early handheld adopter and still has his old Apple Newton MessagePad. But synchronizing data with older handheld devices was a chore. Often, the necessary software wasn't included in the box with the handheld itself and it worked less than optimally anyway. With the Palm, you press a button and all the important stuff you use every day is quickly shared. It couldn't be a whole lot easier.

Now that you've had a chance to explore your Palm device in Chapter 2, it's time to learn about how the device works with your PC. The Palm comes with a slew of tools designed for the desktop, including a synchronization application for making sure the Palm has the same data as the desktop. Let's get started using your PC with the Palm.

Unpacking Your Palm

If you're like us, the first thing you might have thought on seeing the Palm box is it's way too big to hold only a tiny handheld PC—and you'd be right—there's a lot more in the box than just the Palm itself. The most important component, of course, is the HotSync cradle (only a few models don't come with a cradle, and those that don't include a synchronization cable instead). The cradle is the interface that links the Palm to your desktop computer and all its data. In fact, the first thing you should do after unpacking your Palm is to install the cradle.

Installing the HotSync Cradle

The HotSync cradle looks a little different depending on which model of the Palm you're using, but its appearance doesn't matter. Each performs the same function: transferring information between the PC and the Palm. The original cradle, used by models like the PalmPilot Pro, is shown alongside newer cradles, used by the popular Palm V and m125 handhelds, in Figure 3-1.

With rare exceptions, all of today's Palm models use HotSync cradles and cables that connect to your PC via the USB port. Older PDAs used a serial port. What's the difference? USB is easier to use and less prone to installation trouble.

If you have a USB cradle, plug it in to an empty USB port on the computer or a USB hub (but, in most cases, you need to install the Palm Desktop software first. Check the instructions that came with your PDA). You don't even have to turn the computer off first. If you have a serial port cradle (just about the only PDAs still using such a connection are the HandEra 330 and Kyocera 6035 SmartPhone), insert the serial connector from your cradle into a free serial port on the back of your PC.

FIGURE 3-1   HotSync cradles vary in appearance, but they all do essentially the same thing: they let you synchronize the data on your Palm with your desktop computer. Most cradles also charge the batteries in your PDA at the same time.

HotSync

HotSync, a term coined by Palm Computing, refers to the act of synchronizing the data stored on your handheld and desktop computers. These days, all PDA companies use a special term that means more or less the same thing—Microsoft's Pocket PCs, for instance, are called "ActiveSync" instead.

Remember the following information about connecting your HotSync cradle:

- Any compatible port will do. It doesn't matter which serial port you connect your serial cable to, just as it doesn't matter to which USB port you connect your USB cable.

- Two different kinds of serial ports are on the PC, and your computer might have one of each. Modern serial ports have nine pins. Older serial ports are wider, with a whopping 25 pins. Why? You don't want to know. Just remember this: if your nine-pin port is occupied, use a 25 pin-to-9 pin adapter, available at almost any computer store (older Palm models came with just such an adapter).

- If you're making a serial connection, play it safe and turn off the PC before plugging it in. You can leave your PC on to plug in a USB cradle.

NOTE *If you're out of sync with newer computers, all this talk about ports could be a bit confusing. What's USB, for instance, and how is it different from a serial port? In a nutshell, USB stands for the Universal Serial Bus and it's many times faster than the serial port. In addition, it's a plug-and-play port that enables you to connect over 100 devices to your PC without worrying about the kind of ugly configuration issues that have hounded the serial port since the 1980s. USB has gotten so popular that some new computers don't even come with serial ports anymore.*

Powering a Rechargeable Palm

If you have a newish Palm Powered PDA, odds are excellent it has integrated rechargeable batteries. These newer PDAs come with HotSync cradles that can recharge your Palm whenever it's sitting idly at your desk. When you plug the cradle into the PC, make sure you connect the cradle's AC adapter at the same time. If the cradle isn't plugged into the wall, it can't charge your PDA. You can tell your Palm is being recharged because a light on the cradle or the PDA itself lights up. If you don't see the light when the Palm is in the cradle, check to see if the AC adapter has come loose from the wall or the small connector where it plugs into the HotSync cradle.

 TIP *You needn't plug the AC adapter into the HotSync cradle to transfer data between the PC and the Palm. If you don't use the AC adapter, though, the batteries in the Palm won't recharge and, eventually, its batteries will die and cost you your data.*

3

Troubleshooting the USB Port

If your HotSync cradle has a USB connector—and it probably does—don't worry. USB is usually pretty reliable and any potential problems that crop up generally boil down to only a few things. For starters, you might not have anywhere to plug in your cradle, especially if you already have a few other USB devices. If that's the case, you need to run over to a local computer store and buy a USB hub. This device plugs into a USB port on your PC and gives you several extra USB connectors for additional devices. If you plugged in your HotSync cradle and it doesn't seem to work, two likely causes exist:

- Your USB port doesn't have enough power to run the cradle. If your USB port has several devices connected to it, such as through a hub, it might be unable to handle the power requirements of the connected devices. Make sure you're using a "powered" hub (it will come with its own AC adapter) and that it's plugged into the wall. If this checks out, you might need to swap some devices around between your PC's two USB ports to move some high-power devices to the other port. This could take a little experimentation.

- A related problem: your USB port might have run out of bandwidth. This can happen if you have some high-performance USB devices connected to the same port. Again, the solution is to move some things around between the two USB ports. Dave found he simply couldn't run all the USB devices he wants on his PC because they demand more total bandwidth than his PC's USB ports could deliver. If you have lots of USB devices and need more bandwidth, you can simply buy a PCI card that gives you more USB ports.

- One other possibility: something we like to call Windows Funkiness. Reboot your PC and it might work just fine.

NOTE   *Many new PCs have USB 2.0 ports, which are much more robust and have far greater bandwidth than older USB 1.1 ports. Nonetheless, USB 2.0 ports work like older USB 1.1 ports unless USB 2.0-compatible devices are plugged in. Right now, all Palm models are plain old USB 1.1 devices.*

Know Your PC's Serial Ports

Still using serial? Your Palm's installation program will want to know which serial port your HotSync cradle is using. And, 99 percent of the time, the software can figure out what serial port is in use just fine all by itself. If the software encounters trouble, though, you might need to do a little detective work and figure it out yourself. This isn't as hard as it sounds. Use this table as a quick reference to decrypting your serial port:

If...	Then...
There's only one serial port on my PC.	It's COM1.
My cradle is plugged into the small 9-pin port.	It's COM1.
My cradle is plugged into the big 25-pin port.	It's COM2.
I added a new serial port with an expansion card or a serial USB adapter and plugged the cradle into that.	It's a little hard to say from here. Experiment!

Installing the Desktop Software

Before you can synchronize your Palm and your desktop PC, you first need to install the Palm Desktop software suite on your computer. The Palm Desktop software is sort of like a personal information manager (PIM). It duplicates all the core applications from your Palm and serves as the headquarters from which you can use synchronized information from your Palm. While you do need to install the Palm Desktop, you don't need to use it. If you already use Microsoft Outlook or another PIM, you can synchronize your Palm to that program instead and avoid the Palm Desktop entirely.

The CD-ROM that accompanies your Palm includes everything you need to connect the handheld to your desktop, including your choice of synchronization to Palm Desktop or Outlook. Installation is straightforward. Follow the installation instructions that appear after you insert the CD-ROM.

Installing Palm Desktop

The Palm Desktop CD-ROM includes an installer that places most (but, depending on which version of the software you have, not all) of the key components on your hard disk. Most of the main installation is completely automated, but you have to make a few decisions:

- **Outlook or Palm Desktop?** If you have a copy of Microsoft Outlook installed on your PC, the installer detects it and gives you the option of synchronizing your data to it, if you so desire. What data are we talking about? Stuff like contacts from the address book and appointments from the calendar, as well as notes and tasks. If you're a regular Outlook user, you should certainly choose to synchronize your Palm with Outlook. Palm Desktop, on the other hand, is a serviceable PIM, though it's not as comprehensive as Outlook.

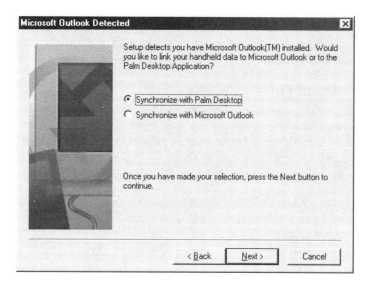

■ **Assign a Unique User Name**   The User Name is the name of your Palm. You can use your own name or give your Palm a unique descriptor—anything from **Dave's Palm** to **Palm 33A** to just plain **Mike** is acceptable. Is the name important? Yup. If you have more than one Palm, each one absolutely must have a different name. If you give two or more Palms the same name, you can end up destroying all the synchronized data on the desktop PC and all the PDAs during a HotSync.

> **TIP**   *If you're upgrading to a new PDA, you probably want to use the same name as your old unit. This way, registered software that depends on the device name will still work on the new Palm. But, if you do that, be sure to reset the old Palm and give it a different name.*

■ **Select a COM Port**   If you have a serial HotSync cradle, the installer can locate the cradle and determine what COM port it belongs to. In some rare cases, a unique hardware configuration might make it impossible for the software to find the cradle or you might not have connected the cradle yet for some reason. In that case, you need to choose a COM port from a list of options. If you have a USB cradle, you needn't worry about this step at all.

■ **Configure Mail**   The installer offers you a list of mail programs with which to synchronize your Palm. Remember, you might not even have many of the programs in the list on your PC. Just choose the one you want to use (if you want to synchronize e-mail at all—see Chapter 9 for more information). Unless you have a wireless model, the Palm's mail program will only let you read and write messages. Sensing and receiving happens when you HotSync to the desktop.

■ **Set Up Wireless Services**   If you have a wireless model like the Palm i705, you might need to activate your wireless service, download Web applications, and perform other setup steps. Follow the instructions in the user guide.

> **TIP**   *Bonus software probably won't be installed automatically. We suggest you browse the CD's main menu for cool programs like Documents To Go and AvantGo, which are bundled with many Palm Powered handhelds.*

Your First HotSync

After you install your cradle, load the software on to your computer, and have a nice, relaxing break watching television (Dave recommends *Andromeda*, Rick prefers *Britney Spears in Concert*)—it's time to perform your first HotSync.

HotSyncing is pretty cool because it transfers all your desktop-based data like appointments, contacts, and to-dos to your Palm, so you don't have to enter any data to get started with your new PDA. Here's what you need to do to make sure you're ready:

1. Make sure your HotSync cradle is connected to the PC.

2. Place the Palm in the cradle.

3. If you have a rechargeable Palm, the AC adapter should also be connected. You see a charging light when the Palm is in the cradle.

4. Make sure the HotSync Manager software is running. You should see the HotSync icon in the System Tray. If you don't see it, start it now. Choose Start | Programs | Palm Desktop | HotSync Manager or, if you're on the Mac, it's located in the Chooser or the Palm folder.

 The System Tray is the region at the bottom of the Windows Desktop that's found to the right of the Taskbar. It contains the clock and icons for special programs like the HotSync Manager.

Pressing the HotSync Button

Depending on what kind of PDA you have, press the button on the HotSync cradle or cable (see Figure 3-2).

After you press the HotSync button, here's what should happen:

1. Your Palm turns itself on (if it wasn't on already).

2. You hear three tones indicating the HotSync has begun.

3. A message box appears on the Windows desktop, which informs you of the HotSync status.

4. You hear another set of tones when the HotSync is complete.

5. The Palm displays a message indicating the HotSync is complete.

Exploring the HotSync Manager

The HotSync Manager software does exactly what it sounds like—it manages the connection between your Palm and your computer, enabling you to HotSync. It contains all the options and configurations needed to keep the two devices talking to each other. To HotSync, you needn't mess with anything on the Palm at all. You only need to tweak the HotSync Manager.

To get to the HotSync Manager's options in Windows, you need to see the HotSync menu. Click the HotSync Manager icon in the System Tray and a context menu appears.

You can click the HotSync Manager icon with either the right or left mouse button. The result is the same.

These options are the first thing you encounter in the HotSync menu:

- Local USB
- Local Serial
- Modem
- Network
- Infrared

FIGURE 3-2   Most Palms have a cradle with a single HotSync button. A few models rely on a cable with the HotSync button instead.

The Best Films of All Time

Taking that TV break before the HotSync got us just a tad distracted. Truth be told, we took the opportunity to go watch some movies. And, that led to the inevitable arguments . . . what are the best movies of all time?

Dave: There's no way a rational person could disagree . . . *Aliens* is the best movie of all time. Space Marines fighting xenomorphs with twenty-third century machine guns! Woo hoo! What could possibly be cooler than that? And it has some of the best movie lines ever. This, mind you, is the film in which Bill Paxton made the words, "Game over, man," a part of my daily lexicon. After *Aliens,* my list gets a bit more introspective. *The Matrix, The Sixth Sense, Almost Famous,* and *O Brother, Where Art Thou?* have to be four of the most amazing films ever made. Now let's see what lame movies Rick thinks are cool. My prediction: His favorite films include *Tron, Dirty Dancing,* and *Weekend at Bernie's 2.*

Rick: I've had just about enough of your *Weekend at Bernie's 2* bashing, Mister. Don't make me tell everyone about your strange fondness for Will Smith. Anyway, in no particular order, my Top Five Movies are as follows: *Life is Beautiful, City Lights, The Shawshank Redemption, Toy Story 2,* and *Star Trek II: The Wrath of Khan.* Yes, I know only one of those movies has things blowing up, which means you won't care for the other four. The age of *Ah*-nold has passed, leatherneck. Grow up already.

For now, the only one that must be checked is the Local option (Serial or USB). This means you can perform a HotSync using the serial or USB port.

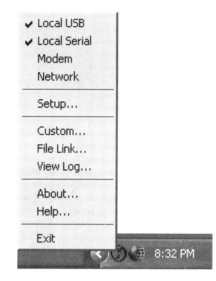

Configuring HotSync Setup

Click the Setup option on the HotSync menu. You should now see the Setup dialog box. This is the place where you get to configure how the HotSync manager behaves. Four tabs are on the Setup dialog box.

General The *General tab* lets you specify how often the HotSync Manager listens to the USB or serial port for a HotSync request. It has three options, as you can see in Figure 3-3.

- **Always available** This is the default setting. As soon as you press the HotSync button on the cradle, you synchronize your data. It's fast and convenient, and it's probably the way most people use their Palms. But you needn't give in to peer pressure because this has a downside: if you're using the serial port, HotSync Manager locks it up, so you can't share the port with another serial device, like a modem.

- **Available only when the Palm Desktop is running** If you often share your serial port with another device, this might be a better solution. The HotSync Manager won't lock the port unless Palm Desktop is running. But, what if you don't use Palm Desktop? Then keep reading, because option number three is the one for you. . . .

- **Manual** Just like it sounds, the HotSync Manager doesn't run at all unless you choose it from the Start menu (Start | Programs | Palm Desktop | HotSync Manager). This is the least convenient of all the options, but you might want to choose it if you only HotSync on rare occasion, if your serial port is frequently used by another device, or if you don't use the Palm Desktop (meaning the second option doesn't work for you).

3

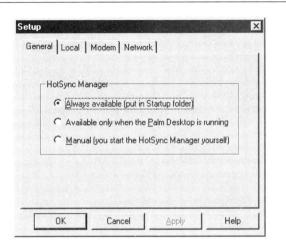

FIGURE 3-3   The General tab determines when the HotSync manager runs and how easy it is to perform a HotSync.

TIP   *If you try to use another serial device like a modem, but Windows reports the serial port is in use, click the HotSync Manager icon and choose Exit. Then try your serial device again.*

On the Macintosh, these options are slightly different. Start HotSync Manager and choose HotSync | Options. On the HotSync Controls tab, you can enable or disable HotSyncing, and specify whether the HotSync Manager should start when you turn on the computer.

Local   The *Local Serial tab* is where you specify the serial port and speed for your HotSync. Most of the time, the installation process correctly determines your serial port and it's all taken care of. If you move the HotSync cable to another serial port, though, this is where you tell the HotSync Manager what the proper COM port is. The correct COM port is almost always COM1 or COM2, and you can either experiment or use the table (see the section "Know Your PC's Serial Ports" earlier in this chapter) to determine your port name.

You can almost always leave the speed set to As Fast As Possible. If you need to troubleshoot connection problems, though, this is where you can specify a slower speed.

Modem and Network   Both of these tabs are used to specify settings for more advanced HotSync techniques. After you've seen all the tabs in the Setup dialog box, click OK to save changes or click Cancel to leave the dialog box without changing anything.

What's a Conduit?

Conduit is the term Palm uses to describe the software that connects data on your Palm with similar data on your computer. The *Calendar conduit,* for instance, makes sure the Palm's Date Book and the computer's Outlook Calendar stay completely in sync. Every application on your Palm with a corresponding program on the PC is connected with its own conduit and the Custom menu option is where you turn to adjust these conduits.

Customizing the HotSync Operation

From the HotSync Manager menu, choose Custom.

TIP   *On the Mac, choose HotSync | Conduit Settings.*

This is arguably the most important dialog box in the HotSync software because it enables you to specify with great detail exactly what data will get transferred. Before you look at this dialog box, however, let's define a few essential terms the Palm uses to perform data synchronizations. If you make the wrong choice, you can destroy data you need.

HotSync Term	Meaning
Synchronize the files	Suppose you added new files to both the PC and the Palm since the last HotSync. The new data from the Palm is copied to the PC and the new data from the PC is copied to the Palm. Both devices will have a copy of everything. *This is the best setting to use most of the time and is, in fact, the default for most conduits.*
Desktop overwrites handheld	This option supposes the desktop data is correct at the expense of anything that might be on the handheld. If you add new files to both the PC and the handheld, for instance, and then perform this kind of synch, the new files on the Palm will be lost. The desktop data overwrites whatever was on the Palm.
Handheld overwrites desktop	This is exactly the opposite of the previous case. Assuming the handheld data is more correct for some reason (we assume you have your reasons), any files that are different or new on the desktop PC are lost after the synchronization. Both systems will have the Palm data.
Do nothing	With this option selected, no changes are made to either device during this HotSync.

Remember, each conduit can be adjusted separately. This means you can set the Date Book to overwrite the PC's Address Book, while the e-mail conduit is set to Do Nothing and the Notes conduit synchronizes.

TIP   *If you're ever in doubt about the state of your conduits, be sure to check the action before you press the HotSync button by right-clicking the HotSync icon and choosing Custom. If you accidentally configure the HotSync Manager to Handheld Overwrites Desktop, for instance, you'll lose changes you made to the Palm Desktop or Outlook when you HotSync.*

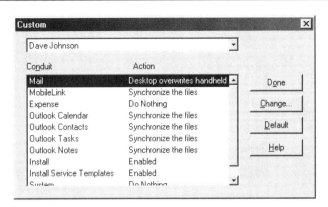

FIGURE 3-4   The Custom dialog box enables you to specify how each conduit behaves when you HotSync.

With those terms in mind, let's look at the Custom dialog box. As you can see in Figure 3-4, the top of the box displays the name of the Palm unit. Managing more than one Palm from each PC is possible, so you select the proper unit from the list menu before continuing. If you only have a single Palm, don't worry about this option.

This dialog box displays a list of conduits and their actions. As you can see from the list, a unique conduit exists for each kind of application on the Palm. Most Palms include these conduits:

- **Calendar**   Shares data between the Palm and desktop calendars.
- **Contacts**   Shares data between the Palm and desktop address books.
- **Tasks**   Shares data between the Palm and desktop to-do lists.
- **Notes**   Shares data between the Palm and desktop memo pads.
- **Expense**   Shares expense entries between the Palm and an application like Excel.
- **Install**   Transfers Palm OS applications from your PC's hard disk to the Palm.
- **Mail**   E-mail messages are synchronized between your desktop mail application and the Palm.
- **AvantGo Connect**   Used by the optional AvantGo application to transfer Web-based documents to your Palm.
- **System**   Transfers other files created by Palm applications between the PC and Palm.

NOTE   *If you install new software, you could end up with more conduits. Many programs come with their own conduits to control the flow of information between your Palm and desktop applications.*

To configure a conduit, either double-click an entry or select it, and then click the Change button. Depending on which conduit you open, you'll find you might have all four synchronization options or, perhaps, fewer (see Figure 3-5).

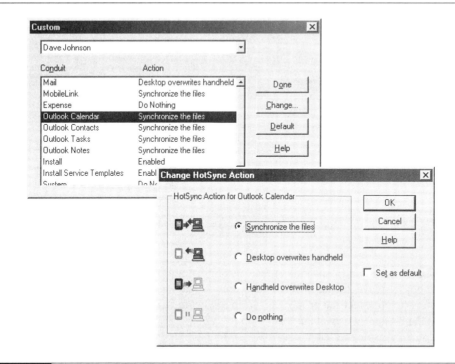

FIGURE 3-5 You can configure each conduit before a HotSync

When you configure a conduit, whatever selection you make applies only to the next time you HotSync, unless you check the box for Set as default.

HotSync with a Cable

You don't need a cradle to synchronize your Palm. You can also use a modem, a Bluetooth access point, or your laptop's IR port. Here's a low-tech alternative for the road warrior: try a HotSync cable. Cables are handy because they take up less room in a suitcase than the bulky cradle and they don't rely on finicky modems or IR ports. A HotSync cable costs about $20 and is an essential tool for the frequent traveler. You can buy peripherals like the HotSync cable from a number of online stores, including Targus (**www.targus.com**) and the Palm web site, **www.palm.com**. Better still, check out the new breed of USB HotSync cables that will also charge your handheld. See Chapter 20 for details.

Reading the HotSync Log

Did your HotSync session go as planned? Did all your data get transferred properly and did files get copied the way you expected? Usually, it's pretty obvious if everything went well, but sometimes it's nice if your computer can tell you what happened, especially if the HotSync dialog box reports some sort of error.

During every HotSync, the HotSync Manager makes a record of everything that happened. This log is easy to read and it can answer that nagging question, "Why didn't the calendar update after I added an entry for the Sandra Bullock fan club?" If the HotSync manager noticed that something went wrong during a HotSync, it'll even tell you. Figure 3-6, for instance, shows the result of a HotSync that generated an error. The log reveals what happened.

To see the log at any time, right-click the HotSync icon in the System Tray and choose View Log (if you're using Windows). On the Mac, choose HotSync | Log from the menu. The HotSync Log window should then appear.

TIP   *You can't perform a HotSync when the log is open.*

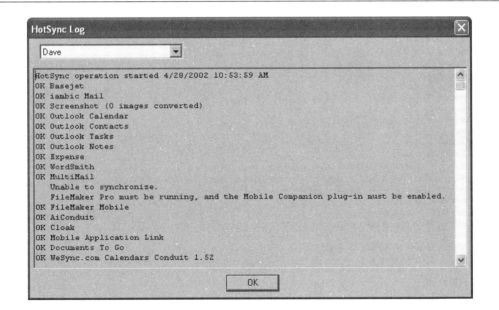

FIGURE 3-6   The HotSync log records the details of the last ten HotSyncs, along with any errors that occurred along the way.

The log displays a list of the actions that occurred for each of your last ten HotSync sessions. The top of the log is the most recent, and older sessions are listed as you scroll down the page. Each session is separated by a text message that indicates when it started and ended.

What kind of information does a log reveal? Each conduit reports its status and these are the messages you're most likely to see:

- **OK** This is good news; the conduit's action succeeded with no errors.
- **Sync configured to Do Nothing** If something didn't happen, this might be the cause—the conduit was intentionally or mistakenly set to do nothing.
- **Truncated** This means a file stored on the PC (such as e-mail or an address book entry) was so long that not all of it would fit on the Palm.
- **Records were modified in both Handheld and PC** You made changes to the same file on both the PC and the Palm. Because the HotSync Manager doesn't know which change is correct, it duplicated both files on both systems. You now have a chance to update the file and delete the one you don't want.
- **Synchronization failed** Any number of reasons can exist for this, but it's probably because the COM ports were misconfigured, so the PC couldn't find the Palm.

TIP *The HotSync log is also available on the Palm itself, albeit only for the most recent HotSync session. To reach it, tap the HotSync application, and then tap the Log button.*

How to ... HotSync

The HotSync process is fast and easy. Once you get used to it, you'll find it's a one-button, one-step process. Here it is in all of its gory detail, though:

1. Plug the cradle into your PC.
2. Set the Palm in the cradle.
3. Make sure the HotSync Manager software is running (by default, it should always be running).
4. Verify the conduits are set properly to transfer and synchronize data just the way you want.
5. Press the HotSync button on the cradle.
6. Wait until you hear the HotSync complete tones before removing the Palm from the cradle.

HotSync as a Way of Life

After your first HotSync, you could begin to see how convenient it is to have a duplicate of your desktop data on your Palm. But how often should you HotSync? The short answer is as frequently as you like. Some people HotSync daily, while others—whose data changes much less frequently—update their Palm only once a week or even less. Use this guide as a rule of thumb:

- HotSync anytime you leave the office with your PDA.
- HotSync when you return from a trip to update your PC with new info stored on the Palm.
- HotSync each day to stay current with the newest content in AvantGo Web channels, which are updated daily.
- HotSync to install new applications on your Palm (this is discussed in Chapter 4).

Changing Conduits on-the-Fly

You might often change all the conduits in your HotSync Manager, except one or two. You might want to disable everything except the Install conduit to get a new program on to your Palm quickly, for instance, or to set everything except AvantGo to Do Nothing, so you can get your news on to the PDA as you're running out the door to lunch.

Whatever the reason, you'll soon find no easy way exists to disable several conduits at once. Successively changing five conduits to Do Nothing is almost as time-consuming as doping the whole darned HotSync to start.

There's an easier way. Download the tremendously useful program called Ultrasoft NotSync from **PalmGear.com**. This program lets you quickly and easily change your conduits in seconds. The change only applies to the next HotSync, so it never affects your default settings.

What HotSync Does to Files

After your first HotSync, you have a set of data on both your Palm and your desktop. The goal of the HotSync process is to make sure the data stays the same on both systems. So what happens when you change data on one or both of the computers? This table, which assumes the conduit is set to synchronize the files, should help you understand the subtleties of the HotSync.

Before the HotSync	After the HotSync
You add a file to the Palm (or the PC).	That file is added to the PC (or the Palm).
You delete a file from the Palm (or PC).	The file is also deleted from the PC (or Palm).
You change a file on the Palm.	The file is changed on the PC.
You change the same file on both the Palm and PC—they're now different.	Both versions of the file are added to both the Palm and PC. You need to modify the file and delete the one you don't want to keep.

With this in mind, you might not always want to use the Synchronize the Files option for all your conduits. Why not? Any number of reasons. Here are a few situations:

- You might rely on your Palm to take notes that you have no interest in copying to your PC. In other words, you want to keep one set of notes on the PC, which are relevant to what you do at your desk, and another set of notes for when you're on the road. In such a case, Do Nothing is probably the best option for your needs.

- You might take notes you don't need to keep after a trip is over. In such an instance, you can use Desktop Overwrites Handheld for that conduit. After your trip is over, the handheld notes are erased during the HotSync and replaced by the desktop notes.

 Don't forget, you can configure each conduit individually so, for instance, the Address Book might be set to Synchronize the files, while the Date Book is set to Desktop Overwrites Handheld.

HotSync Using a Notebook's IR Port

Do you travel with both a laptop and your Palm? If you do, you can wirelessly synchronize the data between the two devices using the IR port built into your laptop (if it has one—many newer laptop's don't) and your Palm. Being able to HotSync without carting a cradle around means you can easily keep your notebook and Palm current no matter where you're located.

NOTE *The capability to IR HotSync doesn't exist in older versions of the Palm operating system, so you might have to upgrade to take advantage of this capability.*

Prepping the Notebook

To HotSync your Palm to a notebook, you first need to prepare your notebook. Namely, it must have the necessary infrared hardware and driver. Here's what you need to do:

1. Start by installing the Palm Desktop software if it isn't already on the system. We obviously need that later.

2. Does your notebook have an IR port? This could sound silly, but check visually for the port. It's a small, reddish plastic bubble that's usually in back of the system, but also might be located on the side.

IrDA port

3. If you have the IR port, you next need to verify the IR driver is installed. To do this, open the Control Panel by choosing Start | Settings Control Panel. Look for an icon named Infrared. If it's there, great. The necessary software is installed.

TIP   *If you don't have the Infrared Driver installed, you need to download it from Microsoft's Web site. Go to **www.microsoft.com/windows/downloads** and click the Windows 95 link. Then find the Windows 95 IrDA 2.0 Infrared Driver and install it. This should only apply to older laptops.*

4. Next, make sure the infrared port is enabled. Double-click the Infrared icon in the Control Panel (seen in Figure 3-7). You should see the Infrared Monitor dialog box. Click the Options tab and make sure the Enable Infrared Communication option is checked. If not, your notebook won't be able to communicate with the Palm.

5. While you're on this tab, make a note of what COM port the infrared device is using. This should be displayed near the option you selected in Step 4.

Before you go any further, be sure you perform at least one normal Local HotSync with the Palm and this notebook. That's right: you need to connect the HotSync cradle and press the button the old-fashioned way. After that, you can put the cradle back on your desktop PC and forget

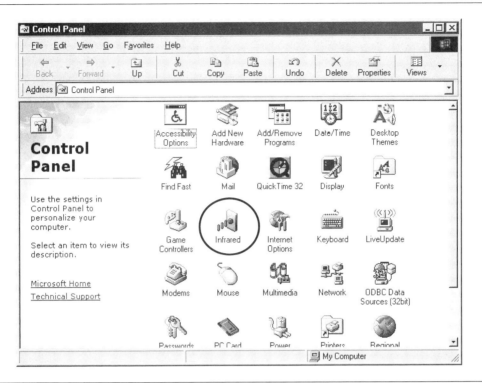

FIGURE 3-7   The Control Panel is where you need to go to configure your infrared settings before you start HotSyncing.

about it. Your first HotSync on a PC can't be an IR HotSync, so if you arrive in Topeka with a brand-new notebook and plan to IR HotSync with it, you're in for a big surprise.

Your PC is ready to start performing IR HotSyncs.

Configure the HotSync Manager

Now that your IR port is ready, you need to configure the HotSync Manager for IR communications. This part is easy. All you need to do is change the COM to the same one the IR port is accessing. Do this:

1.   Click the HotSync Manager icon in the System Tray and choose Setup from the menu. You should see the Setup dialog box.

2.   Switch to the Local tab. Change the serial port to whatever COM port the Infrared driver is using. You can find out by opening the Infrared icon in the Control Panel, as discussed in the previous section.

3.   Click OK to close the Setup dialog box.

Perform the HotSync

Now it's time to perform the HotSync. Turn on your Palm and tap the HotSync icon. Make sure it's set to Local (not Modem) and choose IR to a PC/Handheld from the menu.

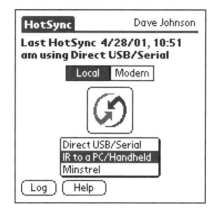

Point the Palm at the IR port on the notebook and tap the HotSync button in the middle of the Palm's screen. You should see the HotSync operation start. That's it!

Where to Find It

Web Site	Address	What's There
Palm Computing	**www.palm.com**	Software updates, news, and accessories
AvantGo	**www.avantgo.com**	Web page-like news and information channels you can carry on your Palm

Chapter 4

Get Information in and out of Your Palm

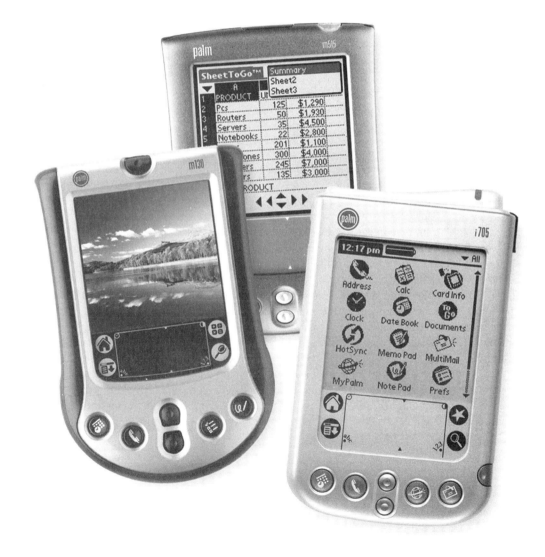

How to...

- Use Graffiti to enter data into your Palm
- Type using the onscreen Palm keyboard
- Enter data using the Palm Desktop
- Use alternative gestures to write in Graffiti more effectively
- Turn abbreviations into long text using shortcuts
- Display Graffiti help
- Receive data from another Palm via the IR port
- Beam items to another Palm
- Beam your business card to another Palm
- Lock your Palm so it can't receive beams
- Install new software on your Palm
- Delete old applications from your Palm

A handheld computer is only as good as the information you store inside it. Or, perhaps more to the point, it's only as good as the methods you have for getting information into it. After all, if you make storing your appointments on the computer too difficult, you won't bother doing it—and then you own an expensive paperweight with the word "calendar" written on it.

Case in point is a tiny, credit card–sized PDA called the Rex. This device debuted a few years ago to somewhat favorable reviews. This little guy was so small that it slipped easily into a wallet, yet it carried contacts and appointments like a champ. The problem? You couldn't update it away from your PC, so a schedule change or a new contact couldn't be entered on-the-fly. For some people, this wasn't a big deal, but public reaction was underwhelming. The Palm sells like hotcakes (the good ones, with the pecans in them) because of the very fact that it can be updated on the go, and quite easily as well.

You already know about some of the tools at your disposal for getting data in and out of your Palm. We talked in detail about how to HotSync (some would say too much detail, but we ignore those people) in Chapter 3 and you know you can enter data directly into the device using Graffiti, an almost-ordinary style of handwriting. In this chapter, you learn everything you might ever need to know about Graffiti. We also cover other data entry methods, including the onscreen keyboard and beaming data directly between Palms using the built-in IR port.

The Three Ways to Enter Data

Without a doubt, one of the first things you want to do with your new Palm is enter data—text and numbers—into your various applications. Hey, don't look so surprised. The core applications—Date Book, Address List, Memo Pad, and To Do List—rely on you to fill them with interesting things you can later reference.

Certainly, you can use the Palm's HotSync capability to enter data, but HotSyncing is only part of the story. Unlike some handheld computers, the Palm doesn't include a keyboard. Instead, you can use any one of three completely different methods for entering information into your Palm:

- Enter text using Graffiti.
- Enter text using the onscreen keyboard.
- Enter text into the Palm Desktop, and then HotSync the data to your Palm.

TIP *You can also connect a real keyboard to your Palm and type the ordinary way. For information on Palm keyboards, see Chapter 20. A fifth way to get data into your handheld is by beaming, which we discuss in the upcoming section, "Beam Data Between Palms."*

If you're on the go, you definitely need to use either Graffiti or the keyboard to enter data. If you're at your desk, though, you might find entering data into the Palm Desktop and then HotSyncing easier because your desktop computer sports a full-sized keyboard.

Using Graffiti

Graffiti is a specialized handwriting recognition system that enables you to enter text into the Palm almost error-free. Unlike other handwriting recognition systems, Graffiti neither interprets your ordinary handwriting nor learns or adapts to the way you write. Instead, you need to modify the way you write slightly and make specific kinds of keystrokes that represent the letters, numbers, and punctuation you're trying to write. Don't worry, though, this isn't hard to do. You can learn the basics of Graffiti inside of a day—heck, you can probably master most of the characters in an hour or less.

$\wedge$ = A

$\daleth$ = T

When entering text into your Palm, you can't write directly on the part of the screen the Palm uses to display data. Instead, you write inside the small rectangle at the bottom of the display—the one that sits between the four icons. We call this the "Graffiti area."

TIP *A Palm utility, called a* Hack, *is available that enables you to write above the Graffiti area, right on the main screen. Some people find this way of entering text more intuitive because the characters appear directly under where they're writing. See Chapter 15 for more information on this tool.*

The rectangle is divided roughly in half: the left side is used to enter letters, while the right side is used to enter numbers.

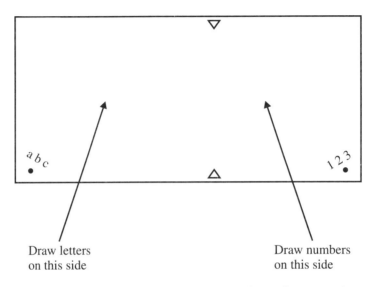

Draw letters
on this side

Draw numbers
on this side

If you aren't getting the results you expect from Graffiti, make sure you're writing on the correct side of the rectangle. The right side is for numbers, the left side is for letters, and either side works for punctuation.

Your Palm came with a Graffiti "cheat sheet," either as a laminated card or a sticker. Take a look at this guide and you'll see most characters are single-stroke shapes (called *gestures* in Graffiti-ese). The characters must be drawn in the direction indicated on the Graffiti guide: the heavy dot indicates the starting position. To write a character, mimic the Graffiti guide by drawing the shape starting with the dot and—in most cases—finish the character in a single stroke without lifting the stylus.

For more details on writing in Graffiti, see the section "Getting to Know Graffiti," later in this chapter.

Using the Onscreen Keyboard

Even after you get comfortable writing with Graffiti, at times you'll need or want to input specific characters without using pen strokes. After all, remembering how to make some rarely used characters in the middle of taking real-time notes can be hard and having access to a keyboard can be a real lifesaver.

When you have to enter a password, tapping it out on the keyboard is easier than writing it with Graffiti. Using the keyboard, you can be sure you're entering the right characters, error free.

HandEra Changes Everything

The HandEra 330 was the first Palm OS device to radically change the way the Graffiti area operates. The HandEra has a high-resolution 320 × 240–pixel screen, which is significantly sharper than the standard 160 × 160–pixel Palm screen. That's pretty neat, but what's even better is the 330 has no silk-screened Graffiti area. Instead, the Graffiti writing area can "pop up" in the LCD whenever it's needed.

Sony's latest CLIE handheld, the NR70, offers a similar "virtual" Graffiti area, this time with higher resolution (320 × 480) and a color screen.

To open and close the Graffiti area on these PDAs, tap the arrow at the bottom of the screen. In many cases, the current application should shrink or enlarge to accommodate it. On the CLIE, applications need to be "aware" of this feature to take advantage of the collapsible Graffiti area.

Here's what the CLIE NR70 looks like with the Graffiti area open and closed:

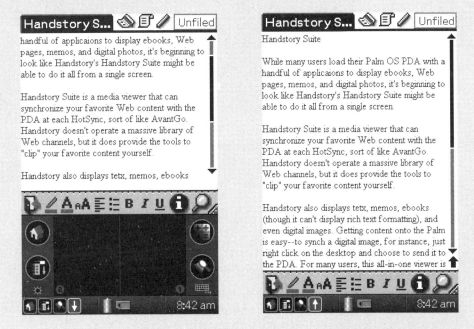

One of the coolest features in these new PDAs is that you see what you're drawing as you enter it on the Graffiti area, which, many people say, improves their accuracy.

All it takes to use the onscreen keyboard is a tap. At the bottom of the Graffiti area, you see the letters *ABC* wrapped around a small dot on the left and the numbers 123 on the right, also curved around a dot. Tap either spot to call up the appropriate keyboard (alpha or numeric).

The keyboard only appears in situations where it's appropriate—specifically, when a cursor is in a data field. If no application is open into which you can insert text, you simply hear a beep when you tap the keyboard dots.

Once the keyboard is open, note that you can switch between letters and numbers by tapping the selector at the bottom of the screen. A set of international characters is available as well.

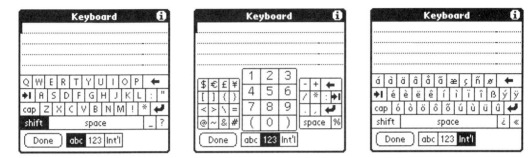

Remember the following tips about the onscreen keyboard:

■ In handhelds that use versions of the Palm OS prior to 4.0, you can't use Graffiti at the same time you have the keyboard open. Drawing on the Graffiti area has no effect.

■ Use the SHIFT key on the keyboard in the same way you'd use a real keyboard: tap it to create an uppercase letter.

■ The CAP key is actually a CAPS LOCK key, which makes all subsequent letters uppercase until you tap it again.

■ If you're typing with the CAPS LOCK on and you want to make a single character lowercase, tap the SHIFT key.

■ The Numeric keyboard provides access to special symbols and punctuation.

Using the Palm Desktop

Those other methods are great when you're on the go, but what about getting data into your Palm when you're comfortably sitting at your desk? Nothing's wrong with entering notes into the Palm with Graffiti, even in the office, but long notes can get tiresome. Instead, you can use the keyboard on your desktop PC to type into the Palm much more quickly and efficiently.

How? By using the Palm Desktop or another program with a HotSync conduit. In other words, suppose you need to enter a long note into your Palm. Instead of writing it slowly using Graffiti, create a note in the Palm Desktop or Outlook, depending on which program you use with your Palm, and then HotSync.

 If you configured your Palm to synchronize with Microsoft Outlook or another PIM, use that program to copy data to your Palm instead.

Let's add a note to the Palm's Memo List using the Palm Desktop. Do this:

1. Start the Palm Desktop in Windows by choosing Start | Programs | Palm Desktop | Palm Desktop. On the Mac, you can find it in the Chooser or in the Palm folder.

2. In Windows, switch to the Memo Pad view by clicking the Memo button on the left side of the screen. On the Mac, choose View | Note List instead.

3. If you're using Windows, click the Memo Pad and type a note, as in Figure 4-1. On the Mac, click the Create Note button on the toolbar at the top of the screen.

4. When you finish typing your note, close the New Note dialog box (on the Mac) or click anywhere in the Memo list (in Windows). The note is automatically saved and the memo's subject line shows as much of the note as would fit on the line in the list.

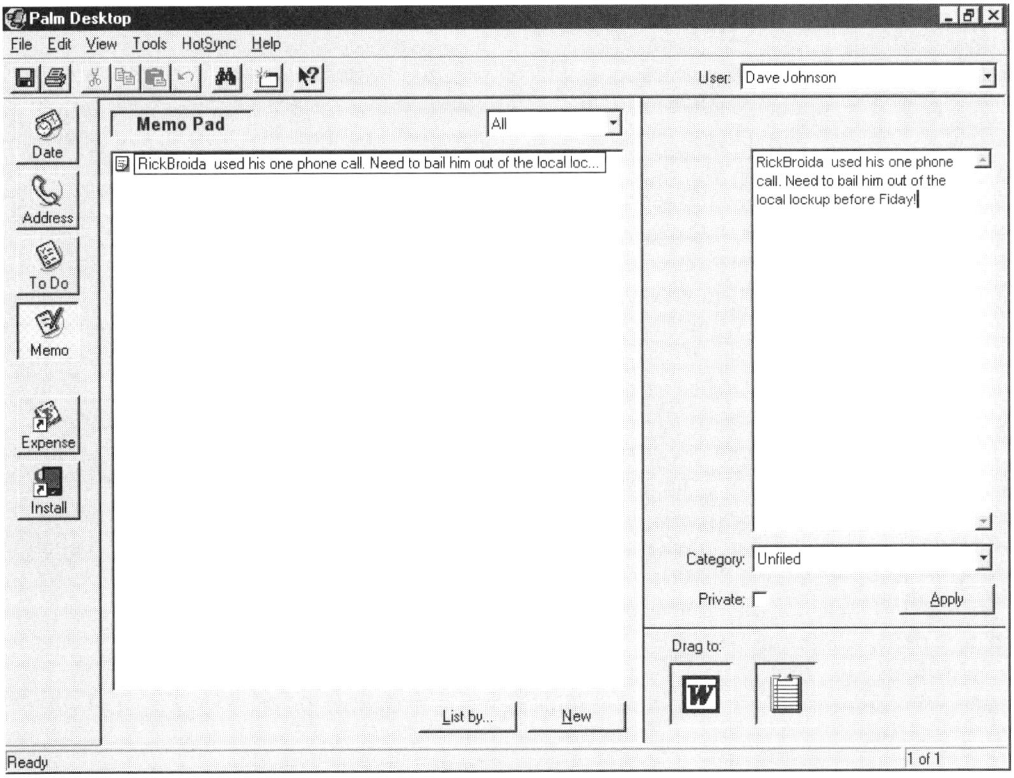

4

FIGURE 4-1   If you want to enter long notes or work with a keyboard, just enter the text using your PC and then HotSync it to the Palm.

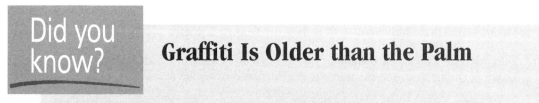

Graffiti Is Older than the Palm

The Graffiti recognition system now used on almost all Palm devices was first created as an alternative text input system for the Apple Newton MessagePad!

5. Enter any additional notes, tasks, calendar appointments, or contacts in the Address List.

6. When you finish entering data, place the Palm in its HotSync cradle and press the HotSync button. For details on how to HotSync, see Chapter 3.

Getting to Know Graffiti

Earlier in the chapter, we took a quick look at using Graffiti to enter data into your Palm. Graffiti deserves a lot of attention, though, because it's your principal way of interfacing with your favorite handheld PC. We're willing to bet that more than 90 percent of the time you need to add a note, contact, or to-do, you end up whipping out the Palm stylus and entering your info with good old Graffiti. Knowing Graffiti like the back of your hand is essential to using your Palm effectively.

As we pointed out earlier in this chapter, Graffiti doesn't rely on interpreting whatever chicken-like scrawl you happen to draw into the Palm's Graffiti area. While it might be nice if the Palm could interpret unmodified handwriting, we've all seen what happened to that technology.

Specifically, Apple's Newton MessagePad was a great little PDA that understood free-form handwriting. And, while it did a darned good job, first-time users faced an uphill battle getting it to understand them. Not until you had a chance to use the Newton for a few hours did it start behaving like it comprehended English. To make matters worse, Apple insisted on putting MessagePads in stores with big signs inviting people to saunter over and try them. The result? People would scratch out a sentence in sloppy handwriting and the Newton would convert the result into total gibberish, kind of like what you think Lou Reed might be muttering in a Velvet Underground song. The public never got any confidence that Apple had a workable handwriting recognition engine and, though the Newton was a great little PDA, it failed largely because of public perception.

Palm didn't make the same mistake. Its handwriting recognition engine is designed to recognize particular gestures as specific characters, thus reducing the possibility of error. In fact, if you routinely draw the characters according to the template, you should get about 100 percent accuracy. Graffiti doesn't have to understand 50 different ways of making the letter *T*, so it's both fast and accurate.

> **TIP** *There's a Graffiti cheat sheet built into the Palm. By default, you can see it by making an upstroke from the Graffiti area to the top of the LCD screen.*

General Tips and Tricks for Graffiti

Before we get started with the nuts and bolts of writing with Graffiti, it might help to remember a few things. Despite Graffiti's simplicity, a few tips and tricks can make writing on the Palm a lot easier.

- Draw your characters as large as possible, especially if you're having trouble with Graffiti misinterpreting what you're writing. Use all the Graffiti area, if necessary.

- Don't cross the line between the letter and number portion of the Graffiti area. Make sure you make your gestures on the correct side of the fence to get the characters you want.

- Don't write at a slant. Some handwriting recognition engines can account for characters being drawn at an angle to the baseline, but Graffiti can't. Vertical lines should be perpendicular to the Graffiti area baseline.

- Don't write too fast. Graffiti doesn't care about your speed; but if you write too fast, you won't have sufficient control over the shape of your gestures and you can make mistakes.

- If you have a hard time making certain gestures consistently, try the character a different way. Specifically, refer to Table 4-1 for a list of primary and secondary gestures for each character. Use the gestures that work best for you.

Writing Letters and Numbers

The genius behind Graffiti—if that's not too strong a word—is almost every letter and number at your disposal has two important characteristics:

- Every letter and number can be drawn in a single stroke of the stylus (with one exception— the letter *X*).

- Every letter and number bears a strong resemblance to its normal, plain English counterpart.

The easiest way to learn Graffiti is simply to practice writing the alphabet a few times. Use the Graffiti reference card that came with your Palm or refer to Table 4-1 as a guide on how to draw each character. The advantage of using this book, of course, is we show you a few alternative gestures that might make certain characters easier to draw consistently. Give them a shot.

Only one exception exists to the single stroke rule: the letter *X.* When you make an *X,* you can pick the stylus up off the screen to cross the letter in the traditional way. Of course, you can use a single-stroke alternative, as well (see Table 4-1 for the scoop on that).

You might notice some letters and numbers have identical gestures. The letter *L* and the number 4, for instance, are both made in the same way (see Figure 4-2). How does Graffiti tell the difference? That's an easy one—don't forget, the Graffiti area is divided into a number side and a letter side.

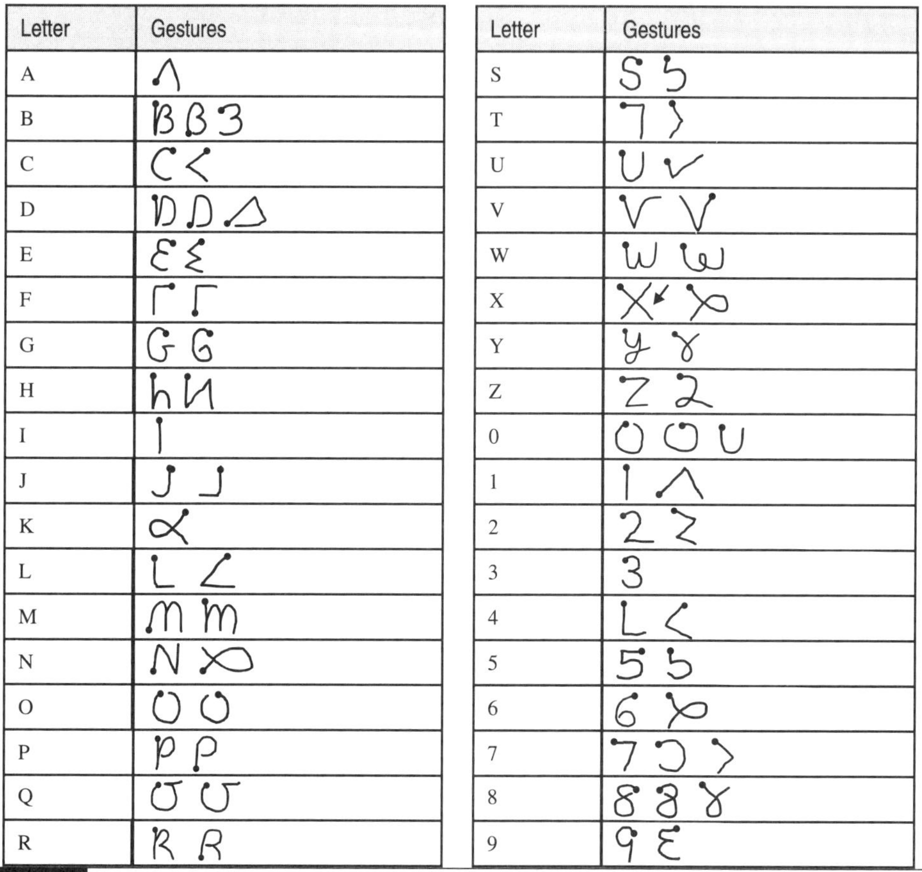

Letter	Gestures		Letter	Gestures
A	∧		S	S 5
B	B B 3		T	7 ⟩
C	C <		U	U ∨
D	D D △		V	V V
E	ε ξ		W	ω ω
F	Γ Γ		X	X ✕
G	G G		Y	y γ
H	h ᴎ		Z	Z 2
I	l		0	O O U
J	J J		1	l ∧
K	⍺		2	2 2
L	L ∠		3	3
M	m m		4	L <
N	N ✕		5	5 5
O	O O		6	6 ✕
P	P P		7	7 ⊃ ⟩
Q	℧ ℧		8	8 8 γ
R	R R		9	9 ξ

TABLE 4-1   The Graffiti Numbers and Letters

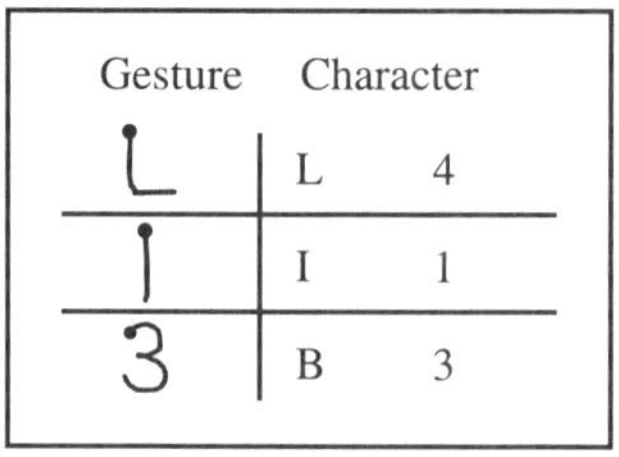

Gesture	Character	
L	L	4
l	I	1
3	B	3

FIGURE 4-2   The letter *L* and the number 4 are made exactly the same way, as are the letter *I* and the number 1.

The Hardest Characters

Everyone seems to have trouble with some Graffiti character. Even if you can never get your Palm to recognize your letter *B,* that doesn't make you a freak—it simply means you should learn an alternative stroke for that letter or put extra care into drawing it carefully and slowly. Even we have trouble with some letters. . . .

Dave: It's unfortunate my last name is "Johnson," because I can't get Graffiti to take my letter *J* to save my life. Half the time, it's my own fault. As many times as I've made the *J,* I can't remember it starts at the top and curves down. I always try to start at the bottom and hook up—which gives me a letter *U* every time. But, even when I remember how to do it, I end up with a *V* or a new paragraph. Of course, now that I'm drawing it for this chapter, I can't seem to do it wrong—ten perfect Js out of ten. I think the letter hates me. And I know I'm not crazy, by the way, despite what my dog keeps telling me.

Rick: If you'd ever seen Dave's chicken-scratch excuse for handwriting, you'd understand why he sometimes has trouble with Graffiti. To be fair, though, a few characters seem tougher to make than others. It's the *V* that drives me up the wall—I always forget to put the little tail on the end of the upstroke. But I know a secret: if you write the letter backward, it comes out perfectly every time—and you don't need to draw the tail!

TIP *If you're really having trouble mastering Graffiti, there's a great tutorial program called PenJammer (**www.penjammer.com**). It's not for Windows or Macintosh—Penjammer works right on your handheld, teaching you every Graffiti character via animated helpers. It's cool, helpful, and inexpensive (only $7.95).*

Capitalize Letters

You probably noticed no distinction exists in the Graffiti gestures for lowercase and uppercase characters. That's a good thing—you don't have to learn over 100 gestures because uppercase and lowercase letters are drawn the same way. Here's how to tell Graffiti you want to make an uppercase letter:

■ **One capital letter**   To make the next character, draw an uppercase gesture: draw a vertical line from the bottom of the Graffiti area to the top. This only works on the left side of the screen. It won't work in the number area. You see a symbol like this one, which indicates you're now in Uppercase mode:

Indicates next letter will be a capital

■ **All capital letters**   To switch to All Caps mode and type in all capital letters, draw the vertical gesture twice. You see this symbol to indicate All Caps mode:

Indicates All Caps mode

■ **Lowercase letters**   If you're already in All Caps mode, you can exit and write in lowercase again by making one more vertical gesture. The All Caps symbol should disappear to show you changed modes.

NOTE   *Uppercase mode doesn't affect numbers, so it doesn't matter which mode you're in when writing numbers. This means you needn't drop out of Uppercase mode just to write numbers amid a bunch of capital letters.*

TIP   *One of our all-time favorite Hacks (see Chapter 15) is called MiddleCaps. It saves you having to write the upstroke before each capital letter. Just write the letter across the imaginary line separating the letter and number sides of the Graffiti area. Absolutely indispensable and it's a freebie! Find it at PalmGear (**www.palmgear.com**).*

Spaces, Backspaces, and Deleting Text

Words are arguably more useful when you can put a space between them, thus enabling the casual reader to discern where each one ends and the next one begins. In Graffiti, it's easy to insert spaces. So easy, in fact, you might be able to figure it out on your own (but we'll tell you anyway). Draw a dash that starts on the left and goes to the right, and the cursor skips ahead a space. You can use this gesture to insert spaces between words or to perform any other space-making task you might need. And, yes, you can insert multiple spaces simply by performing this gesture as many times as needed.

The backspace, not surprisingly, is exactly the opposite. Draw a gesture from right to left and the cursor backs up, deleting any text it encounters along the way.

TIP   *Space and backspace gestures work fine in both the letter and number sides of the Graffiti area.*

Using the backspace gesture is great if you want to delete one or two characters, but what if you want to delete a whole sentence? That backspace swipe can get tiring if you have a lot of text to kill or replace all at once. Luckily, an easy solution exists: select the text you want to delete. The next thing you write replaces the selected text. Here's how to do it:

1. On the Palm, find a region of text you want to replace.

2. Tap and hold the stylus down at the start of the text you want to select, and then drag the stylus across the text. Pick the stylus up when you've selected all the text in question.

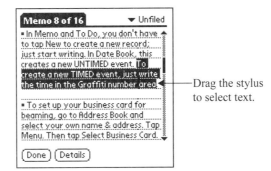

Drag the stylus
to select text.

3. In the Graffiti area, write some new text. The old text is immediately erased and replaced with the new text. If you simply want to delete the text, use the backspace gesture instead.

Adding Punctuation

To add punctuation to your prose, you need to (surprise, surprise) enter Graffiti's special Punctuation mode. All this takes is a tap in the Graffiti area. You see a dot appear, which indicates you can now enter punctuation. Table 4-2 displays the punctuation gestures you commonly need.

The most common punctuation mark is a period and, because it's simply a dot, you can add a period to the end of a sentence by performing a quick double-tap. Some other symbols are trickier, though, and might take some practice. The comma, parenthesis bracket, and apostrophe are so similar, for instance, getting one when you're trying to gesture another isn't unusual.

If you have a lot of trouble with specific symbols, you can always use the onscreen keyboard along with Graffiti to write your text.

If you enter the Punctuation mode by tapping on one side of the Graffiti area, you need to complete the punctuation gesture on the same side. For instance, tapping once on the number side and again on the letter side has no effect.

Using Shortcuts

Everyone seems to love shortcuts. In desktop applications like Microsoft Office, many folks eschew the mouse for keyboard shortcuts that speed tasks like text formatting and saving files. The Palm also has the capability to save you time and effort using shortcuts. Even better, Palm shortcuts are user-definable, so you can create your own library of them and you needn't be satisfied with whatever came in the box.

So what are *shortcuts,* exactly? If you have a word or phrase you frequently write over and over (such as "Rick throws like his baby girl"), you can assign an abbreviation to it and let Graffiti

Punctuation	Gestures
Period	•
Comma	/ (draw low)
Question mark	? ⌐
Exclamation point	↓
Colon	V
Semicolon	⟋
Open parenthesis	C
Close parenthesis	)
Tab	⌐
Apostrophe	↑ (draw high)
Quotes	N
Slash	/
Backslash	\
At symbol	∪
Asterisk	⅋
Number sign	∿ ⌂
Greater than	<
Less than	>
Percent	∪∪ ∞
Equal sign	z
Plus sign	∝
Dollar sign	S

TABLE 4-2   The Most Common Graffiti Punctuation Gestures

do the hard work of writing the phrase in its entirety. To see how easy using shortcuts is, try this, using one of the shortcuts that comes built into your Palm:

1. Open the Memo Pad and tap the New button to open a new memo page.

2. Draw the shortcut gesture (shown at the left). The *shortcut gesture* tells Graffiti that the next thing you write is going to be an abbreviation, which should be expanded in accordance with the shortcut library.

3. Write **br**, which is the shortcut for "breakfast." As soon as you finish writing it, the text should expand into the word "breakfast."

That's all there is to it. We hope you can see the value of creating shortcuts that are relevant to what you frequently write.

Storing Your Own Shortcuts

Your Palm comes with half a dozen shortcuts and you can easily create new ones whenever you want. To create a shortcut, do this:

1. Display Preferences by tapping the Prefs icon.

2. Choose Shortcuts from the list of Preferences in the upper-right corner of the screen.

```
Preferences              Buttons
                         Connection
br - Breakfast           Digitizer
di - Dinner              Formats
ds - [Date Stamp]        General
dts - [Date and Time St] Network
lu - Lunch               Owner
me - Meeting             ShortCuts
ts - [Time Stamp]


  ( New )  ( Edit )  ( Delete... )
```

3. Tap the New button to display the Shortcut Entry window.

4. Give your shortcut a name. This is the abbreviation you write to summon the entire shortcut text. If you want to create a shortcut that reads "Dear Sir," for instance, you might want to use "ds."

```
Preferences          ▼ ShortCuts
       ShortCut Entry        ⓘ
ShortCut Name:
ds

ShortCut Text:
dear sir



  ( OK )  ( Cancel )
```

5. Enter the complete shortcut text. Remember, you're limited to a maximum length of 45 characters. If you reach that limit, you hear a beep when you try to write additional text.

6. Tap the OK button to save your shortcut.

Once you create a shortcut, you can use it anywhere in your Palm that you can write with Graffiti.

Don't go overboard with shortcuts right away. Shortcuts become a lot less cool if you have so many of them that you can't remember what the abbreviation is to summon the entire text. Start with two or three, and, once you know them like the back of your hand, add a few more.

Another Kind of Shortcut: Menu Commands

If you're a big fan of choosing CTRL-S in Microsoft Word to save your work, then you should love this. The Palm has its own menu shortcuts you can access with Graffiti. To do that, though, you must be prepared by remembering two important items:

■ How to draw the Graffiti command stroke

■ What the shortcut character is for the menu command you want to invoke

The command stroke is easy. To put your Palm in Command mode, draw the gesture on the left. After you draw the gesture, your Palm displays the Command bar. You simply need to write the proper character to invoke the menu item.

To learn what the shortcuts are for each menu item, display the menu (tap the Menu soft button on your Palm and you see something similar to Figure 4-3). You'll see many menu items have associated shortcuts.

FIGURE 4-3   Many menu items have Graffiti shortcuts associated with them.

NOTE   *The Command mode only lasts for about two seconds. If you don't write the shortcut character quickly, Command mode is deactivated and you need to perform the command stoke again.*

Get Help with Graffiti

Graffiti help is never far away. You should know about a few resources that can help you master this almost, but not quite, normal alphabet.

4

■ **Play a game**   When you start out with Graffiti, you might want to use one of the core applications that comes with your Palm. Called *Giraffe,* it's a game that enables you to get up to speed quickly on the art of shaping Graffiti characters. You need to draw the correct gesture for letters that fall from the sky. Time is limited, so a few rounds of Giraffe can build up your speed and accuracy at drawing letters and numbers. Install Giraffe from the CD-ROM that comes with your PDA to hone your handwriting skills.

■ **Display the help screen**   There's a Graffiti reference built into the Palm. To display it, start your stylus at the bottom of the Graffiti area and draw a vertical line that extends all the way up to the top of the Palm screen.

■ **Use the guides**   Keep a copy of the Graffiti guide that came with your Palm in your Palm carrying case or in your wallet. The tables (Table 4-1 and 4-2) in this chapter are also handy for learning the ropes, though we know you're not likely to carry our book around with you everywhere you go (though we hear that's what all the cool kids in SOHO are doing).

Beam Data Between Palms

On *Star Trek,* transporters are used to beam people and equipment from one location to another. While we're a long way from being able to beam physical things around, the Palm makes it possible to beam almost any kind of data between handheld PC users.

All Palm models (except for first-generation Palm Pilots) have an infrared port. On most models, you can find the infrared port on the front edge of the case. Handspring models put the IR port on the left side of the case of many of its PDAs. If you haven't seen your Palm device's IR port yet, find it now. It's a small, red, translucent strip of plastic. Using this IR port, you can beam information in a surprising number of ways. You can do the following:

■ Use your Palm as a TV and stereo remote control.

■ Control an MP3 player on your laptop.

■ Send data between your Palm and a cell phone or pager.

■ Print Palm data on an IR-equipped printer.

■ Beam data to other Palm users.

■ Give another Palm user your "business card."

■ Play two-player games "head-to-head."

The Command Bar

So, you tried entering a command, but you're curious about the Command bar. What are all those little symbols and what do they do?

The *Command bar* is a clever tool you can use to access common features of your Palm rapidly. It's context-sensitive, which means the bar will look different—it'll have different icons—depending on when you make the command stroke.

Try this: make the command stroke when you're on the Applications screen. The three icons on the right side of the Command bar represent Info, Beam, and Delete (just as if you tapped the Menu button and selected Info, Beam, or Delete from the App menu).

Now open the Date Book and select an appointment by dragging the stylus across some text. Make the command stroke again. Voila! You now have all new choices, like cut, copy, and paste. You can experiment with the Command bar in various locales around your Palm to see what kinds of shortcuts you can create.

While you can do a lot of things with your Palm's IR port, usually you'll want to exchange mundane business data with other Palm users. All the core applications support beaming, so you can beam

- Address List entries
- Your own "business card" from the Address Book
- Appointments and meetings
- Memos
- Tasks

to other users. In addition, you can beam entire applications to other Palm users. If you download a freeware program from the Internet and you want to share it with friends or coworkers, go ahead: it's a snap to transmit the item wirelessly.

How to Beam

No matter what you're planning to beam—or receive—the process is essentially the same. Seeing the process demonstrated is faster than reading about it but, because neither Dave nor Rick is handy to stop by your office today, here's the process in a nutshell:

1. Orient the two Palms so their IR ports face each other, and are between about four inches and three feet apart. If you're any closer than four inches, the Palms could have a hard time locking onto each other. If you're too far away, the signal won't be strong enough to reach.

2. As the sender, you should choose the item you want to beam.

3. Choose the Beam command from the menu.

TIP   *If you beam often, you might want to use the beam shortcut—a command slash gesture followed by the letter B. Or, you can configure your Palm so a stroke from the bottom of the Graffiti area to the top of the screen can start a beam. To do that, tap the Prefs icon, and then select the Buttons item in the list at the top-right corner of the screen. Tap the Pen button and choose Beam Data.*

4. A dialog box appears to indicate the beam is in progress. First, you see a message that your Palm is searching for the other Palm. This message then goes away and the data is transmitted.

5. After the beam, your Palm goes back to business as usual—you won't get a message indicating the beam was successful. The receiver Palm, on the other hand, gets a dialog box that asks permission to accept the beamed data. As the receiver, you need to decide what category to file the information into, and then tap either Yes or No, depending on whether you want to keep the item. If you tap Yes, the data is integrated into your Palm in the category you specified.

TIP   *As the receiver, a good idea is to specify a category in which to file the data you just received. If you let stuff like Address Book entries accumulate in the Unfiled category, it can later become difficult to find what you're looking for.*

To Accept or Not to Accept

By default, your Palm is set to accept beamed items. Two reasons exist why you might want to disable autoreceive for beaming, though:

- Because the IR port is constantly on and searching for transmissions from other Palms, your Palm uses slightly more battery power when it's set to the default autoreceive. Is this a big deal, though? We don't think so. The extra power consumption is marginal.

- With all the concerns about viruses and other malicious programs that exist for PCs today, some folks are nervous about leaving their Palms in a state that receives software all the time. Our call: viruses for the Palm aren't a threat (yet) and you have to accept a beamed program explicitly after reception anyway. Don't worry about it.

So, while we obviously don't think autoreceiving beamed items is a big deal, here's how to disable that feature if you want to:

1. Open the Palm's Preferences by tapping the Prefs icon.

2. Choose the General category from the list at the top-right of the screen.

3. Change Beam Receive from Yes to No.

After changing your preferences to disable beaming, other Palms can't send you data unless you reenable beaming from Preferences.

TIP *You can receive a beam from someone even if you've disabled beaming in Preferences. When someone starts to beam something to you that you want to receive, draw the shortcut gesture and double-tap to make a period. Then draw the letter I. You receive the beam only that one time. You must receive a beam signal within about five seconds or you revert to no-beaming mode.*

Selecting Items for Beaming

So, now that you know the rudiments of beaming, you're no doubt eager to start. While we're usually a pretty down-to-earth couple of guys, we have to admit a certain coolness factor is involved in beaming things in the middle of a meeting or on the show floor at a trade show. It's definitely better than writing notes by hand or trading easily scrunched business cards.

Beaming Appointments

If you work with other Palm users, you can make sure everyone is on the same schedule by beaming entries from the Date Book. To do that, select an appointment, and then choose Beam Event from the menu.

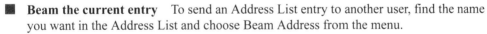

Beaming Contacts

If you're like most people, the Address List is the most well-exercised part of your Palm. And, instead of exchanging paper-based business cards, now you can beam the information between Palms, which can later be HotSynced back to your PC's contact manager. In recognition of just how important the Address List is, you have not one, not two, but three options for sending data from this application:

■ **Beam the current entry**   To send an Address List entry to another user, find the name you want in the Address List and choose Beam Address from the menu.

■ **Beam a whole bunch of entries**   You can send any number of contacts to someone else all at once—every name in your Palm, in fact—using Beam Category. To do that, first choose the category you want to beam by picking the category from the list at the top-right corner of the screen. Then choose the Beam Category from the menu. To beam all the entries in your entire Address List, you should (obviously) set the category to All—but, if you do that, you lose the categories and everything ends up on the new Palm as Unfiled.

CAUTION *Be careful before you beam or try to receive a whole category's worth of contacts—make sure it's something you need to do. This operation could include hundreds of entries, which will take more time than either of you are willing to spend pointing your PDAs at each other.*

■ **Beam your own entry** What's more common than handing your business card to someone? You can configure your own Address List entry as your personal business card and beam it to other Palms. For details on configuring an entry as your business card, see Chapter 6. Once configured, however, you can send it by opening the Address List and choosing Beam Business Card from the menu.

TIP *There's a faster way to beam your business card to someone: hold down the Address List button for two seconds. This automatically tells the Palm to beam your business card.*

Beaming Memos and Tasks

Memos are handy to pass off to other Palm users. You can give them notes, action items, short documents, and even meeting minutes in this way. Likewise, if you want to delegate a task to someone else in your office, tell that person to "visit my cubicle—and don't forget to bring your Palm." Two ways exist to beam memos and To Do items:

■ **Beam a Memo or a To Do** To beam a single item, select it and choose Beam Memo (for a Memo) or Beam Item (for a To Do) from the menu.

■ **Beam a bunch of stuff at once** Like the Address List, you can select a category in the Memo List or the To Do List, and then choose Beam Category from the menu. To beam all your memos or tasks at once, remember to set the category list to All.

Beaming Applications

Now for the best part. You can use the Palm's beaming prowess to transfer entire applications from one Palm to another. If you meet someone who shows you his cool new Palm game or utility, for instance, you can ask him to send the game to you instantly so you can have it, too.

NOTE *Not all applications are free, so don't use your Palm's beaming capability for piracy. Many commercial programs are "locked" to prevent beaming and shareware applications often require an unlock code to access all the features in the registered version. You can beam trial versions around, but don't share registration codes—that's piracy.*

Not all programs can, in fact, be beamed. The core applications that come with your Palm are "locked," making them nonbeamable. Many commercial programs are also locked and some programs have a resistance to beaming—like Hacks (discussed in Chapter 15). In addition, if you have a program that requires supporting database files, the files won't be beamable. This means you must go home and install the program the old-fashioned way, using your PC.

If You Have No Friends

Rick is a lonely guy. While he loves the capability to beam stuff to other Palms, Rick is hampered by the fact that he never leaves the house. Thankfully, Dave has turned him on to a hidden feature in the Palm that enables you to, well, beam things to yourself. If you want to experiment with beaming stuff and you don't have a second Palm, you can now do the same thing Rick does for amusement.

Create the shortcut gesture, and then tap twice to write a period. Now write the letter *T*. When you try to beam, your Palm simulates the process of beaming and "receives" the item all by itself. You're asked if you want to accept the item, to which you can answer Yes or No. When you tire of beaming things to yourself, just repeat the shortcut to return to the ordinary Beaming mode.

Now that we've told you what you can't do, let's talk about what you can do. Beaming an application isn't much different than beaming data from one of the Palm's programs. Do this:

1. Tap the Home button on your Palm to return to applications.

2. From the menu, choose Beam. You see a dialog box with a list of all the applications on your Palm, as in Figure 4-4. Some applications have little locks; these aren't beamable.

3. Select an application, and then tap the Beam button.

Get a program called Beam Box if you beam lots of stuff. Beam Box simplifies the process of beaming programs and makes it possible to beam certain kinds of apps (like Hacks) that the Palm can't do on its own.

Beam	
Address	89K
AmusePark	38K
Astroids	28K
AvantGo	681K
Beam Box	14K
CharonClock	6K
Connection	2K
Cuepert	39K
Date Book	52K
Expense	1K

Done   Beam

FIGURE 4-4   Choose an app from the list to beam it to another Palm.

Installing New Software on Your Palm

Did you know you can install tons of additional programs on your Palm? Thousands of free and commercial applications are out there, just waiting to be installed. They include enhancements to the core applications, utilities, games, and more. In fact, one of the best reasons for choosing a Palm OS device (instead of a competing Windows CE device or some other kind of organizer) is that such a wealth of software exists.

But you might wonder: how the heck do I get all this cool stuff on to my Palm?

The answer is this: the Palm Desktop includes a handy Install tool for loading Palm apps.

Install Tool Shortcuts in Windows

Not everyone likes to use the Palm Desktop. If you use Microsoft Outlook, for instance, and you don't need to open the Palm Desktop to HotSync or enter data, then don't feel compelled to open the Palm Desktop simply to install Palm applications. Instead, you can start the Install tool directly. Choose Start | Programs | Palm Desktop | Install Tool. The Install tool starts without the Palm Desktop running at all.

And, while you can use the Add button to select files for installation, a much easier way exists. On the desktop, open the folder that includes the files you want to install and drag the program icons to the Install Tool dialog box. Drop the icons and they appear automatically in the list of files to be installed. Dave doesn't use the Palm Desktop, so he added the Install tool to the Microsoft Office Shortcut bar that appears on the Windows Desktop. This way, the Install tool is always only one click away.

> NOTE *You might have discovered a folder called Install. If you don't know where it is, look in C:\Palm\your username\Install. This folder holds applications waiting for the next HotSync to be installed on the Palm. Don't mess with this folder! You can't simply drag files to this folder because the Install tool needs to tell Windows files are waiting to be installed.*

You can install an application quickly in another way: double-click it, which automatically adds it to the Install Tool queue.

Prepping Applications for Installation

As we've said, a ton of Palm applications are available—many free, some for a commercial fee. Throughout this book, we make reference to our favorite applications and we recommend you try them. Perhaps the single best resource for Palm applications is a web site called **PalmGear.com** (see Figure 4-5).

Often, downloaded applications aren't immediately ready for installation. If you download an application from the Internet, it usually arrives in the form of a SIT file (if you're a Mac user) or a ZIP file (if you use Windows). You need to expand these SIT and ZIP files before they can be installed on your Palm. We recommend these tools for managing compressed files:

- **Windows** Use WinZip to uncompress ZIP files.
- **Macintosh** Use Aladdin StuffIt Expander to manage SIT files.

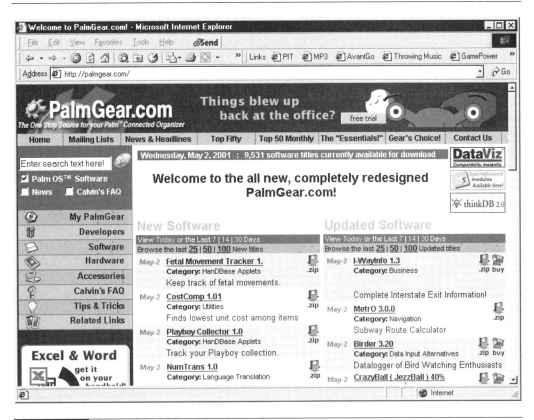

FIGURE 4-5 **PalmGear.com** is where Dave and Rick typically go to look for Palm software.

Of course, if you already happily expand compressed files with another program, keep up the good work. These are just our favorites.

Once expanded, most Palm files bear the file extension .prc. In a ZIP or SIT with lots of little files, you can generally grab the PRC file and install that. Of course, if in doubt, read whatever documentation accompanied the application.

After the HotSync

Any programs you want to install are stored in the Install tool's queue until you HotSync. After the HotSync, the programs are copied to your Palm, as long as the Install conduit is set to Install handheld applications (see Chapter 3 for details on configuring conduits).

After the HotSync, remember two things about your applications:

- New applications end up in the Unfiled category on your Palm.

- On your PC, the files are moved to a folder called Backup. The Backup folder can be found at C:\Pilot\your palm's folder\Backup. This folder is used by the Palm Desktop to reinstall

all your applications, just in case your Palm suffers a total memory failure and you need to reinstall programs from scratch. In a bizarre twist on logic, though, you can't always count on the Palm Desktop to restore 100 percent of these apps when you have a total failure. If you want more backup security, one alternative is a program called BackupBuddy, which is covered in detail in Chapter 15.

Installing to a Memory Card

If your Palm has a memory card, you can install applications directly to the external memory. That's handy, especially if you want to install a huge application or data file that simply wouldn't fit if copied to the Palm's more limited internal memory.

When you open the Install Tool dialog box, click the Change Destination button. You'll see the Change Destination dialog box. Then, click the program you want to copy directly to the memory card, and then click the arrow to move it to the right side of the screen, which represents the PDA's memory card. (The Change Destination option appears only if you're using a handheld that runs Palm OS 4.0 or later.)

When you've configured your to-be-installed applications to your liking, click OK, close the Install Tool, and HotSync.

How to ... Install New Palm Applications

Discovering new software for your Palm is one of the real joys of having a PDA. Here's how to install new programs:

1. Start the Palm Desktop by choosing Start | Programs | Palm Desktop | Palm Desktop. On the Mac, select the Palm Desktop from the Chooser or the Palm folder.

2. Click the Install button on the left side of the Palm Desktop screen. The Install tool appears. If you're using a Mac, choose HotSync | Install from the menu.

3. Click the Add button. You see the Open dialog box for selecting Palm applications.

4. Locate the program you want to install and select it. Click the Open button.

TIP *You can select multiple applications at once by holding down the* CTRL *key as you click programs in the file list.*

5. With your application displayed in the Install Tool dialog box, click Done.

6. The next time you HotSync your Palm, the selected application is installed.

Removing Applications from the Palm

You won't want every application you install on your Palm forever. Some programs you won't like, while others will outlive their usefulness. And, quite often, you need to eliminate some apps to make room for more, because the Palm has limited storage space.

Deleting programs from the Palm is easy. Tap the Applications soft button on your Palm and choose Delete from the menu. You see a list of all the applications currently stored on the handheld. At the top of the screen, you also see a bar that shows how much memory remains on your Palm.

```
┌─────────────────────────────┐
│        Delete          ⓘ    │
│ Free Memory: 6011K of 8064K │
│ ┌─────────────────────────┐ │
│ └─────────────────────────┘ │
│ AmusePark          38K ▲    │
│ Astroids           28K ▐    │
│ AvantGo           681K ░    │
│ Beam Box           14K ░    │
│ CharonClock         6K ░    │
│ Cuepert            39K ░    │
│ GetRom2             1K ▼    │
│ ( Done ) ( Delete... )      │
└─────────────────────────────┘
```

NOTE   *If you have a first-generation PalmPilot, switch to Applications and tap the Memory icon to get to the Delete Apps option.*

To delete an application, select it and tap the Delete button. This is similar to the Beam interface and, in fact, it's so similar, you should be careful you don't accidentally delete an app you're trying to beam to a friend.

TIP   *When you delete an application, you also delete all the data it generated. If you have a document reader, for instance, deleting the app also trashes any Docs it might contain. To preserve these files, HotSync before deleting anything.*

Part II

Get Things Done

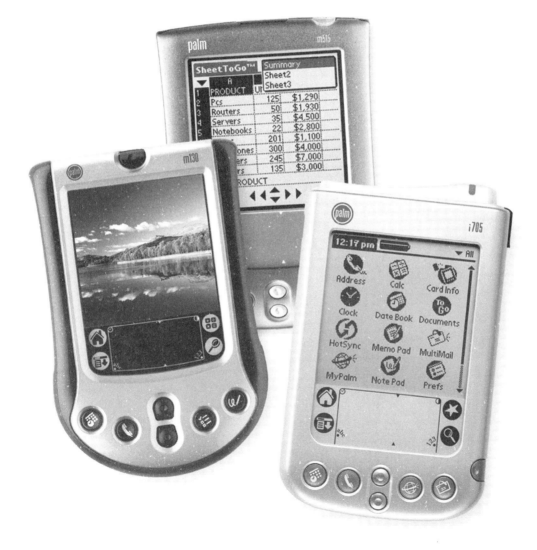

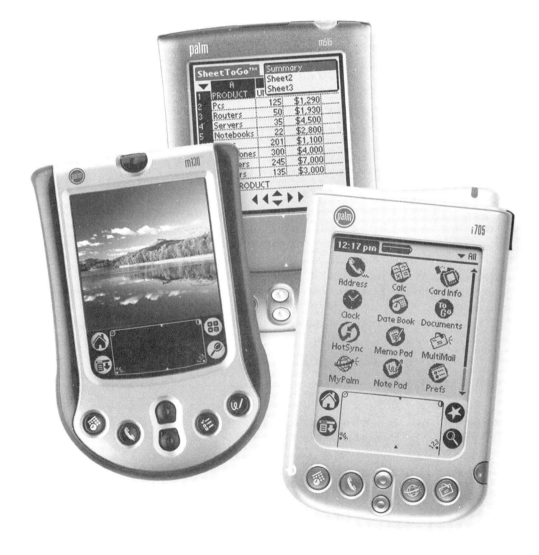

How to...

- Use the Day, Week, Month, and Agenda Views
- Customize the Date Book's appearance
- Add appointments to the Date Book
- Beam an appointment to someone else
- Create an appointment using the Address Book
- Create Repeating Events
- Add a note to an appointment
- Make an appointment private
- Edit Appointments in the Date Book
- Delete events in the Date Book
- Set an alarm for an appointment
- Use the Windows Date Book
- Use the Palm with Outlook
- Use the Macintosh Date Book

Are you busy on Tuesday at 3 P.M.? If you have your Palm handy, you'd probably already know the answer to that question. In an informal survey, we found the Date Book is the single most popular core application on the Palm. Heck—some people buy the Palm just for its scheduling prowess.

The Date Book is a modern miracle. That might sound like an overstatement, but consider how useful it is. The Date Book can track all your appointments. It can show you your schedule by day, week, or month. The Date Book handles recurring appointments and can alarm you about upcoming events. It synchronizes precisely with your desktop calendar. And the Date Book fits in the palm of your hand. It's better, Rick might tell you, than *Star Trek*. Dave, on the other hand, would be inclined to say it's better than *Babylon 5.*

View Your Appointments

When you switch to the Date Book, by default, it starts by showing you any appointments you have for today. Start the Date Book by pressing the Date Book button on your Palm or tapping the Date Book icon in the Palm's Application screen.

Navigate the Day View

When you start the Date Book, the first thing you see is the Day View. You can see it shows the currently selected date in the tab at the top of the screen. Next to that are seven icons, one for each day of the week.

Operating System Oddities

Although Palm devices all work more or less the same way, they don't all use exactly the same operating system (OS). Likewise, the Palm Desktop software on your PC could vary a bit, depending on which model you own. We wrote the next few chapters with Palm OS 4 in mind because that's what comes in all the coolest new gadgets, like the m500, m515, and i705. If you have an older PDA or one that runs a different version of the OS, don't worry: the differences are minor.

5

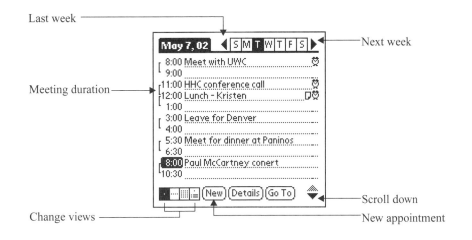

TIP   *Tap and hold the date tab to see the current time. If you let go too quickly, the Record menu will drop instead.*

In the middle of the screen, you see the current day's calendar. You can enter new events on the blank lines. If you have any appointments already entered, note that long appointments (those lasting for more than 30 minutes) have *duration brackets,* which appear to the immediate left of the appointment time and show you what time an appointment is scheduled to end.

Other icons also appear near appointments. In fact, you should get used to seeing these three icons:

- ■ **Alarms**   This icon indicates you'll get notified by the Palm alarm sound that the appointment is due to start.

- ■ **Notes**   If you attach a note to your appointment (perhaps with directions to the location or agenda details, for instance) you see this icon.

- ■ **Repeating meetings**   If the meeting is configured to happen more than once, this icon appears.

If you tap any of these icons, seen in Figure 5-1, you see the Event Details dialog box, which we discuss in the section "Make Your Appointments Repeat."

Finally, the bottom of the screen has several important controls. Icons exist to change the current view, as well as to create a new appointment, to view the Event Details dialog box, and to go to a specific day.

Change View Options

By default, the Day View compresses your calendar by not showing blank times of the day. This way, you can have appointments that span from 6 A.M. to 11 P.M. and have them all appear onscreen without needing to scroll at all. Whenever it can, it includes blank events between existing events for better readability.

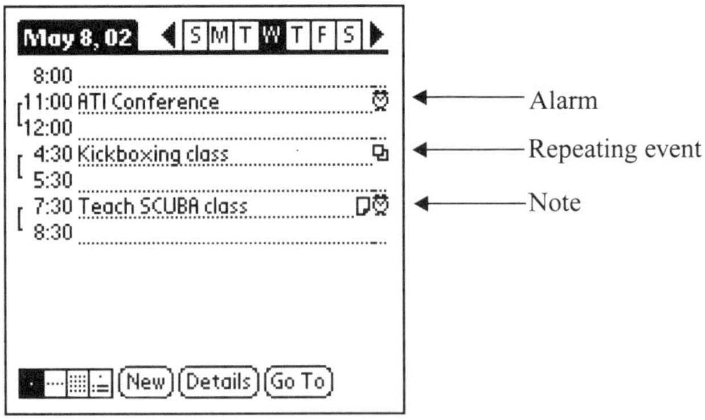

FIGURE 5-1 These icons tell you valuable information about your appointment. Tap them to edit the details.

What happens if you have such a busy day that all your appointments won't fit onscreen at once, even with the Palm's compression in place? You need to tap the scroll button at the bottom of the screen. It only appears when needed.

> **NOTE**   *Many users try using the Scroll button on the Palm's case to see more appointments in the same day. Of course, pressing the scroll button simply changes the view to the next day.*

Not everyone likes the Day View compression. If you frequently add events to your schedule during the day, for instance, you might want to have blank lines available for all the hours of the day. If this sounds like you, here's how to turn off compression:

1. Choose Options | Display Options from the menu.

2. Uncheck the Compress Day View option.

```
┌─────────────────────────────────┐
│    Display Options        ℹ     │
│ Day View:                        │
│   ☑ Show Time Bars               │
│   ☐ Compress Day View            │
│                                  │
│ Month View:                      │
│   ☑ Show Timed Events            │
│   ☐ Show Untimed Events          │
│   ☐ Show Daily Repeating Evts    │
│  ( OK )  ( Cancel )              │
└─────────────────────────────────┘
```

3. Tap the OK button.

Now, when you use the Day View, you see all the blank lines for your day. On the other hand, using this setting virtually guarantees you need to use the stylus to surf around your daily schedule.

When you configure your Day View, you also have to decide what kind of person you are. Are you:

■ Neat and orderly—and opt for less clutter whenever possible?

■ Impatient—and want everything at your fingertips all the time?

■ Apathetic—and don't want to bother changing the default settings?

You can change the display of the Date Book to accommodate the way you want your Palm to look. If you're the neat and orderly sort, for instance, you might want the Date Book to be a blank screen, unless it has appointments already scheduled for that day. If this is the case, choose Options | Preferences and set the Start Time and End Time as the same thing—like 7:00 A.M.

After configuring your Palm in this way, you should find days without appointments are essentially a blank screen with a single blank line—the time you set in Preferences.

More of an impatient sort? Then choose Options | Preferences and configure your Start Time and End Time to span the full range of hours you plan to use. If you ever add events to the evening, for instance, set the End Time for 10 P.M. or later. This way, you have a blank line available immediately for writing a new entry.

If all this sounds extremely pointless to you, leave the Preferences alone. The default settings cover most of the hours you routinely need.

Getting Around the Days of the Week

As you might expect, several ways exist to change the view to a different day. You can figure out most of them on your own, but we bet you can't find 'em all. Here's how you can do it—use the method that's easiest for you:

- To switch to a specific day, tap the appropriate day icon at the top of the screen (see Figure 5-2).

- To move ahead one week at a time, use the forward button to the right of the week icons, as seen in Figure 5-2. If you're currently on Tuesday, for instance, tapping the arrow takes you one week ahead to the following Tuesday. Obviously, you can go back a week at a time by tapping the Back arrow instead.

- To move forward or backward one day at a time, press the hard Scroll button. If you hold it down, you scroll quickly, like holding down a repeating key on a computer keyboard.

- To find a specific day quickly, tap the Go To button and enter the date directly in the Go to Date dialog box. When you use Go To, remember to choose the year and month first, because you go to the selected date as soon as you tap a date.

- To get back to "today" from somewhere else in the calendar, tap Go To, and then tap Today on the Go to Date calendar dialog box.

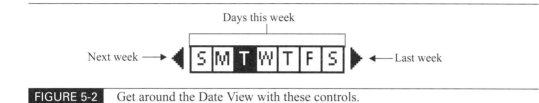

Days this week

Next week ⟶ S M T W T F S ⟵ Last week

FIGURE 5-2   Get around the Date View with these controls.

Navigate the Week View

Now that you're used to the Day View, we'll let you in on a little secret: there's more where that came from. That's where the icons at the bottom of the screen come in. Tap the second one to change to the Week View.

> **TIP**   *The Date Book button also serves as a view changer. Every time you press the button, the view cycles from Day View to Week View to Month View to Agenda View, and then back to Day View again. It's convenient to jab with your thumb as you view your various schedule screens.*

This screen uses a grid to display your appointments. The top of the grid is labeled by day and date, while the left side contains time blocks throughout the day. The gray blocks represent scheduled events. Obviously, this view isn't ideal for determining your daily schedule in detail, but it's handy for getting your week's availability at a glance. Use it to pick a free day or to clear an afternoon, for instance, when you're in a meeting and trying to choose a good time to get together with an equally busy person.

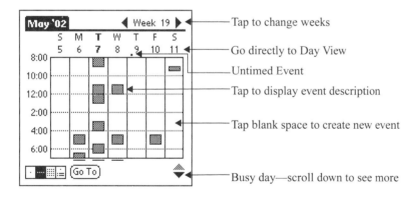

Tap to change weeks
Go directly to Day View
Untimed Event
Tap to display event description
Tap blank space to create new event
Busy day—scroll down to see more

> **TIP**   *If you have an appointment you need to move to another time anywhere in the week, tap the event, hold the stylus down, and then drag it to another place on the schedule. As you move the block around, you can see the exact time to which the event is being moved. To abort this process without changing anything, move it back to its original location without lifting the stylus.*

Navigate the Month View

If you press the Date Book button again or tap the third icon at the bottom of the screen, you're transported to the Month View. It displays an entire month at a time.

Blocks of busy time are now replaced by little hash marks. You can't tap on these marks to see the appointment details because they don't represent individual events. Instead, the three possible marks represent events in the morning, afternoon, and evening, as seen in Figure 5-3. In addition, this view shows untimed events as plus (+) signs and multiday events as a series of dots that span several days. If you tap any day in this view, you're automatically taken to the Day View for that day.

NOTE   *By default, both of these special display features are disabled on your Palm. To turn them on, choose Options | Display Options from the Day View screen. Then, in the Month View section of the Display Options dialog box, enable Show Untimed Events and Show Daily Repeating Events.*

Manage Your Day from the Agenda View

The last of the Date Book views—the Agenda View—is a favorite for many people. Why is the Agenda View so cool? Because, like some desktop day planners, it combines your appointments and to-do tasks into a single screen. At a single glance, you can see all your responsibilities for the day without switching screens or pressing buttons.

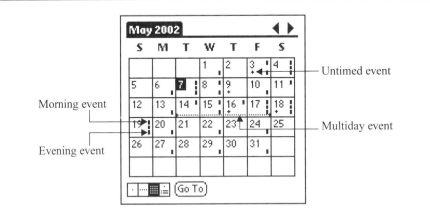

FIGURE 5-3   If you enable the right features in preferences, you can see untimed and multiday events in the monthly calendar.

Take a look at the Agenda View:

As you can see, the top of the screen shows you any appointments and untimed events that might be scheduled for the day. After a horizontal line, your Palm lists your To Dos.

You can change the current day by tapping the arrows at the top of the screen to change a day at a time. If you want to hop directly to another day, tap the date between the arrows. This displays the Go To Date dialog box, just as if you'd tapped the Go To button at the bottom of the screen.

TIP *To jump to the current date, tap the Go To button, and then tap the Today button at the bottom of the Go to Date dialog box.*

Filtering Your To Dos

You might not always want to see all the To Do tasks stored in your Palm. If you're at work, for instance, you might not want to see any To Dos filed in a personal category.

To fine-tune the To Do List, tap the down arrow for the category list and choose the category you want to see displayed. You can choose any category you like, including All.

The Agenda Zoom

The Agenda View is great for viewing your day's schedule, but it's also a cool way to make changes to your daily itinerary. Just tap on a calendar item to switch to the Day View so you can make schedule changes. Or tap a To Do item to go directly to the To Do List for editing.

NOTE *It would be great if you could automatically start your Palm in Agenda View all the time. Alas, you can't quite do that. But, if you set your Palm to the Agenda View, and then visit another application, the Agenda View automatically returns the next time you start the Date Book. If you're in a hurry, remember, you can always press the Date Book button several times to cycle through the Date Book's various screens to arrive at the Agenda View.*

Create New Appointments

Now that you've mastered the fine art of viewing your schedule from every conceivable angle and perspective, you probably want to know how to add new events to the schedule. As you can probably guess, two ways exist to add appointments to your Palm: via the Palm Desktop—which we discuss in the section "Import Alarm Settings"—and right from the Palm itself. The only place you can enter data about a meeting is from the Day View.

Add Timed Events

Most of the time, your schedule will be full of meetings that take place at a specific time of day, such as

```
Meet with Susan from accounting
3-5 pm in Conference Room A.
```

The Best Sci-Fi

Dave: The Palm is like science fiction come alive, which begs the question, which sci-fi? Rick obsesses over some of the lamest sci-fi shows ever, like *Star Trek: Deep Space Nine* and *The West Wing* (Martin Sheen as the president? Yeah, that's gotta be sci-fi). I'm partial to shows with plausible technology, engaging plots, and a real sense of drama—that's why *Babylon 5* ranks up there among the best television ever. Meanwhile, Rick is watching a repeat of another "very special" episode about Kira. Apparently, she lost the bracelet her mom gave her this week.

Rick: Speaking of sci-fi, aliens have taken over Dave's brain. I know because for years...*years*...I've stated my disdain for *Deep Space Nine* and my total love for *Star Trek: Voyager*. But alien-Dave can't seem to compute that. And, obviously, anyone who doesn't like *The West Wing* must be controlled by some evil influence. Oh, that's right, Dave's a Republican.

This is what the Palm refers to as a *timed event*—but most people call it an appointment. In any event, several ways exist to add an event like this to your Palm:

- **Use the New button**   Tap the New button on the Day View. Then, within the Set Time dialog box, select a Start Time and an End Time, and then tap OK. Now, enter the meeting information on the blank line provided for you.

Set Time		
Start Time:	8 ↑	▪00
	9	05
	10	10
End Time:	11	15
	12P	20
	1	25
	2	▪30
[All Day]	3	35
	4	40
[No Time]	5	45
	6	50
[OK] [Cancel]	7 ↓	55

- **Start writing**   Tap on a blank line that corresponds to the meeting start time and write the details of the meeting on the line.

- **Pick a time from the Week View**   If you're looking for a free space to place a meeting, the Week View is a good place to look because it gives you the "big picture" of your schedule. When you find a spot you like, tap it and the Day View should open to the desired start time. Then write the meeting info.

A Closer Look at the Set Time Dialog Box

To set a time in this dialog box, tap an hour (in the selector on the left) and a minute (on the right) for both the Start Time and End Time. You can change your mind as often as you like, but the time must be in increments no smaller than five minutes. You can't set a Start Time of 11:33, for instance.

You can also use Graffiti to set the time, a real convenience for folks who are faster at writing than tapping. 335 is interpreted as 3:35. To change between A.M. and P.M., write an *A* or a *P* in the letter side of the Graffiti area.

If you need to back up and start over, use the backspace gesture. When you want to move between the Start Time and the End Time box, use the Next Field gesture. Finally, when you finish entering times, use the Return gesture to simulate tapping OK. Now, you're back at the Day View, ready to write in your meeting name.

A fast way to create a new event at a specific time is to write the start time in the Graffiti area. A Set Time dialog box appears and you can proceed from there. For example, writing a numeral 4 automatically launches the Set Time dialog box for 4 P.M.

Adding Untimed Events

If we wrote about something called a timed event, you must have assumed we'd get to something called an untimed event, right? *Untimed events* are pretty much what you'd expect—they're events associated with a day, but not with a specific time. Typical untimed events include birthdays and anniversaries, reminders to pick up the dry cleaning, and deadline reminders (though you might also consider putting those kinds of things in the To Do List, described in Chapter 7). To create an untimed event, perform one of these two techniques:

■ On the Day View with no time selected (in other words, the cursor isn't waiting in a blank line for you already), just start writing. The event appears at the top of the screen as an untimed event.

■ Tap New to display the Set Time dialog box. Instead of setting a Start Time and an End Time, though, tap the No Time button, and then tap OK.

Make Your Appointments Repeat

Some schedule events simply don't go away. Weekly meetings, semiannual employee reviews, and the monthly dog-grooming sessions are all examples of events you might want the Palm to automate. After all, you don't have the time or energy to write the same weekly event into your Palm 52 times to get it entered for a whole year. An easier way exists. To create a recurring event, do this:

1. Select the entry you want to turn into a recurring event and tap the Details button at the bottom of the Day View screen.

2. In the Event Details dialog box, the Repeat box is currently set to None; tap it. The Change Repeat dialog box should now appear.

How to ... **Make a Date**

If you're setting up an appointment with someone in particular, you can have a lot of fun with your Palm. Okay, it's not better than listening to Pink Floyd with the lights out, but it's pretty cool, nonetheless. Suppose you need to meet with someone who's already in your Address Book. Switch to the Day View and tap on a blank line at the time you want to start your meeting. Then choose Options | Phone Lookup. You see the Phone Number Lookup dialog box, which displays all the names in your Address Book. Find the name of the person you're meeting with and tap it. Now tap Add. What do you get? The person's name and phone number positioned at the start time of the meeting.

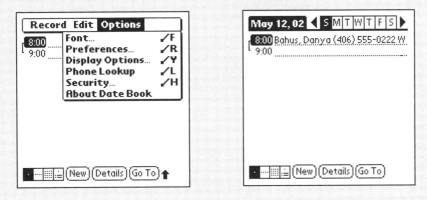

Now it gets even better. Does your associate have a Palm? If so, make sure the appointment is still selected and choose Record | Beam Event. You've just given your associate a copy of your meeting in her Palm. She has no excuse now if she's late.

3. Now you need to tap a repeat interval. Will the event repeat daily, weekly, monthly, or annually? In other words, if the event takes place only once a year or once every five years, tap Year. If you have a meeting that takes place once a month or every other month, tap Month. For meetings that occur every week or every five weeks, use the Week button. Finally, if you need to schedule daily, every other day, or every ten-day meetings, tap Day.

```
┌────────────────────────────────────┐
│      Change Repeat        ⓘ         │
│  ┌────┬───┬────┬─────┬────┐          │
│  │None│Day│Week│Month│Year│          │
│  └────┴───┴────┴─────┴────┘          │
│       Every:  ___1| Week(s)          │
│       End on:  ▼ No End Date         │
│   Repeat on: │S│M│T│W│T│F│S│         │
│  ┌──────────────────────────────┐   │
│  │ Every week on Wed and Fri     │   │
│  │                               │   │
│  └──────────────────────────────┘   │
│  ( OK )  ( Cancel )                  │
└────────────────────────────────────┘
```

4. You now have more options, depending on which interval you choose. A comm on interval is Week, which would enable you to set up a weekly meeting. Tell the Change Repeat dialog box how often the meeting will occur, such as Every 1 Week or Every 3 Weeks.

5. If you chose a monthly interval, you can also choose whether the meeting will repeat by day (such as the first Monday of every month) or by date (as in the 11th of every month).

6. If the event will repeat more or less forever (or at least as long as you can imagine going to work every day), then leave the End On setting at the default, which is No End Date. If you are creating an event with a clear conclusion, tap End On to set the End Date for this repeating event.

7. Your selection is turned into a plain English description. If you agree the repeat settings are what you want, tap OK.

TIP   *If you're attending a multiday event, such as a trade show, you can display this in your Palm by creating an untimed event and setting it to repeat daily (Every 1 Day). Don't forget to set an End Date.*

Make an Appointment Private

You might not want all your appointments to be available to the public. While we generally believe honesty is the best policy, you can flag certain appointments as private—and they'll be hidden from everyone except you. If you want to hide an appointment, do this:

1. On the Day View screen, select an appointment.

2. Tap the Details button.

3. On the Event Details dialog box, tap the Private box to add a check mark. Once you select this option, the current record is flagged for privacy. Tap the OK button and you see this dialog box:

Event Details ⓘ

Time: 8:00 am - 9:00 am
Date: Sun 5/12/02
Alarm: ☐
Repeat: None
Private: ☐

(OK) (Cancel) (Delete...) (Note)

4. Tap OK to close the dialog box.

You might notice the event probably isn't hidden yet. To make it go away, you need to enable the Private Records feature in the Security app. For details on how to do this, see Chapter 9. Using this feature, you can hide and show private data whenever you want.

Edit Recurring Meetings

With most appointments or events, you can make a change just by tapping and entering the needed change with a little Graffiti. Changes to repeating meetings require a little more care. In general, when you change some aspect of a meeting that repeats, the Palm asks you whether you want to change only this one meeting, future meetings, or every meeting in the series.

If you need to move a specific meeting—like the one in November—to a different time, but all the other meetings continue to be held at the traditional time, select Current. This event is unlinked from the series and any changes you subsequently make to the rest of the repeating event don't affect the one you changed. On the other hand, if the meeting is moving to a new day permanently, choose All.

There's an exception to this rule: if you change any of the text in the name of the appointment, Palm then makes the change to the entire series without asking. If you want to change the text of one instance of the event without changing the rest, you need to unlink it from the series. To do that, try this:

1. Change something else about the event, like its time.

2. You're asked if you want to change the current event or all of the events. Choose Current. The event is now unlinked from the series.

3. Change the name of the unlinked event.

4. If you need to, fix whatever you changed in Step 2.

Delete Old Appointments

As time goes on, your Palm starts to accumulate a considerable number of appointments. Often, after an event has passed, you no longer need a record of it. If that's the case, you might want to delete it to save memory. Granted, each appointment takes up a miniscule amount of memory but, eventually, this can add up. Even if you don't care about memory savings, meetings do sometimes get canceled—and you need a way to delete them. A few ways exist to get these events off your Palm:

■ **Erase it** Open the Day View. Tap the stylus at the end of the line and backspace over it to delete all the characters. Or, you can highlight the text by dragging the stylus over the name of the meeting, and then use a single backspace gesture to erase it.

 Watch out! If you use this method to delete a repeating event, the Palm erases all the events in the series without warning.

■ **Use the Delete button** Select the event and tap the Details button. Then tap Delete (or select the item and choose Delete from the menu).

■ **Purge a bunch at once** If you want to delete a bunch of appointments at once, a special tool was designed especially for this task. Choose Record | Purge from the Day View. Then choose how much data to delete—you can choose to delete events that are more than a week old or, if you want more of a safety cushion, delete events more than a month old.

 If you purge your appointments, you have the option to "save an archive copy on PC." If you do that, you can always restore those appointments from the desktop later.

Work with Alarms

If you need a reminder about upcoming events, you should use the Palm's built-in alarm feature. Any event you enter can be set to beep shortly before the event, giving you enough time to jump in your car, pick up the phone, or start saving for the big day. You can assign an alarm setting to your events as you create the event or at any time afterward.

 Timed events play an audible sound. Untimed events don't play a sound, but simply display a screen advising you the event is pending.

Pick Your Own Alarm Sound

If, like us, you're easily bored, you might be interested in changing your Palm's default alarm sound. This is easy to do—simply visit **PalmGear.com** and search for alarm sounds. You'll find tons of downloads that give your Palm alternative sounds. Here are a few of the most popular:

- Creationzone Alarm Collection
- System Sound Plus
- GeeSounds

We've listed only three, but the choices are almost limitless. Some apps give you special effects like science fiction or animal sounds, while others are complete songs. If you've ever wanted your Palm to sound like a *Star Trek* communicator, here's your chance.

Of course, it's not all fun and games—a distinctive alarm sound can make your Palm easier to hear in a crowd. If you have a new Palm device like a Sony CLIÉ with enhanced sound, many of these programs may not work on your PDA. That's the cost of progress!

Set Alarms for Specific Events

To enable the alarm for a particular appointment, do this:

1. In the Day View, select an appointment.

2. Tap Details.

3. In the Event Details dialog box, tap the Alarm check box. You should see a new control appear that enables you to set the advance warning for the event.

4. Select how much advanced warning you want. You can choose no warning (enter a zero) or set a time up to 99 days ahead of time. The default is five minutes.

5. Tap OK.

Set Alarms for Everything

By default, the Palm doesn't turn the alarm on for your appointments. Instead, you need to turn the alarm on for each event individually. If you like using the alarm, though, you can tell the Palm to turn the alarm on automatically for all your appointments. Then, it's up to you to turn the alarm off on a case-by-case basis when you don't want to be notified for any events.

To enable the default alarm setting, do this:

1. In the Day View, choose Options | Preferences.

2. Tap the check box for the Alarm Preset. Set your alarm preference. Now configure the alarm time, the kind of alarm sound, and how many times the alarm will sound before giving up.

> **TIP** *You can try out each of the alarm sounds by selecting them from the list. After you choose a sound, it plays so you can hear what it sounds like.*

3. Tap OK.

Import Alarm Settings

Much of the time, you probably get appointments into your Palm via your PC—you HotSync them in from the Palm Desktop or Outlook. In that case, the rules are different. The Palm keeps whatever alarm settings were assigned on the PC and doesn't use the Preference settings on the Palm. If you want a specific alarm setting, you need to change the alarm setting on the desktop application before HotSyncing or change the alarm on the Palm after you HotSync.

> **TIP** *Some folks would like to have two separate sets of alarms for their appointments: one for the Palm and another for their desktop calendar program. If you have a PC and Microsoft Outlook, try* Desktop to Go, *which enables you to configure the Palm to use a completely independent set of alarms from Outlook.*

Control Your Alarm

If you use an alarm clock, you must surely know the only thing better than having an alarm is being able to turn it off.

Remember, the Palm isn't all that loud. If you need to hear your Palm, don't bury it in a backpack or a briefcase, where the sound will be hopelessly muffled. But what if you're in a quiet meeting room and the last thing you need is for your Palm to start chirping in front of the CEO? In that case, temporarily silence it. Open Prefs and choose the General view, where there's an option for Alarm Sound. Choose Off from the Alarm Sound list. Some Palm models even have a vibrating alarm, which is a great way to keep on top of alarms without disturbing the people around you.

5

Work with the Palm Desktop

If you use the Palm Desktop as the calendar on your desktop PC, you benefit because it looks similar to the version on your Palm. Granted, the Palm Desktop is much bigger than your Palm screen and it's in color. But, aside from that, you find the modules share a common appearance and the overall philosophy of the program is similar.

> TIP *You can display more than one calendar on your Palm at once. If you collaborate with coworkers or a spouse and you want to see their calendars side by side with yours, try* **www.wesync.com**.

The Windows Date Book

The Date Book in the Windows version of the Palm Desktop uses a few unique control elements—but they're quite intuitive. After you start the Palm Desktop, you can switch to the Date Book by clicking the Date icon on the right side of the screen or by choosing View | Date Book. To change views, click the tabs at the right edge of the screen. You should see three tabs: Day, Week, and Month.

Use the Day View

The Day View looks similar to the Palm display. Look at Figure 5-4 for an overview of the major elements in this display.

> TIP *The easiest way to double-book a time slot is to click the Time box. A new blank appears to the right of the existing appointment.*

You might recall that on the Palm, you can create an appointment by using the Phone Lookup feature—this grabs a name and phone number from the Address Book, and places it in a time slot in the Date Book. You can do the same thing in the Palm Desktop. Under the calendar, you can see the To Do List and Address Book minilists. Choose which one you want to see by clicking Address or To Do. Then drag a name (or even a To Do) into a time slot.

Go to Today

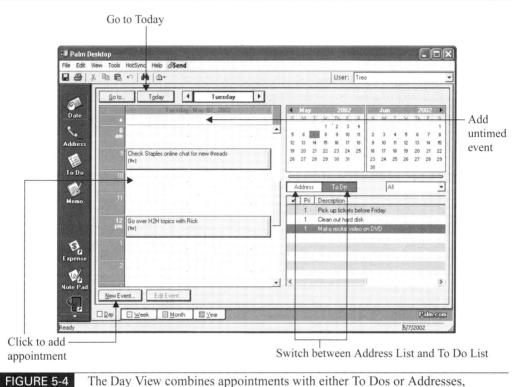

Add untimed event

Click to add appointment

Switch between Address List and To Do List

FIGURE 5-4 The Day View combines appointments with either To Dos or Addresses, depending on how you configure the screen.

Edit Appointments

You can make lots of changes with the mouse. To change the duration of an event, drag the arrow-shaped duration handle up or down. To move the appointment, drag it by its event handle on the right edge. And, to see the Edit Event dialog box, which lets you edit the text and includes alarm and privacy controls, double-click anywhere in the event.

> **TIP**
>
> *You can move an appointment to another day by dragging it via the event handle to the calendar and dropping it on the desired day.*

Use the Week and Month Views

Both of these views are quite similar to their Palm counterparts. When in the Week View (seen in Figure 5-5), though, the event blocks work a little differently than you might expect:

- To move an event to a different time, drag it by the event handle.
- To display the Edit Event dialog box and change options like text, time, repeat settings, or the alarm, double-click the event.
- To change the duration of the event, drag its duration handle up or down.

The Month View is a bit more helpful than the one in your Palm. The Month View shows you what events are scheduled, not only that you have a mysterious "something" scheduled. You can't edit the events in this view, though. Instead, you can double-click the appropriate day to get to the Day View or add a new event to a specific day by right-clicking the day and choosing New Event from the menu.

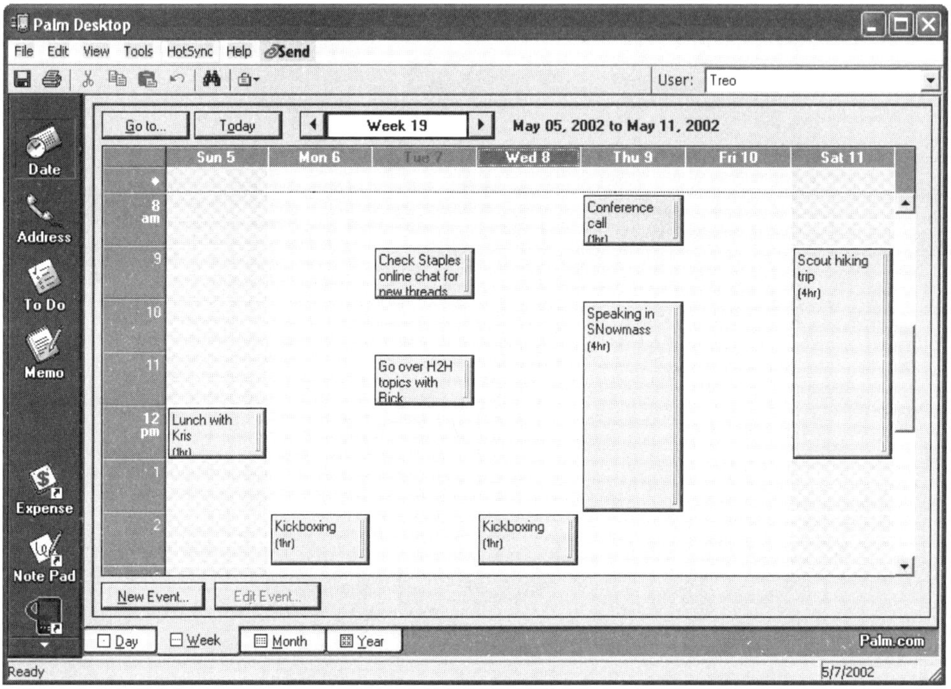

FIGURE 5-5   The Week View enables you to add and edit appointments.

Using Alarms on the Desktop

Want to be notified about upcoming events while working at your desk? You need to use the Palm Desktop's Alarm Manager (a new feature in Palm OS 4). While Alarm Manager is linked to the Palm Desktop, it's technically not a part of it. What we mean is Alarm Manager runs outside the program and hangs out in the Windows System Tray, just like HotSync Manager.

To activate the Alarm Manager, choose Tools | Options, and then click the Alarm tab. You see three choices in the Options dialog box:

- **Always Available**   When you choose this option, Alarm Manager loads when you start Windows, even if Palm Desktop itself isn't running. It ensures you hear all your alarms. Most folks, we think, want this option.

- **Available only when the Palm Desktop is running**   This is pretty self-explanatory—but we can't think of many reasons why you'd use this option.

- **Disabled**   Alarms won't ring at all—which makes sense if you don't need to worry about event alarms or you use another PIM, like Outlook.

Once you set up the Alarm Manager to your liking, you can configure alarms in the Palm Desktop when you create new events. At the bottom of the New Event or Edit Event window, you'll find the alarm options (which work just like they do on the Palm itself).

Using Outlook

Of course, Microsoft Outlook synchronizes with the Palm just fine and many people use it instead of the Palm Desktop. We should point out, though, that some people categorize appointments in Outlook. The Palm doesn't let you categorize events in the Date Book, but you can add this capability by upgrading to a HotSync conduit like Chapura's PocketMirror Professional.

Navigating Around Outlook

The Outlook Calendar View is a handy tool for seeing your current and upcoming events. By default, you see today's appointments. To switch to a specific day, click the date you want in the minicalendar (see Figure 5-6). You can also see several days at a time. To do this, click-and-drag a range of days in the minicalendar.

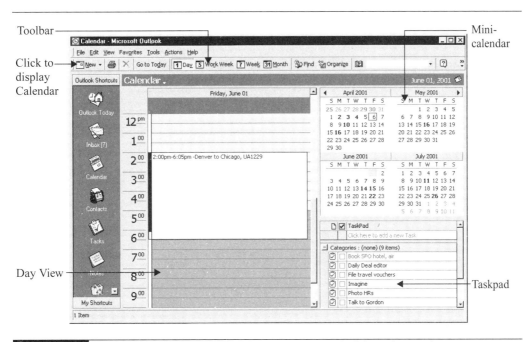

FIGURE 5-6   Many users synchronize with Outlook instead of the Palm Desktop.

TIP
The toolbar includes buttons for viewing the work week, an entire week, and a month at a glance. To switch back to a single view of today, you need to click both Day (to switch to a single-day view), and then Go to Today (to view the current day).

Adding Appointments

You can add an appointment to Outlook in several ways. Pick the method that's easiest for the kind of event you want to add.

- Create a simple 30-minute meeting: simply click a time slot and start typing. Press the ENTER key when you finish.

- Create a simple meeting that lasts for 60 minutes or more: click a time slot and drag the mouse down to extend the length of the appointment for an hour or more. When a block of time is selected, type the subject of the meeting and press ENTER.

- Create a meeting that repeats or has detailed notes: find the start time of the meeting and double-click the block. An untitled Appointment window should appear, as in Figure 5-7. Fill in all the meeting details as needed.

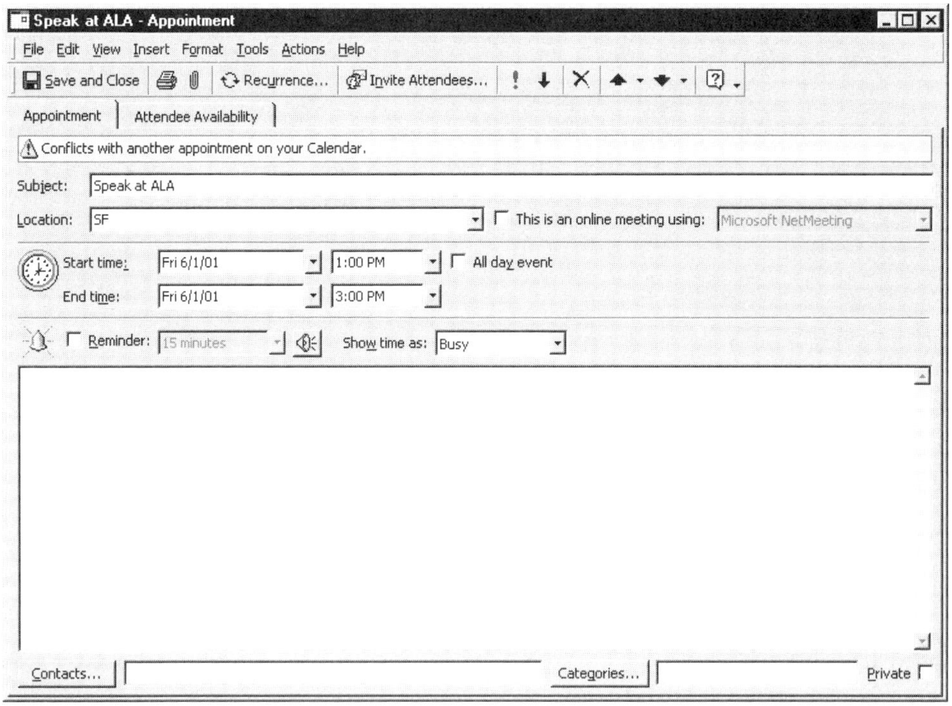

FIGURE 5-7 All of the information in an Outlook appointment gets transferred to the PDA after a HotSync.

NOTE   *If you use the Location line of the Outlook appointment box, this information appears in parentheses after the subject text on your Palm.*

Tweaking Alarms for the Palm

By default, every Outlook appointment comes with an alarm that sounds 15 minutes before the event. If you create most of your appointments within Outlook, you might end up with alarms you don't want on the Palm after a HotSync. To change the length of the default alarm—or to disable alarms entirely—choose Tools | Options from the Outlook menu, and then click the Preferences tab. In the Calendar section, edit the Default Reminder option to suit your needs. If you remove the check mark, the alarm is then disabled for new appointments.

5

Disable alarms

The Macintosh Date Book

Right off the bat, the Macintosh Date Book is something of a misnomer. The Mac version of the Palm Desktop calls the Date Book the "Calendar." That's okay. We're all adults and we can adjust pretty well. Well, everyone except Rick, who insists on calling it the Date Book anyway.

To see the Calendar, click the View Calendar button on the Palm Desktop toolbar. Like the Palm's Date Book button, you can click this button over and over to cycle among the Day View, Week View, and Month Views. Also, note you can see all the appointments you have scheduled for today by clicking the Instant Palm Desktop icon on the Desktop's menu bar.

Use the Daily View

The Daily View (in Figure 5-8) is divided into two parts: the Daily Calendar and the Task View. You can create a new event in this view in two ways:

- Click-and-drag the mouse to define the start and end time of the appointment. When you release the mouse, you can write in the appointment name.

- Double-click in a time slot to display the Appointment dialog box. You can fill out the event time, alarm, and frequency information here. Click OK to save the appointment.

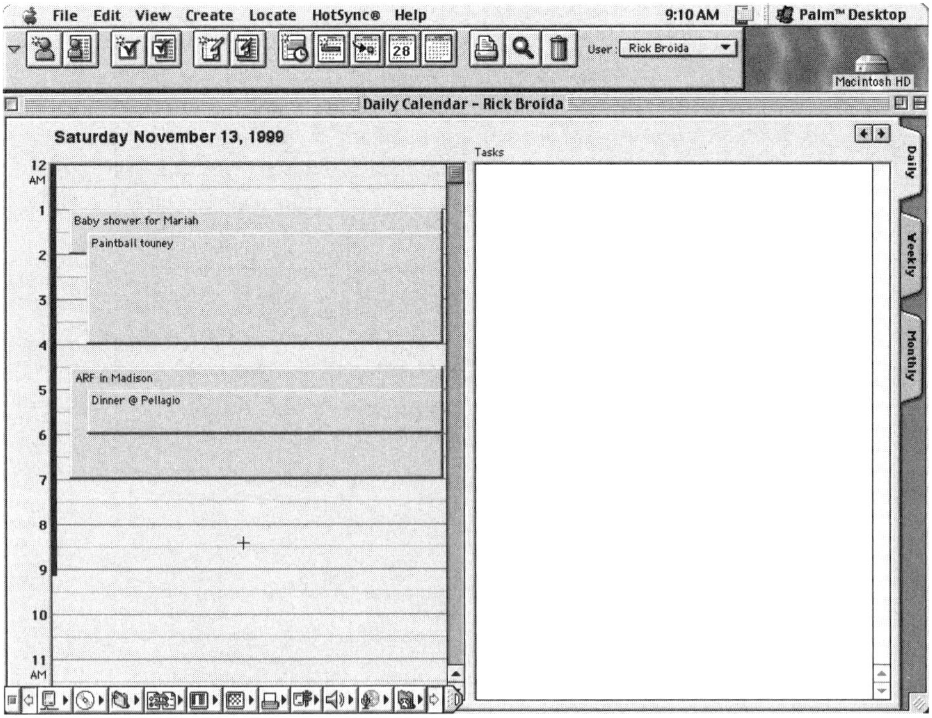

FIGURE 5-8   The Daily View stacks appointments in layers for better readability.

If you need to add an appointment in the same time slot as an existing event, you can either double-click or click-and-drag in the space between the event and the hour markers, at the left-hand edge of the window.

 To change the increment of the time slots (say, from 30-minute blocks to 10-minute blocks), choose Edit | Preferences, and then click the Calendars button. Now you can change the interval to suit your needs.

Add an Untimed Event

In the Palm Desktop, untimed events are called *Event Banners.* To add an Event Banner to the current day, double-click above the time slots, but below the date. You then see the Event Banner dialog box. Fill it in and click OK.

Use the Weekly and Monthly Views

The Weekly View works much the same as the Daily View. Adding and editing appointments—both timed events and untimed events—is done in the same way.

 If you want to see more or less days in the Weekly View, click the plus and minus buttons on the right edge of the window. Depending on your preferences, you can see as few as one day or as many as seven days onscreen at once.

The Monthly View has the most surprises. Unlike on the Palm, this Monthly View is fully editable and enables you to see the contents of your appointments (they don't simply appear as gray blocks). Here's what you can do with the Monthly View:

■ Double-click an empty space to display this dialog box:

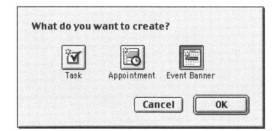

■ Click the item you want to create in the designated day.
■ Click-and-drag an appointment to move it to another time.
■ Double-click an appointment to open the Appointment dialog box and edit the event details.
■ Double-click the gray date bar across the top of any day to switch to the Daily View.

 Gray events in the Weekly and Monthly Views are untimed events (also called Banner Events).

A Better Date Book

Looking for an alternative to the Date Book that comes with your Palm? Then look no further than DateBk5 (which you can download from **www.datebk.com**), probably the most popular replacement for the built-in Palm applications.

The program replaces more than only the Date Book—it's a combination Date Book, To Do List, and Memo Pad application that's more full-featured and tightly integrated than the Palm's own programs. We love this program, so you might want to try it and see if, in your opinion, it beats the Palm's own applications.

DateBk5 uses a split-screen approach to display information from multiple applications at once. It also includes a number of ways to view your calendar and To Do items, as well as handy features like a "recently used" list for quickly accessing contacts from the Address Book. It supports fancy icons and text formatting that make your appointments stand out in the calendar, along with dozens of other clever features. Give this program a try!

Where to Find It

Web Site	Address	What's There
Chapura	**www.chapura.com**	PocketMirror Professional lets you sort events by category
Pimlico	**www.datebk.com**	DateBk5, the best Date Book substitute on the market (in our humble opinion)
WeSync	**www.wesync.com**	Sync with other peoples' calendars

Chapter 6

The Address Book

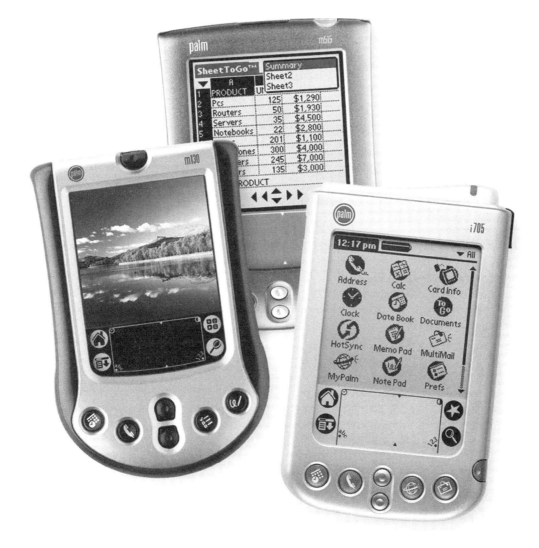

How to...

- View Address Book entries
- Customize the Address List display
- Search for an entry by name
- Search for an entry by keyword
- Create new Address Book entries
- Display a specific phone number in the Address List
- Use the custom fields
- Assign a category to an entry
- Delete Address Book entries
- Use the Windows Address Book
- Use your Palm with Outlook
- Use the Macintosh Address Book

What's the big deal? It's only an address book. Yes, but as one of the four big "core" applications—the main programs that ship with your Palm—you'll use this Address Book a lot. And the Address Book is an elegant program, designed to get the information you need quickly, perhaps more quickly than any other contact manager on the market.

We're sure you'll get a lot of mileage from the Address Book. You can store literally thousands of entries (about 10,000, to be precise) and not run out of memory. Despite how many names you add to the list, your Palm never slows down—that's a claim desktop applications simply can't make. In addition, the Address Book isn't really a stand-alone application (though it can be if you want). The Address Book synchronizes with desktop applications like the Palm Desktop and Microsoft Outlook. This means you only need to create a contact list once, and then it's maintained on both your PC and your Palm.

View Your Addresses

When you switch to the Address Book, the program displays all the entries in your list onscreen. As you might expect, you can start the Address Book by pressing the Address List button on your Palm or tapping the onscreen Address icon in the Palm's applications.

NOTE *If you have a Palm smartphone, the Address Book button might launch the Speed Dial screen. You might have to press the button several times to get to the Address Book.*

As you can see in Figure 6-1, the Palm lists your contacts alphabetically in a view called the Address List. Room exists for 11 entries onscreen at one time. The rest appear above or below the screen, depending on where you are within the Address List. To get around in the Address List, just use the scroll buttons. Each time you scroll, the Palm moves the list by one complete page of entries.

Address List   ▼ Airline 800 #s ◄——— Category list

A O M French Airline	800-892-9136 W
Access Air	877-462-2237 W
Aces	800-846-2237 W
Action Air Lines	800-243-8623 W
Aer Lingus	800-223-6537 W
Aero California	800-237-6225 W
Aeroejecutivo SA-D	800-735-5396 W
Aeroflot	800-995-5555 W
Aeroflot Cargo Sale	800-506-5544 W
Aerolineas Argentin	800-333-0276 W
Aeromar	800-950-0747 W

Look Up: ....   (New)   ◆ ◄——— Scroll
                        ▲
                 Create new contact

FIGURE 6-1   The Address List is a database of all your contact information.

You can also get around with categories. If your contacts are divided into more than one category, every time you press the Address button, you switch categories. You can cycle through the first page of names in each category by repeatedly pressing the Address Book button.

View by Company Name

For most folks, the default Address List is great. This list displays the entries by name (last, first) and a phone number. If you prefer to work with your contacts according to the company they work with, you can change the Address List.

To change the View mode of the Address List, do this:

1. Display the Address List View.

2. Choose Options | Preferences from the menu.

3. Choose Company, Last Name from the List By list.

Address List   ▼ Airline 800 #s

Bahamas Air	800-222-4262 W
Balair/CTA	800-322-5247 W
Balkan Bulgarian Air	800-852-0944 W

Address Book Preferences

☐ **Remember last category**

List By:

Last Name, First Name
Company, Last Name

(OK) (Cancel)

4. Tap OK to save your changes.

Notice that after making the change, you can see the company name in the list. If no company is associated with a particular entry, then you only see the individual's name, as you did before. You can switch back to the default view at any time.

Find a Specific Name

If you're looking for a specific entry in the Address List, you can simply scroll down until you find it. If you only have a few dozen contacts, that's not so hard. But what if you're like us and your Address List is brimming with over a thousand contacts? Scrolling might take a while, especially if the guy you're looking for is named Nigel Walthers or Earnest Zanthers. That's when you use the Look Up function.

To search for a specific name, start writing the person's last name in the Look Up field at the bottom of the screen. The Address Book adjusts the display as you write, so if you enter the letter **J**, it displays all the names that begin with the letter *J*. If you enter **JO**, it narrows the search and shows names that begin with those letters.

If you're using the List By: Company, Last Name option in the Address List View, it's a little more complicated. If the entry has a company name, you need to search for that entry by company name. If the entry doesn't have a company name, though, you must find it by the last name.

Once you start searching, you can keep writing letters until the Palm displays exactly the name you want or you can write one or two letters, and then use the Scroll button to find the name you need. If you want to clear the Look Up field to write in a new name, just press one of the Scroll buttons.

If you try writing a letter, but your Palm beeps at you, this means no name in the list is spelled with the letter you're trying to add. You've probably misspelled the name.

Conduct a Detailed Search

You might have noticed the Look Up field only searches by last name. What happens if you want to find someone, but you can only remember that person's first name or the company where they work? The Look Up field won't do any good.

In this case, use the Find tool. Tap the Find button, enter the word you want to search for, and then tap OK. You get a list of every entry in the Palm with that word—even items from the other Palm applications—as shown in Figure 6-2. The current application is searched first, so make sure you're in the Address Book before you start using the Find tool.

View a Name

Once you locate the name you were looking for, tap on it. You see the Address View, which displays the contact's name, address, and phone numbers, as shown in Figure 6-3.

If you're using a Palm smartphone, you can dial a phone number from this screen.

FIGURE 6-2   The Find Tool is a powerful way to locate an entry, even if you don't remember the person's exact name.

Create New Entries

To create a new Address List entry on the Palm, tap the New button at the bottom of the screen. From there, start filling in the blanks. Start by writing the last name of the person you're adding. When you're ready to move on to the first name, you need to change fields. You can do this in two ways:

- Tap the next field with the stylus, and then write in the Graffiti area.
- Use the Next Field gesture to move to the next field.

The Next Field gesture takes a little practice because it's easy to get the letter U *by mistake. Although the gesture template shows a curve in the first part of the stroke, you get the best results by going straight down, and then straight up again.*

FIGURE 6-3   The Address View shows you all the details about the selected individual.

Even though you only see a single line for text in each field, the Address List secretly supports multiple lines of text in each field. If you're entering the company name, for instance, you can use two or more lines to enter all the information you need about the company, department, and so on for the individual. To write multiple lines of text in a field, use the Return gesture to create a new line. You won't see the multiple lines in the Address List, but you can see them when you select the entry and view the Address View.

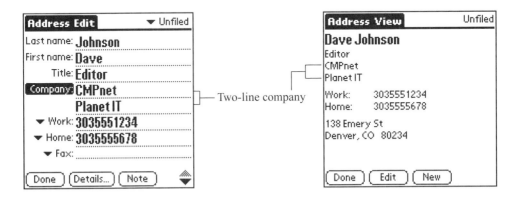

When you finish adding information about this new person, tap the Done button.

TIP *What if you're Canadian, French, or living in some other non-American location? The Palm defaults to address details like city, state, and ZIP code—which might be inappropriate for your locale. The solution is to tap on the Prefs icon in Apps and select Formats from the menu. Then, set the Preset To: menu to whatever country you choose.*

Use Multiple Phone Numbers

The Address List gives you a few options when you enter contact information. Specifically, you can set what kinds of phone numbers your Palm has for each contact. Conveniently, this needn't be the same for everyone. For one person, you might list a home phone and a pager, for instance, while another entry might have a work number and an e-mail address. The Palm keeps track of everything for you.

To control these numbers, tap on the phone number list and choose the desired label. Then, write the number or e-mail address in the field next to the label. You can specify up to five entries for each person in your Address List.

If you're on the ball, you might wonder which of those numbers shows up in the Address List View. Remember, the list shows the name and a phone number for each contact—this means you might not have to open an entry simply to dial a phone number because it's right there in the List view. The answer, though, is this: the first phone number you enter into the Edit view is the one that appears in the List view—no matter where it appears in the list of phone numbers.

SHORTCUT *If you later decide you want a different number to appear in the list view, tap the Details button and select the number label you want from the Show in List menu.*

Use Extra Fields

The Address List has plenty of preconfigured fields (like name, company, and phone numbers) for most users, but it's flexible enough also to accommodate the special needs of everyone else. You might want to track birthdays, Web pages, spouse names, or other personal information. If so, you're in luck—four custom fields are at the bottom of the Address Edit view, which you can rename as you like.

To label these four bonus fields into something more useful, do this:

1. Choose the Address Book. Any view will do.

2. Choose Options | Rename Custom Fields from the menu.

3. Select the text on the first line (which should say Custom 1) and write a name for the field. Name the other fields—or as many as you need—in the same way.

4. Tap OK when you finish.

Dialing Your Phone with a Palm

Now that you have hundreds of phone numbers stored on your Palm, it's better-equipped to place phone calls for you than the speed-dial feature on your desktop phone. If you don't mind investing in a gadget called the Parlay Autodialer, you can point your Palm at your phone and automatically dial phone numbers.

The *Autodialer* is a small infrared receiver that plugs into your telephone (sort of like an answering machine) and intercepts beams from your Palm. Beam an Address Book entry toward your phone and it dials the associated phone number. It's as simple as that.

If you change the Palm's preferences so a single upstroke across the display starts the beaming process (that's something you can configure in the Palm's Prefs program, explained in Chapter 4), dialing is effortless: just find an Address Book entry, point your PDA at the Autodialer, and beam. Pick up your handset or turn on the speakerphone to complete the call.

Once you create labels for these fields, you can find them at the bottom of the list of contact info in the Address Edit view.

NOTE   *The custom fields are global. This means you can't have different custom fields for each entry or even for each category. Once named, the custom fields apply to all entries in the Address List. You needn't fill them out for every entry, though.*

Assign Categories

Your new contact can easily get lost within a sea of names and addresses if you aren't careful. With only a few names to manage, this isn't a big deal. But what if you have 500 or 1,000 contacts in your Address List? This is when categories could come in handy.

Choose a Category

As you might remember from Chapter 2, categories are simply a way of organizing your Palm data more logically into groups you frequently use. To assign a contact to a specific category, do this:

1. From the Address Edit screen, tap Details. The Address Entry Details dialog box should appear.

2. Tap the Category List and choose the category name you want to assign to this contact.

3. Tap OK to close the dialog box.

Of course, you needn't assign a category if you don't want to do so. By default, new contacts are placed in the Unfiled category.

Edit and Delete Addresses

In this fast-paced world, a contact once entered in an address book isn't likely to stay that way for long. You might need to update an address, phone number, or e-mail address, or delete the entry entirely.

To edit an entry, all you must do is find the entry in the Address List and tap it. You're taken to the Address View where you can see the existing information. Then, tap on the screen and the display changes to the Address Edit screen, which you can change to suit your needs.

If you have a contact you simply don't need anymore, you can delete it from the Palm to save memory and reduce data clutter. To delete a contact, do this:

1. Choose the entry from the Address List. You see the Address View.

2. Choose Record | Delete Address from the menu.

Create and Beam Your Business Card

As mentioned in Chapter 4, one of the coolest things about taking your Palm to meetings and trade shows is the capability to beam your personal information into other peoples' Palms. This is a lot easier and more convenient than exchanging a business card. Heck, a paper business card? That's so . . . '80s! Use your Palm instead.

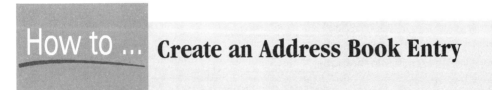

How to ... Create an Address Book Entry

In summary, here's how you can create entries in the Address Book:

1. Press the Address Book button on your Palm to switch to that app.

2. Tap the New button on the bottom of the Address List view.

3. Enter all the information to create an entry for the person in question.

4. Tap the Details button and assign the entry to a category, and then tap OK.

Before you can beam your personal information around, though, you need to create a business card. That's not hard to do. Find your own personal information in the Address List (or, if you haven't done this yet, create an entry for yourself). After you select your card and you can see your personal information on the Address View screen, choose Record | Select Business Card from the menu.

From here on, you can beam your card to others either by choosing Record | Beam Business Card from the Address List menu or, more simply, by holding the Address List button down for two seconds.

TIP   *Is your Address List entry selected as your business card? It's easy to tell. On the Address View, you can see an icon representing a Rolodex page at the top of the screen, to the right of the title.*

Work with the Palm Desktop

The Palm Desktop obviously has its own counterpart to the Address Book found in the Palm. Using the Palm Desktop, you cannot only create, edit, and refer to entries on your PC, but you can also put them to use in ways unavailable on the Palm itself. Next, we look at the Palm Desktop—both on the PC and the Mac.

The Windows Address Book

Using the Address Book in the Palm Desktop is a radically different experience than using the Palm. In most respects, it's better because the larger desktop screen, keyboard, and mouse enable you to enter and use the data in a more flexible way. After you start the Palm Desktop, you can switch to the Address Book by clicking the Address icon on the right side of the screen or by choosing View | Address Book (see Figure 6-4).

The Address Book interface enables you to see both the Address List and Address View simultaneously. To see a specific record's contents, click it in the list and the information then appears in the column on the right.

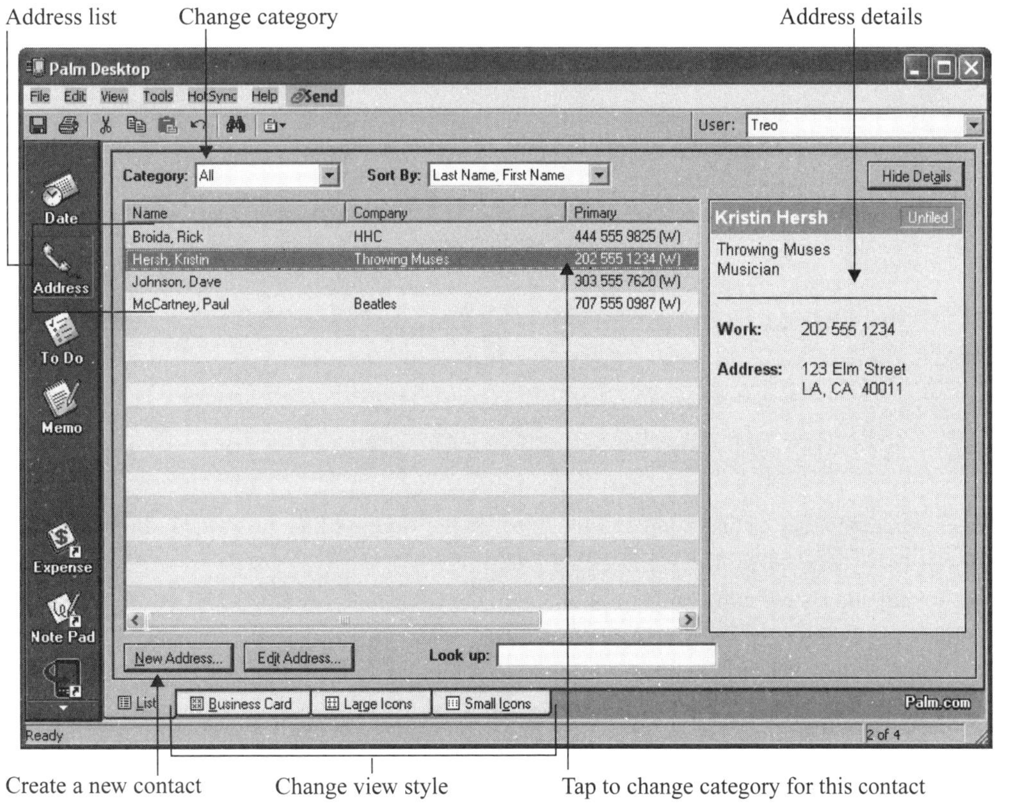

6

Address list   Change category   Address details

Create a new contact   Change view style   Tap to change category for this contact

FIGURE 6-4   The Address Book looks sparse, but it has more features than the Palm itself.

You can print a detailed address book based on your Palm contacts by choosing File | Print. The address book is nicely formatted.

Create and Edit Entries

Some of the most dramatic differences in the Address Book appear when you create and use the Address Book. Remember these notes:

- To create a new entry, click the New button at the bottom of the screen or double-click a blank spot in the Address List.

- The Edit and New dialog boxes enable you to enter the same information as on the Palm. The dialog box also has a list box for specifying the category and a check box to make the entry private.

![New Address dialog box with General and Note tabs. Name section shows Last name: Gruber, First name: Hans, Title: Thief, Company: Die Hard. Address section with Street, City, State, Zip, Country fields. Contact Info section shows radio buttons for Work (selected), Home, Fax, Other, E-Mail, with "Work is the primary contact." Custom 1-4 fields. Buttons: OK, Cancel, New, Help. Category: Unfiled. Private checkbox.]

- To specify which phone number will appear in the Address List, click the radio button to the left of the appropriate phone number.

- To edit an existing entry, either double-click the entry in the Address List or its equivalent in the Address View on the right.

- You can also change the custom fields on the Palm Desktop. To do that, choose Tools | Options and click the Address tab.

Import Contacts into the Palm Desktop

If you have a history with another contact manager, you could have dozens or even hundreds of names and addresses that should be copied over to the Palm Desktop to be synchronized with the

Palm. Thankfully, the Palm Desktop makes importing all those contacts possible with a minimum of fuss. All you need is a contact manager capable of saving its data in either a comma-separated (CSV) or a tab-separated (TSV) format. To import your data from another program, do this:

1. In your old contact manager, find the menu option to export your data in either CSV or TSV format. If the program gives you an option to remap your data as it's saved, don't worry. We'll map it properly as it's imported into the Palm Desktop. Save the exported data to a file on your hard disk. Make a note of where you save this file because you need to find it again in about two steps.

2. In the Palm Desktop, choose File | Import. The Import dialog box should appear.

3. Select the file you just created with the old contact manager. You might have to choose the proper file extension (like CSV or TSV) from the Type of File list box to see the file you created. Choose Open.

4. Now you see a Specify Import Fields dialog box, as shown in Figure 6-5. This is the hardest part of the process and the one part that isn't terribly automated. Here's the deal: the data in a typical contact entry includes items like name, phone numbers, and address. But those fields won't be in the same order in any two contact management programs, which means you need to help the Palm Desktop put the old data in the right fields as it imports. To map the fields properly, drag each field on the left (which is the Palm Desktop) until it's lined up with the proper field on the right (which represents the old program). Line up last name with last name, for instance, and match phone numbers, e-mail addresses, and any other important fields. If you don't want to import a certain field, deselect its check box.

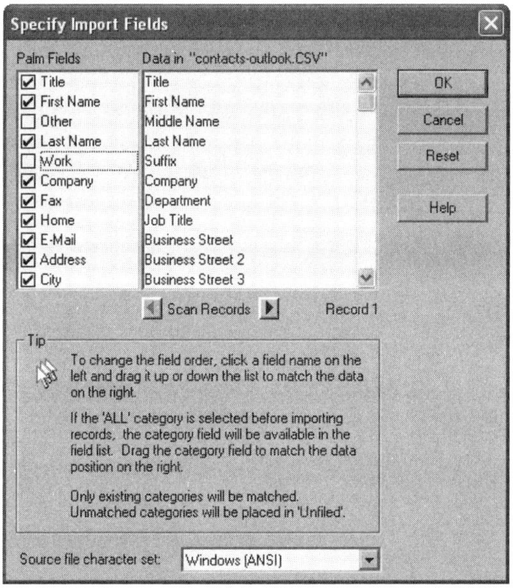

FIGURE 6-5 Carefully rearrange the fields in the Specify Import Fields dialog box so your old data is imported properly into the Palm Desktop.

> **TIP** *You can use the arrows to cycle forward through the database and make sure you assigned the fields properly.*

5. When you finish lining up the fields, click the OK button.

If you did everything right, you should see your contacts in the Palm Desktop. Any newly imported entries are highlighted. If you messed something up, all isn't lost. Simply delete all your records, and then try to import your contacts file again.

Using Outlook

As we mentioned in Chapter 5, Outlook is a perfectly good alternative to the Palm Desktop. To see your contacts in Outlook, start by clicking the Contacts icon in the Outlook Shortcut bar. Outlook should switch to the Contacts view, and then you see a complete list of your names and addresses.

You can view your contacts in many ways. That's good, because if you're anything like us, you have hundreds of entries—and sorting through them can be like finding a virtual needle in a digital haystack. To see your options, click the Organize button in the Outlook toolbar. The Organize pane should open. Click Using Views, and then you can experiment with arranging your contacts by category, by company, or nearly any other way imaginable.

SHORTCUT *To find a contact quickly from any view in Outlook, type the person's name in the Find a Contact field on the Outlook toolbar and press* ENTER. *Outlook displays a list of names that matches your criteria or, if only one name appears, displays its entry.*

Working with the Palm

Outlook can hold a wealth of information, but it's important for you to understand the Palm's limitations when synchronizing to Outlook. Not all the fields in Outlook get transferred to the Palm because there simply aren't enough fields. Specifically, the limitations in the HotSync from Outlook to the Palm are the following:

- By default, only the business address is stored on the Palm. You can upgrade to other HotSync conduits that let you synchronize the personal address. Specifically, try PocketMirror Professional or IntelliSync.

- Work, Home, Fax, Mobile, and E-mail are typically the only contact fields transferred to the Palm. If you create a contact with alternative fields, like Business 2 or alternative e-mail addresses, Palm tries to include these entries, space permitting.

- None of the data from the Details tab is stored on the Palm.

This illustration should help you see how the Palm's Address Book entries correlate to Outlook:

The Macintosh Address Book

Like the other applications in the Palm Desktop, the Address Book doesn't precisely match the name or even the function of its related Palm core app. On the Mac, the Address Book is called Contacts. Its appearance is quite different as well. To see the Contacts program, you need to click the View Contact List button on the Palm Desktop toolbar.

The Macintosh Blues

Dave: Okay, this is totally lame. Here we have a program that's available for the Mac and for Windows, and they're so radically different, you'd never know they were supposed to be the same application. None of the menus or buttons are the same. Heck, you can't even expect to do the same *kinds* of things with the Mac version of Palm Desktop as you can with the Windows version. It's enough to make me cry. If I have a Mac at home and a PC at the office, I have to learn two completely different ways of working with my Palm data on the desktop. Was there ever anything more annoying than this? Huh? Answer me already!

Rick: As you can see, Dave agitates easily. The Mac version of Palm Desktop is a lot more capable than the Windows version, so I don't see what the fuss is about. Granted, it would be nice for people who have Macs at home and Windows PCs at work to have some continuity between them, but, as I like to say: there's no such thing as perfect!

The Contact List is essentially the only view or module in the program—you needn't learn to switch between multiple views to use all the features in the Address Book:

TIP   *When you create a new contact, the first phone number in the list (not the first one you complete) is the one the Palm uses in the Address List as the main number. Also, to synchronize with the Palm properly, you should enter the e-mail address in the field in Other Information.*

Sort and Filter Your Contacts

You can customize the way your contacts are displayed by using the controls at the top of each column. If you only want to see some of the contacts, for instance, you can filter the display to show only certain entries. You can establish filters based on any column. To see only contacts in your own area code, for instance, choose Phone 1 and set the filter accordingly. Here's how:

1. Click the menu for the column you want to use as the filter criteria. You should see the filter and sorting menu.

2. If the criteria you want to sort appears in the menu, click it. If not, click Custom Filter. That displays the Custom Filter dialog box.

3. Choose the filter operator that can accomplish what you want to do. If you want to display contacts with an area code of 303, for instance, choose Starts With and enter **303** in the field. If you want to display contacts that work at a company called OmniCorp, then choose Contains and type **OmniCorp** in the blank field.

4. Click OK to close the dialog box and display the results.

> TIP
>
> *You can create detailed filters by combining different columns. You can apply a filter to both the Phone 1 and Company columns, for instance. Anything that passes the first filter must then also pass the second filter to appear in the Contact List.*

If you create a filter set you want to use often, you can tell the Address Book to memorize it. To do this, click the View menu and choose Memorize View. Give this view a name, and then you can display it in the future without going thorough the process of setting up one or more filters every time. To exit this memorized view and revert to the normal view, click Show All.

You can also sort your results alphabetically. To sort, decide which column you want to use as the sorting column. Then click the column menu and choose Sort.

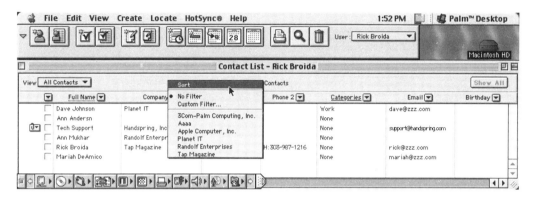

Address Book Alternatives and Enhancements

Don't think you have to stick with the Address Book just because it came with your trusty old Palm. Personally, we prefer the Palm Address Book to most of the alternatives, but here are a few you might want to look into if you feel like expanding your contact management horizons:

- **KeyContacts**   This new program from Chapura could well be the answer to every power user's dreams. While the ordinary Address Book doesn't synchronize many of Outlook's fields, KeyContacts is an Address Book replacement that transfers absolutely everything—including all those extra fields in the other Outlook Contact tabs and all the categories as well. If you live and die by your contacts, this might be as essential a replacement for the Address Book as DateBk5 is for the Date Book.

- **Action Names Datebook**   This Address Book replacement combines the To Do List, Date Book, and Address Book to deliver a single, integrated interface for tracking, alarming, and viewing your daily itinerary. This program has lots of die-hard fans because of its many powerful features for managing contacts. You can try it out at **www.iambic.com**.

- **Contacts-M**   This Address Book alternative provides a number of tabs for storing all kinds of stuff the Palm Address Book doesn't include—like ICQ numbers and AOL Instant Messenger screen names. It also lets you link *commitments*—essentially appointments—to names in your contact list. Download it from **dpi.hypermart.net**.

- **PopUp Names**   Using Hackmaster (which we discuss in Chapter 15), this program pops the Palm Address Book on to the screen with a simple stroke of the stylus, and then puts it away when you're done—letting you keep the application you were using open, so you don't lose your place or have to hunt around to get back to what you were doing. Find it at **www.benc.hr**.

Where to Find It

Web Site	Address	What's There
Chapura	**www.chapura.com**	PocketMirror Professional and KeyContacts
Pumatech	**www.pumatech.com**	IntelliSync
Synchroscan	**www.pda2phone.com**	Parlay Autodialer

6

Chapter 7

The To Do List

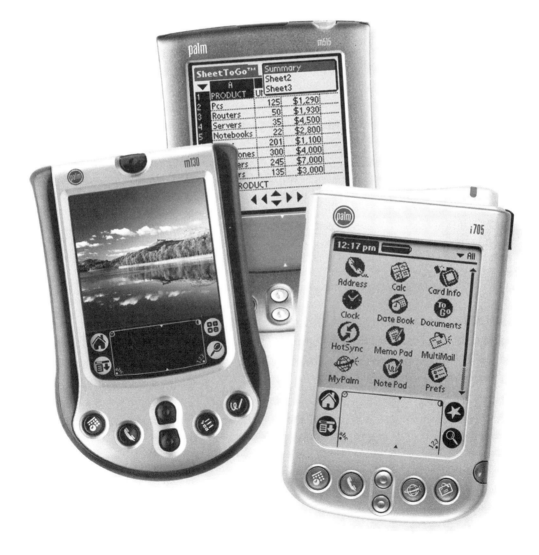

How to...

- Create new To Dos
- Create a To Do based on an Address Book entry
- Prioritize your To Dos
- Add notes to your To Dos
- Edit To Dos from the List View
- Customize the To Do List View
- Beam To Dos to others
- Use the Palm Desktop for Windows
- Export To Dos to Word and Excel
- Using Outlook with the Palm
- Create Tasks on the Mac
- Sort and display tasks on the Palm Desktop for the Mac

The To Do List is admittedly one of the smallest of the core Palm applications, but don't let that fool you. There's a lot of convenience under the hood. What good is this little program? Well, think of it this way: would you be more organized if you carried a list of things you needed to do—big and small—with you all the time? Finish a task and cross it off the list for a sense of immediate gratification. Or, think of something you need to do while you're away from the office and add it immediately to the Palm, knowing the entry will be added to your PC's master To Do List as soon as you HotSync. The To Do List is a way to take charge of all the little things that make up your daily agenda.

View the To Do List

As with most of the core applications in your Palm, you can start the To Do List by pressing its button on the Palm (it's the one to the right of the scroll buttons) or by tapping its icon on the Application screen.

As you can see in Figure 7-1, the Palm lists your To Dos in a fairly straightforward list, which you can use to see what tasks you have coming up or, in some cases, past due (you might want to take care of those pretty soon). A standard Palm screen has room for 11 entries at one time. The rest appear above or below the screen, depending on where you are within the To Do List (high-resolution displays can fit more). Getting around is easy. Simply scroll down to see more names, either with the onscreen scroll arrows or the scroll buttons on the Palm's case.

Each time you scroll, the Palm moves the list by one complete page. This means if you scroll down, the bottom entry on the page becomes the top entry after scrolling.

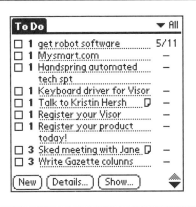

FIGURE 7-1   The To Do List displays all your pending tasks.

Another way to get around is by using the categories. If your tasks are divided into more than one category, every time you press the To Do button, you switch categories. You can cycle through the first page of tasks in each category by repeatedly pressing this button.

Create a To Do

To add a To Do to your Palm, start writing in the Graffiti area. The text appears automatically in a brand new To Do entry.

If you want to create a task with a specific priority, tap on a To Do entry that has the priority you want, and then tap New. The new To Do takes the priority of the previously selected task, saving you the trouble of choosing a priority later.

While most tasks can be summarized in only one line of text, there's no reasonable limit to how long you can make a To Do entry. If you need more than one line of text to describe your task, you can use the Enter gesture to get the Palm to display a new blank line in the same To Do.

Did you know?

The Agenda Shows To Dos

You can view your To Do items in the Date Book. The Agenda View lets you see all of today's appointments and upcoming To Dos at a glance, all on the same screen. See Chapter 5.

Remember, though, creating multiline To Dos might make it hard for you to read your tasks later, as you can see here:

Instead of making long, multiline tasks, we recommend you add a note to your task instead (this is explained in the next Tip).

Add Some Details

Once you finish entering the name of the task, tap elsewhere on the screen to save the entry. If you prefer, you can add additional information, like a priority, category, and due date. You don't have to enter any of these special settings, but using them enables you to track your tasks with greater accuracy. Here's what you need to do.

1. Select the task you want to edit by tapping the name of the To Do.

2. Tap the Details button.

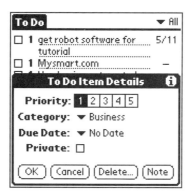

3. Tap a number to represent the priority of your task. You can select any number from one to five (the lower the number, the higher the priority).

Friends Are a Chore

It's true! Having friends and coworkers can be actual work. Suppose you need to meet with Ed Grimpley from accounting sometime this week to talk about why you've gone through 18 mouse pads in the space of one week. You don't have an appointment in your calendar—you'd rather pop in sometime when it's convenient. The To Do List is your answer. Create a new To Do and choose Options | Phone Lookup from the menu. Find Ed in the Phone Number Lookup dialog box and tap Add. What you get is Ed's name and phone number in the To Do entry. It's a handy way to remind yourself to call someone without setting up a rigid appointment in the Date Book.

4. Choose a category from the Category list.

5. Choose a due date from the Due Date list. You can choose to make a task due today, tomorrow, or in a week, or you can choose a date directly from the Calendar dialog box.

6. Tap OK to save your changes to the task.

7

TIP   *While you can make a task almost any length, most people find it's better to keep the To Do short and add a note. To add a note to a To Do, select your To Do, tap the Details button, and then tap Note.*

Work with the List View

When you switch to the To Do List, all of your existing tasks are arranged onscreen, usually in order of importance (as determined by the priority number assigned to each To Do). As you can see in Figure 7-2, six elements are associated with each task:

■ **Check box**   If you complete a task, you can indicate it's done by tapping the check box. That places a check mark in the task. Depending on how you configured the To Do Preferences, the entry either disappears or remains onscreen, but is marked as done.

To Do or Appointment?

We know what you're thinking—if you can assign due dates to items in the To Do List, why bother with appointments? Or, from the other perspective, why use To Dos if you have the Date Book? That's a good question. We use the To Do List whenever we have tasks that need doing by a certain date—but not at a certain time of day. If it requires a time slot, we put it in the Date Book. So, stuff like "buy lemons" and "finish Chapter 20" (hint, hint, Rick . . .) are To Dos. "Meet with Laura for lunch at 11:30" is a Date Book entry. There's also the matter of alarms: your Palm has an alarm for appointments, but not for To Dos.

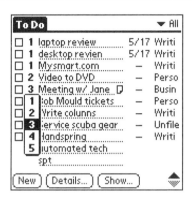

FIGURE 7-2   The To Do List lets you modify your tasks without tapping the Details button.

- **Priority**   Not everything is the most important thing on your task list. If you want to arrange your tasks by importance or urgency, use the priority numbers, from one through five. Tap the number to get a list of all the priority choices.

  We recommend you use priority numbers for your tasks—they help you sort through the clutter of your various To Dos and determine what's important from one day to the next.

- **To Do description**   You can edit the description of the task by tapping in this field and editing the existing text.

- **Note icon**   If you already created a note for the task, you can read the note or edit it by tapping the icon to the right of the To Do name field. If no note already exists, you can add one by selecting the task and choosing Record | Attach Note from the menu.

- **Due date**   You might have tasks that need to be accomplished by a specific date. If this is the case, use the final column. If a dash is in that slot, this means you haven't yet assigned a due date. Tap it and choose a date. You can also change the due date in the same way.

Watch out! The To Do List uses date/month, an unusual format in the United States.

- **Category**   Change the category to which a task is assigned by tapping the category column and choosing the desired category from the list.

Some of these columns aren't displayed by default—to enable them, tap the Show button and choose the columns you want to appear in the To Do Preferences dialog box.

Change the View Options

If you're anything like us (and that could be a very, very bad thing, if you know what we mean), you could be perfectly happy with the default look of the To Do List. It's easy to modify, though. Tap the Show button and you see the To Do Preferences dialog box. Here are your options:

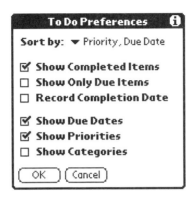

Sorting Options

The first item you encounter in the Preferences dialog box is a Sort By list. This determines the way the To Do List shows the tasks onscreen.

- ■ **Priority, Due Date**   This groups all the priority 1 tasks first, then priority 2, and so on. Within each priority group, the earliest deadlines are listed first, and no deadline tasks are listed last. This option works best if you need to work on tasks with the highest priority and due dates aren't particularly important to you.

- ■ **Due Date, Priority**   This selection arranges all the tasks by due date, with the soonest due dates listed first and no due dates listed last. If several tasks have the same due date, they're listed by priority order. This is probably the best display option for most people— it lists your tasks with the ones due soonest at the top of the page and, within each due date, you can see the top priorities arranged first.

- ■ **Category, Priority**   Arranges your tasks by category. The categories are arranged in alphabetical order. If you have more than one task in a given category, they're arranged in priority order within the category. Use this category if seeing tasks visually arranged into different categories—like work and personal—is more important for you than arranging them by due date or category.

- ■ **Category, Due Date**   This selection also arranges your tasks by category and the categories are arranged in alphabetical order. If you have more than one task in a given category, they're arranged by due date within the category. Soonest deadlines appear first and no due date tasks are placed last within each category.

Use Filters to Customize the Display

The next section in the To Do Preferences dialog box controls what kind of tasks are displayed onscreen. Actually, that's not true, but we're trying to apply some logic to the way Palm chooses to group the items on this screen. Here's what each of these three items does.

■ **Show Completed Items** As you check off tasks you complete, slowly but surely, they clutter up your screen unless you do something about them. If you uncheck this option, completed items are hidden. If you need to see items you've completed, simply check Show Completed Items and they reappear.

 If you hide completed tasks in this way, they're not deleted. They still take up memory on the Palm. The upcoming section "Delete Old To Dos" tells you how to eliminate them.

■ **Show Only Due Items** If you're only concerned about tasks due today, check this item. Any tasks with a due date after today disappear from the screen and only reappear on the day they're due.

 Be careful with this option because it hides To Dos that aren't due today from the screen, regardless of priority. It's easy to get caught off guard by a major deadline this way.

■ **Record Completion Date** This interesting little feature changes the due date of a completed item to the date it was completed. If you didn't assign a due date to a task, the completion date becomes the due date. In this way, you can track what day you completed each of your tasks.

CAUTION *This option overwrites the due date with the completion date. You can't get the original due date back, even if you uncheck the task or turn off the Record Completion Date option.*

Modify the Task Columns

As you probably already saw, you can tweak the data the To Do List shows you for each task in the list. That tweaking occurs here, in the last three options of the To Do Preferences dialog box. Your To Do List can look sparse, highly decorated, or anything in between by changing the Show options.

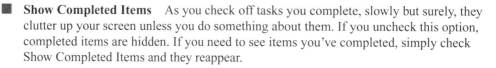

- **Show Due Dates**   The due date format is day/month, which takes some getting used to. If you don't assign a due date to a task, you see a dash instead. On the To Do List, if you tap a due date, you see a list for changing the date.

- **Show Priorities**   This displays the priority to the left of the To Do name. The priority can be adjusted by tapping the number on the To Do List View.

- **Show Categories**   The category of the task appears on the right edge of the To Do List View if you use this option. You can assign a category to an unfiled To Do (or change the category of a previously filed entry) by tapping the category name on the To Do List View.

Delete Old To Dos

For most people, To Dos are not like diamonds—they don't last forever. After you check off a task that says "pick up a loaf of bread," how long do you need a record of having accomplished that goal? That's why your Palm provides a method of removing tasks you no longer want. The Palm offers you two ways to eliminate tasks:

- **Delete them one at a time**   If you need to delete only one To Do, tap in the To Do to select it. Now choose Record | Delete Item from the menu and the To Do is gone forever.

- **Delete a whole bunch at once**   If you use the To Do List a lot and develop a back list of dozens or hundreds of completed tasks occasionally, axing them one at a time could become a full-time job. Instead, purge them. A *purge* deletes all completed tasks, so be sure you want to do this. To purge your To Do List, choose Record | Purge from the

Where's All the Color?

Dave: I wept with happiness when I got my color Palm. I can play arcade games in color, read text more easily against the white background, and show off color pictures of my cat to total strangers at the bus stop. But I'm stumped: where's all the color in the built-in apps? I mean, think about it . . . if you assign a due date to a To Do, wouldn't you want it to appear in red if it's late? But Palm's color support is so slight, it hardly seems worth having a color model at all—unless you buy lots of additional Palm software that's optimized for color.

Rick: I'm stumped by this as well. Palm should have added more color-related features to the core apps. Fortunately, third-party developers have filled in the gaps. Pimlico Software's DateBk5, for instance, makes extensive use of color. So does Electric Pocket's BugMe, a program that simulates Sticky Notes. I think one reason the Palm platform is so popular among software developers is they feel like part of the team, pitching in in areas Palm neglected.

menu. The Purge dialog box appears, asking if you really want to delete your completed To Dos. Tap OK.

TIP *If you want to preserve a copy of your completed tasks, check Save Archive Copy on PC, and then load the archive into the Palm Desktop when you need to refer to the entries.*

Share Your To Dos

Delegation is the key to successful management. At least that's what we've been told. We don't actually supervise anyone, but it sounds like solid business advice, nonetheless. You can use your Palm as a solid delegation tool by beaming tasks to other people. Just like in other applications, you can beam a single item or all the items in a specific category. Here's the skinny:

■ **Beam a single To Do** To beam one To Do to someone, choose a task by tapping inside the To Do name. Then choose Record | Beam Item from the menu.

■ **Beam a whole bunch of items** You can beam an entire category's worth of To Dos at once. To do this, switch the current view to show the category you want to beam. You can choose a category from the list at the top right of the screen or press the hard To Do button several times until the category you want appears. Then choose Record | Beam Category from the menu.

Work with the Palm Desktop

Who says the only place you can enter To Dos is on your Palm? Not us! The Palm Desktop—both the Windows and Mac versions—has a module dedicated to tracking your tasks. Using the Palm Desktop, you can enter To Dos and have them appear on your Palm when you're away from your desk.

How to ... Create Tasks on Your Handheld

We've talked a lot about To Dos, so here's a summary of how to create tasks on your Palm:

1. Press the To Do button on the Palm.
2. Start writing in the Graffiti area—this creates a new To Do.
3. Tap the Details button.

If you want to, assign a priority, category, and due date on the Details dialog box. Tap OK to close this dialog box.

7

The Windows To Do List

The To Do List's interface is a bit more spacious than the one in your Palm. As a result, the Palm Desktop pulls off a cool trick—it displays both the list itself and the contents of the Details dialog box onscreen simultaneously, as you can see in Figure 7-3. Click a To Do and the details on the right automatically update to show you more information about the particular task you selected.

Create and Edit To Dos

To create a new To Do, click the New To Do button at the bottom of the screen. You'll see the New To Do dialog box, where you can enter text, assign priorities, and even set a due date for your task.

Using Outlook

If you're an Outlook user, you probably already know that Palm's To Do items become Tasks in Outlook. In fact, that's pretty much all you need to know to use Outlook with your Palm. To see your To Dos in Outlook, click the Tasks icon in the Outlook Shortcuts bar. The tasks are also displayed in the Taskbar section of the Calendar.

 When you mark a task as completed in Outlook, it isn't deleted. To reduce clutter and save disk space, you might want to delete tasks occasionally. To do this, right-click a completed task and choose Delete from the menu.

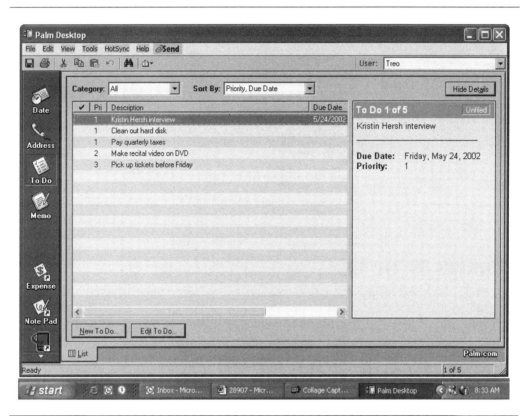

FIGURE 7-3   You can see the details on any To Do by clicking the appropriate description on the left side of the screen.

Understanding Task Priorities

The Palm and Outlook use two slightly different ways of assigning priority to tasks and To Dos. Thankfully, the two systems work together and are easy to figure out. Use this guide to correlate the Palm and Outlook systems:

Palm	Outlook
1	High
2	Normal
3	Normal
4	Normal
5	Low

Turn To Dos into Appointments

Your Palm understands there's a tight relationship between your calendar and your To Do tasks. Switch to the Date Book in the Palm Desktop and you'll find the right side of the screen has a window for displaying either addresses or To Dos. Click the To Do box to show To Dos and click Address to return to the Phone Number Lookup mode. What good is that? Well, you can grab a To Do, and then drag-and-drop it into a calendar appointment. That lets you turn a task into a bona fide appointment. You can't go the other way, though, and turn an appointment into a task.

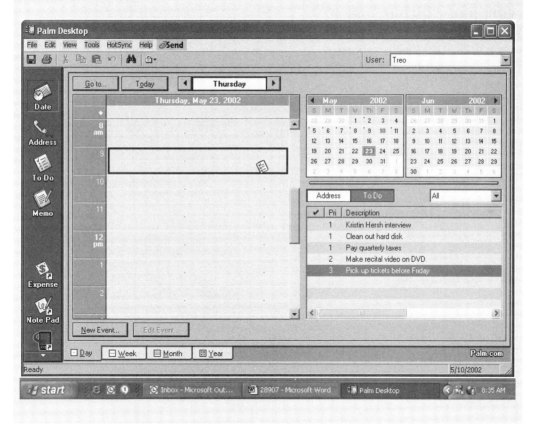

The Macintosh Task List

This should come as no particular surprise to you: the To Do List on the Mac is quite different than the Palm's version—after all, they come from two completely different heritages. On the plus side, the Mac is powerful and easy to use, so we don't think you'll complain a whole lot about it. On the Mac, the To Do List is called the Task List. To see the Task List, you need to click the View Task List button on the Palm Desktop toolbar.

The Task List is composed of a few key elements and is shown in Figure 7-4.

 A View control for displaying only specific tasks

 Filters for sorting and displaying the tasks, found at the top of each column

 The task entry, which includes the name, priority, date, category, completion status, and note

Create and Editing Tasks

You can create a new task either by double-clicking anywhere in the Task View or by clicking the Create Task icon in the Palm Desktop toolbar. The Task dialog box has everything you need to complete your task, but it looks somewhat different than the Palm equivalent.

Here are a few things to watch for:

 Priority   The Mac uses a word-based priority system (highest to lowest) instead of numbers (1 to 5). Highest corresponds to 1, and Lowest corresponds to 5.

 Categories   Two categories are in the Mac's Palm Desktop, but only the first one is used by the Palm when you HotSync.

 Carry Over After Due   Use this item to make sure the task is still visible after its deadline has passed. On the Palm, though, To Dos are always carried over anyway, so the Palm ignores this option.

 Remind   You can set up the Palm Desktop to remind you about upcoming tasks, but the Palm doesn't use this feature.

The Task List displays all the pertinent information about your tasks on one screen.

SHORTCUT *If you need to create a task exactly like the one you just made—complete with scheduling and priority information—use the Add Another button on the Task dialog box instead of clicking OK. The current task gets saved and a new task is created in the same mold as the one you just made.*

Repeat a Task

You can create a task that, like the Repeating Events in the Date Book, occurs over and over on a schedule you determine. To do this, create a new task and click Repeat Task in the Task dialog box. Select the kind of repetition you want from the List menu and you can set the task to repeat indefinitely or to repeat until a date you specify.

All the instances of a repeating task are transferred to your Palm when you HotSync, but they aren't related to each other on the Palm. This means if you later decide to change the series, the change only occurs to one task, not all of them. For this reason, use the Repeating Tasks with care.

Sort and Filter Your Tasks

You can customize the way your tasks are displayed by using the controls at the top of each column. If you only want to see some of the tasks, for instance, you can filter the display to only show certain entries. You can establish filters based on any column. To see only tasks with a priority of 1 (highest), for instance, choose Highest from the Priority column. Here's how:

1. Click the menu for the column you want to use as the filter criteria. You should see the filter and sorting menu.

2. If the criteria you want to sort appears on the menu, click it. If not, click Custom filter. This displays the Custom Filter dialog box.

3. Choose the filter operator to accomplish what you want to do. If you want to display tasks that include the word "meeting," for instance, choose Contains and enter **meeting** in the field.

```
┌──────────────────────────────────────────┐
│ ═══════  Custom Filter on Title  ═══════  │
│                                            │
│ Filter Tasks whose Title                   │
│ ┌──────────────────────────┬───┐          │
│ │ Contains                 │ ◆ │          │
│ └──────────────────────────┴───┘          │
│                                            │
│ ┌──────────────────────────────┐  ◁       │
│ │ meeting                      │          │
│ └──────────────────────────────┘          │
│ ┌───┐              ┌────────┐ ┌────────┐  │
│ │ ? │              │ Cancel │ │   OK   │  │
│ └───┘              └────────┘ └────────┘  │
└──────────────────────────────────────────┘
```

4. Click OK to close the dialog box and display the results.

If you create a filter set you want to use often, you can tell the Task Book to memorize it. To do this, click the View menu and choose Memorize View. Give this view a name, and then you can display it in the future without going through the process of setting up one or more filters every time. To exit this memorized view and revert to the normal view, click Show All.

You can also sort your results alphabetically or numerically. To sort, simply decide which column you want to use as the sorting column. Then click the column menu and choose Sort.

A Better To Do List

We hear what you're saying (figuratively, not literally, of course). The To Do List simply isn't powerful enough. Well, there's a great alterative called ToDo Plus (from Hands High Software at **www.handshigh.com**).

ToDo Plus enables you to attach drawings to your tasks, use templates to customize your entries, add alarms, and much more. One of the most interesting features is a comprehensive set of filters that lets you display your tasks in a variety of useful ways. Give it a try and you might never want to use the built-in To Do List again.

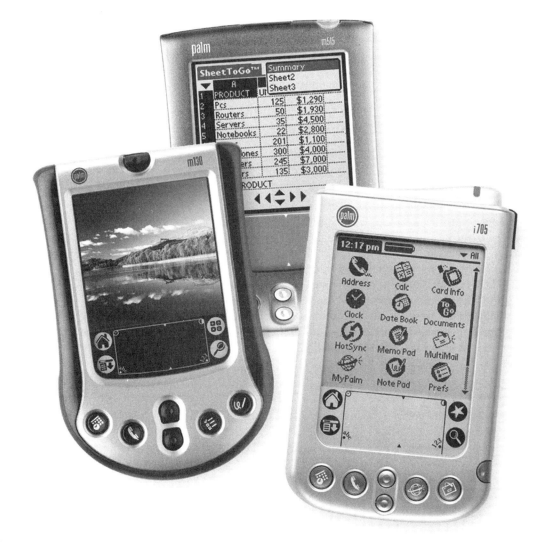

How to...

- View the Memo List
- Create new memos
- Cut, copy, and paste text in a memo
- Assign categories to memos
- Customize the appearance of memos in the Memo List
- Beam memos
- Make memos private
- Delete old memos
- Import text files into Windows memos
- Use memos in other Windows applications
- Attach any item to any other item
- Configure attachments to HotSync properly
- Use Outlook with the Palm
- Sort and filter notes on the Mac

As you've already seen, applications like the Date Book, Address Book, and To Do List let you attach long notes to your entries. A note in the Address Book, for instance, enables you to list directions to the person's house, the names of all their kids, or ten reasons not to visit them for Thanksgiving. But there's also an application designed to do nothing but create notes. These memos can be memory joggers, information you need to take on a trip, or anything not explicitly connected to an address, an appointment, or a To Do. The Memo Pad is your chance, in a sense, to color outside the lines and leave yourself any kind of message you want. And speaking of coloring, the newer Palm models—particularly ones running Palm OS 4 or greater—also let you draw, sketch, doodle, and write notes in the Note Pad with "digital ink." We'll talk about both of these apps in this chapter. Let's start with the Memo Pad.

The Last Button

You know the drill by now. Four buttons are on the front of your Palm and the last one should start the Memo Pad, right? Right.

Unless your new Palm is preprogrammed to launch the Note Pad, that is. Traditionally, the rightmost button looks like a little notebook—but if yours looks like a pen making a scribble, it'll start the Note Pad when you press it. The following shows the difference between old Palms and new Palms.

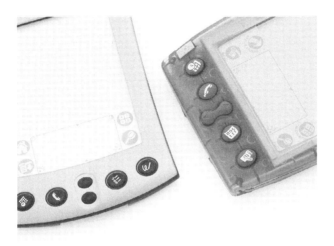

After you get comfortable with both programs and decide which one you use most often, you can leave your Palm the way it is or reassign that program to launch the Memo Pad instead. It's up to you. If you want the Note Pad button to start the Memo Pad, start the Prefs app and choose the Buttons category. Then tap the drop-down menu next to the onscreen Note Pad button and choose the Memo Pad instead.

Whichever program doesn't get the distinction of being associated with that popular button will have to be launched via its icon on the Application screen. It's no big deal, but we thought you'd want to know.

Viewing the Memo Pad

The Memo Pad has two views—the *Memo List* (which is, not surprisingly, a list of all the memos you created) and the *Memo View,* which shows you the contents of whatever memo you select from the Memo List. When you start the Memo Pad, it always starts in the Memo List View. As you can see in Figure 8-1, the Palm displays each of your memos in a list, with the first line of the memo visible as a kind of title that lets you know what's inside. Getting around is easy—just scroll up or down to see more memos.

SHORTCUT *Another way to get around the Memo List is by using the categories. If your memos are divided into more than one category, every time you press the hard Memo Pad button, you switch categories. You can cycle through the first page of tasks in each category by repeatedly pressing this button.*

Creating New Memos

Sure, a New button is at the bottom of the Memo List—but you don't need to use it. Start writing in the Graffiti area, and the Palm automatically switches from the Memo List View to the Memo View.

FIGURE 8-1 The Memo List displays all your memos.

Cool Things to Do with the Memo Pad

Do you know what surprises us? Lots of things, actually. Dave is surprised Rick has no appreciation for the fine arts—specifically, bands like Pink Floyd, the Velvet Underground, Kristin Hersh, and Throwing Muses. (Inexplicably, Rick has an entirely different definition of "fine arts.")

More to the point, we're surprised at how many people can't seem to come up with good uses for the Memo Pad. They let it languish, while they use the Address Book and Date Book all the time. To help you fully realize the potential of this cool little application, here are some helpful suggestions for how to use the Memo Pad:

- **A Million Dollar Idea memo** Create a memo with a header that says "Million Dollar Ideas." No matter when or where you come up with one of those incredibly amazing ideas to help you retire before you turn 50, pull out your Palm and jot it down.

- **Trade show category** Got a lot of booths to visit at next month's lawn care trade show? Create a category and put all the memos for that event in the category. As you walk the show floor, you can reference your notes about the show in one easy-to-find set of memos.

- **Store passwords** This one is dangerous, so make sure you make it private. But, if you have a lot of passwords you routinely need—for your ISP, web sites, computer logons, and that kind of thing, you can store them all in one place in a memo for passwords. Note, we have to reiterate this is kind of dangerous—if your Palm is stolen, you can give all your passwords away if they're not protected properly. No IT department on Earth would sanction this particular tip, and we won't even admit to writing it down if questioned in court.

- ■ **Meeting notes**   Take notes during a meeting and beam the memo to others when the meeting is over.

- ■ **A Phone Messages memo**   Name a memo Phone Messages and when you check voice mail, jot down the notes in your Palm in this memo. If you're diligent about this, you won't end up with a million yellow stickies all over your desk after each VM-checking session. And names and phone numbers will be in your Palm where you need them, not splayed out all over your desk.

- ■ **Store your new words**   Dave makes up new words in an effort to evolve the English language at a grass roots level. If you, too, make up new words frequently (and that's a beautiquious thing to do), store them in a New Words memo, so you don't accidentally forget them. Chizzy! (Rick is working on a way to delete that particular memo from Dave's Palm, perhaps by using a large hammer.)

The memo can be as long as you want—up to 4,096 characters, or about 700 words. That's pretty long and it should suit your needs most of the time. You can include blank lines and divide your memo into paragraphs—anything you need to make it logical and readable.

TIP   *You can't name your memos in the sense that you can save files on the PC with a specific filename, but the first line of the memo is what appears in the Memo List. To keep things neat and organized, you can write a brief description of the memo on the top line, and then start the memo itself on the next line.*

Using Editing Tools

The familiar cut, copy, and paste tools are available in every Palm app. But nowhere are they more important than in the Memo Pad, where you're likely to be writing more than a sentence or two. Remember, you needn't create text from scratch all the time. Using these edit tools, you can move text from other applications and rearrange it to suit your needs.

Suppose, for example, you previously had a Date Book appointment that read

```
Meeting with Ted
```

Within that appointment, you might have created a note that looked like this:

```
Discuss performance review
Get feedback on budget for 2Q
Agree on approach for marketing plan
```

If you want to have a record of your meeting with Ted, take notes in a memo. Open the appointment note and select the three lines of text from the note. With the text selected, choose Edit | Copy from the menu (or you can use the Command gesture and write *C*). Then switch to the Memo Pad, create a new memo, and paste the text into the memo using Edit | Paste (or COMMAND-P using the Graffiti shortcut).

Memo Pad Assistants

Many tools can enhance the experience of creating long notes in the Memo Pad. Here are a few examples you might want to try.

A pair of programs—*TextPlus* and *WordComplete*—can suggest common words as you write, even before a word is complete. By offering likely options for what you might be writing, either of these apps can significantly reduce the time you spend creating text in the Memo Pad.

MultiClipHack expands the Palm's clipboard. It keeps track of your last 16 cut-and-copy operations, and it enables you to pick them from a drop-down menu to insert in your memo as you write.

After pasting the text into the memo, you can use it as your agenda items—and insert notes as needed, giving you a complete record of the meeting. When you HotSync your Palm, you can paste that data into Word or some other application and generate a formal report.

Assigning Categories

After you accumulate a few memos, you might find the Memo List View getting a bit crowded. Clean it up with the Palm's ever-helpful category filing system. Assign a category like this:

1. Create a new memo.

2. Tap the Details button. The Memo Details dialog box appears.

3. Choose a category from the Category list.

4. Tap OK to close the Memo Details dialog box.

After your memos are arranged into categories, you can cycle through them easily by pressing the Memo Pad hard button on the Palm case.

Arranging Memos in the Memo List

Computer users are, for the most part, fanatical organizers. We tend to spend hours straightening up the Desktop, so icons appear in exactly the right place when the computer starts each morning. That said, we're sure you want to organize your memos. This isn't pointless busy work: if you need to open the same memo over and over, having the memo appear at the top of the list whenever you open the Memo List can help. At the very least, we're sure you'll want to understand how to take control of the way memos appear onscreen.

Peering into Madness: Dave's and Rick's Memos

Dave: I have a Memo Pad category called Lists. In this category, I have a bunch of memos I refer to all the time. I have a list of movies—whenever I think of a film I want to rent, I add it to the list. Then, when I go to **Netflix.com**, I can add that movie to my queue. I also have a Songs memo where I can jot down the names of songs I hear on the radio that I might want to download from an MP3 service. I have a list called meals—things I'd like to eat—that I can refer to when I go grocery shopping and get the appropriate ingredients. Finally, I have a Top 10 list. When I think of a funny Top 10 topic—like "Restaurants you won't want to eat at" or "Reasons to own a Palm"—I jot it down, so I have something funny to start a speaking engagement.

Rick: I compile similar lists of books I want to read, movies I want to rent, and wines my wife and I have tried and liked. I also use memos to jot down business ideas, and any other brainstorms I don't want to forget.

When you add memos to the Memo List, by default the newest ones always appear at the end of the list. The default order of Memo List entries is essentially chronological, with the oldest entries at the top and the newest ones at the bottom.

It's a little more complicated than that, though. You can specify the sort order of memos by choosing Options | Preferences. You get two choices:

- **Manual** This is the default mode your Palm uses out of the box. New memos are added to the bottom of the list, but you can drag-and-drop memos to different positions in the list. Suppose you have a frequently used memo you want to appear at the top of the screen. Tap and hold the stylus on the entry, and then drag the stylus up to the position where you want it to appear. You should see a line move with the stylus, indicating where the memo will land if you release the stylus.

- **Alphabetic** This option sorts all entries into alphabetical order. If you select this option, the drag-and-drop method of moving memos won't work unless you revert to the manual method.

Blank Lines for Emphasis

Here's a trick you can try if you think the Memo List is too cluttered. If you use the manual-ordering method and arrange your memos in a specific order in a near-fanatical way, you might be bothered because memo number 4 is "touching" memo number 5. Rick, for instance, is adamant about not eating his mashed potatoes if they come in contact with his peas. Maybe you suffer from the same kind of problem with your Palm.

Try this: Create a new memo with a blank first line. You have to enter at least one character on the second line because the Palm doesn't let you create a completely blank memo. Close the memo and you see you've made a new memo with a blank header. Drag this memo between two memos you want separated and—voilà—you've found a way to separate memos.

```
┌──────────────────────────────────┐
│ Memo          ▼ Personal         │
│  1. Palm book notes              │
│  2. Digital camera book notes    │
│  3. Robot notes                  │
│  4.                              │
│  5. Linux stuff                  │
│  6. IT interviews                │
│  7. Radio guests                 │
│  8.                              │
│  9. Scuba sked                   │
│                                  │
│                                  │
│  ( New )                         │
└──────────────────────────────────┘
```

Working with Your Memos

You have the same 4,096-character limit on writing memos as you have with notes in other parts of the Palm suite of applications. That's plenty of space to write, as long as you're not trying to draft your autobiography (if you are, in fact, trying to create an extremely long document, see Chapter 14 for details on applications that enable you to do that).

Beaming Memos

You can send a memo or a group of memos to another Palm owner just as easily as beaming any other kind of information. Here's how:

■ **Beam one memo** To beam a memo, you need to tap on the memo you want to beam—this displays the memo in the Memo View. Then choose Record | Beam from the menu. That's all there is to it.

■ **Beam a bunch of memos**   To beam more than one memo, they all must be in the same category. Make sure you're in the Memo List View and switch to the category you want to beam. You can do this by choosing the category from the list at the top right of the screen or by pressing the Memo List hard button on the Palm case until you see the category you want. Then choose Record | Beam Category from the menu.

Make a Memo Private

If you have private information stored in a memo, you can easily hide specific memos from prying eyes. The procedure is essentially the same as with other Palm applications. Do this:

1. In the Memo List, select a memo by tapping it.

2. Tap the Details button. You see the To Memo Details dialog box.

3. Tap the Private box to add a check mark. Now the entry is marked as private. Tap OK and you see this dialog box.

4. Tap OK to close the dialog box.

The memo probably isn't hidden yet—you still have one more step to go. To make your memo disappear, you need to enable the Private Records feature in the Security app. For details on how to do this, see Chapter 9.

Deleting Memos

No matter how much you like your memos, eventually you might need to delete some. To delete a memo, tap the memo you want to delete. Now, choose Record | Delete Memo from the menu. The memo is then deleted from your Palm. If you prefer, you can save a backup of this memo to the Palm Desktop by choosing Save archive copy on PC.

Working with Notes

The Note Pad is similar to the Memo Pad. The major difference is this: instead of writing long messages in Graffiti, you're sketching or writing them directly on the screen, as if the stylus were a pen writing on paper. Although Note Pad gives you the freedom to write anything on the screen

How to ... Create New Memos

Working with the Memo Pad is a snap. In summary, here's what you need to do to create memos:

1. Press the Memo Pad button on your Palm.

2. Start writing in the Graffiti area to create a new memo.

3. Tap the Details button and assign your new memo to a specific category.

4. Tap the Done button to close your new memo.

5. Drag the memo to put it in a specific place in the Memo List.

any way you like, remember, you can't transform this digital ink into Graffiti. Your scribbles stay scribbles. When Note Pad starts, you'll see the Note List View (which looks a lot like the Memo Pad's Memo List View).

Creating a Note

To create a note, tap the New button at the bottom of the screen (you can also simply start writing in the Graffiti area). Start your note by giving it a name. Unlike memos, all notes get their own unique subject line. By default, this subject begins with a "time stamp," though you can erase that if you want to.

When you're ready to draw, write or sketch in the main part of the Palm display. Here are the controls at your disposal.

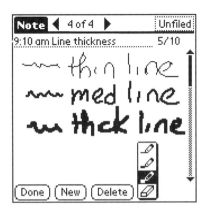

Alarming a Note

Unlike those yellow sticky notes you leave all over your office walls (clean up already—it looks like a pig sty!), the notes you leave in your Palm can buzz you at a certain time and date. Why on Earth would you want that to happen, you ask? Well, here's a good example:

You're stopped at a red light when you hear on the car radio that Diana Darby is playing a show in town in a few weeks. You'd love to go to the concert, so you whip out your Palm. The light will turn green in a moment, though, so you don't have a lot of time to write. Instead of trying your luck with Graffiti, you simply press the Note Pad button and scrawl Diana Darby on the screen. Then you quickly choose Options | Alarm from the menu and choose Saturday at 10 A.M., which is when the tickets go on sale. Tap OK and, when Saturday morning rolls around, the Palm will turn on, bring your note to the front, and play the alarm. As you probably expect, you can accept the alarm or tap the snooze button.

Working in the Palm Desktop

You can create and review your notes and memos on the Palm Desktop. That's good because many kinds of memos might come in handy on the desktop. If you took our advice from earlier in the chapter to create a Phone Messages memo, for instance, you'd appreciate the capability to type directly into the PC when the phone rings.

The Windows Memo Pad

Because the Palm has pretty limited real estate on the small screen, you have to switch between the Memo List and Memo View. But, on the Palm Desktop, you can see both at once. To see a memo, click the header on the left, and the memo's contents appear in the window on the right (see Figure 8-2). Double-clicking a memo header has no effect.

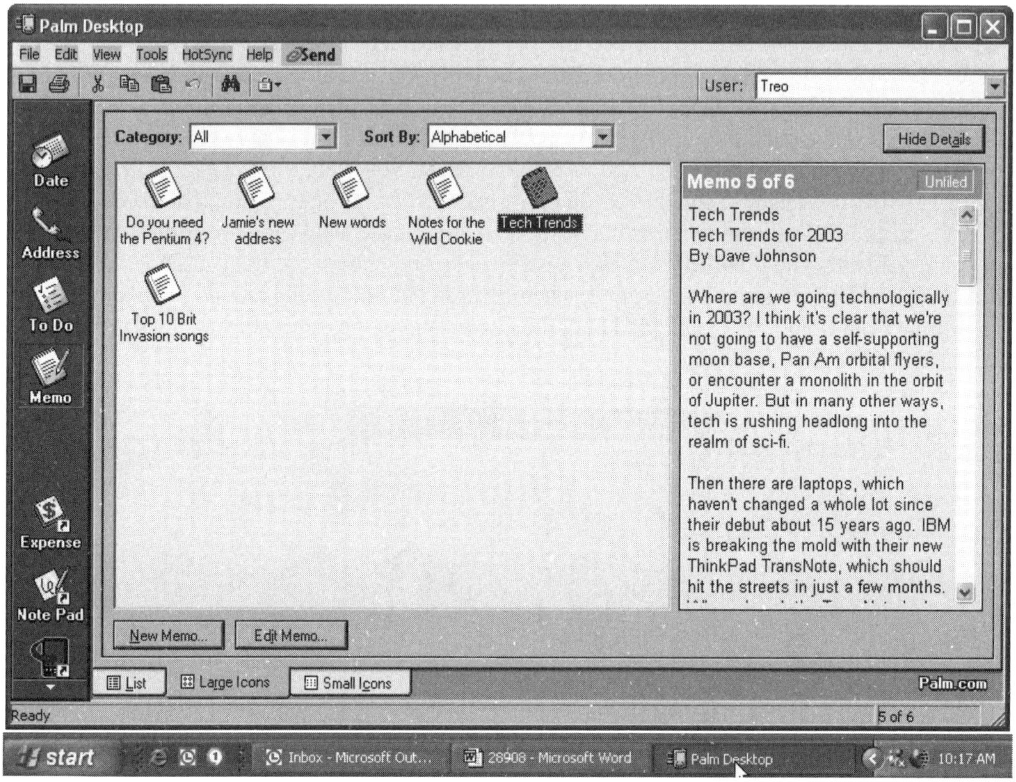

FIGURE 8-2   Palm Desktop's Notes look a lot like the same view in Microsoft Outlook—
except Palm Desktop adds a convenient text window on the right.

Most of the Memo Pad's operation is obvious. The controls aren't identical, though. Here are
some things to remember:

■ You can't rearrange memos. You can sort them alphabetically or by the way they appear
on the Palm. Use the Sort By drop-down menu at the top of the screen.

■ You can display memos in a list or by icons (like Outlook's Notes) using the tabs at the
bottom of the screen.

Importing and Exporting Memos

You don't need to create memos from scratch. Heck, you don't even have to cut-and-paste to
create a memo. The Palm Desktop lets you import text files from elsewhere on the computer.
To import a text file, do this:

1. Choose File | Import. The Import dialog box appears.

2. Choose Text (*.txt) from the File of Type list box.

3. Find the file you want to import (this must be a plain text file in ASCII format—no Word or other specially formatted file types are allowed). Select the file and click the Open button. You then see the Specify Import Fields dialog box.

4. The text file should be ready to import, with the text lined up with the Memo field. If it isn't, drag the Memo field on the left until it lines up, like the one shown here.

5. Click OK.

6. If your text file is too large to fit in a single memo, the Palm Desktop automatically divides it into multiple memos.

7. Click OK.

What about the other case: you have a memo and you'd like to get it into Microsoft Word? Piece of cake! Just right-click a memo and choose Send To | MS Word from the menu. The text will automatically appear in a new blank document in Word.

> **NOTE** *For the Send To feature to work, you need to have the Palmapp.dot template installed in Microsoft Word. Some folks delete that template, and then are mystified why they can't send documents to Word. On the other hand, you can always get text into Word the old-fashioned way: copy-and-paste.*

The Windows Note Pad

The Note Pad is a little more limited. You can't create notes on the desktop, for instance—all you can do is look at ones you created on your Palm. Notes won't alarm on the desktop, either, so if you want to be alerted when a note's time comes up, you'll have to have your Palm with you.

Besides looking at notes, you can also export them to a graphics program. Don't expect to stick one of these sketches into a high-resolution PowerPoint presentation, of course. A Note Pad image measures only 152 × 352 pixels, which isn't enough to fill a computer screen. But getting your handiwork into a graphics program is easy. Just do this:

1. Press the Note Pad button on the left side of the Palm Desktop display. You should see the Note Pad window appear.

2. Find the note in the list you want to export.

3. Right-click the note (whether in the List View or on the image itself) and choose Copy from the menu.

4. Open your favorite image-editing program and choose Edit | Paste from the menu.

Using Outlook with the Palm

Outlook's Notes View is, like the Palm's Memo Pad, a place to store free-form notes of any kind. You can use it to record phone messages, jot down reminders, leave long-term documents (like things to bring on a trip), or to remind yourself about web sites you want to visit. It doesn't matter what you put in these notes. By default, Outlook's notes look like little Post-it notes. You can change their appearance in two ways.

1. To change the color of a single note, right-click it and choose Color from the menu. You can choose from five colors to make certain notes stand out visually.

2. To change the default color and size of all notes, choose Tools | Options from the Outlook menu and click the Preferences tab. Click the Note Options button and set your preferences. Click OK to close the dialog boxes. All new notes you create appear with these settings.

Quirks Between Outlook and Palm

While the Outlook Notes View and Palm Memo Pad are perhaps the simplest of all the features in these two programs, you should know a few things to ensure everything works smoothly when you HotSync:

1. The Palm Memo Pad has a size limit—but Notes in Outlook don't. This means you can create a long note in Outlook that doesn't transfer properly to the Palm. If you create a huge note in Outlook, only the first 4,096 characters appear in the Palm Memo Pad. You also see a warning saying this occurred in the HotSync log.

2. The Palm's categories aren't used by Outlook. This means your Palm memos, when they appear in Outlook as notes, are unfilled. The same is true in the other direction.

Look Ma, No Scroll Bar!

Outlook's notes have an annoying glitch—lacking scroll bars, it's hard to read a long note that trails off the bottom of the sticky note window. Don't know what we're talking about? Copy a long Word document into a new note. Or, create a long Palm memo and HotSync. You'll find the text extends beyond the bottom of the note window in Outlook and there's no scroll bar to scroll down to read it all.

The solution is deceptively simple: click in the note window to place the cursor in the note, and then use the down arrow key on the keyboard to scroll through the document. Or, make the note's window larger, so it can show more text.

Why do we mention this? Rick didn't realize there was any way to scroll through the document at all—he thought anything that didn't fit in the sticky note window was totally inaccessible—until Dave showed him the keyboard arrow trick. So, if you were ever perplexed by the missing memo text, now you are at least as smart as Rick (fill in your own jokes here).

The Macintosh Note List

The Note List is the Mac's unique name for the Note Pad. And not only the name is different—this module is strikingly different than the Palm's equivalent core application. That's good, though, for the most part—if you use the Palm Desktop as your primary information manager, you'll find the Note List is a powerful and flexible tool for creating long or short notes. In addition, the very concept of attaching notes is more open-ended on the Mac, as you'll see in the upcoming section "Attaching Notes."

Creating and Editing Notes

You can use notes on the Mac just like on the Palm—to track phone messages, leave yourself yellow sticky notes, or nearly anything else. To create a new note, you can use either one of these techniques:

- Double-click anywhere in the Note View. The Note dialog box appears, which you can fill in and close when you finish (there's no OK button to save the changes).
- Click the Create Note icon on the Palm Desktop toolbar.

A Memo Pad Alternative

Is the Memo Pad not powerful enough for you? Then flip over to Chapter 14, where we introduce you to a few powerful word-processing alternatives to the Memo Pad, such as Documents To Go and WordSmith. Or, there's a program called Memo PLUS, which enables you to attach drawings to your memos, use templates, and more. Memo PLUS is a good program you might choose to use instead of the Memo Pad. Find it on the Web at **www.handshigh.com**.

To create a note, fill out the Title field, and then enter information in the body of the message. The title becomes the first line of the note on the Palm, not unlike the way we recommended you create a title for your note on the first line of the note, earlier in this chapter. In addition, watch for these other differences between the Palm and Mac versions of the note:

- **Date and time fields**   The date and time fields don't get transferred to the Palm because the Palm doesn't remember when you created a note.

- **Date stamping**   A date stamp icon in the Note dialog box inserts the current date and time in the body of the note. You can use this to create a log or a journal-like note. This data is stored in the body of the message, so it does get transferred to the Palm during a HotSync.

- **Categories**   Two categories are in the Mac's Palm Desktop, but only the first one is used by the Palm when you HotSync.

- **Length**   The Mac can accommodate extremely long notes, but only the first 4,096 characters are transferred to the Palm.

- **Attachment gripper**   You can drag the gripper to another item to attach the note.

Attaching Notes

Attaching notes is a bit different on the Mac than on the PC or Palm. Specifically, you're not limited to notes but, instead, you can attach any kind of item to any other kind of item. You can attach a note to a contact, of course—that even works on the Palm and the PC Palm Desktop—but you can also attach a contact to a note or a task to a calendar appointment. How you attach stuff has no limit or restriction.

NOTE *This might sound odd, but you can attach a memo to another memo. This can come in handy if you have related information in different memos and want to connect them to each other.*

This flexibility makes managing your life on the Mac easy, but an important caveat exists: most of those attachments won't get transferred to the Palm properly. Remember these rules about attachments and the Palm:

■   The only kind of attachment that will HotSync to your Palm is a note attached to an item created in one of the other three primary apps (Address Book, To Do, or Date Book). Any other kind of attachment (like a task attached to an appointment) is ignored during the HotSync.

■   For the note to attach, you must name it exactly like one of these titles: "Handheld Note: Address Book," "Handheld Note: Date Book," or "Handheld Note: To Do Item," as seen in Figure 8-3. After you name the note with one of those titles, you can attach it to another item.

You can attach a note or other item in several ways on the Palm Desktop. Each way has its advantages: use the method that works best for you at any given time.

■   **Drag an item on to another item**   Can you see both windows onscreen at once? Then the easiest way to attach an item to another one is to grab the first item and drag it onto the second item, and then release the mouse.

■   **Use the Attach To menu item**   Open the item you want to attach to something else, and then click the paperclip icon. Choose Attach To | Existing Item. You should see the Attach Existing Item dialog box appear at the bottom of the screen. Now, open the item you want to attach it to, and drag the item from the Attach Existing Item dialog box onto it. This might sound convoluted, but it makes sense when you can't easily display both items onscreen at once.

| FIGURE 8-3 | You need to give your memo a name if you want to attach it to another item and have it appear on the Palm. |

■ **Drag an item to the toolbar**   If you want to attach an existing item to one you haven't created yet, use this method. Grab the item and drag it to the Palm Desktop toolbar. As you move the item across the toolbar, you find it highlights the Create icons for each kind of item. Drop it on the icon that represents the item you want to create. The new item appears with the old item automatically attached. Or, you can achieve the same result by clicking the item's paperclip icon and choosing Attach To. Then choose the appropriate item, such as New Appointment or New Task.

Sorting and Filtering Your Notes

You can customize the way notes appear on the screen by using the controls at the top of each column. This feature works like the filtering tools you've probably already seen in the Contact List and Task List. Essentially, this lets you hide note entries you don't want to see using a set of easy-to-use filters. Here's how it works:

1. Decide what basis you want to use to filter your notes. Suppose, for instance, you only want to see notes with a specific word in the title. You'd obviously want to use the Title column. Click the menu for the appropriate column. You should see the Sort and Filter menu.

Task List - Rick Broida

View	All Tasks ▼	Sort	12 Tasks			Show All

▼	Task	No Filter · Custom Filter... rity ▼	Date ▼	Categories ▼	Completed
☑	Create your own custom case	Highest	Unscheduled	None	November 25, 1999
☐	Write the Sunday column	Medium	November 28, 1999	Work	
☐	Complete Questionaires	Low	Unscheduled	Work	
☐	Write game review — Indiana...	High	November 30, 1999	None	
☐	Planet IT meeting	Low	November 1, 1999	Work	
☐	Planet IT meeting	Low	November 2, 1999	Work	
☐	Planet IT meeting	Low	November 3, 1999	Work	
☐	Planet IT meeting	Low	November 4, 1999	Work	
☐	Planet IT meeting	Low	November 5, 1999	Work	
☐	Planet IT meeting	Low	November 6, 1999	Work	
☐	Planet IT meeting	Low	November 7, 1999	Work	
☐	Planet IT meeting	Low	November 8, 1999	Work	

2. If the criteria you want to filter appears in the menu, click it (if you were displaying only today's notes, for instance, there's an entry for that in the Date menu). If not, click Custom filter, which displays the Custom Filter dialog box.

3. Choose the filter operator to accomplish what you want to do. If you want to display memos that include the word "home," for instance, choose Contains and enter **home** in the field.

Custom Filter on Title

Filter Notes whose Title

Contains	⬍

home	◁

[?]		Cancel	OK

4. Click OK to close the dialog box and display the results.

TIP

You can create detailed filters by combining different columns. You can apply a filter to both the Title and Date columns, for instance. Anything that passes the first filter must then also pass the second filter to appear in the Memo List.

If you create a filter set you want to use often, you can tell the Memo List to memorize it. To do that, click the View menu and choose Memorize View. Give this view a name, and then you can display it in the future without going thorough the process of setting up one or more filters every time. To exit this memorized view and revert to the normal view, click Show All.

The View menu includes another option you might want to use. As we already discussed, attached notes on the Palm look different and can get in the way. That's why the View menu features an option to display only Desktop Notes. If you choose this option, an entry that conforms to the Palm standard for attachments—that is, it starts with the words "Handheld Notes:"—won't appear in the list.

Where to Find It

Web Site	Address	What's There
SmartCell Technology	**www.smartcell.com**	TextPlus
High Hands Software	**www.handshigh.com**	Memo PLUS
PalmGear	**www.palmgear.com**	Tons of additional software

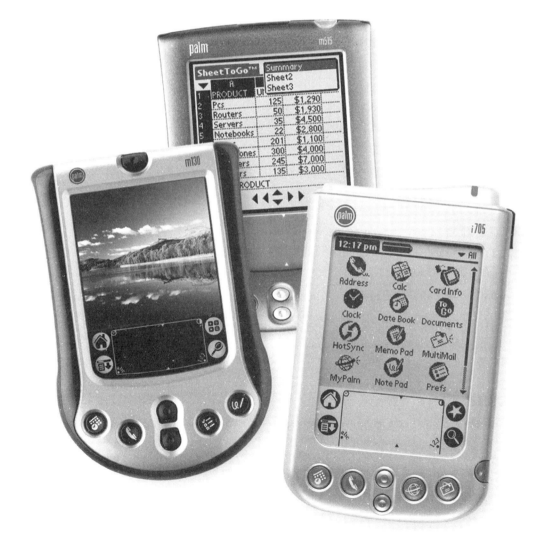

How to...

- ■ Access security features
- ■ Set records as private
- ■ Hide or show private records
- ■ Set a security password
- ■ Password-protect your Palm device
- ■ Find third-party security measures for your Palm and data
- ■ Use the Find feature
- ■ Find third-party utilities that extend your search capabilities
- ■ Use the calculator
- ■ Find third-party calculators
- ■ Decide whether or not to use the Mail applet
- ■ Use a Palm device to track expenses
- ■ Use Expense
- ■ Use Expense to track mileage
- ■ Make effective use of categories
- ■ Synchronize your expenses with Excel
- ■ Synchronize your expenses on a Macintosh
- ■ Find other expense-management software and solutions

Now that we've looked at the stars of the Palm OS—the Address Book, Date Book, Memo Pad and To Do List—let's turn our attention to the supporting cast. We're talking about the Security program, which enables you to hide private records and "lock" your Palm device; the Find feature, a search tool that helps you quickly sift through all your data; the calculator, which, big surprise, calculates; and the potentially mystifying Mail program, which is used to send and receive e-mail—sort of. We also give you the full scoop on the often-ignored Expense program.

Palm Security

At the risk of sounding like a spy novel, listen up, 007. If your data falls into the wrong hands, it could spell disaster for M, Q, and lots of other letters of the alphabet. Fortunately, we've outfitted your Palm device with foolproof security measures. Only you will have the access codes. Only you can view Heather Graham's phone number. (Can we have it? Please? Please?)

In all seriousness, it's not unlikely that you'll be storing some sensitive information in your Palm device, information that should be kept private. Important passwords, account numbers, meeting locations, contact data—these are among the items you'd be loathe to let a stranger see. Fortunately, the Palm OS offers two effective ways to protect your data: marking individual records as private, and locking your Palm every time you turn it off.

In both scenarios, you—or anyone who's trying to access your Palm—must supply a password to gain access. It's a bit of a hassle to have to enter it over and over again, but at least you have the comfort of knowing your Palm and data are totally secure.

Security 101

To get started with Palm security, find and tap the Security icon. You'll see the screen shown in Figure 9-1 (or something like it—it may look a bit different depending on which version of the Palm OS you have). The first step is choosing a password. Notice that the Password box currently says "-Unassigned-"—meaning simply that you haven't entered your password yet. Before you do, read a little further.

What You Should Know About Passwords

The password you choose can be any combination of letters, numbers, symbols, and spaces. You can make it "Spock" or "H4T*Q" or "The quick brown fox." Ideally, it should be something reasonably short, as you'll probably wind up writing it frequently. Don't make it too obvious, like "123," but you could use something as simple as the last four digits of your Social Security number or your spouse's initials.

NOTE *Capitalization doesn't matter. Even if you make a point to capitalize "Spock" when you enter it as your new password, you can write "spock" to unlock your Palm and it'll work just fine.*

CAUTION *Whatever password you decide on, it's vital that it be something you can easily remember. If you forget it, you could wind up unable to access certain records—or your entire Palm device! Thus, if you have even the slightest concern that you might forget your password, write it down on a piece of paper and store it in a safe place. Better safe than sorry.*

9

Security

Password:
-Unassigned-

Auto Lock Handheld:
Never

Current Privacy:
▾ Show Records

[Lock & Turn Off...] [Help]

FIGURE 9-1   In Security, you select a password for use in hiding private records and locking your Palm device.

Working with Passwords

Okay, let's enter a new password on your Palm device. Just tap the "-Unassigned-" box, and then use Graffiti or the onscreen keyboard to enter your desired password.

NOTE *At this time you're also asked to supply a hint. If you use, say, your mother's maiden name as your password, you should put "mother's maiden name" in the hint field. This hint appears when an incorrect password is entered.*

Note the warning that's included here: "If you assign a password, you must enter it to show private records." This sounds a little scary, but don't worry—none of your existing records will immediately be effected by your selection of a password. Only when you mark one as private, as we explain later, does your password enter into play.

After you tap OK, you'll be asked to verify the new password by entering it again. And you'll see another warning about what'll happen if your password is forgotten. The moral of the story is, *don't forget your password!*

Tap OK again, and notice that the Password box now reads "-Assigned-".

TIP *You can tap this box again at any time to change or delete your password, but you have to supply the original one first.*

The "Lost Password" Button

Oh, the perils of the forgotten password. For the last time, just don't forget yours, okay? If you do, there's a scary but effective way to reestablish access to those records you've marked as private. In Security, when you tap the "-Assigned-" button under Password, you're prompted to enter your password. You also see a "Lost Password" button. Tap it, and your password will be deleted—and all your marked-as-private records along with it. However, those deleted records will be restored on your Palm device the next time you HotSync.

Danger, Will Robinson, Danger!

The Palm Operating System's built-in security features are far too weak for the corporate environment. Consider the password, for instance. There's no mandatory length or required combination of letters or numbers: users can create a password from a single character, sure to send any system administrator into heart failure.

Passwords are also easy to bypass. A free utility called *No Security,* for instance, can easily circumvent the Palm security application, erasing the Palm's password and exposing all of the private records on the device. It's billed as a way to recover data if you've lost your password, but the reality is that such programs make it all too easy for thieves to retrieve sensitive data on a lost, stolen, or unguarded PDA. There's no need even to HotSync the device to install the app; No Security can be beamed from another handheld.

No Security won't let someone turn on a locked Palm, but some Palm hardware vendors have customized the security feature to defeat even that slim measure of security. The Samsung I300 smartphone, for instance, lets users turn on a locked device by resetting the password to the default password, usually the I300's phone number. If you know the phone number, you can get in without a hitch.

The moral of the story? Be careful what kind of data you store on your handheld, and take extra measures to protect it if it's valuable. Read on to learn about the software and techniques you need.

Now, when you mark records as private, they become hidden from view, requiring your password to reveal them. Additionally, if you use the "Lock & Turn Off…" option (as detailed in the following section), you'll need to supply your password next time you turn on your Palm.

SHORTCUT   *If you tap the "abc" button in the bottom-left corner of the Graffiti area, the onscreen keyboard will appear. You can use this to enter your password!*

Password-Protecting Your Entire Handheld

If you really want to secure what's stored in your Palm device, you need to password-protect the entire thing, not just certain records. That's where "locking" comes into play. When activated, your Palm becomes locked the next time it's turned off. Translation: When the Palm is turned on again, a screen pops up requiring the password (see Figure 9-2). Without it, there's no getting past that screen.

NOTE   *You can modify the information that appears on this "locked" startup screen by going to Prefs | Owner (see Chapter 2 for a refresher). We recommend including your name and phone number, and maybe even a reward offer—all so that anyone who might find your lost Palm device will have an easier time returning it (and an incentive to do so). What's a good reward? Considering how much a new Palm would cost you, we think no less than $20.*

Auto Lock Handheld   Palm OS 4.0 includes several automated locking options, all of them accessible by tapping the Auto Lock Handheld button in the main Security screen. Here's a quick rundown:

- **Never**   No automatic locking.
- **On power off**   The moment you turn your handheld off (or it shuts off after a few minutes of inactivity), it locks.
- **At a preset time**   Set the handheld to lock at an exact time. For example, if you use it a lot during the day, but rarely at night, you might set it to lock at, say, 6 P.M. That way, you won't have to keep entering your password all day.
- **After a preset delay**   This is our favorite option. It locks the handheld after a period of inactivity—ten minutes, three hours, whatever you choose.

FIGURE 9-2   When you "lock" your Palm, only the correct password will unlock it.

The "Current Privacy" Menu

We've saved the Current Privacy option till last because it relates to the upcoming section on hiding and masking individual records. Simply put, when the Hide option is selected, all records you've marked as private will disappear from view. When you select Mask, private records are hidden but still listed. When you select Show, which you need your password to do, private records are made visible.

NOTE   *The Mask option was added to Security in Palm OS 3.5. If you have an earlier version, you may want to consider upgrading, as masking is a far better solution than hiding.*

Hiding and Masking Your Records

In the four main applications—Address Book, Date Book, Memo Pad and To Do List—any record can be marked private, meaning it suddenly becomes masked or invisible and, therefore, inaccessible. Here's how:

1. Select a record (just by tapping it) in any of the aforementioned programs.

2. Tap the "Details…" button. (In Address Book, you have to tap Edit to get to the screen with the "Details…" button.) You'll see a window containing some options for that record—and a box labeled Private.

3. Tap that box, noticing the check mark that appears. This indicates that the record will become private after you tap OK.

4. Tap OK.

Remember, marking a record as private has no effect unless you've chosen one of the two privacy options in the Security program. If it's set to "Mask Records," records you've marked as private will turn into a solid gray bars. If you choose "Hide Records," records will just plain disappear. (Don't freak out—they're still in memory, just not visible.)

The Difference Between Masking and Hiding

The Mask Records option provides a middle ground between the visibility of "shown" records and the total invisibility of "hidden" records (which appear to have been wiped from existence— great security, but awfully inconvenient). Masked records still appear in your phone list, memo pad, and so forth but appear as solid gray bars (see Figure 9-3). This remains a less-than-stellar solution, as there's still no way to know what lies beneath until you tap the record and enter your password.

The Hide Records option goes a major step further, removing marked-as-private records from view altogether. To make them visible again, you must return to Security and select Show Records. Naturally, you'll need to supply your password at this time.

Passwords on the Desktop

Security isn't limited to the Palm device itself. It also extends to Palm Desktop, working in much the same ways. Thus, you can hide certain records or password-protect the entire program. The same password you've selected for your Palm device will automatically be used in Desktop.

FIGURE 9-3 When you choose Mask Records, all records marked as private are hidden by gray bars.

NOTE *Unfortunately, this is an area in which Mac users get the short shrift. Palm Desktop for Macintosh doesn't include any security features whatsoever. While you can still keep your data protected on your Palm, anyone who has access to your computer has access to your info (unless you've installed some third-party security software).*

CAUTION *Only Palm Desktop is affected by masked and hidden records. If you synchronize with Microsoft Outlook or another third-party contact manager, records marked as private on your Palm device will still be visible on your PC.*

Hidden Records

Whenever you HotSync, any records marked as private on your Palm will become hidden in Palm Desktop—and vice versa. To change whether private records are visible or not, click the View menu, and then select the desired option: Hide, Mask, or Show.

Password-Protecting Palm Desktop

Just as you can lock your Palm, so can you lock Palm Desktop. When you do, and then exit the program, your password will be required the next time it's started—by you or anyone else. Here's how to activate this setting:

1. Make sure Palm Desktop is running, and then click Tools | Options....
2. In the tabbed dialog box that appears, click the Security tab.
3. Click the box that says "Require password to access the Palm Desktop data."
4. Click OK, and then exit Palm Desktop.

NOTE *This security setting applies only to your data. If multiple users are sharing Palm Desktop on a single PC, they'll need to implement password protection for their own user profiles.*

How to ... **Keep Others from Accessing Palm Desktop**

Suppose you step away from your desk for lunch or a meeting. You don't want coworkers or corporate spies poking around through your records. Fortunately, there's an easy way to password-protect Palm Desktop for Windows (alas, the Macintosh version has no security features). Choose Tools | Options, click the Security tab, and check the box marked Require Password to Access The Palm Desktop Data. Now, whenever someone starts Palm Desktop, they must input the correct password (which is the one you created on your handheld) to access your data.

Other Security Software

While the Palm Operating System's built-in security features are fairly comprehensive, there's always room for improvement. Hence the availability of numerous third-party security programs, which generally offer greater versatility and/or convenience. Here we spotlight some of the more intriguing solutions.

MobileSafe

Your Palm can be a handy place to store account numbers, PIN numbers, passwords, and other secret codes, but stuffing them all into a memo isn't the most practical solution. HandMark's MobileSafe, one of Rick's personal favorites, is designed expressly to organize and protect your important numbers and passwords. You need to remember only one password (different from the one used by Palm Security) to access all this neatly categorized information. MobileSafe also has a Windows-based counterpart, so you can manage and access the information on your PC.

NOTE *While Rick is a fan of MobileSafe, Dave likes Chapura's Cloak—a similar product. It's worth checking out if you're interested in this kind of security.*

OnlyMe

Like Security on steroids, OnlyMe locks your Palm device automatically whenever it's turned off. Your password is entered by tapping on a special six-button keypad, or by pressing the Palm's buttons in a particular sequence, or by entering certain letters or numbers in the Graffiti area. You can even create a password that's based on sliding your stylus over the special keypad. Best of all, OnlyMe lets you set a "lock delay," so that your Palm won't lock until after a designated period of time has elapsed.

Sign-On

Passwords can be guessed or discovered, but it's a lot harder to duplicate your signature. Communication Intelligence Corp.'s Sign-On automatically locks your Palm when it's turned off, and then requires you to sign your name—right on the Palm's screen—to unlock it again. This is a great choice for those concerned about forgetting their password.

The Find Feature

The more you use your Palm device, the more data you're likely to wind up storing. And the more data you have, the harder it can be to expediently find what you're looking for. Some examples:

- A couple days ago, you set up a meeting a few weeks in the future, and now want to check the details of that meeting. Must you page through your calendar a day at a time to find the entry?

- You've got dozens of memos and need to find the ones containing the word "sponge." Must you open each memo individually?

- You have 1,500 names in your address list and want to quickly find the record for that guy named Apu whose last name and company you can't remember. How will you locate him?

Using the Palm Operating System's built-in Find feature, you can unearth all this information in a snap. True to its name, Find sifts through your databases to ferret out exactly what you're looking for, be it a name, a number, a word, a phrase, or even just a few letters.

As we showed you in Chapter 2, Find can be found in the lower-right corner of the Graffiti area, represented by a little magnifying-glass icon. Using it couldn't be simpler: Tap it (at any time, no matter what program you're running), and then write in what you want to search for (see Figure 9-4).

> **NOTE** *Capitalization doesn't matter. Even if you're looking for a proper name like "Caroline," you needn't capitalize the first letter.*

FIGURE 9-4   Looking for a specific word? Just write it in the Find box and the Palm will find it for you.

9

> **TIP** *If you use your stylus to highlight a word or chunk of text (done much the same way you select text using a mouse), that text will automatically appear in the Find field when you tap the Find icon.*

The search process should take no more than a few seconds, depending on how many records you've got on your Palm device and the complexity of your search criteria.

How Find Works

When you execute a search, the Palm OS looks through all stored records (except those marked as private) for whatever text you've specified, starting with whatever program you were in when you tapped the Find icon. It looks not only in the main databases—those used by Address Book, Memo Pad, and so forth—but also in the databases associated with any third-party software you may have installed.

> **TIP** *If you're looking for, say, a phone number, you can save a lot of time by loading the Address Book before tapping Find. That's because Find starts its search in whatever program is currently running.*

Keep in mind that Find searches only the beginnings of words. Thus, if you look up "book," it will find "bookcase" but not "handbook." There are third-party programs that can perform much more thorough searches—we talk about some of them in the next section.

> **TIP** *You can make your data a bit more "Find friendly" by using special modifiers. For instance, you might use the letters AP to preface any memo that has to do with Accounts Payable. Then, when you do a search for "AP," you'll quickly unearth all the relevant records.*

Running a Search

After you've written the desired search text in the Find box and tapped OK, the Palm will get to work. You'll see items appear in a categorized list as they're found. If you see what you're looking for, you can halt the search immediately by tapping the Stop button. Then, simply tap the item to bring up the corresponding record in the corresponding program.

If the Palm finds more instances of the desired item than can fit on the screen at once, it will stop the search until you tap the Find More button. This essentially tells it to look up another screen's worth of records. There's no way to backtrack—to return to the previous screen—so make sure you need to keep searching before tapping Find More. (You can always run the search again if need be, but that's a hassle.)

Third-Party Search Programs

Many users find that Find isn't nearly as robust as it could be. If you want to maximize the search potential of your Palm device, one of the following third-party programs might be in order. They're a little on the advanced side, meaning they require the program X-Master (which we talk about in Chapter 15). That doesn't mean you should shy away from them, just that they might prove a little more complicated to install and operate.

FindHack

The Rolls Royce of search programs, Florent Pillet's FindHack lets you specify whether to search all the installed applications, just the main applications, or just the current application. It also remembers the last six searches you ran, lets you preconfigure up to four "permanent" searches, and supports the use of wildcards. Best of all, it's faster than Find.

Find Ignore Hack

This simple Hack lets you select applications that should *not* be searched during the Find process. Why would you want to do this? E-books are a great example: if you have a few of them loaded on your Palm device, they can slow a search considerably. With Find Ignore Hack, you could exclude your e-book viewer.

PopUp Find

One problem with Find is that it forces you to leave the application you're currently working in (when you open the "found" record). Bozidar Benc's PopUp Find puts the data into a pop-up window, thus enabling you to stay in your current program. It has viewers for the four main applications and can transfer you to any of those programs with the tap of a button.

The Calculator

What's an electronic organizer without a calculator? Not much, so let's take a quick peek at the Palm's. Activated by tapping the icon in the upper-right corner of the Graffiti area, Calculator operates like any other (see Figure 9-5). In fact, it's so self-explanatory that we're not going to insult your intelligence by explaining how to use it.

There are, of course, one or two features we feel obligated to point out. First, you can use the standard Palm copy option to paste the result of any calculation into another program. Second, you can review your last few calculations by tapping Menu | Options | Recent Calculations.

```
┌──────────────────────────────┐
│ Recent Calculations      ⓘ   │
│                  36.     =    │
│               ─────────       │
│                  56.     =    │
│                  45.     *    │
│                  98.     =    │
│               ─────────       │
│                4410.     =    │
│               -4410.    +/-   │
│               -4410.     +    │
│             9558201.     =    │
│               ─────────       │
│             9553791.     =    │
│  ┌─────┐                      │
│  │ OK  │                      │
│  └─────┘                      │
└──────────────────────────────┘
```

FIGURE 9-5   The Palm calculator functions like every other calculator you've ever used.

Calc's buttons are large enough that you can tap them with a fingernail, so save time by leaving the stylus in its silo. Just keep in mind that oil and dirt from your fingers can grubby-up the screen.

Third-Party Calculators

Whether you're a student, realtor, banker, or NASA engineer, there's no debating the value of a good scientific and/or programmable calculator. Your Palm device has ample processing power to fill this role, and the proof is in the dozens of third-party calculators currently available. Let's take a look at some of the best and brightest.

FCPlus Professional and the powerOne Series

Aimed at financial, real estate, and retail professionals, Infinity Softworks' FCPlus Professional is one of the most sophisticated calculators around. It offers more than 400 built-in business, math, finance, and statistics functions, and includes memory worksheets for keeping track of various computations. If anything, FCPlus Professional might be overkill, but if you need this kind of power, you'll love the program.

Infinity Softworks also offers a series of task-specific calculators: powerOne Finance, powerOne Graph, and powerOne Scientific. And don't be surprised to find powerOne Personal bundled with your Palm device, as Palm now has a license agreement with Infinity Softworks.

SynCalc

A fully algebraic calculator, Synergy Solutions' SynCalc offers a unique plug-in architecture that allows new functionality to be added. As it stands, SynCalc is already plenty powerful, with algebraic parsing of expressions, a full suite of trigonometric and logarithmic functions, and support for up to 100 macros that simplify the execution of complex calculations.

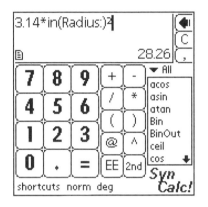

The Mail Program

An underrated member of the Palm's supporting cast of characters—er, programs—is Mail. We're going to teach you to use it in Chapter 13, but a brief bit of explanation is in order now. Specifically, Mail enables you to read, compose, and send e-mail, but not in the traditional sense. That is, Mail isn't capable of connecting to your Internet service provider (ISP) via a Palm modem and conducting e-mail transactions. Rather, it merely synchronizes with your desktop e-mail program, such as Eudora or Outlook Express, absorbing copies of messages you've received and transferring outgoing messages you've written.

> **NOTE**   *The m100 doesn't come with the Mail program, and the m105 and m125 don't have it preloaded. Instead, you must install it separately from the software CD, where it's called HotSync Mail.*

In practical terms, this means that your Palm serves as a kind of portable e-mail viewer. Here's an example: in the morning, before heading off to work or the airport, you HotSync with your PC. All the e-mail messages you received the night before are transferred to your Palm. Throughout the day, you read through those messages and reply to those that require it. You can even compose new messages if the need arises. Later, when you return home, you HotSync once again, and all the outgoing messages are transferred to your desktop e-mail program, and then sent.

```
New Message
    To: rickbroida@magicaldesk.com
    CC:
  Subj: The Palm Mail applet
  Body: When I'm done composing this
        message, I'll have to wait till I
        HotSync before I'll be able to
        send it.

        I

  (Send) (Cancel) (Details...)
```

> **NOTE**   *If you own a Palm modem, you can HotSync from the road, but even this doesn't allow for real-time e-mail transactions. For that you need third-party e-mail software.*

How to Decide If You Should Use Mail

Although the Mail program itself is easy to use and relatively capable (it supports signatures, blind carbon copies, delivery confirmation, filters, and more), its inability to work directly with ISPs is a definite shortcoming. Thus, you'll have to decide if it's the e-mail program for you. As we discuss in Chapter 13, several third-party packages can transact mail in real time.

> **NOTE**   *Many Palm-branded handhelds now come with MultiMail SE, an e-mail program that does allow for direct connections to your ISP. Find out more about this in Chapter 13.*

All About Expense

Introduced with version 2.0 of the Palm OS, Expense is an often-overlooked, but decidedly valuable addition to the Palm software arsenal. With it, you can track and manage all your expenses and mileage, whether for personal reconciliation or reimbursement from your company or clients. While a bit on the rudimentary side, Expense does afford quick and easy item entry and push-button synchronization with Microsoft Excel. Ultimately, it can create detailed and attractive-looking expense reports that are ready to print.

> **NOTE**   *What if you're not an Excel user, or you'd prefer to synchronize your expense data with software like Quicken or Microsoft Money? In that case, Expense might not be for you. However, third-party alternatives offer greater compatibility with desktop software. We discuss some of them in the upcoming section "Alternatives to Expense."*

Expense doesn't come bundled with every Palm model. If yours doesn't have it, consider one of the third-party expense managers discussed in the section "Alternatives to Expense."

Getting Started with Expense

Put simply, *Expense* is like an electronic folder for your receipts and a logbook for your mileage. Whenever you buy something, you simply add it to your expense list. Whenever you take a business-related road trip, you do the same. On the Palm side, using Expense is a piece of cake. (Using it with Palm Desktop is even easier, but we get to that in the section "From Expense to Excel.")

We should note that Expense has remained unchanged since it debuted, so it doesn't matter if your Palm device is running OS 2.0, OS 3.5, or anything in between.

Some Palm models—most notably the m100 series—don't come with Expense. If you have one of those models, read on to learn about some third-party alternatives (many of which are better programs anyway).

Creating New Expense Items

Adding new expense records is a snap. Here's the basic process:

9

1. Tap "New" to create a blank expense item. You see a line appear with the date, the words "-Expense type-", and a blank field next to a dollar sign. Note that your cursor appears in that field.

```
┌─────────────────────────────┐
│ Expense          ▼ Sample   │
│ 11/10 -Expense type-  $ ........ │
│                             │
│                             │
│                             │
│                             │
│                             │
│                             │
│                             │
│                             │
│                             │
│                             │
│ (New) (Details...) (Show...) │
└─────────────────────────────┘
```

2. Write in the amount of the purchase or, if you're recording mileage, the number of miles driven.

3. Now, tap the words "-Expense type-" to see a predefined list of expense categories, and choose the one that most closely matches your purchase. If you're recording mileage, select that option, noticing that the dollar sign changes to the abbreviation "mi."

Expense	▼ Unfiled
1/2	Mileage	✦	6.00
1/5	Other		28.64
1/6	Parking		10.43
1/8	Postage		14.84
1/12	Snack		41.58
1/13	Subway		33.02
1/13	Supplies		22.10
1/13	Taxi		118.91
1/13	Telephone		13.16
1/20	Tips		18.49
1/22	Tolls		35.01
	Train		

(New) (Details...) (Show...)

Unlike most lists that appear in Palm applications, the Expense list cannot be modified or expanded. In short, you're stuck with the categories provided. If you can't find one that fits the situation, there's always the "other" category.

4. By default, any new expense is created with the current date. If, however, you're catching up on previous purchases, you can tap right on the date that's shown to bring up the calendar and select whatever date is appropriate.

There, wasn't that easy? You've just recorded a new expense. Now let's talk about recording the more specific details of that expense.

You can save yourself a step when you create a new expense by not tapping the "New" button first. Instead, just start writing the dollar amount in the numeric portion of the Graffiti area. A new expense item is instantly created. This same practice also works in Date Book, Memo Pad, and To Do List.

Modifying Expense Details

Obviously, any expense report worth its salt needs to have more than just the date, expense type, and amount. As you probably guessed, your next stop after entering these tidbits is the "Details…" button.

Before tapping it, make sure you select the expense item you want to modify. You know when an item is selected because the date is highlighted and a cursor appears in the "amount" field.

The Receipt Details screen (see Figure 9-6) lets you specify the minutiae of your purchase, from the category to which it belongs, to the type of currency used, to the city in which it took place.

FIGURE 9-6   You can record any or all of the crucial details of your expense in the Receipt Details screen.

From Expense to Excel

One key difference between Expense and most of the other core Palm programs is that the data you enter isn't replicated—or even accessible—in Palm Desktop. Certainly the data is transferred to your PC when you HotSync and backed up in a folder on your hard drive. But as for turning those raw numbers into an actual printed expense report, we've got good news and bad news.

The good news is it's a one-step procedure. In Palm Desktop for Windows, you simply click the Expense button on the toolbar. The bad news is you must have Microsoft Excel installed on your computer because the Expense data shoots directly into an Excel spreadsheet—and can't go anywhere else. (Okay, it's bad news only if you're not an Excel user.)

Making the Transfer

As you've already discovered, a toolbar along the left side of the Palm Desktop screen lets you navigate between Date Book, Memo Pad, et al. Near the bottom of the toolbar is a button labeled "Expense"—*but don't click it yet*! Not until we explain exactly what's going to happen when you do.

Expense and the Macintosh

Notice that in our discussion of Expense and Excel, we referenced only Palm Desktop for Windows. Unfortunately, Macintosh users don't have quite the same flexibility in this department. In fact, Expense isn't mentioned anywhere in the help files for Palm Desktop for Macintosh. Inexplicably, the Expense-to-Excel conduit never made it into that version of the software.

Third-party developers to the rescue! WalletWare's ExpensePlus is among a smattering of programs that include support for the Mac, so you're not without options.

9

TIP *You don't have to click the button at all, or even venture into Palm Desktop (helpful if you're using Microsoft Outlook or some other personal information manager). You can launch the expense-report creation procedure by clicking Start | Program Files | Palm Desktop | Expense Report.*

Before commencing, make sure you HotSync, so all your latest Expense data is transferred to your PC. Then, whether you click the Expense button or choose the aforementioned menu option, two actions occur: Microsoft Excel starts, and then opens the Expense database file. This is the file created by Expense and updated every time you HotSync.

NOTE *Depending on the version of Excel you have installed, you may get a warning message about the use of macros and their possible infection by viruses. Because it's impossible for the expense file to become infected, go ahead and click "Enable macros." If you don't, you can't access your Expense data.*

Expense Report Options	? X
Name: Rick Broida	OK
Department: Editorial	Cancel
Phone No.: 719-555-1212	Help
Project: How To Do Everything...	
Bill To: Osborne/McGraw-Hill	

Template
Select an Expense template from the list
SAMPLE1.XLT
DATALIST.XLT
SAMPLE1.XLT
SAMPLE2.XLT
SAMPLE3.XLT
SAMPLE4.XLT

When It Comes Out of Your Pocket...

When you think of your Palm, what applications come to mind? When it comes out of your pocket, what applications do you know you're about to turn on?

Dave: When I first got my Palm, I stuck to the tried-and-true Address Book and Date Book features. These days, though, I use my Palm largely for wireless and Internet kind of applications. When I go out to lunch, I pop the Palm out of my pocket and read my favorite AvantGo news channels. If I run out of news before I run out of lunch, I'll also check e-mail with my wireless modem and read or reply to that. If all else fails, I have a few games installed on my Palm, but they're so addictive that I try to avoid turning them on.

> **Rick**: I'm a To Do List junkie, meaning I'm constantly checking it, adding to it, and, hopefully, tapping to remove completed items. However, if I have a few minutes to kill, I'll either read whatever e-book I currently have loaded in Palm Reader (more on that in Chapter 19) or play one of Astraware's frighteningly addicting games. As I write this, I'm hooked on Bounce Out and Text Twist.

Alternatives to Expense

Truth be told, Expense isn't the most robust expense-management program—especially relative to some of the software created by third-party developers. If your needs extend beyond what Expense has to offer—and for businesspeople who rely heavily on reimbursement reports, they probably do—you should definitely check out one of the many available alternatives.

We've spotlighted some of the major programs, but keep in mind that these are designed for expense-tracking only. There are other programs that manage billing as well as expenses, and that let you track your bank accounts and stock portfolios. (We talk about those in Chapter 16.) So don't be discouraged if none of these packages fit your particular bill. Chances are good there's a program out there that will.

ExpenseDirector

Iambic Software's *ExpenseDirector* lets you track expenses by type, account, payee, client, project, and the currency for the expense. It supports the creation of customized item lists, so your data entry speeds up over time. Particularly noteworthy are the program's filtering and sorting options, which let you view records for a single day or a range of days, and sort by any of the aforementioned tracking criteria. ExpenseDirector even enables you to e-mail expense data directly from your Palm device (if it has a modem or wireless capabilities, of course).

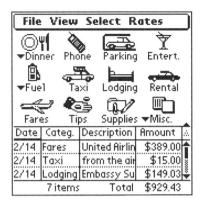

One hitch: ExpenseDirector can synchronize data to your Windows PC, but only with Iambic's ExpenseDirector for Windows—a separate program that's equally robust on the PC side. You can buy ExpenseDirector alone for $29.95 or bundled with its Windows counterpart for $59.95.

ExpensePlus

One of the most robust and versatile expense managers available, WalletWare's *ExpensePlus* uses an icon-based interface to simplify the selection of expense types, and automation to fill in dates and amounts for things like hotel stays and car rentals. More important, it can link directly to any existing company expense forms created in Excel or FileMaker (including the Mac versions), so you needn't contend with nonstandard forms. And, if your company's forms aren't based in Excel, WalletWare can design a custom link (for a fee) to other software programs.

ExpensAble

ExpensAble began as a PC application and has migrated to the Palm. LandWare's software makes it a snap to record reimbursable, nonreimbursable, and personal expenses, and it supports split transactions. Also present is the ever-popular *AutoFill* feature, a Quicken staple that simplifies repetitive data entry.

Naturally, the Palm version of ExpensAble integrates seamlessly with the computer version, the latter offering report submission via e-mail or the ExpensAble web site.

Where to Find It

Web Site	Address	What's There
Handmark	**www.handmark.com**	MobileSafe
Chapura	**www.chapura.com**	Cloak
Tranzoa	**www.tranzoa.com**	OnlyMe
CIC	**www.cic.com**	Sign-On
Florent Pillet	**perso.wanadoo.fr/fpillet/**	FindHack
PalmGear	**www.palmgear.com**	Find Ignore Hack
Bozidar Benc	**www.benc.hr**	PopUp Find
Infinity Softworks	**www.infinitysw.com**	FC Plus Professional, powerOne series
Synergy Solutions	**www.synsolutions.com**	Launch 'Em, SynCalc
Iambic Software	**www.iambic.com**	ExpenseDirector
LandWare	**www.landware.com**	ExpensAble
WalletWare	**www.walletware.com**	ExpensePlus

9

Part III

Beyond the Box

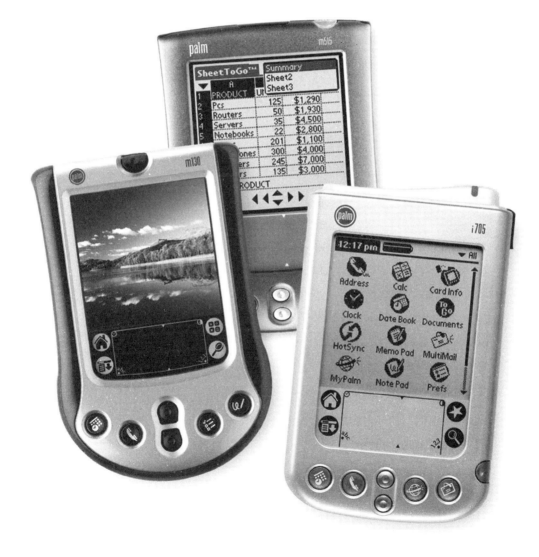

Chapter 10

An Introduction to Palm OS 5

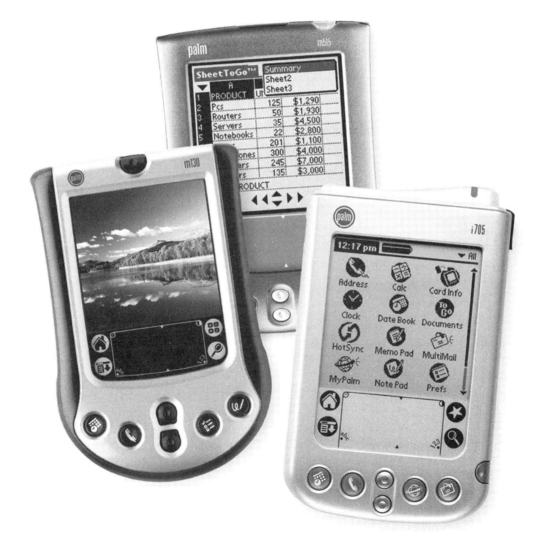

How to...

- Differentiate between OS 5 and earlier versions
- Determine the importance of handheld speed
- Determine if older software is compatible with OS 5
- Avoid potentially damaging software
- Upgrade to OS 5 (sort of)

As we put the wraps on this book, PalmSource (the spun-off division of Palm, Inc., that's responsible for the Palm Operating System) had just finished work on the most significant new version of the Palm OS since, well, the first one. OS 5 promises everything from faster performance to better screen resolution to more robust multimedia and security features. In short, it's a major step forward for Palm, and it will lead to handheld PCs that are even more versatile than they are now.

Why a standalone chapter on OS 5? Why not just integrate the info into the rest of the book? As they say, timing is everything: we just missed getting our hands on an OS 5–equipped device prior to publication. However, all is not lost. We know all the important stuff about the new OS, so we've compiled it here. If you're thinking of upgrading to a new model or just cracked the shrink-wrap on one, this is the chapter for you.

NOTE   *If you're not sure what an operating system is or why it's significant, see Chapter 1 for an explanation.*

As major an upgrade as OS 5 is, it doesn't change the fundamental operation or capabilities of your handheld. The user interface remains largely unchanged (though it looks a bit spiffier), and you'll still be able to run all that great third-party software we discuss in later chapters (with a few caveats).

What's New in OS 5

When Microsoft unveils a new version of Windows, the company usually touts features like improved performance, easier operation, more stability, and so on. (And most of these claims usually turn out to be bogus, heh, heh.) In the case of OS 5, performance definitely gets a boost—but that's just the tip of the iceberg. The OS is already remarkably easy to use and fairly crash-proof, so Palm looked at other areas where improvements were warranted. Let's get the scoop on each.

Speed

Until now, all Palm Powered handhelds have had one thing in common: their processor. They've all used some iteration of Motorola's Dragonball chip. With OS 5, Palm has said goodbye to Dragonball and hello to a faster, more versatile processor: the ARM. Manufactured by companies like Intel, Motorola, and Texas Instruments, the ARM chip will be at the core of all Palm Powered devices that run OS 5.

In terms of raw computing horsepower, ARM processors leave Dragonballs in the dust. Most current Palm handhelds run at a clock speed of 20 MHz or 33 MHz (though some of the newest PDAs, like Sony's CLIÉ NR70 series, rev to 66 MHz), but those with ARM inside will *start* at

206 MHz. Intel's Xscale version of the ARM processor clocks in at 400 MHz. That's an awful lot of computing power in the palm of your hand (make that the Palm of your hand).

On the software side, OS 5 itself represents a huge leap in speed, from a 16-bit to a 32-bit operating system. Combine that with the speedier processors and OS 5-based devices will run anywhere from 2 to 20 times faster than they do now (though, admittedly, this has a bit more to do with the hardware than the OS). As Dave likes to say, while imitating Keanu Reeves, "Whoa!"

At this point you might be thinking, "Big deal. My handheld already runs pretty fast." We call that Thinking Like Rick, which is a good thing. Just how fast does a handheld PC need to be, anyway? It's not like you have to wait for the thing to boot up or load an application. You press the power button and boom, it's on. You tap an icon and boom, the program loads. Indeed, for handheld computing as we now know it, all this acceleration may seem like fool's gold.

Until you consider what handhelds are really capable of doing. For instance, it's nice to have a screen that runs at a high resolution (say, 320 × 320 pixels) and displays loads of colors (upwards of 65,000). But these features bog down the processor, making the handheld run slower overall. And consider software that lets you watch full-motion video—with so many colors and pixels to push around, speed suddenly becomes a crucial element. For businesses, more speed means more efficient access to large documents like spreadsheets and databases, as well as better support for charts, graphs, and other kinds of graphics. Consider the fact that it can take many seconds for a large Word or Excel document to appear on the Palm's screen. With an OS 5-compatible processor, those documents will snap onto the screen more or less instantly, eliminating the "lag" that can make your PDA seem sluggish and unresponsive.

Screen Resolution

As you learned in Chapter 2, most Palm Powered handhelds have a screen resolution of 160 × 160 pixels. Sony's color CLIÉ models are among a handful of exceptions, but they required special tweaks to the OS to achieve their higher resolutions. OS 5 has innate support for 320 × 320-pixel screens (and, for that matter, 480 × 480—but don't expect to see that resolution for quite some time). 320 × 320 is actually four times the resolution of current models, meaning everything looks much sharper. As a result, it's much more practical to view items like photographs, maps, PDF files, and so on. What's more, the higher resolution allows the use of more varied fonts, which helps for word processing, book reading, and the like.

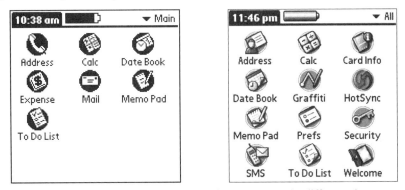

Even in these black and white screenshots, it's easy to see the difference between
160 × 160-pixel (left) and 320 × 320-pixel screens (right).

NOTE   *Even software that was written for 160 × 160-pixel screens will work at the higher resolutions—just one of many compatibility efforts Palm built into OS 5. Read on to learn more about software compatibility.*

Multimedia

Despite the strides made by Sony's CLIÉ series, audio and video have never been a forte of the Palm OS. That changes with OS 5, which boasts enhanced audio features (right out of the box, alarms and other system sounds will sound vastly improved) and the potential for far superior video playback. We say "potential" because the OS has no built-in video capabilities, but the ARM processor will allow third-party developers to work their magic. Expect full-motion handheld video to become a big deal in the not-too-distant future.

Security

OS 4 has decent security features (see Chapter 9), but they're not robust enough to satisfy corporate users. OS 5 offers 128-bit encryption, Secure Sockets Layer (SSL), RC4, SHA-1, and signature verification using RSA-verify. We have no idea what any of that means, but all those letters and numbers should keep the corporate crowd happy. One thing we do know is that all this stuff adds up to safe, secure Internet transactions, so you can, say, order books from Amazon without having to worry about your credit card number falling into the wrong hands.

Wireless

Palm wants to make OS 5 as wireless as it can be. That is, the new operating system has built-in support for popular and emerging wireless technologies such as 802.11b (also known as Wi-Fi) and Bluetooth. Unless you're an enterprise (that is, business) user, this probably won't seem too important. But consider: many modern home networks employ 802.11b wireless access points or routers. All you'd need to do is slip an 802.11b card (there aren't any available as of this writing, but they're coming soon) into your Palm, and you could send and receive e-mail from anywhere in the house. Similarly, if you have one of the new generation of Bluetooth-equipped printers, you could print contact listings or memos straight from your handheld—no wires or computer required. The possibilities are tantalizing, to be sure.

Lack of Innovation?

Dave: I have to admit I had horribly inflated expectations for OS 5. I wished for a revised interface that would add a little modern juice to the plain old Palm application screen. I hoped for some better core applications—like a version of the Address Book that supports all of Outlook's categories. I wanted better support for high-resolution screens. After all, I love the CLIÉ's 320 × 480-pixel display (which, thanks to the collapsible Graffiti area, makes the CLIÉ the highest-resolution PDA on the market—even better than Pocket PC devices), and that's totally unsupported in OS 5. I know you're going to apologize for Palm as usual, but the fact is that Palm is hampering innovation by locking partners into rigid, specific screen resolutions. Shouldn't Palm have built OS 5 with support for *any* screen resolution that hardware manufacturers want to build? Sigh. So much opportunity lost.

Rick: Methinks you dost protest too much. Certainly Sony has achieved something wonderful with the ultra-high-res CLIÉ, but at what price? The NR70V currently costs $600 and has mediocre battery life—direct results of the fancy screen. Plus, the thing is downright huge, and most people want their PDAs compact. That said, the collapsible Graffiti area is the best thing since sliced bread, and it's too bad Palm didn't pick up on it. As for better interfaces and applications, Palm has wisely left that to the third-party developers, as they've done since the beginning. OS 5 already looks much nicer than its predecessors, and its level of Outlook integration is fine for most users. As always, you want the moon, when most people are happy with moonlight.

Compatibility

A key concern for any longtime Palm user is compatibility—specifically, will all your favorite software still work on an OS 5 model? The answer is a resounding "probably." Despite the major differences between ARM and DragonBall processors (which would normally render older software inoperable), Palm took pains to incorporate backward compatibility into the new OS. Therefore, most software written for OS 4.0 and earlier should run fine under OS 5. We say "should" because we've yet to test it firsthand, but the lack of any outcry from the developer community suggests that all is well on the compatibility front. Yes, friends, you'll still be able to play Bejeweled (hallelujah!).

Of course, there are a few caveats. Palm's official estimate is that roughly 80 percent of today's third-party software will run properly under OS 5. Software makers who didn't closely adhere to the "rules" of Palm OS programming may find that their programs no longer function.

> **TIP**   *Before installing any third-party application on your OS 5-based handheld, visit the developer's Web site to investigate its compatibility. There may be a newer version available or in the works or you may learn that it simply won't run with OS 5—in which case you shouldn't install it.*

> **CAUTION**   *Hacks (see Chapter 15), which represent some of our favorite third-party programs, won't work under OS 5—period. Yes, we're disappointed about this, too, but that's the price of change. Fortunately, it's only a matter of time before the developer community whips up a fresh batch of OS 5-compatible Hacks. But, in the meantime, steer clear.*

Can I Upgrade to OS 5?

Alas, no you can't. While many previous Palm models allowed you to install the latest version of the Palm OS, it's not possible with OS 5. Have you guessed why? Yep, it's because of the shift to

ARM-based processors. OS 5 requires one—it just plain won't work with a Dragonball chip. If you want the new OS, you have to buy a new handheld that comes with it. This may be frustrating to learn, especially if you just bought a model with OS 4. Our advice: use it, enjoy it, do what you were planning to do with it, and don't succumb to feature lust. OS 5 will still be waiting if and when you have a compelling need to upgrade.

Are Older Palm Devices Useless?

Absolutely not! Models that run OS 4.0, 3.5, and even 3.0 are as robust and capable as ever, and they'll be supported by third-party software and accessory developers for a long time to come. Dave and Rick are smitten with Sony's NR70 family, and that still runs good-old OS 4.1. Heck, don't be surprised to see several more OS 4.0-based handhelds hit the streets alongside OS 5 models.

Chapter 11

Going on a Trip

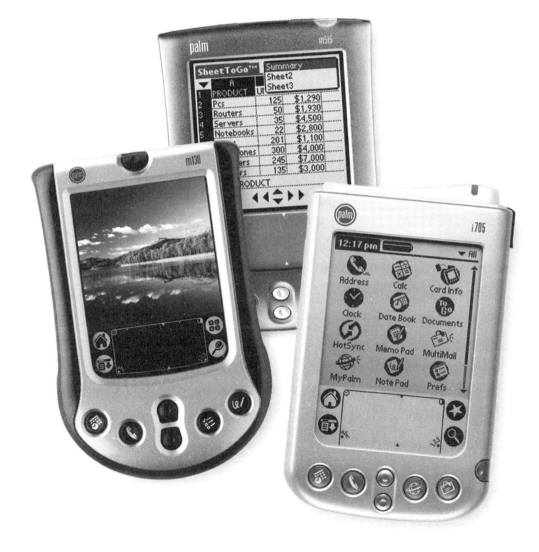

How to...

- Organize your Palm's categories and data for travel
- Pack smartly so you're prepared for Palm trouble
- Make sure your Palm doesn't run out of power during the trip
- Prepare for HotSync opportunities away from home
- Enhance the core apps for life on the road
- View your coworkers' Date Book entries on your own Palm
- Load your Palm with essential travel phone numbers
- Use the Palm as an alarm clock
- Use the Palm as a subway map
- Communicate in a foreign language with your Palm
- Navigate your way around town and country with a Palm
- Use your Palm as a compass
- Get star charts on your Palm
- Read books on your Palm

Some people find their Palm so useful that—imagine this—they put it in their pocket and take it on trips away from the home and office! Daring, we know. And, as it turns out, the Palm is even designed for these kinds of "away missions." Its batteries mean you needn't plug it in and, because it synchronizes with your desktop PC, you can bring important information with you wherever you go. The Palm even has a built-in clock in case you forget your watch. What could be better?

Seriously, we know you already carry your Palm around town. But, if you plan to take it on an extended trip, you might want to read this chapter. We have all kinds of suggestions for how to prepare your Palm for a grueling business trip, as well as what kind of software you might need to make the trip a little smoother. And how about a camping trip? Your Palm might not be the first accessory that springs to mind when you consider roughing it in the Rocky Mountains, but your trusty little handheld has a lot to offer in the wilderness, too.

Preparing Your Palm for the Road

When we go on a business trip, it's usually such absolute pandemonium—running around at the last minute, throwing power cords and HotSync cables in the travel bag—it's a wonder we ever make it to the airport in time. Because of our experiences with forgetting data, bringing dead batteries, and being unable to connect to the Internet in strange cites, we offer the following checklist to you for bringing your Palm on trips.

Set Up Your Data

Make sure your Palm is ready for the details of your upcoming trip. Specifically, consider the kinds of data you need to create while you're on the road and prepare your Palm ahead of time. Here's how you can make sure you're ready:

1. In the To Do List, create a trip checklist and enter everything you need to do before you leave, plus what you need to bring with you. If you have a comprehensive checklist, you're less likely to forget something important before you go.

```
To Do List                    ▼ Trip
☐ 1 Bring tickets             —
☐ 2 Install DB on laptop      —
☐ 2 Charge cell phone         —
☐ 3 Palm Battery              —
☐ 3 Modem                     —
☐ 3 HotSync                   —
☐ 3 Serial cable              —
☐ 4 Bring suit                —


( New ) ( Details... ) ( Show... )
```

TIP *You probably don't want to build your travel list from scratch each time. One solution is to create a comprehensive list of travel tasks and leave it in the Memo Pad. You can copy the entire memo and paste it into a new memo before a trip, and then erase individual lines as you complete them. The master list is still safely stored in a different memo entry.*

11

2. Create a new category in which you can store data related to your trip. If you're going to Chicago for a convention, for instance, create a category on the Address Book, the To Do List, and the Memo Pad called Chicago. (If you want to call it something else, that's okay too.) By using a special category on the road, you can find data related to your trip more quickly—both during the trip and after you return home. When you get back, you can recategorize the data any way you like.

3. Create a new category for the Expense app. While you might be able to get by with lobbing all your To Dos or contacts in the same Unfiled category, don't try that with expenses. After all, how are you going to distinguish among a dozen cab receipts? We don't want to see you up late at night with a calendar and your Palm, trying to figure out what city you were in when you paid $14 for a cab ride, especially if you don't fill in the details for each entry. A much easier way is simply to create a category for your upcoming trip and put all your expenses in there.

4. Enter your itinerary in the Date Book. If you're flying, enter each flight's number, departure, and arrival time in your Palm, so it's available when you need it. An easy way to do this is to enter the flight number in the Date Book at the scheduled departure time and note

the arrival time there as well. That way, you can check your Palm in flight to see how much longer you have to grit your teeth and eat peanuts.

 You can block out the dates of your trip on the Palm using an untimed event. The trip appears at the top of the Date Book and still lets you schedule actual appointments during those days.

Get the Hardware Ready

When you leave on a trip, make sure your Palm is fully prepared to go the distance. There's nothing like being a thousand miles from home and remembering you forgot to bring some data from your desktop PC or discovering you forgot an important cable.

To save yourself from calamity, remember these tips:

- Always bring a stylus with a reset pin. Most Palm models include a reset pin in the metal stylus—just unscrew the end to get to it. If you don't have one, bring a paperclip or a thin pin instead. And test the pin before you go! Rick once traveled with a paperclip too thick to fit in the hole. D'oh! Bottom line: there's nothing worse than having your Palm crash when you're away from home and discovering you have nothing small enough to fit in the reset hole.

- Perform a HotSync right before you leave. This way, you're sure to have the latest info on your Palm and you also have a current backup in case something unfortunate happens to your trusty handheld while you're away.

- Do you plan to do a lot of typing? If so, pack a keyboard for the Palm. You have over a dozen options to choose from, from the fold-up Targus Stowaway to the cloth, flexible Logitech Key Case. See Chapter 20 for more details.

- Be prepared to restore. Call us paranoid, but . . . hey, wait a minute, did you just call us paranoid? Sheesh, the nerve. . . . Anyway, if your Palm should lose all its data for some reason, you might want to have the capability to restore it while you're on the go. Depending on what model Palm you have, you can do that in a few ways. A HotSync cable can let you restore data from a laptop, for instance, but a better bet might be a backup device. For some Palm models, you can get a backup card, described in Chapter 12.

Have a Backup Plan

Call us Luddites, but we don't like to rely 100 percent on a fragile piece of electronic gizmotry (and yes, that's a word. Don't look it up, just trust us). What if you drop your Palm in the airport and it shatters on the nice marble floor? You'd better have a Plan B.

Dave: For me, the most important document to have access to on a trip is my flight itinerary. I always buy e-tickets—so I have no written record of my flight—and then I enter the flight information in my Palm. But, to be on the safe side, I also print a copy of my flight info and stick it in the back of my bag somewhere. That way, if my Palm batteries die before I finish my trip or my Palm falls out of a five-story window, I can always refer to the piece of paper and get myself home.

Rick: If your Palm has a memory slot or you own a Handspring Visor, HandEra 330, or Sony CLIÉ, do yourself a favor and purchase a backup card. With just a few stylus taps, you can back up the complete contents of your handheld's memory. Then, in the event that some catastrophe left you with a wiped handheld (it's been known to happen), you could pop the card in and restore everything in a matter of minutes. Well worth the $30–$40 you'll spend for a backup card. See Chapter 20 for more information.

Stay Powered

A dead Palm is no good to anyone. Take these steps to keep it working when you're away:

- Recharge your Palm right before you leave and bring some sort of charging solution with you. There are many options, from Electric Fuel's Instant Power system (available for most Palm models) to Tech Center Labs' Palm V Emergency Charger, which connects a 9-volt battery to your Palm's HotSync cradle port. You can also get a USB cable that charges your PDA from a nearby laptop or desktop PC.

- If your Palm takes replaceable batteries, change them before you go. If you're going to be away for a week or more, bring a spare set of batteries with you—better safe than sorry. If you generally leave a spare set of batteries in your travel case, score ten points for preparedness. But use a battery tester before each trip to make sure your backup batteries are still in good shape.

- Remember to bring batteries for any Palm accessories you use. This includes your modem, keyboard, cell phone, and GPS receiver.

HotSyncing on the Go

You don't have to be satisfied with the last HotSync you performed at home before you jumped on a plane, of course. You can perform a remote HotSync to connect to your desktop PC from anywhere or you can use the IR HotSync tool to connect your Palm to a laptop PC while you're on the go. For details on this kind of HotSync, see Chapter 4.

Real-Life Tragedy

Not that long ago, Dave spent a week in sunny Florida in the dead of winter to see a photography trade show and do a bit of scuba diving. While there, his trusty Visor Prism held all his data—contact info, schedules, even flight information for the return trip. Well, thanks to a bitterly frustrating glitch in the OmniSky modem, two days into the trip, the Visor performed a hard reset, erasing all the data on the device.

"I had thrown caution to the wind," Dave reports. "I thought I could trust my Prism and I had no backup of any kind—no laptop, no backup module, not even a printout of my schedule."

In fact, Dave had to call home repeatedly to be updated on his daily schedule and to know what time to show up to the airport at the end of the trip. He reports that he plans to follow his own advice in the future.

You need at least version 3.3 of the Palm OS to perform an IR HotSync to a notebook PC.

- If you plan to perform a Remote HotSync, be sure to test your connection before leaving home. You can never anticipate everything that might go wrong with a modem connection, but you can at least verify the system works before you leave.

- Check with your hotel concierge to see if the phone lines in your room are PBX or analog. PBX lines can damage your Palm's modem, so don't experiment with a connection unless you know for sure.

TIP   *If your room phone has a data port built in, the room is modem-friendly and you needn't check with the front desk.*

- If your laptop doesn't have an IR port or if you want to HotSync with a desktop PC at your remote location, bring a HotSync cable. You can buy the appropriate cable from Palm or Targus. Another alternative: bring a HotSync cradle. The standard-issue Palm cradles are a bit bulky for travel, so you might want to look into a folding cradle from DS International. They make folding cradles for a variety of Palm and Visor models.

- If you plan to perform either a Remote or an IR HotSync, remember to perform a normal Local HotSync using the cradle first. Also, don't forget to turn your PC on before you go and leave it ready to receive incoming calls. For more details on IR HotSyncs, see Chapter 4.

CAUTION   *Check what the room charge will be for each call. It can be as much as a dollar per call just to dial the phone, so those communication charges can add up quickly.*

Road Tips

We've done our share of traveling and we've amassed a few handy tips for making the best use of your Palm on the road. Not all these suggestions will appeal to you, but you're sure to find a few things to make your next trip a little more enjoyable.

■ If you're planning to stay at your destination for more than a few hours, reset the time on your Palm. Otherwise, all your appointments will alarm at the wrong time and you'll show up late everywhere you need to be. To change the time, tap the Prefs app and choose the Time & Date page. Tap the Set Time Zone box and set it to your new location. The time will automatically update for you.

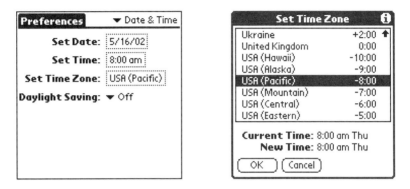

NOTE *If you have an older Palm without the Time Zone option, change the time on the General page of the Prefs app.*

■ If you have a Palm V, using the stock cover in your pocket or in a tightly packed travel bag can be bad for your Palm's battery life. Why? The cover can press against the power button and the scroll button, causing a constant power drain. Two solutions exist. First, a number of software products can help keep the battery from draining. You can use PalmOffHack, StayOffHack, or Stay Off If Up Hack, for instance, all programs that safeguard—in one way or another—from accidentally turning your Palm on by bumping the power switch. Second, you can get a hard-shelled case to enclose your PDA, which keeps the power button from getting triggered accidentally. Worst case: you can cut a slot in the cover that prevents the power button from getting activated, but that's an ugly fix for the problem. Dave knows: his Palm V was once the laughingstock of taxi drivers all over the country.

■ Your Palm could set off the metal detector at the airport. To save yourself time and hassle, go ahead and pop it into one of those little trays, along with all your change, time travel portal control, roll of aluminum foil, and other personal items, right at the outset when you go through a metal detector.

■ The Palm is considered a "portable electronic device" and you shouldn't use it at the beginning or the end of a flight. You probably already knew that, but your Palm can get you in trouble anyway if you're not careful. Specifically, don't enable any alarms for the start or end of the flight, or your Palm will come to life and start beeping during the forbidden times.

■ You might need to print something stored on your Palm while you're on your trip and you can print in several ways. The easiest solution is to get a print driver for your Palm, such as PalmPrint, PrintBoy, or IS/Print, especially if you have access to a portable printer. If that's the case, aim your Palm and print. If you do a lot of printing, get a portable model

11

and carry it with you (see Chapter 14 for details). If you can get to a printer, but it isn't IR-capable, you still have options. First, if you have a few extra bucks, you might want to carry the PrintBoy InfraReady Adapter from Bachmann Software. This is a little device that fits in your pocket (or your travel bag) and plugs into the parallel port of any printer. Its infrared port lets you instantly convert any printer into an IR-ready printer for your Palm. When you finish printing, remove the adapter and put it back in your travel bag. It's a cool solution for printing anything anywhere you can find a printer when you travel. The next best thing is to carry a serial cable for your Palm and a serial-to-parallel converter (this is available from Stevens Creek, the company that sells PalmPrint). As a last resort, you might install a fax program like Mark/Space Fax. Equipped with a Palm modem, you can fax to your hotel's front desk, and then pick up the printout.

Software to Bring Along

Don't rely on the software that comes with your Palm to get you through your extended trips away from home. Most of the software we discuss in this next section is available from **palmgear.com**. Experiment and see what applications are useful.

CAUTION   *Don't install a new application as you're walking out the door to go to the airport. Some applications might cause your Palm to misbehave. Others can change the way your Palm functions or make it hard to access data you've already created. You don't need to discover those kinds of things on an airplane bound for Topeka. Bottom line: install and experiment with new software well in advance of a trip.*

Address and Date Book Enhancements

Sure, you love the Address Book and the Date Book. But, by enhancing these core applications, you might find you can significantly improve the way you work when you're away from home.

Synchronize with the Web

Believe it or not, you can synchronize your Palm's Date Book and Address Book with web-based information managers. Why would you want to do that? Well, when you're on the road, you might want to access your schedule and contacts from a PC that isn't yours. And, if you can get to any web-enabled PC, you can log on to a web-based calendar and address book. Here are some cool reasons to try this:

- Send e-mail from a web-based e-mail system using contact information culled from your Palm.
- Add calendar appointments on the PC and synchronize it to the Palm later.
- If something happens to your Palm on a trip, access all your data from a PC that's connected to the Internet.

The web site **Yahoo.com** offers the best Palm synchronization support on the Internet. By installing a small utility on your home or office-based PC, you can sync the Palm's Date Book, Address Book, and To Do List with equivalent applications on the Yahoo! site. Because Yahoo! also offers free e-mail, you can use the Palm Address Book to send messages without reentering any data.

To get started with web synchronization, visit **www.yahoo.com**. If you don't already have an account there, create one. You'll need to find the site's synchronization tools, which are buried a few layers deep. Click the link for Yahoo's Address Book or Calendar, and then click the Options link (at the top-right corner of the page). You should then see a list of links. Click the Synchronize link to be taken to your Sync options. Follow the instructions to download and install TrueSync for Yahoo!

TIP   *Once you install and synchronize, you might find you can't see entries on your Palm that were created in Yahoo! That's because, by default, Yahoo! marks its records private. You have to display private records on the Palm to see them. For details on how to do that, see Chapter 5.*

Share Your Appointments

You're meeting with coworkers at a trade show to review the newest, most innovative pencil sharpeners. If your associates are as busy as you plan to be, how can you reconcile your schedules to meet for lunch? Or, if you're a little more business-minded, how can you find out where everyone is during the day and schedule meetings everyone can attend?

One solution is to use WeSync (see Figure 11-1). This web-based calendaring and contact tool lets you sync your Palm data with a web-based information manager and share it with coworkers. The best part is WeSync takes the form of a new Date Book–style app on your Palm that can display multiple schedules side by side. So, you can visually evaluate free and busy times on two schedules on the same screen.

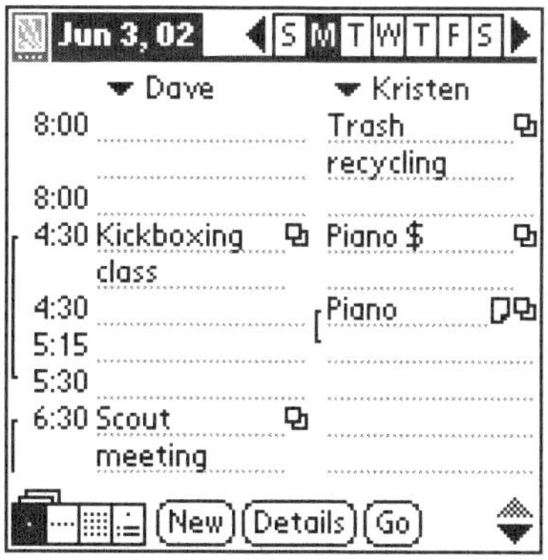

FIGURE 11-1   WeSync lets you share your Date Book data with others via the Internet.

To try out WeSync, visit **www.wesync.com** and install the WeSync application. After you and at least one other person are using the app, you can share your calendar in this way:

1. Start by creating a private community. Visit the WeSync web site and log on with the user name you selected. Then click Create a New Community.

2. Give the community a name and description, and then enter your user name as the Member/Administrator Name. Now, click Create Community. After that, you should be in the My Community tab.

3. Click Manage Community, and then click Invite New Members. Enter the e-mail and user name of the person you want to invite, and then click Invite.

4. Now it's time to share your calendar with this private community. Start the WeSync Desktop Viewer and choose Edit | Calendar Manager from the menu. You should see the WeSync Calendar Manager dialog box.

5. Select your calendar (it should currently be configured as Local). Click the Published button, and then click Close.

6. HotSync your Palm. Your calendar will be transferred to the web calendar, ready to be shared with others.

After this setup process, any time you change your calendar, the data is updated on the WeSync web site at the next HotSync, and then updated on all the shared Palms. Of course, if you're invited to join a community, as in Step 3, you need to accept the invitation before you can see a shared calendar. To join, click the Your Invitations link on the web site and place a check mark next to the community you've been invited to join (as in Figure 11-2).

To see calendars side by side on your Palm, start the wsCalendar app and choose +Cal | Calendar Manager from the menu. Check all the calendar entries you want to see onscreen at once, and then click OK.

Get Rental Car Phone Numbers

The Palm can hold lots of phone numbers, so why not take advantage of this? Several databases of phone numbers exist to services like rental car companies, airlines, and hotels. If you travel frequently, you probably want to try one of them:

Application	Data Included
WeSync.com	The WeSync Contact Manager has hundreds of phone numbers to airlines, hotels, and rental car companies. When you implement this feature, these entries are automatically added to the Palm's Date Book in categories.
Travel Telephone Numbers	A smaller list (about 100) of the most popular hotels, car rentals, and airlines.
Palm Rent-a-Car	List of rental car companies and their 800 numbers.

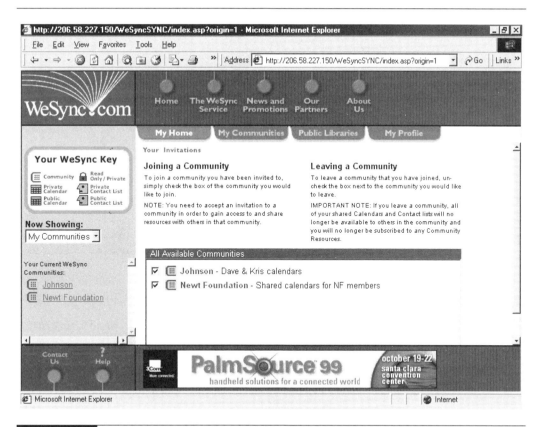

FIGURE 11-2	You can share your calendar with friends, family, and co-workers by synchronizing it with a WeSync "community."

*These apps are all available from **www.palmgear.com**.*

TIP *If you have a Palm with wireless Internet capabilities, don't forget about web-clipping applications. A number of clipping apps were custom designed for on-the-go reference. Check out Chapter 13 for details on these wireless wonders that can help you order a taxi, find a gas station, get airline information, or satisfy nearly any other travel need.*

Itinerary Tracking

While you can certainly store your itinerary information in the Date Book, using a specialized program is more efficient for many people. Many applications at a site like PalmGear fit the bill. Some of our favorites include TravelTracker and Travel Pal, both seen in the following.

The Ultimate Alarm Clock

You can set alarms with the Palm, but the somewhat-anemic alarm system built into the Date Book isn't terribly useful in a lot of situations. Instead, you should download a copy of *BigClock* (see Figure 11-3), a free application that displays the time, has a timer, and four independent alarms. BigClock also lets you easily change time zones.

BigClock's alarm is good enough to serve as your morning alarm clock, either on its own or as a safety backup to a hotel wake-up call. To use BigClock's alarm function, follow these steps:

1. Start BigClock and tap on the Alarm tab at the bottom of the screen. Four different alarms are available. We'll set Alarm 1.

2. Highlight the Alarm 1 title at the top of the screen and rename it **Wake Up**.

3. Set the time you want to wake. Tap the top half of a number to increase its value or tap the bottom half to decrease it. Do this for both minutes and hours.

4. Make sure the A.M./P.M. indicator is set to A.M. for your morning alarm. Tap it to switch between the two.

5. Tap the day or days you want the alarm. If the day is highlighted in black, it's selected.

11

FIGURE 11-3   BigClock has multiple alarms and time zones—the perfect companion for life on the road.

6. To enable the alarm, tap the large check box to the left. The alarm will now trigger at the designated time.

You should test your alarm before trusting it to get you out of bed the next morning. Specifically, be sure you haven't disabled system sounds in the Palm's Prefs app. If you did, then you'll never hear the alarm. Also, you want to be sure you remembered to set the alarm up for the right day of the week and the right half of the day.

Getting a Snooze

You can set BigClock's alarm to snooze, that is, to realarm after a few minutes if you want to nab a few extra minutes of sleep. To enable the snooze feature, choose Options | Alarm from the menu, and then tap the appropriate alarm number at the top of the screen. Now tap the Snooze check box. You can set how long the snooze will last (a common length is about ten minutes, if you're setting a wake up) and how many times the snooze goes off before turning off completely. When the alarm goes off, tap anywhere on the Palm screen and the snooze resets the alarm to go off again a few minutes later.

CAUTION *The snooze only works if you tap the screen. Because the alarm only sounds several times, and then shuts off, BigClock runs the danger of letting you fall asleep without tapping the screen to activate the next snooze cycle. To avoid oversleeping, you should modify the alarm sound, so it chimes for a long time. To do that, choose Sounds | Sound 1 (or whatever sound you want the alarm to play) from the menu, and then set the repeat value to a large number—like 100.*

Other Clocks

Quite a few timekeeping applications are available for the Palm and you might want to check out some of these others to see which you like the best:

■ **WorldMate**   This cool program lets you compare four world clocks to your local time. It also synchronizes the Palm with an online atomic clock at each HotSync, retrieves weather forecasts, and includes a currency converter.

- **CityTime**   We like the gorgeous color display that graphically shows the day/night line as it moves across the globe. CityTime displays four world clocks and lets you change your location and time easily without entering the Prefs app.

- **Time 2.0**   For those who want a simpler, calendar-based view, Time 2.0 shows the time and a calendar, along with a second time zone and upcoming appointments.

Finding Your Way Around

Many Palm tools can help you find your way around in a strange place. In fact, you can connect your Palm to a GPS navigation system (see the upcoming section, "Wilderness Survival Tools")! Most people need more mundane assistance, though, so we've collected a few interesting applications for you here.

Get Metro and Subway Routes

Do subway routes leave you scratching your head? Those maps they put in the train stops aren't exactly intuitive and finding the best route from one end of Paris to the other can be a nerve-wracking experience. That's why you should install *Metro,* a free utility that calculates the best route between any two stations in over 100 cities. The application comes with database files for cities like New York, London, Paris, Chicago, and Hong Kong, and you only need to install the files for cities you're visiting.

Many other travel guides specific to certain cities exist. Try some of these:

Region	Service	Program Name
200 cities worldwide	Several	MetrO
Montreal	Map of the subway system	Montreal Subway Map
Moscow	Metro guide to the city of Moscow, including maps	TealInfo Moscow Metro Guide
New York	Enter a Manhattan address and program provides the nearest cross street	X-Man

Region	Service	Program Name
Paris	Metro paths between monuments, museums, and stations	Paris
Southern California	MetroLink schedule	MetroLink

Language Translators

In the past, traveling abroad often resulted in serious communication difficulties. Do you know how to ask for the bathroom in French? If not, try one of these applications.

- **Small Talk**   This program is a real-time, two-way translator. Hold the Palm up to the person you want to communicate with. *Small Talk* presents you with complete sentences organized into situation-based categories, such as Basics, Lodging, Emergency, Food, and Entertainment. Select a phrase in English and it's translated into the target language, as you can see in Figure 11-4. The person you're communicating with can then select a response from a menu, which is translated back into English. Small Talk supports French, Italian, Spanish, German, and Japanese.

- **TourMate**   Available in several versions (including English-Spanish and English-Italian, English-French, and English-German), *TourMate* is easy to use. Choose a common greeting, expression, or question in English, and read the phonetically spelled foreign-language equivalent expression to the person with whom you're trying to communicate.

- **Translate**   This application enables you to enter a word and instantly translate it among 18 languages. The translator works in both directions, so you can go from English to Italian or Italian to English, for instance.

FIGURE 11-4   Choose a phrase from a list, divided by topic (left), and your associate can choose a response (right) that's translated back into English for you.

Unit Conversions

If you're an American in Europe, you need to contend with an alien set of measurements: not only is the currency different, but even the length, weight, and volume of common items are unusual. Heck, unless you're a scientist or an engineer, you might not know if 40 degrees Celsius is hot or cold. Try *Conversions* (see Figure 11-5), a calculator utility that lets you instantly make conversions among measurements like currency, temperature, length, area, and volume.

Wilderness Survival Tools

It's not surprising to walk into a fancy hotel and see a dozen executives standing around in fancy suits, checking their schedules via the Palms. But how often do you go camping in the middle of the woods and see people bring their Palms? Not that often, we're willing to bet. And that's too bad because the Palm is a handy survival tool. It does almost everything, except open cans of beans or start campfires.

Navigate with Your Palm

Have you ever gotten lost in a strange town or some deserted stretch of highway? Have you wished you hadn't seen the *Blair Witch Project* because it reminds you of exactly how bad you are at navigating in the wilderness? If so, you might benefit from a GPS navigation system. Combined with a GPS system, your Palm is perfectly capable of telling you exactly where to go.

Several popular GPS solutions are available for the Palm and other Palm-powered PDAs. The *Navman* is a GPS solution that's available for m-Series Palm models like the m125, m500, and m515. It's a sled design that clips on to the back of the PDA. Delorme sells the *Earthmate Road Warrior* package, which is a stand-alone, palm-sized GPS receiver, which attaches to the

11

| FIGURE 11-5 | Conversions makes it easy for an American to get by in a metric world.

What Is GPS?

GPS stands for Global Positioning System and it's comprised of 24 satellites flying around the earth in semisynchronous orbit (each trip around the Earth takes 12 hours). These satellites transmit extremely precise timing signals toward the Earth.

On the ground, an inexpensive GPS receiver simply listens for these timing signals. At any given moment, the time broadcast from each satellite in the GPS system's field of view is slightly different because the satellites are at different distances from the receiver and, consequently, some signals take longer to reach the receiver from the satellite. Because the orbit of each GPS satellite is very precisely known, the GPS receiver can process the different timing signals and determine its own position through simple triangulation.

The bottom line is this: through this process, a GPS receiver can narrow its position to an accuracy of about 100 feet—not bad for a system that works anywhere on Earth.

For GPS to do its magic, though, you must be able to see enough satellites. You need to see no less than three satellites for accurate position data, which isn't a problem in clearings. In a skyscraper-infested metropolitan area or in a forest with lots of tree cover, though, GPS can have trouble working. Even obstacles like trees can block the GPS signal.

PDA via a serial cable that plugs into the HotSync port. The *StreetFinder GPS* from Rand McNally, is another sled that snaps on to the back of older Palms like the Palm III and Palm V. For Handspring Visor users, Magellan sells its *GPS Companion,* a module that slides into the Springboard slot. You can see several of these units in Figure 11-6. Sony CLIÉ owners might eventually be able to use a GPS Memory Stick, but when we wrote this, it wasn't clear if or when Sony would sell it outside of Japan.

These GPS receivers generally work in two different modes:

- The bundled software lets you plan a door-to-door route on your PC and upload the turn-by-turn directions to your Palm when you HotSync. Once on the Palm, you can read these direction to find your way to the destination. Attach the GPS receiver to your Palm and it uses satellite data to alert you about each upcoming turn.

- Or, you can choose a region of the United States map and transfer it to the Palm during a HotSync. If the GPS system is attached to the Palm, you not only see the map on the Palm's screen, but your position on the map will also be visible, updated constantly as you move.

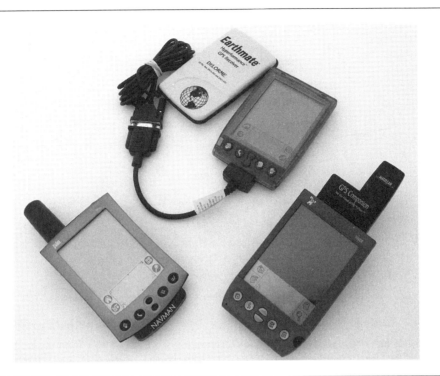

FIGURE 11-6   From left to right, the Delorme, Navman, and Magellan GPS systems

Use Your Palm as a Compass

While we're quite sure you know a Palm won't open a can of beans, we suspect you wouldn't believe it could be a compass, either. But you'd be wrong. Using a program like *Sun Compass,* you can get an immediate onscreen indication of north any time, anywhere (during daylight hours).

Unfortunately, Sun Compass comes with virtually no documentation, which might make it confusing for new users. To use Sun Compass, all you need to do is input a few pieces of information:

- ■ **Tz**   This is the time zone you're in currently. Time zones are calculated from −12 to 0, and then on up to +12. Your time zone value is simply the number of hours you're located away from Greenwich, England, home of Greenwich Mean Time (GMT). GMT is a time zone of 0. New York is −5, and California is −8. You can find a complete list of time zones in Windows by opening the Date/Time Properties dialog box (in the Control panel) and looking on the Time Zone tab.

- **La** Enter your latitude. Latitude is measured from 0 degrees (the equator) to 90N and 90S.

- **Lo** Enter your longitude. Longitude is commonly measured from 0 (at the longitude line that cuts through Greenwich, England) to 180E and 180W.

> **TIP** *Looking for your latitude and longitude? Visit **www.census.gov/cgi-bin/gazetteer**. Enter your city or ZIP code to find out your lat/long.*

- **DST** DST stands for daylight saving time, and it needs to be set either on or off, depending on the time of year. Daylight saving time is on between the first Sunday in April and the last Sunday in October.

> **TIP** *A few locations in the United States don't observe daylight saving time at all. These include Arizona, Hawaii, and parts of Indiana.*

Once you enter these values, point the front of your Palm at the sun (keep the Palm level with the ground) and the compass indicates which way is north. That's all there is to it!

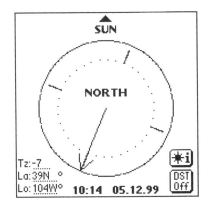

Find Stars

You can also use Sun Compass to find the North Star. Choose Misc | Polarstar from the menu and you see a dark screen with the Big and Little Dipper constellations. By aligning them with what you see in the sky, you can find the North Star and, thus, get a northerly orientation even at night.

That's great, but you can also use your Palm for some real star gazing. Here are a few programs you can try the next time you're far away from city lights with your Palm:

- ■ **Planetarium**   This program calculates the position of the sun, the moon, the planets, and over 1,500 of the brightest stars and deep sky objects in the sky. You can enter any location and any time period—you needn't use the present system clock. In addition to using this program for stargazing, it can also be used as a compass when the sun or moon is visible (much like Sun Compass).

- ■ **Star Pilot**   This program lets you specify your location, and then see the planets, the moon, and 500 stars in a compact star map. You can identify objects by clicking them, and search for celestial objects by name.

Read Late at Night

When all your tent buddies are trying to sleep while wondering if that odd sound is an approaching bear, you can relax in your sleeping bag and read a good book—with your Palm. The Palm's efficient backlighting makes it easy to read both in total darkness and in bright sunlight. What you need is a document reader. While you can see Chapter 19 for details on electronic books and document readers, we think it's worth pointing out right now that there's nothing like curling up

11

with a good e-book on a camping trip. You can store lots of reading on one Palm, so you can travel light and still have a lot to read on those quiet, lonely nights.

Where to Find It

Web Site	Address	What's There
DSI International	**www.dsi-usa.com**	Compact, folding HotSync cradles
Tech Center Labs	**www.talestuff.com**	Chargers for the Palm V
Electric Fuel	**www.instant-power.com**	Instant Power Charger
RGPS	**www.rgps.com**	StayOffHack
BigClock site	**www.gacel.de/palmpilot.htm**	BigClock
Mark/Space	**www.markspace.com**	Mark/Space Fax
Stevens Creek Software	**www.stevenscreek.com**	PalmPrint
Bachmann Software	**www.bachmannsoftware.com**	PrintBoy
IS/Complete	**www.iscomplete.com**	IS/Print
Yahoo!	**www.yahoo.com**	Web-based information management that HotSyncs to the Palm
WeSync.com	**www.wesync.com**	Side-by-side calendaring
SilverWare	**www.silverware.com**	TravelTracker
Delorme	**www.delorme.com**	Earthmate GPS
Rand McNally	**www.randmcnally.com**	StreetFinder GPS
Navman	**www.navman.com**	Navman GPS
Magellan	**www.magellangps.com**	Magellan GPS

Chapter 12

Working with Memory Media

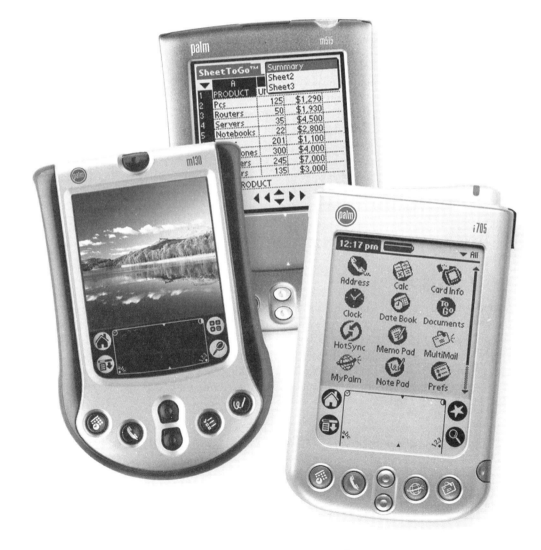

How to…

- Distinguish between different types of memory media
- Distinguish between memory cards and backup cards
- Find media preloaded with software
- Work with the Virtual File System
- Transfer programs and data to and from memory cards
- Find program launchers that support memory cards

By now, you know the 21st-century spin on the old adage: you can never be too rich, too thin, or have too much memory. Sure, it's grammatically iffy—but it is accurate. What with RAM-devouring e-books, games, AvantGo channels, productivity software, and even MP3 files, 8MB just don't go as far as they used to. Fortunately, the latest and greatest Palm Powered handhelds offer simple, inexpensive, potentially limitless memory expansion.

And not just memory expansion. The Visor's Springboard socket, for instance, can host MP3 players, GPS receivers, reference libraries, and plenty more. Palm offers expansion cards packed with games, e-books, road atlases, and travel guides—and promises hardware, such as Secure Digital Input/Output (SDIO) devices like digital cameras and barcode scanners, in the future. As for Sony, most Memory Sticks are exactly that—memory—but you can also find a Bluetooth networking card (which, at press time, is being sold only in Japan, but may be available elsewhere by now) and a digital camera mounted right on a stick.

In this chapter, we teach you the ins and outs of Palm OS memory media (see Figure 12-1), and give you a peek at some nifty expansion-slot extras.

It's in the Cards

It all started with Handspring's Visor, the first Palm Powered device to shatter the storage barrier. Simply pop an 8MB module into its Springboard socket and you immediately double your available memory (or quintuple it, if you have a 2MB Visor). Then came the TRGpro, which served up an industry-standard CompactFlash (CF) slot. Finally, Palm got into the act, equipping the Palm m125, m130, m500 series, and i705 with a slot for razor-thin MultiMediaCard (MMC) and Secure Digital (SD) media. In the interim, Sony kept things in the family with its proprietary Memory Stick cards for the CLIÉ series.

NOTE   *What's the difference between MMC and SD cards? Physically, they're almost identical: about the size of a postage stamp. MMC media tends to cost a bit less, while SD media offers faster data transfer rates and more capabilities. If you're just looking to add more memory to your Palm, go for MMC. It's the older of the two technologies, but it works just fine.*

Yep, the good news is that virtually every Palm Powered handheld introduced in 2001 featured some flavor of expansion slot—and it's a good bet most future models will do the same. The bad

FIGURE 12-1   Pick a card, any card. Different Palm Powered handhelds use different kinds of memory media, including (from left to right) CompactFlash, Secure Digital, and Memory Stick.

news is these slots are largely incompatible with one another. You can't, for instance, stick a Springboard module into a Memory Stick socket or slide your digital camera's CF card into your Palm m505's SD slot. This isn't a major issue, but you may want to do a little planning as you shop for your next handheld PC, digital camera, MP3 player, and even notebook PC. By making sure all your hardware supports the same media, you'll lower your operating expenses and have an easier time sharing files between devices.

What Price Memory?

Speaking of expenses, just what will it cost you to add, say, 8MB or 32MB or 128MB to your handheld? For starters, it depends on the media. We spent some time shopping at **Buy.com**, where we found a 32MB SD card selling for about $28, a 32MB Memory Stick for about $23, and a 32MB CF card for about $22. (Visor users can expect to pay about $80 for a 16MB flash module—though you can also opt for Springboard modules that let you utilize less-expensive CF and SmartMedia cards.)

Keep in mind that you needn't buy media directly from Palm or Sony just because you own, say, an m505 or CLIÉ 760C. Memory cards from companies like Lexar Media and SanDisk tend to cost a lot less and work just as well. SanDisk's 32MB Memory Stick, for instance, sells for just $23 at **Buy.com**, but you'll pay $35 for a 32MB card direct from Sony. CLIÉ users should also steer clear of Sony's MagicGate-flavor Memory Stick cards. They cost more and offer absolutely zero benefit.

As with most kinds of computer storage, your cost per megabyte usually decreases the more you buy. If a 32MB Memory Stick costs $30, you can probably get a 64MB card for $50. Buy as much storage capacity as you can afford because, as you may recall, you can never have too much. And make sure to shop online, as prices tend to be dramatically lower than in retail stores.

Handheld Expansion at a Glance

Model	Expansion/ Memory Type	Maximum External Storage Capacity	Lowest Price Per Megabyte*	Added Benefits
Palm i705/m125/ m130/m500 series	MultiMediaCard and Secure Digital	256MB	$0.46	Palm has been promising SD-based expansion hardware for a long time but, so far, there's only a Bluetooth card.
Handspring Visor series	Springboard	16MB**	$4.93 (16MB DataQuake module purchased from **PalmGear.com**)	Oodles of expansion modules, including MP3 players, GPS receivers, digital cameras, and more.
Handspring Treo 90	MultiMediaCard and Secure Digital	256MB	$0.46	This is Handspring's first model to use an expansion technology other than Springboard, but the Treo 90 doesn't support SDIO.
HandEra 330	CompactFlash and Secure Digital	1GB	$0.42	How about a memory card in one slot and a wireless LAN module in the other? Killer convenience for the corporate user.
Sony CLIÉ series	Memory Stick	128MB	$0.46	Memory Stick-based Bluetooth and digital camera cards available now. More expansion hardware to come.

*Approximate—based on 128MB card purchased from **Buy.com**, unless noted otherwise

**Optional CompactFlash, Memory Stick, and SmartMedia modules enable use of higher-capacity media

Memory 101

For purposes of our introduction to Palm OS memory expansion, we're going to exclude Visor users for a moment. That's because the Visor has a somewhat specialized version of the OS, and it handles external storage a bit differently.

With the introduction of Palm OS 4.0 (found on models like the Palm m125, Palm m505, and Sony CLIÉ N760C), Palm also introduced the Virtual File System (VFS)—a way for the operating

Should You Buy Software on a Card?

Handspring and Palm sell a variety of memory cards that come preloaded with software. Because the software resides on the card, you can run it without sacrificing any of your handheld's internal memory. But if memory conservation is your only concern, don't bother with software cards. Usually it's a better bet to buy a blank memory card, and then load it up as you see fit. Same end result, but you can get a lot more storage capacity for the money.

However, there are some good deals to be had. Some of Palm's eBook and Game cards, for instance, pack multiple titles onto a single card—titles that would cost more if purchased separately. The key thing to remember is that virtually any software you can buy on a card, you can buy electronically.

system to recognize removable memory cards, and access the programs and data stored therein. Thus, you could relocate, say, Palm Reader and all your e-books to a card, freeing a fair chunk of your handheld's valuable internal memory.

Working with Memory Cards

You can get programs and data onto a memory card in two basic ways. First, if you have software that's already loaded in internal memory, you can use the Palm OS Copy tool to copy it to the card. (This works both ways: you can copy items from a card back to internal memory as well.) To access it, tap the Applications button to return to the main screen, and then tap Menu | App | Copy. Select the program you want to copy (you have to copy them one at a time), making sure to select the desired Copy To and From destinations. Tap Copy to begin the process.

Copy	
Copy To: ▼ ▢ Card	
From: ▼ Handheld	
Beam Box	**14K**
Graffiti	**15K**
ScreenShot	**0K**
Tweak User	**10K**
X-Master	**52K**
(Done) (Copy)	

Alas, because there's no "move" option, the original file remains on your handheld. To claim the extra storage space you were after, you must then delete the software from internal memory.

This is exactly as tedious as it sounds, which is why we strongly recommend a third-party file manager like FilePoint (**www.bachmannsoftware.com**) or PocketFolder (**www.palmgear.com**). These programs make it much easier to move, copy, beam, and delete files than the Palm OS.

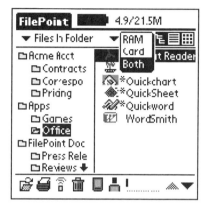

A better way to place apps into external storage is by installing them there directly. The Palm OS Install Tool lets you specify the destination for new software at the time you install it, meaning you can HotSync apps right onto a memory card.

Click here to load programs directly onto a memory card

More Memory on the Inside

If you own a Palm OS device that doesn't have an expansion slot or you're simply not satisfied with its 2MB, 4MB, or 8MB of internal memory, take heart. It's possible to increase the internal memory—provided you're willing to part with your handheld for a few days. Just send it to STNE (**www.stnecorp.com**) or Tony Rudenko (**www.palmpilotupgrade.com**). Both can upgrade virtually any model.

STNE, for instance, will install 8MB in a Palm VII or m100 for $55.95. The same upgrade for a Palm V costs $79.95. To bump a Visor Edge, Platinum, or Prism to 16MB will cost you $99.95. Check the site for the latest prices and more details.

It's important to note that utilizing either service will void your handheld's warranty, but both vendors offer a 90-day warranty of their own.

Ah, but what happens to them after that? Novice users often fall into the same trap: they install programs on their memory cards, and then can't understand why they don't see the icons in the Apps screen. The answer lies in a quirk of VFS: all applications stored on a memory card are automatically segregated into a category called Card. Thus, you must look in that category to find your newly installed stuff.

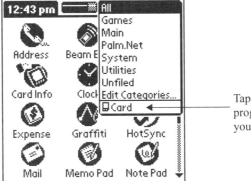

Tap here to access programs stored on your memory card

This can be inconvenient, to be sure, especially for users who like to keep their icons orderly. If you wind up with, say, 30 apps on a storage card, now you've got an organization problem— you can't subcategorize the Card category. Fortunately, there's a solution in the form of third-party launchers, many of which now support external storage. One of our longtime favorites, Launcher III, lets you organize your icons however you see fit, regardless of where the actual applications are stored. MegaLauncher and Silver Screen, two more launchers we like, offer VFS support as well.

It's a somewhat different story for Visor users. Applications stored on "flash" memory modules aren't grouped into a special category because the slightly tweaked OS "sees" them as part of main memory. Thus, you don't necessarily need a third-party launcher to categorize them alongside your other apps. However, flash modules do share a limitation with VFS memory cards, which we discuss in the next section.

How to ... Make a Backup Using a Regular Memory Card

Psst! Have we got a great tip for you. Let us preface this by saying that if your handheld has an expansion slot, you should be making regular backups of your data. Glitches and catastrophes happen—consider yourself warned. However, you needn't buy one of those special backup cards or modules (like the ones offered by Palm and Handspring). Instead, buy a standard memory card and use Portable Innovation Technology's PiBackup II. It creates a backup of your entire handheld (or just specific files), storing the data in a folder on the memory card. Now you have only one card to keep track of and one less thing to buy!

Memory 102

While memory cards open the door to carrying much more software than you ever could before, there are a couple hitches. Suppose you have a favorite document reader and a fairly large collection of Doc files that go with it. You decide to move the files to your memory card to free some internal storage space. But the next time you fire up the Doc reader, you discover your Doc files are gone. Why? Because the Doc reader doesn't know to look for them on the memory card. They're still stored there, but the software can't see them. This is true of many older programs (and by "older" we mean those written prior to summer, 2001). The good news is that developers are rapidly updating their wares to support VFS, meaning this problem should disappear before long. (For the record, plenty of Doc readers already support VFS, including Palm Reader, TealDoc and WordSmith.)

To overcome VFS-related issues like this one (and have an easier time overall working with applications and data stored on memory cards), power users should check out utilities like MSMount (**www.palmgear.com**), PiDirect (**www.pitech.com**), and PowerRun (**www.tt.rim.or.jp/~tatsushi/ powerrun/index-e.html**). In a nutshell, these programs trick the operating system into thinking that programs and data stored on a memory card are actually stored in main memory, so everything is accessible all the time.

Where to Find It

Web Site	Address	What's There
Benc Software	**www.benc.hr**	Launcher III
Lexar Media	**www.lexarmedia.com**	Memory cards
Megasoft 2000	**www.megasoft2000.com**	MegaLauncher
Pocket Sensei	**www.pocketsensei.com**	Silver Screen
Portable Innovation Technology	**www.pitech.com**	PiBackup II, PiDirect
SanDisk	**www.sandisk.com**	Memory cards

Chapter 13 — Handheld Communications

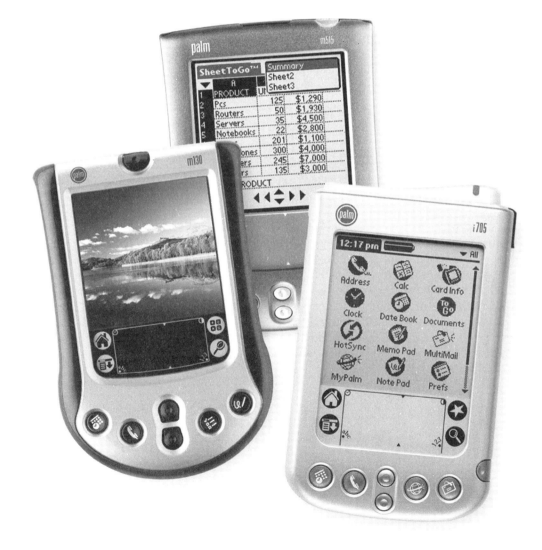

How to...

- Choose a smartphone or connected organizer
- Decide between landline, wireless, and cell phone connections
- Use a Kyocera smartphone as a wireless modem
- Turn your Visor into a cell phone
- Connect your cell phone to your handheld
- Configure your handheld for Web and e-mail access
- Find and download Web clipping apps
- Work with the Palm Mail program
- Access America Online
- Use AvantGo to take the Web with you
- Choose and work with handheld Web browsers
- Work with Bluetooth technology

The world it is a changin'. A few years ago, when PDAs were the hot new thing, it was enough to be able to check your schedule from an electronic organizer kept tucked in your pocket. These days, "connected" organizers are the new thing, and everyone, it seems, wants one. A connected organizer is simply a PDA that has access to the Internet. Such a gadget can retrieve e-mail, let you surf the Web, and perhaps even make phone calls. The possibilities are staggering.

There are all kinds of ways to get your Palm online. You can connect to a cell phone with a connection cable and let the phone act like a modem. If you're a bit more adventurous, you can link your phone and Palm wirelessly with infrared or Bluetooth. If you don't mind looking like you're still in the 1990s, you can always use a traditional "landline" modem and jack into a phone outlet. Of course, one of the most exciting trends in PDAs is the smartphone—a combination of PDA and cell phone that does it all in one smart little box. With so many options at your fingertips, this chapter is here to help you figure out how to connect your Palm and join the fast-growing world of the Internet. (For a brochure on how *you* can make money on the Internet, send $5, cash only, to Dave or Rick. Allow 6 weeks for delivery.)

NOTE *A lot of the information in this chapter, particularly the stuff about e-mail and Web clipping, is applicable to all wireless Palm devices and configurations. Whether you have an Earthlink Minstrel for your Palm m515 or a Mobile Internet Kit linking your m100 to your cell phone, you're likely to find some worthwhile stuff in these pages.*

Wireless PDAs

It's too expensive. It doesn't do real Web browsing. It forces you to work with a special e-mail account. The monthly service plans are too limiting and too costly. It'll be Palm's first flop.

Those were some of the things that people said about the Palm VII, Palm's first wireless-enabled PDA. And though it did indeed get off to a slow start, the Palm VII family eventually sold so well that it led the entire PDA industry to make wireless PDAs. The Palm VII is now discontinued (though a lot of people still use it, and you can find the 2MB Palm VII and 8MB Palm VIIx selling for great prices online), but it has been replaced by Palm's more advanced i705. At the same time, companies like Kyocera, Samsung, and Handspring have all released PDAs that have Internet capabilities of their own. How to choose?

For starters, we should probably explain that there are really two kinds of Internet-enabled PDAs out there:

- **Smartphones**   A smartphone is a gadget that combines aspects of a PDA with a mobile phone handset. You can use a smartphone like a regular cell phone to place calls, but it also has all the guts of a Palm. That means you can track your schedule, dial the phone directly from the Address Book, and even run Palm applications and games. Smartphones are for people who want to carry one device, not two, and have all the advantages of both.

- **Connected organizers**   Not all Palms with Internet access can place phone calls—some are just designed to use the Internet for data transactions, like e-mail and the Web. These gadgets are for folks who think that two devices are better than one; they may really like their existing cell phone and not want to trade up to a smartphone.

The good news is that no matter what your preference, you can find a smartphone or connected organizer to satisfy your needs. There are several excellent models to choose from today, and the following table outlines the most popular ones:

13

Model	Style	Features
Palm i705	Connected organizer	Always-on Internet access for e-mail and Web browsing. It comes with 8MB of memory and is fully compatible with Palm's universal connector and SD memory cards.
Handspring Treo	Smartphone	Voice, e-mail, and Web access. Available in grayscale or color; thumb keyboard or Graffiti. Available with GSM or CDMA service plans. 16MB of memory, but no memory slot.
Kyocera 7135	Smartphone	Voice, e-mail, and Web access. Color screen, 16MB of memory, SD slot, MP3 player. Supports newer CDMA2000 1X network.
Samsung I300	Smartphone	Voice, e-mail, and Web access. Comes with color screen and common CDMA service plans. 8MB of RAM, and no memory slot.

Choosing a Handheld

Before you pick a smartphone or connected organizer, we suggest that you play with them a bit. All of these models are popular enough that you can find them on display in office supply stores, computer shops, and cellular provider outlets. Here are some things to consider:

- **Coverage areas**   There are two major kinds of service offered by cell phones today: GSM and CDMA. CDMA is significantly more popular and has broad coverage throughout the U.S. It's an aging technology, though, and newer smartphones use GSM service, which is the same network used in Europe. The advantage of GSM is that it is an international standard, allowing you to use the same phone almost worldwide (though, because of regional differences in the way GSM works, you need a "tri-mode" GSM phone to get service both in the U.S. and Europe). GSM should also offer high-speed Internet access over your cell phone and PDA sooner than CDMA-based networks. For now, though, you may have difficulty getting coverage outside of major metro areas.

- **Size and shape**   How does it fit in your hand and against your head? The Treo, for instance, has a clamshell cover that folds open to fit the contour of the human head quite well. The Samsung I300 is a flat, brick-like device that may not be as comfortable without using a headset.

- **PDA features**   This is an important consideration. Do you want a color screen? What about 16MB of internal memory or memory cards? Some smartphones are built on a rather closed PDA base that doesn't let you back up your data on the road or expand past 8MB. Fortunately, most of the newest models offer some form of expansion capability, usually in the form of a Secure Digital slot.

- **Price**   There are some excellent deals to be had on older models. The Palm VIIx routinely shows up in online auctions for a steal, for instance, and the older Kyocera smartphone sells for under $100. Don't forget to compare the monthly service plan costs. Factor in data access—you may have to pay your ISP to "dial up" your e-mail account from your smartphone. Of course, the i705's monthly fee is for data since it doesn't have voice capabilities.

A Closer Look at the i705

The i705, seen in the following illustration, is Palm's successor to the Palm VII series—a PDA that delivers e-mail and Web access without changing all of the applications and capabilities people expect in a Palm. It still has four quick-access buttons on the front of the case, but they've been reprogrammed a bit. What used to open the To Do List and Memo Pad, for instance, now launch the MyPalm Internet portal (a screen that gives you quick access to popular Web services like sports, weather, travel, and shopping) and Palm's MultiMail e-mail client, which lets you retrieve messages from up to six Internet and corporate e-mail accounts. Rather than using a cellular network for your Internet activities, the i705 uses a proprietary data network that has outstanding coverage throughout the U.S.

The handheld comes in two flavors: an over-the-counter consumer version that you can pick up in any computer or office store (as well as via the Internet), and a special enterprise model that corporations can deploy in an organized rollout to their road warriors. This is the cool part: the enterprise version can be configured such that new e-mail messages are automatically pushed from the corporate mail server directly to the i705, with no need to manually check for new messages.

If you have a typical home PC like Dave and Rick, though, don't look to the i705 for "push" e-mail. In order to receive messages on the road, you need to close your mail client on the home PC so mail accumulates at your ISP's server. Then you need to press a button on the i705 to retrieve a copy of your messages.

A Closer Look at the Handspring Treo

Like the i705, the Treo is equipped with all of the familiar Palm core applications—but it's also a cell phone. Thus, the Address Book has been renamed the PhoneBook and is enhanced to let you dial calls more easily using an onscreen number pad, choose a call history, or dial from your contacts.

NOTE *The Treo 90 is a bit different from the other models in that it has no phone capabilities. It does, however, have the same design, a built-in keyboard, a color screen, and a Secure Digital expansion slot (which, interestingly, is not found in the other Treos).*

When you open the Treo's hinged flip cover (which you can see in all its hinged glory in the following illustration), the unit automatically turns on and switches to the PhoneBook. Even with

13

the cover closed, though, you can operate the Treo using the power switch and a scroll wheel on the side of the case.

One of the most unusual features of the Treo is the lack of a Graffiti area; instead, it has a small, thumb-operated keyboard that makes it look like a pager. (Handspring sells a Graffiti version, but is clearly marketing the keyboard version more aggressively.) Which to choose is largely a matter of taste, but we suspect you'll like the Graffiti version better if you already use a Palm.

The Treo comes in both color and grayscale versions, and works with a number of different cellular networks and service plans. The only thing it really lacks is a memory expansion slot; at least as of press time, there was no version of the Treo that could be expanded or backed up on the road.

A Closer Look at Other Smartphones

Other choices abound. The Samsung I300, for instance, is popular because it features a bright, colorful Palm display embedded in the middle of what looks like a traditional cell phone handset. The phone has a lot of very traditional cell-phone-style features, like voice dialing, voice memos, and a small LCD display on the top of the phone that displays phone status and Caller ID for incoming calls. You can even mute the ringer with a swift tap on the volume control, and just wait for the call to go to voice-mail—a cool feature that the Treo also has, but that all mobile phones should someday include. It uses the common CDMA network, and the phone can fall back on analog cellular service if you travel outside the digital network. There's just one major flaw: no expansion capability beyond the 8MB that is built in.

As we were putting the finishing touches on this book, Kyocera Wireless introduced its third-generation smartphone, the 7135. This is a particularly exciting model, as it offers just about everything a user could want: 16MB of memory, a Secure Digital slot for expansion, a color screen, a built-in MP3 player, and all the great phone features found in its predecessor (the Kyocera 6035). Like the Treo, the 7135 (shown in the following illustration) employs a clamshell design, with the screen in the upper half and the Graffiti area and dial pad in the lower. The 7135 is among the first smartphones to support the emerging CDMA2000 1X network,

Mail Alternatives for i705 and Treo

Right out of the box, you can retrieve Internet mail from any of the smartphone and connected organizers—including the i705 and Treo. Both Palm and Handspring realized you might want to get messages from your corporate e-mail account, though, and that's pretty hard to do without special software. If you use your i705 or Treo both at work and at home, there's good news: both Palm and Handspring have special e-mail solutions for you.

If you own a Treo, for instance, you can subscribe to Handspring's Treo Mail. The Corporate Edition of Treo Mail lets business professionals who need to access Microsoft Exchange automatically get mail, even if it's stored behind a corporate firewall.

IT managers who have Palm i705 users can install the Palm Wireless Desktop Server. It sits behind the corporate firewall and connects the mail server to the fleet of i705s; as e-mail arrives on the server, a copy is encrypted and transmitted to the appropriate device. But what if your IT department doesn't want to invest in the Wireless Desktop Server? That's where the Palm MultiMail Deluxe Desktop Link comes in. The Desktop Link is a free application, available on the Palm Web site, that you can install on your desktop PC. It intercepts incoming mail from the Microsoft Exchange server and sends an encrypted copy to your i705.

13

which opens the door to data transfer speeds of up to 153 Kbps. Translation: e-mail messages and Web data should arrive on the 7135 at a very fast clip. (By contrast, the best speed the Kyocera 6035 can manage is about 14.4 Kbps, so the 7135 is more than 10 times faster for data transfers.)

How to ... Use a Kyocera Smartphone as a Wireless Modem

One of the best features of the Kyocera 6035 and 7135 is that they can double as a wireless modem. Why is this such a big deal? If you own a notebook PC, you could use the Kyocera to send and receive e-mail, surf the Web, connect to a corporate LAN, and so on. Trust us: these activities are far more enjoyable—and usually more practical—on a notebook than on the tiny Kyocera.

In order to make this work, you need a cable that will link your notebook to your phone. They're available from several sources; we found one at TeleAdapt (**www.teleadaptusa.com**) for $59, which includes the necessary Windows drivers.

Next, you need Kyocera's modem setup guide. It's available online at the following link: **www.kyocera-wireless.com/pdf/modem_setup.pdf**. This is an Adobe PDF file, so you need the Adobe Acrobat Reader to view it. If it's not already installed on your system, you can download it free from Adobe (**www.adobe.com**).

Connecting Other Handhelds

So you've already invested in a non-wireless handheld. Does that mean you have to toss it out the nearest window and buy something new if you want wireless Internet access? Of course not! This is the Palm universe we're talking about. There are a number of ways to get your handheld connected, including landline modems, wireless modems, and cell-phone cables.

Landline, Wireless, or Something Else?

There are two kinds of modems available for Palm devices: landline and wireless. The former are similar to what most computers have, and make their connections via standard telephone lines (or "*landlines*," as we in the biz call them). *Wireless* modems require no wires at all, relying instead on cellular and/or radio towers to make their connections. Naturally, there are pros and cons to each technology—and some alternatives to consider as well. Here's what you need to know.

Landline Modems

Landline modems, which are what most computers have, clip onto (or into) your Palm device, then plug into a phone jack using traditional RJ-11 cable.

The Pros:

- Reasonably inexpensive.
- Phone jacks are downright ubiquitous.
- Supports the use of America Online and/or your existing ISP.
- Speed—most Palm modems support connections of up to 56 Kbps.
- Reliability—99.9 percent of the time, a landline connection works right.

The Cons:

- Okay, so phone jacks aren't really ubiquitous. They're not in trains, bus depots, grocery stores, the beach, or other places you may find yourself.
- Even when you find a phone line, some—like the "PBX" variety in hotel rooms—can be deadly to computer modems.
- You're tethered to a wall while you're online.

What Are Your Choices?   Of the various landline modems currently available, not all are compatible with all Palm devices. In the chart below, you'll get a general idea for which modems work with which models.

Modem	Compatible With
PalmModem Connectivity Kit	Most Palm models
Card Access Thinmodem/Thinmodem Plus	Handspring Visor series
Sony Modem for CLIÉ Handheld	CLIÉ N series, S series

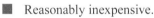

13

These modems all sell for around $100, though the Thinmodem Plus costs $149. That's because in addition to a 56 Kbps modem, this Springboard module includes an extra 8MB of memory.

Wireless Modems

Wireless modems, which are no doubt the wave of the future, rely on existing cellular and radio technologies to transmit and receive data through the ether. Keep in mind that there are several different kinds of wireless options for Palm devices, including mobile phones and dedicated modems. In this section we focus on the latter.

The Pros:

- Unsurpassed convenience—no phone jacks to seek out, no wires tethering you to a wall. And because there's no lengthy dial-up procedure, you get connected almost instantaneously.

The Cons:

- Performance—most wireless solutions top out at 19.2 Kbps, if that. Such speeds are okay for e-mail, but can make Web browsing a chore.

- Cost—The hardware itself can cost hundreds of dollars, and you also have to pay monthly service charges.

- Coverage can be an issue. If you live and/or work in a rural environment, you may have weak service or no service at all. Even in urban areas, there can be "dead zones" where you simply can't connect. The convenience factor can go right out the window if you're faced with uneven coverage.

What Are Your Choices?   If you're shopping for a dedicated wireless modem for your handheld, you'll soon find you have relatively few choices. That's one reason cell phones are becoming more popular as surrogate wireless modems.

Modem/Service	Compatible With
Novatel Minstrel/Earthlink	Palm m500 series, Palm Vx
Novatel Minstrel/Earthlink	Handspring Visor series

If you own a model that's compatible with Earthlink's offerings, you'd do well to consider the service. It includes excellent software for your handheld, giving you quick and easy access to e-mail, Web, chat and other services. Modem prices vary quite a bit depending on which handheld you have, but the monthly service is just $39.95 for unlimited access.

Cell Phones

You probably already own a cell phone—most people do. And it's already wireless, so wouldn't it be great if you could link it to your handheld for Web browsing and e-mail? You can, and it's easier than you might think. Here's what you need:

■ A phone that supports data calls. Most modern phones do (those that work with CDMA and GSM networks), but check with your service provider to be sure. You may also have to pay a little extra per month to make data calls, though some companies build the cost into their standard service plans.

Turn Your Visor Into a Cell Phone

Have we got a Springboard module for Visor owners! Handspring's VisorPhone turns your handheld into a full-featured GSM cell phone, complete with Caller ID, call waiting, voice mail, and more. The module doubles as a wireless modem, so you can dial into your ISP to send and receive e-mail and surf the Web. At press time, Handspring was offering the module absolutely free—yes, free!—with service activation via Cingular Wireless and VoiceStream. That's a pretty impressive deal—so long as you don't mind walking around with your Visor stuck to your head.

If you live in an area that doesn't have access to the GSM network, check out the Sprint PCS Wireless Web Digital Link—a phone module that utilizes CDMA technology. Unfortunately, it's nowhere near free, selling for about $250 (plus service).

13

■ A cable to link your handheld to your phone, or a phone with an infrared port (found almost exclusively on GSM phones, and only a handful of those). We think a cable is the best bet, as it gives you greater flexibility in positioning the two devices. (With an IR connection, the phone and handheld need to lie on an even surface so they can communicate.)

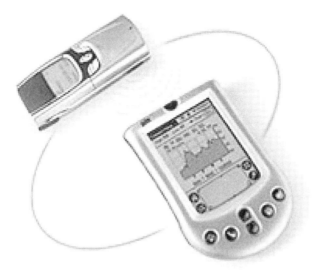

■ Palm OS 3.5 or later. That version of the operating system includes the necessary components (known as the Mobile Internet Kit) for data communications via cell phone. Keep reading to learn how to install these components and start using your cell phone with your handheld.

Finding Connection Cables   Unless you're lucky enough to have an IR-equipped phone, you'll need a cable to make the connection to your handheld. We know of two good sources for them:

Site	URL
Purple Data Cables	**www.pcables.com**
SupplyNet	**www.thesupplynet.com**

You may also be able to find cables at your local computer or office superstore, or at one of your cell phone company's outlet stores.

A Neat Little Number Called BackFlip

Not a modem in the traditional sense of the word, the PocketMail BackFlip is a unique e-mail accessory that works with ordinary telephone handsets. That is, you hold the device next to any handset (pay phone, cell phone, Mickey Mouse phone—whatever) and dial a toll-free number.

13

Did you know?

Swap Contacts with Nokia Phones

Here's a little-known secret about Nokia cell phones—those that have infrared ports. They can receive contact info beamed from your handheld, and can also beam its own address book entries to your handheld. While you're limited to sending one contact at a time, this would ultimately be a timesaving way to transfer important phone numbers into your phone (much quicker than entering them manually). Consult your phone's instruction manual for information on beaming (it's a little different on each phone).

After a minute or two of beeping and booping, your e-mail is sent and received. Then you can toss the BackFlip back in your briefcase—no fuss, no muss.

The BackFlip is available only for older Palm models—namely, the Palm III series, Palm V series and Palm VII series. It's $149 for the hardware and 12 months of service—a decent deal if you need a quick and easy way to transact e-mail while traveling. You can use the PocketMail e-mail account that you get when you sign up, or access up to three corporate, POP3, Yahoo, or America Online accounts.

Introduction to Web Clipping

Most Internet-capable Palm devices can access the Internet two different ways: with a standard Web browser, or using a more efficient Palm-invented technology called *Web clipping*. The concept behind Web clipping is simple. Most of us turn to the Web for specific bits of information. We look for news, sports scores, stock quotes, airline flight information, weather reports, and so on. But when we visit sites that provide this information, there's always "fluff" that goes with it: big splashy graphics, banner ads, tables, and links to other sites. These flourishes are time-consuming to download and typically work best with a large display.

Web clipping dispenses with Web fluff, pulling down only the raw information that's needed. Thus, connection speed becomes less of an issue, because only tiny amounts of data are actually being transmitted. And because the data is mostly text, screen size becomes largely irrelevant.

Web clipping also dispenses with the Web browser, instead employing specialized programs called Web clipping apps (which in their early days were known as Palm Query Apps). These little gophers pull specific bits of information from the Internet, then present that information to you on neatly formatted screens. They're used to obtain everything from news and weather to movie times and traffic reports (see Figure 13-1).

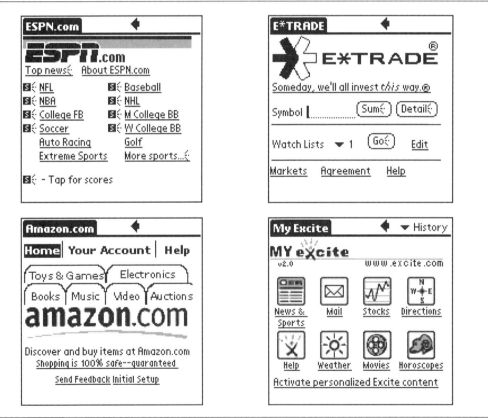

FIGURE 13-1 With Web clipping apps, you can access a wide range of information and services.

Web clipping was originally limited to models like the Palm VII, but with the arrival of Palm OS 3.5 and the Mobile Internet Kit, it's now available for all Palm Powered handhelds. In fact, if your handheld comes with OS 4.0 or later, everything you need for Web clipping is already installed. You just need to download a few Web clipping apps and get online (using either a modem or cell phone, as described in the previous sections).

Finding and Installing Web Clipping Applets

Hundreds of Web clipping apps are available from third-party developers. You can get news from ABC and ESPN, stock quotes from E*Trade, driving directions from MapQuest, and so on. Most of these apps are free, but some cost a few dollars up front or have subscription-related fees.

Web clipping apps are as easy to find and install as any other Palm software. We suggest starting with Palm (**www.palm.com/wireless/apps**), which boasts a collection of over 500 Web clipping apps. You can also find them on software sites such as Handango (**www.handango.com**) and PalmGear H.Q. (**www.palmgear.com**). Once you download a clipping app, you install it exactly as you would any Palm application (as detailed in Chapter 4).

Introduction to MultiMail SE

MultiMail SE, a full-featured e-mail program designed to work with modem and cell-phone connections, resides on the software CD that came with your handheld. Find the folder and double-click the Setup.exe icon to install it. In that same folder, there's an electronic instruction manual that will help you configure MultiMail for use with your ISP.

> **TIP**
>
> *If you have broadband Internet access for your PC, there's probably no dial-up connection involved (unlike with traditional ISPs and services like America Online). Thus, you're probably wondering where your modem or cell phone should call. Many broadband ISPs do offer dial-up numbers for their subscribers, ostensibly to allow Internet access while traveling. Check with your provider to see if such a number is available.*

13

A Word About E-Mail on Your Handheld

This could be the single most important sidebar in the entire chapter. When we talk about doing e-mail on your handheld, it's a somewhat complicated conversation. That's because there's e-mail in the traditional sense (a modem, an e-mail program like MultiMail, your ISP, and so on), and then there's Mail. Notice how we capitalized it there. That's because most Palm models come with an e-mail application with that very name. It's pretty cool, but quite different from the aforementioned e-mail scenario. Find out more in the next section.

Introduction to the Palm Mail Program

It's hard to remember life before e-mail, isn't it? Imagine, having to actually pick up the *phone* every time you wanted to communicate with someone. Now we just fire off e-mail messages. And with Mail (also known as Palm Mail and HotSync Mail), we needn't wait till we're sitting at our PC to conduct e-mail business.

What Mail does, in a nutshell, is link to the e-mail program on your desktop computer. Just as Memo Pad, Address List, and the other apps synchronize with Palm Desktop, Mail synchronizes with Outlook Express, Eudora Pro, and various other e-mail programs. The end result is that Mail becomes a portable extension of that program, allowing you to view, delete, and reply to messages and write new ones.

Mail is not a stand-alone e-mail client. That is, it works only when it's linked to desktop software. You'd think if you purchased a modem for your Palm device, you could use Mail to dial into your ISP and transact messages. In reality, Mail has no use for a modem whatsoever (unless you're dialing into your PC for a remote HotSync).

This is not to say that Mail is an underpowered or valueless piece of software—quite the opposite. It comes in very handy when you're on the road and suddenly think of a message you need to send—presto: you can compose it on the spot, knowing it'll be sent the next time you HotSync. Additionally, if you take the train to work every morning, you can HotSync before you leave and read all your e-mail from the night before.

Mail also sports some reasonably advanced features, such as blind carbon copies, signatures, and delivery confirmation. And because it's a Palm program, the interface is streamlined and familiar. Let's get you up and running with this great little e-mail manager.

Setting Up the Palm Mail Program

Although Mail comes preinstalled on most Palm devices (one notable exception being the m100), you must set it up for use with your desktop e-mail program. It's possible you did this already while installing the Palm Desktop software, which gives you a choice of configuring your e-mail settings then and there or skipping it till later. In either case, you can access the Mail Setup program in Windows by clicking Start | Programs | Palm Desktop | Mail Setup.

NOTE *Palm Desktop for Macintosh doesn't inherently support synchronization with Palm Mail, but it does include a third-party utility that enables you to synchronize Palm Mail with Qualcomm's Eudora e-mail client. We talk more about it later in this chapter.*

The only real step involved in this setup procedure is choosing which e-mail program you use, as shown next:

Which Desktop E-Mail Programs Does Mail Support?

The bad news is that Mail doesn't work with every e-mail manager on the planet. The good news is that it works with the most popular ones, as listed below:

- Lotus cc:Mail, versions 2.5, 6.0 and 7.0
- Microsoft Exchange 4.0 or later
- Microsoft Outlook (all versions)
- Microsoft Outlook Express (all versions)
- Microsoft Windows Messaging 4.0
- Qualcomm Eudora 3.03 or later

For sake of continuity, most of our explanations will center around Outlook Express, one of the most popular e-mail programs. There may be some slight differences if you're using an enterprise-based program like Lotus cc:Mail. Consult your IT manager if you need assistance.

Palm Mail and HotSync Manager

After you run Mail Setup, check your HotSync Manager settings to make sure they're properly configured. To open HotSync Manager, click the HotSync icon in your Windows System Tray and choose Custom. (You can also access it from within Palm Desktop by choosing HotSync | Custom.) You see a dialog box listing the installed conduits (which handle the actual synchronization for each program) and the setting (that is, action) for each one.

If the action for the Mail conduit reads Synchronize the Files, you're all set. (But don't HotSync yet! We still have to configure the settings on the Palm side.) If, for some reason, it still reads Do Nothing, click on the conduit to highlight it and then click the Change button. In the resulting dialog box, choose Synchronize the Files, then check the box that says Set as Default.

> **TIP** *If you ever decide to stop using Mail, you can simply return to this setup screen and select Do Nothing. Regardless of how you've configured your Palm, this single HotSync Manager setting overrides all others.*

Configuring Mail Settings on the Palm

Synchronizing your desktop mail with the Mail applet is not an all-or-nothing proposition. For instance, you can elect to pull only unread messages into your Palm device, or create filters so that only messages tagged as "high priority" will be synchronized. The settings for such options are found in the HotSync Options screen on your handheld, which is accessible by choosing Menu | Options from within the Mail program.

Note that you can configure Mail settings for both local and remote HotSyncs, just by tapping the Settings For arrow at the top of the screen. If you do plan to HotSync remotely, you may indeed want to have different synchronization settings in order to minimize the connection time.

Figure 13-2 shows the HotSync Options screen. Let's take a look at the four choices therein.

All

This option forces all messages to be synchronized between your Palm device and your desktop e-mail program. Take caution when selecting this option—if you have more than a couple dozen messages in you PC's Inbox, your HotSyncs may take quite a bit longer (a few minutes instead of a few seconds), and you'll eat up that much more of your Palm's memory.

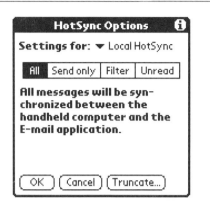

| FIGURE 13-2 | The HotSync Options screen contains important settings for use with Palm Mail |

Send Only

This one-way solution sends any messages composed on your Palm, but doesn't retrieve messages from your desktop mailbox. Use this if you don't wish to view your mail on your Palm.

Filter

The most complex of the e-mail options, Filter lets you choose to ignore messages that meet certain criteria or retrieve messages that meet certain criteria. Suppose, for instance, you want to retrieve e-mail that comes only from your coworkers. Or you want to ignore messages that originate from a specific address. Filter makes such options possible, all in the interests of giving you greater control over the mail that's retrieved from your desktop mailbox. Let's examine the workings of this choice, which is shown in Figure 13-3.

- **Retrieve All High Priority**   When you check this box, it overrides any other filter settings you may have specified. Any e-mail marked as high priority by the sender will be received on your Palm.

- **Ignore Messages Containing**   With this option selected, you're essentially telling HotSync Manager not to retrieve e-mails that meet the criteria laid out in the To, From, and/or Subj fields.

- **Retrieve Only Messages Containing**   With this option selected, you're essentially telling HotSync Manager to retrieve only the e-mails that meet the criteria laid out in the To, From, and/or Subj fields. This will generally download much less e-mail than the Ignore Messages option, as you're requesting a specific subset of messages.

- **To, From, Subj**   These three fields are used to specify *filter strings*—the exact information that the filter should look for in excluding or accepting messages. Thus, if you wanted to ignore all messages from *dave@johnson.com*, you'd enter that e-mail

13

FIGURE 13-3   Mail's Filter option lets you decide which e-mail messages do or don't get transferred during a HotSync.

address in the From field. If you use multiple e-mail accounts on your desktop PC but want to receive messages sent only to a specific account, you'd enter that e-mail address in the To field. In Figure 13-3, we've configured our Palm device to receive e-mails only from *denise.richards@babe.com*. All others will be ignored.

> **TIP**   *You can specify multiple e-mail addresses in the To and From fields, just by separating them with a comma. And if you run out of room in either field, just tap the field name to access a larger data-entry screen (and the Palm Lookup function, should you wish to pull e-mail addresses from your contact list).*

> **NOTE**   *If you plan to use filters, plan on experimenting a bit to get them set up right. There's always the concern that you might accidentally miss an important message if, say, the sender misspells the subject name or sends the e-mail using a different-than-expected account. So, use them with caution.*

Unread

Rather than transferring all the e-mail from your Inbox to your Palm, this option transfers only those messages that are marked as unread. This is an excellent choice if you tend to retain mail after reading it, as it won't download your entire Inbox.

Truncate

If you find that HotSyncs are taking too long because you often receive lengthy e-mails, or you're just concerned about messages eating up too much of your Palm's memory, you can instruct Mail to truncate (that is, trim) messages that exceed a certain size. By default, Mail truncates messages longer than 4,000 characters, but you can change the value by tapping the Truncate button in the HotSync Options screen.

NOTE   *This has nothing to do with file attachments, which Mail never downloads. If an e-mail in your Inbox has an attachment, it is simply ignored during HotSync.*

The Relationship Between Palm and Desktop

It's important to understand that Mail and your desktop e-mail program are not just mimicking each other; they're actually linked together. Thus, when you delete a message on your Palm, it gets deleted on your desktop the next time you HotSync. When you mark a message as read on your desktop, it subsequently gets marked as read on your Palm.

Key Consideration #1

In whatever e-mail program you use on your PC, it's not uncommon to have a variety of different mailboxes set up. You might have one marked "personal," another for "work," and so on. This helps you keep inbound messages better organized, rather than lumping them all into a single folder.

However, regardless of how you've configured Mail's options or filters, the only place it will retrieve messages from is your main Inbox. Hey, we never said the program was perfect.

Key Consideration #2

When you compose or reply to a message, the resulting outbound e-mail is sent via Outlook Express (or whatever desktop program you use). Unfortunately, you don't have any control over which desktop e-mail account is used—it's automatically sent via your default account. This might pose a problem if you use multiple accounts, and need to send messages using one that's not the default. Hey, we never said the program was perfect.

Mail's Mailboxes

Like all e-mail programs, Mail uses mailboxes to keep messages organized. Thus, it has the standard Inbox and Outbox, plus folders for draft, deleted, and filed items (see Figure 13-4).

13

FIGURE 13-4   Tap the arrow in the upper-right corner of the screen to access Mail's message folders.

Alas, you can't edit the names of the mailboxes or create new ones, but you can still meet most of your basic organizational needs. Here's a guide to the ins and outs of the Inbox, Outbox, and so forth.

Inbox

When you load the Mail applet, the Inbox is the first thing you see. If you haven't set up and synchronized your desktop e-mail program yet, your Inbox will look rather empty. If you have, however, you'll see a list of messages:

The first column shows the name (or e-mail address) of the sender, the second an abbreviation of the subject heading, and the third the date the message was received. If you tap the Show button at the bottom of the screen, you can change whether your messages are sorted by date, sender, or subject. You can also uncheck the Show Date box, which will eliminate the third column from the message list (making the other two a bit bigger).

Tap any message to open it. A check mark next to any message in the list denotes that it has been read. At the top of the screen, you see a numerical description of how many messages are in the list and how many of those remain unread.

Outbox

When you tap Send after composing a new message or reply, the message is directed to the Outbox. There it stays until the next time you HotSync, after which it's transferred to your desktop e-mail program and sent. You can tap any message in the list to view, edit, or delete it.

The Show button affords the same options here as in the Inbox (and is, in fact, the same in all the folders).

Deleted

As noted earlier, when you delete a message on your Palm device, it gets deleted from your desktop e-mail program as well. But that doesn't happen until your next HotSync, and in the meantime all deleted messages are stored in the Deleted folder. You can undelete a message from this folder by tapping it, then tapping the Undelete button at the bottom of the screen.

Filed

Want to keep a message for later reference, but don't want to clutter up your Inbox? Just file it in the Filed folder. With any e-mail message open, simply choose Menu | Message | File. You're then asked if you want to keep the e-mail in the Inbox as well—tap Yes or No (or Cancel if you've changed your mind about the whole thing). The Filed folder has no connection with your desktop e-mail program, so messages stored there are not synchronized. (They are, however, backed up on your computer's hard drive, along with other Palm data.)

Draft

Suppose you're composing a love letter (make that e-mail) to Denise Richards. You've written the first draft, but don't want to send it right away in case it sounds too corny. You can file it away in the Draft folder, where it stays until you're ready to edit it.

There are two ways to direct an e-mail to this folder. First, you can choose Menu | Message | Save Draft. Second, if you tap Cancel while working on a new e-mail, you'll be given the option of saving it to the Draft folder instead of deleting it. To continue work on a message filed in Draft, just tap it once, then tap the Edit button. (You can also tap the Delete button to get rid of it.)

SHORTCUT *Instead of venturing into the drop-down menus when you want to save an outgoing e-mail in the Draft folder, tap Cancel.*

As with the Filed folder, the contents of Draft are not synchronized with your PC—despite the fact that your desktop e-mail program may have a similar folder (as does Outlook Express).

Composing New Messages

Okay, so you've configured Mail to your liking, and now you're ready to start writing messages. There are two ways to go about this: Tap the New button, or choose Menu | Message | New. You can't simply start writing in the Graffiti area, as you can with most of the other core Palm apps.

The New Message screen consists of four fields, which should be quite familiar to anyone who's worked with e-mail on a PC:

```
┌─────────────────────────────────┐
│ New Message                     │
│  To: rickbroida@magicaldesk.com│
│  CC:                            │
│ Subj: The Palm Mail applet      │
│ Body: When I'm done composing this│
│       message, I'll have to wait till I│
│       HotSync before I'll be able to│
│       send it.                  │
│                                 │
│                                 │
│                                 │
│                                 │
│ (Send) (Cancel) (Details...)    │
└─────────────────────────────────┘
```

■ **To**   Enter the address of the recipient here. You can send the same message to multiple recipients simply by writing more e-mail addresses, separating them with a comma. Tap the To field button for access to a larger address-entry screen (and the Palm Lookup function, should you care to pull e-mail addresses from your contact list).

■ **CC**   Want this message to reach additional recipients? Enter their e-mail addresses here in the "carbon copy" field. Tap the CC field button for access to a larger address-entry screen (and the Palm Lookup function, should you care to pull e-mail addresses from your contact list).

- **Subj**   Enter the subject of the message here. Tap the Subj field button for access to a larger data-entry screen.
- **Body**   Enter the full message here. Tap the Body field button for access to a larger data-entry screen.

The buttons at the bottom of the New Message screen should be equally self-explanatory. But let's take a peek at them anyway.

Send
When you tap it, your message is placed in the Mail outbox. The next time you HotSync, all messages in the Outbox are transferred to your PC and sent via your desktop e-mail program.

Cancel
This is actually a two-function button. When you tap it, the Palm will ask if you want save the message in the Draft folder. If so, tap Yes; if not, tap No. The latter action will erase the message and return you to the Inbox screen. The former will file the message in the Draft folder, a kind of holding tank for messages that aren't ready to be sent.

Details
There are a few additional sending options you can apply to outgoing messages, all of them accessible by tapping the Details button.

- **Priority**   Want the recipient(s) to know that this message is of high priority? Or low? Or just normal? Tap here to select one.
- **BCC**   Checking this box adds a Blind Carbon Copy field to your message, which you see when you return to the New Message screen. This is a way to secretly send copies of the message to additional recipients, without the other recipients being able to see their e-mail addresses.

NOTE *The following three options are "sticky," meaning if you select them for one message, they stay selected for all future messages (unless you subsequently deselect them again).*

- ■ **Signature** When this box is checked, your "signature" (as specified in the Mail Preferences screen) is appended to the end of the message. Though it doesn't appear when you return to the New Message screen, it is added.

- ■ **Confirm Read** Kind of like an RSVP, this option requests an e-mail reply that your message was read by the recipient(s).

- ■ **Confirm Delivery** This option requests e-mail notification that your message was delivered to the intended recipient(s).

NOTE *All five of these features will work only if your desktop e-mail program supports them.*

Viewing Messages

Regardless of which mailbox or folder you have open, viewing a message is as simple as tapping it. However, the options associated with that message vary a bit depending on the folder that contains it. In the Inbox and Filed folders, for instance, you can tap Reply or Delete. In the Outbox and Draft folders, your options are Edit and Delete. And in the Deleted folder, you can choose Edit if the message was originally composed on your Palm, and Undelete if it's one that was in your Inbox.

Header Information

When you open any e-mail message, regardless of its folder location, you see a pair of icons in the upper-right corner of the screen. These control how much of the message's *header* is displayed. If you'd like to see more information, such as the sender's reply-to address, the date and time the message was sent, and the e-mail addresses of all recipients (if there were others beside yourself), tap the right icon. Tap the left one to "shorten" the display again.

```
Inbox  Message 4 of 7          ▣▤
From: Amy Nemechek
 Subj: Palm CEO named: Carl
        Yankowski

Dear all,
3Com announced this morning it has
named Carl Yankowski to the new
post of CEO of the Palm Computing
division. Alan Kessler will continue in
his role as president. The press
release follows.
(Done) (Reply) (Delete)   ◀▶
```

```
Inbox  Message 4 of 7          ▣▤
   To: palm@arpartners.com
From: anemechek@arpartners.com
       (Amy Nemechek)
 Subj: Palm CEO named: Carl
        Yankowski
Date: 12/2/99 12:30 pm

Dear all,
3Com announced this morning it has
named Carl Yankowski to the new
post of CEO of the Palm Computing
(Done) (Reply) (Delete)   ◀▶
```

Replying To and Forwarding Messages

Hey, wait a second. You've seen the Reply button, which is used to answer e-mails. But what if you want to forward a message to someone else? Where's the Forward button?

Surprise—there isn't one, at least not where you'd expect it to be. Though most people would agree that replying and forwarding are two very different animals, Mail inexplicably buries the Forward option in the Reply Options menu. Let's take a look at that menu, as shown in Figure 13-5.

- **Reply to**   To whom should this reply go? The person who sent it? Everyone else who received it? Maybe you just want to forward the message to someone else. Choose the desired option by tapping Sender, All, or Forward, respectively.

- **Include original text**   It's a common courtesy to include a copy of the original message when replying to or forwarding one. By checking this box, Mail will do exactly that, as you see in the body of the new message that appears.

- **Comment original text**   Of course, it can be difficult to distinguish the old text from the new, which is why it's a good idea to "comment" the original message. Translation: the old text is marked and indented using ">" symbols. Mail even adds a descriptor ("So and so wrote on 12/2/01 at 12:30 p.m:") before the commented text, as illustrated below:

Mail's Other Options

While perusing the Mail menus, you may have noticed a few choices other than HotSync Options (which we covered in great detail a few pages back). Let's check 'em out, and then you can go back to playing Giraffe.

- **Purge Deleted**   Accessed by choosing Menu | Message | Purge Deleted, this option empties the contents of the Deleted folder. Said messages are still deleted from your desktop e-mail program the next time you HotSync. So, why bother with this option? There's no particularly compelling reason, except that if you have a lot of lengthy messages stored in the Deleted folder, they're probably eating up some of your precious RAM.

FIGURE 13-5 When you reply to a message, Mail lets you specify who gets the reply and whether or not to include the original message.

■ **Font** As with all the core Palm OS programs, Mail lets you choose one of three fonts for viewing data. The procedure here is the same as elsewhere: choose Menu | Options | Font, then tap the font you want.

■ **Preferences** Remember a few pages ago, when we told you about the Details screen for new messages? That bit about appending your "signature"? Here in the Preferences screen, you get to create that signature. It can be anything you want, from a standard closing ("Very truly yours," for example) to your opinion about which is the best *Star Trek* series (it's *Voyager*, as everyone knows). For some reason, Dave likes to include obscure song lyrics in his signature.

Put Palm Mail on Steroids

If you like the concept behind Palm Mail (synchronization with your desktop e-mail program) but wish the software was a little more robust, check out Network Orion's Mail Plus. It's a Palm Mail substitute that offers similar functionality, but with more features.

For instance, Mail Plus enables you to preview messages and beam them to other Palm users. Better still, it supports unlimited mail folders, so you're not stuck with the handful that come with Palm Mail.

Accessing America Online

At last count, America Online (AOL) had something like 70 billion subscribers. Okay, we may be off by a few billion, but there's no debating the popularity of the service. With AOL for Palm OS, you can access your e-mail account(s) as well as some of the service's more popular areas. Get it from within AOL at keyword **Anywhere**, or on the Web at **www.aol.com/anywhere/ index.html**.

NOTE   *Hey, guess what! AOL for Palm is available for both Windows and Macintosh. Way to go, America Online!*

13

Web Browsing with the Palm

Typically, Palm-powered PDAs don't come with any built-in Web browsing software (the exception is Palm smartphones and connected organizers, which include browsers because they're wireless devices right out of the box).

That's okay—you can add your own. The most popular browsers include Eudora Internet Suite, AvantGo, Blazer, and Xiino. All of them are available for download from PalmGear.com. Some—like AvantGo and Eudora—are free, but Blazer and Xiino offer more features.

Surfing Limitations

Once you have a browser installed and some sort of modem (either wired or wireless) attached, you're ready to start surfing. Surfing with your PDA is radically different than surfing with your PC, though. Keep these limitations in mind as you start exploring the Internet with your Palm:

- **Graphics are much more limited**   It doesn't take a rocket scientist to deduce this one, but you don't have a lot of room to work with. Most browsers can squeeze large graphics to fit on the small screen, but it can make them hard to see clearly.

- **Color**   Unless you have a color model, you'll be looking at everything in shades of gray. The good news? Most browsers support color, so armed with the right handheld model, you can surf the Web in full color.

Essential Web Sites

There are a bunch of Web sites that are dedicated to the Palm OS family of handheld devices. If you're surfing for good Palm-related content, give some of these sites a try:

- The best collection of downloadable Palm software on the Internet can be found at **www.palmgear.com**.

- There are lively discussion forums, news, feature stories, and reviews at **www.pdabuzz.com**, a site that caters to all kinds of handheld PCs.

- The only magazine that covers Palm OS handhelds exclusively, **www.hhcmag.com** is a good source of news about your Palm.

- You can find news, product reviews, software, and other Palm stuff at **www.handango.com**.

- Thanks to news and message boards, **www.palmpower.com** is an interesting place to stop for Palm information.

- Your home for Web clipping apps is **www.palm.net**.

- **Connection speeds are much lower**   Your overall Web surfing experience may be a lot more sluggish than you're used to, especially if your desktop PC has a corporate T1 line or some other form of high-speed surfing. Palm modems—especially wireless ones—are quite slow and it can take minutes, not seconds, for a Web page to display.

- **Don't download**   The Palm isn't really equipped to handle ordinary Mac or Windows applications or data files—so don't bother trying to download anything. (Actually, you can download Palm apps and Web clipping apps using the Xiino browser.)

Channel Surf with AvantGo

Buy all the modems you want—the Web just doesn't fit on a 2-inch screen. Enter AvantGo, a free service that not only delivers Web-based content to your Palm, but also formats it to look pretty (and readable). With every HotSync, the software downloads your preselected channels—everything from news and stock reports to driving directions and movie showtimes—using your computer's modem to ferry the data. Pretty slick—and did we mention it's free?

Set Up AvantGo

To install the AvantGo software, visit the AvantGo Web site and download the software. Install it per the directions in the package and configure your AvantGo account. You'll need to set up an AvantGo account, complete with username and password.

NOTE   *AvantGo is included on the installation CD-ROM with some Palm devices.*

13

    To set up the channels you want to transfer to your Palm, go to the AvantGo Web site and log in. The AvantGo site should look something like the one shown in Figure 13-6, in which your currently selected channels appear on the left in a column called Your Channels. You can browse the AvantGo Web site and click on any channel you like to add it to your personal AvantGo hot list.

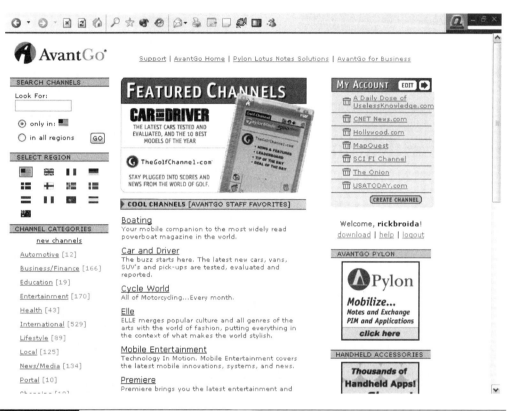

FIGURE 13-6   AvantGo lets you transfer Web "channels" to your Palm for offline reading.

Edit Your Channel Content

Most AvantGo channels are configured to work well on a handheld device with limited memory. Sometimes you might want to customize the way channel content is delivered to your Palm, though. Take *The Onion*, for instance—Dave loves to read this news parody Web site each week while eating lunch, but the site is so large that many of the stories often aren't downloaded to the Palm in their entirety. The solution? Dave increased the Maximum Channel Size from the default of 100KB to 500KB so it all fits on his Palm. To edit your channels as cleverly as Dave, open the AvantGo Web page, log in, and click on a channel in the My Account box. You should see the Channel Properties page, as in Figure 13-7. Make your changes and click the Save Channel Changes button.

Use AvantGo on Your Palm

While we've spent a lot of time talking about configuring AvantGo channels on your desktop's Web browser, in truth all the fun stuff really happens on your Palm. Start

AvantGo on your Palm and you should see all the channels that you selected and configured on the Web.

FIGURE 13-7   You can modify the amount of data contained in each channel from this page.

Wireless Channels

AvantGo is mainly known for its offline browsing capabilities, but it also supports both real-time browsing in the form of Web page access and wireless channels. Visit the Wireless section of the AvantGo site and you'll find a collection of channels that are interactive when used with a wireless device like the Earthlink Minstrel modem. You can request real-time stock quotes, find movies playing in your area, get map data, and more. In fact, here are some of our favorite wireless channels:

- **White Pages and Yellow Pages**   The "killer app" for wireless handheld devices! You can look up people and companies using this channel—just enter their name and city to get an address and phone number. Or, if you already have a phone number but need the street address, you can search that way too.

- **Hollywood.com**   This channel lets you find movie listings, theaters, and show times for movies wherever you happen to be.

- **Trip.com**   Want to know details about a flight—like its airspeed, flight path, and arrival time? This channel lets you find that data.

NOTE   *If you don't see any channels in AvantGo, it's probably because you haven't HotSynced yet.*

To use AvantGo, just tap on one of the channels in the My Channels list. You can read text, view pictures, and drill deeper into the channel by tapping on links. There are two navigational tools built into each and every channel page:

- Tap the navigational arrows to move forward and backward through the current channel.
- Tap the Home icon to return to the My Channels list.

In addition to reading cached channels on your Palm, AvantGo can also be used to open live Web pages if you have a modem attached. To do that, follow these steps:

1. Start AvantGo.

2. Choose Channels | Connect from the menu. This tells AvantGo to activate your modem.

3. Choose Channels | Open Page from the menu. Enter the URL you would like to visit and tap OK.

NOTE   *Some users prefer using a program called Plucker (available at **PalmGear.com**, of course) instead of AvantGo. Feel free to try it out, but be advised that you'll need to edit the channels manually in a text file—not a very friendly way to set up the program.*

All About Bluetooth

Bluetooth is a short-range wireless technology that allows devices to communicate with each other up to a distance of about 30 feet. That's really just a fancy way of saying that Bluetooth is a technology designed to replace connection cables. By using Bluetooth, handheld gadgets like your Palm and cell phone can communicate with each other without wires and without even getting in line-of-sight with each other.

That said, Bluetooth is a new technology that is just starting to hit the streets. When we wrote this chapter, no Palm devices were yet shipping with Bluetooth built in, but Bluetooth add-ons are available to turn many PDAs into Bluetooth gadgets (see the next section, "Adding Bluetooth to Your Palm").

The first applications designed for Bluetooth are wireless headsets that let you talk on your mobile phone and provide Internet access solutions for your Palm via a mobile phone. You can do other stuff with Bluetooth as well, like print, access a LAN, and even send digital images from Bluetooth cameras—but those applications won't get real popular for a while. For the moment, Bluetooth is all about making your PDA and cell phone communicate wirelessly.

Adding Bluetooth to Your Palm

Interested in Bluetooth? There are a number of Bluetooth peripherals that enable Palm devices for wireless communication. Here's a handy list:

- **Palm Bluetooth Card**   This $129 device is an SD card that fits in any Palm with the standard SD memory card slot. It's available directly from Palm.

- **Blade**   Red-M's $199 add-ons are available both as a sled for the Palm V series and a Springboard model for the Handspring Visor.
- **BlueM**   TDK sells a sled-style Bluetooth adapter for Palm m-series PDAs (or any model with the Palm universal connector).

So, suppose you have a Palm m515 and you add a Bluetooth adapter. What can you do with it? Right now, the killer app is connecting your Palm to a Bluetooth mobile phone to get Internet access. That means you need to get a phone with built-in Bluetooth. Sony Ericsson, Motorola, and Nokia have a small array of phones to choose from.

Once your Bluetooth adapter is installed, here are some of the things you can do with your Palm:

- ■ **Dial the phone**   Just tap on a phone number to dial the phone from your Palm's Address Book. Red-M includes a special Bluetooth-aware Address Book for dialing the phone with a Blade module. If you have a Palm running OS 4 or higher, though, you'll find that you can dial directly from the built-in Address Book.

- ■ **Access the Internet for Web and E-mail**   Once you properly configure your Bluetooth card to recognize your Bluetooth cell phone and activate dial-up Internet access, you can use your Bluetooth connection like any PDA modem to access the Internet.

- ■ **Print**   Armed with a Bluetooth-aware printer driver, you can print to a Bluetooth-enabled desktop printer. Epson, for instance, sells a Bluetooth Print Adapter that works with the Epson C80 inkjet printer. Likewise, you can get MPI Tech's Bluetooth Printer Adapter to print from a number of printers, including HPs. There are a few Bluetooth printer drivers you can choose from, including BtPrint (from IS/Complete) and PrintBoy (from Bachmann Software).

- ■ **Chat**   The Palm Bluetooth Card comes with whiteboard and chat software that lets several people collaborate from up to 30 feet away from each other.

Where to Find It

Web Site	Address	What's There
Palm.Net	**www.palm.net**	Service coverage maps, additional Web clipping apps, instructions on creating clipping apps
Handango	**www.handango.com**	Web clipping apps (and lots of other Palm software)
PalmGear H.Q.	**www.palmgear.com**	Web clipping apps (and lots of other Palm software)
MPI Tech	**www.mpitech.com**	Bluetooth Printer Adapter
Epson	**www.epson.com**	Bluetooth Print Adapter
IS/Complete	**www.iscomplete**	Bluetooth printer driver
Bachmann Software	**www.bachmannsoftware.com**	Bluetooth printer driver
AvantGo	**www.avantgo.com**	AvantGo browser and channel management

Chapter 14

Your Palm as a PC Replacement

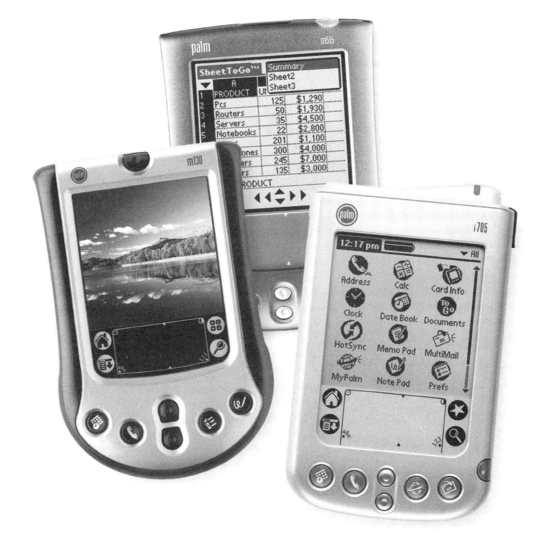

How to...

- 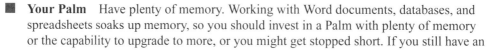 Use your Palm as a complete business application computer
- Read and edit Word and Excel documents on your Palm
- Distinguish between Palm Doc and Word .doc files
- Import Palm documents into Microsoft Word
- Generate graphs and charts on the Palm
- View Adobe Acrobat files
- Project PowerPoint slides via your Palm
- Print to wireless printers
- Print to serial and parallel printers

The core applications that come with your Palm are fine for many people—they offer all the basic functionality you need to stay on top of contact information and schedules while on the go. But, as you've already seen in this book, your Palm can do so much more. In fact, it's possible to use your Palm as a full-fledged alternative PC, capable of running applications as varied as a word processor, a spreadsheet, and a database program.

Why on Earth would you want to do that? Well, which would you rather carry around—a Palm that fits in your pocket or a seven-pound laptop? Which is easier to store in a hotel room? Which is more easily stolen? Which lasts longer on a set of batteries? We think you get the idea. Obviously, using a suite of "office" applications on your Palm isn't for everyone and won't work all the time. After all, a Palm has a limited amount of storage space, so you can't fit a whole lot of documents on it. And most Palm document editors don't support an extremely extensive array of formatting options. So, even if you exchange documents with your desktop apps, your text and format options could be somewhat limited. But, if you're intrigued by the thought of leaving your PC at home and traveling only with a Palm, then read on. This chapter is all about creating the perfect Palm office.

Building the Perfect Beast

No, we weren't really big fans of that Don Henley solo album either. But that does describe your Palm if you want to outfit it to be a mobile office, complete with office applications.

The name of the game when it comes to creating a Palm office is convenience and compatibility. What good is it, for instance, to generate documents on your Palm if they're not readable by the word processor on your PC? And why bother trying to do office-style work on your Palm if you can't do it easily, efficiently, and in all the apps and formats you're used to on your desktop? With this in mind, here's a list of products you should have if you plan to do serious work on your Palm:

- **Your Palm**   Have plenty of memory. Working with Word documents, databases, and spreadsheets soaks up memory, so you should invest in a Palm with plenty of memory or the capability to upgrade to more, or you might get stopped short. If you still have an old 2MB Palm, consider upgrading to a modern device with 8MB or 16MB. We also recommend investing in expansion memory—like an SD card or Memory Stick—if your PDA is compatible.

■ **A keyboard**   As much as we love Graffiti, the fact remains you'll hate writing long documents or entering data in a spreadsheet with the stylus alone. Invest in a Palm keyboard. Many compact, yet comfortable, keyboards are available for Palm-powered PDAs. See Chapter 20 for a rundown of the best ones.

■ **Document reader**   If you mainly need to read documents on your Palm and don't care about creating or editing them, then you can get by with a document reader like the Palm Reader, TealDoc, or AportisDoc. These programs let you read large documents that don't fit in the Palm's Memo Pad. Thousands of books and other documents are in the DOC format, which you can download and read on your Palm. While certainly a popular use for the Palm, this isn't all that interesting from an office-application point of view. What you probably want is a full-featured office application—or, in other words, a document editor.

■ **Office suite**   If you want to create new documents or edit files you made in Microsoft Word, then a simple document reader like AportisDoc won't be enough. You should try an office suite instead. Although these applications for the Palm aren't quite full-featured suites—at least not in the sense that Microsoft Office on the desktop is—some programs deliver sophisticated tools like spelling checkers, rich text formatting, charting tools for your spreadsheet, and more. Most importantly, these programs break through the file-size limit imposed by the Memo Pad and let you edit documents of almost unlimited length that can be shared with Word and Excel.

■ **Adobe Acrobat**   If your office makes extensive use of PDF files, you should have an Acrobat reader on your Palm so you can view those documents on the go.

■ **Database**   Yes, database applications are available even for the Palm. A slew of popular programs are available for the Palm that let you create new databases from scratch, and most even let you import existing databases from programs like Access, FileMaker, and other ODBC-complaint applications. Some of the most popular database engines for the Palm include HanDBase, JFile, MobileDB, ThinkDB, and dbNow. FileMaker also has its own PDA "companion" to Filemaker, called (not too surprisingly) FileMaker Mobile. If you're a FileMaker user, FileMaker Mobile might be all you need.

14

Top Ten Reasons to Use a Palm

Dave: With all the neat office-like applications available for Palm devices, it got us thinking. What are the top ten uses for a handheld computer? So, here goes (and if you imagine us reading this off blue cards at your local book store, you've pretty much experienced a *How to Do Everything with Your Palm Handheld* book signing):

10. New excuse at work: I was writing the weekly status report, but I dropped it and it broke.

9. Too old for a Game Boy, but can still play Pac Man on your Palm.

8. Snap-in gadgets for the Visor make you look like a spy.

7. As a *Star Trek: The Next Generation* fan, you like to pretend you're an Enterprise crewmember on an away mission.

6. As a *Star Trek: The Original Series* fan, you like to pretend you're an Enterprise crewmember in a landing party.

You know, for me, the funny thing is you have to be a *Star Trek* fan to even appreciate the difference between those last two items.

Rick: For me, it's funny to hear Dave describe any of his half of the list as "funny."

5. Gives you a great pickup line: "Hey, let's HotSync!"

4. When tipping the pizza guy, now you can calculate 15 percent of $36.87 to the exact penny.

3. No one can tell you're reading Monica Lewinsky's biography.

2. You can look busy in a board meeting when you're actually playing a game of SimCity.

1. They don't put a single penny into Bill Gates's pocket!

Dealing with Documents

If you're like most business travelers, you're used to carting a laptop around with you to edit Word documents. If you have a 14-inch or 15-inch display, then you know what it's like trying to get the laptop screen open in the cramped space on an airplane seat. Heck, sometimes we can't get it open far enough to read what we're typing.

Thankfully, there's an easier solution. Your Palm—combined with a keyboard—can take the place of your laptop for text entry. You can even synchronize specific Word documents with your Palm, edit them on the road, and update your desktop PC with the latest versions of your work when you get home.

Understanding the Doc Format

All Doc files aren't created alike. Specifically, when Palm users talk about Doc files—text documents in the Doc format—they're not gabbing about Microsoft Word's .doc format but, instead, about a text format originally popularized by a program called AportisDoc. These days, programs like TealDoc (from TealPoint) and Palm's own Palm Reader are generally considered the de facto standard among Palm text readers today. While any Doc file can be read by almost any Doc reader/editor for the Palm (and vice versa), the Doc format is totally incompatible with the version used by Microsoft Word. On the plus side, you can generally get converters for most of these readers that convert desktop .doc to Palm Doc files and back again.

Using an Office Suite

Pocket PC users have one small advantage over Palm users—a Microsoft-branded office suite that includes Pocket Word and Pocket Excel. People can trust those apps to be compatible with Microsoft Office on the desktop.

What a lot of people don't realize, though, is that there are several excellent Office-compatible suites for the Palm. Most Palm models come with one right in the box, in fact: Documents to Go, from DataViz. If your Palm-powered PDA didn't come with an office suite—or you want to try another, you'll be happy to know you can choose from three popular suites:

- **Documents to Go (www.dataviz.com)**   Documents to Go is quite popular by virtue of the fact that Palm has chosen to put it in the box of every new Palm model it sells. In addition to a word processor (Word to Go) and spreadsheet (Sheets to Go), the Professional edition of Documents to Go includes the capability to view (but not edit) PowerPoint slides and Adobe Acrobat (PDF) files.

- **Iambic Office (www.iambic.com)**   Comprised of FastWriter and TinySheet, these programs offer Word and Excel connectivity for your Palm. In addition, the suite includes *Iambic Mail,* an e-mail client that lets you synchronize messages with your

14

desktop e-mail program or check mail on the go with a modem. Iambic Mail uses FastWriter and TinySheet to let you read Word and Excel attachments in e-mail.

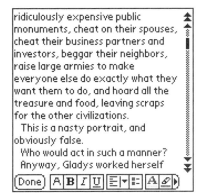

■ **Quickoffice (www.cesinc.com)** This suite includes Quickword and Quicksheet for reading and editing Word and Excel documents. *Quickword* has its own thesaurus and spelling checker and you can install custom fonts as well. *Quickoffice* also enables Palm users to collaborate wirelessly on documents via cell phones and modems—so you can invite other people to view and make changes to a document, even if you're in different cities.

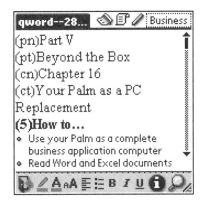

> **NOTE** *Older versions of Documents To Go don't support document editing. They simply provided the capability to view Microsoft Office files. If you don't have Documents To Go 3.0 or higher, consider upgrading to a different office suite.*

> **TIP** *If you don't want the entire suite, you can usually buy the word processor and spreadsheet separately by visiting the vendor's web site. Cutting Edge Software sells Quickword all by itself, for instance, if you don't need Quicksheet.*

Transferring Documents Between the Palm and Desktop

No matter which suite you choose, they all work more or less the same way: you use a desktop application to manage the documents you want to work with on the Palm. Just drag the document you want to move into the suite manager (the following shows several of them) and it'll be copied to the Palm at the next HotSync. When you make a change to the document on either the Palm or the desktop, it'll be synchronized after the following HotSync, keeping the two documents exactly the same.

TIP *Bachmann Software's* FilePoint *is a file management program for the Palm that lets you install documents from the desktop as well. So, if you have several different Office-style applications, you can transfer files on the Palm to all of them using only one program—*FilePoint—*instead of loading each office suite's desktop component separately.*

If you prefer not to synchronize your Palm documents with their cousins on the desktop, that's fine as well. In each suite manager, you can disable synchronization and select familiar options like Handheld overwrites, Desktop overwrites, and Do nothing, as you can see in Figure 14-1.

What if you create a new document from scratch on the Palm? No problem. On the next HotSync after you create the document, you'll find it's been synchronized with the desktop. To find it, simply open your suite manager software and double-click the new file. The file will automatically open in Word.

Working with Documents and Spreadsheets

If you want to leave your laptop at home and only carry a PDA, being able to read and edit Word and Excel files on the go is essential. Any of the suites we've already mentioned will work and if all you care about is text, you have a fourth excellent option as well—a program from Blue Nomad called WordSmith (pictured in the following illustration). WordSmith doesn't come as part of a suite with a spreadsheet. Instead, *WordSmith* is a stand-alone word processor for the Palm that,

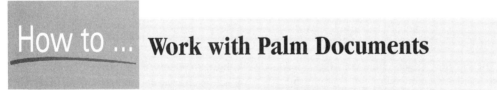

FIGURE 14-1 Most office suites give you a lot of control over how documewnts are synchronized with the PDA and desktop.

How to ... Work with Palm Documents

In a nutshell, here's what you need to know to work with text documents on the Palm:

- To create or edit long documents on your Palm, you need a program like Documents To Go, Quickoffice, Iambic Office, or WordSmith.

- On the desktop, open your office suite's manager application.

- Click the button to add a file, or simply drag-and-drop a document into the suite's manager's window.

- Close the program, and then HotSync to transfer the files to the Palm.

- Edit the files on your Palm.

- HotSync to carry the changes you made to the Palm back to the desktop versions of the affected files.

like Quickoffice, includes font support, a spelling checker, a thesaurus, and sophisticated formatting controls. Many users choose WordSmith as their word processor of choice, especially if they don't also need a spreadsheet.

While most Palm word processors try hard to preserve all the formatting in your document, remember, these programs do it with varying levels of success. You might find, for instance, that group annotations or graphics like "boxes" around text could be stripped out when the files are synchronized back to the PC. As a consequence, word processing on the Palm is often best reserved for documents with fairly conservative levels of formatting. In addition, some word processors have more formatting features than others. Documents to Go, for instance, might be popular, but it can't hold a candle to WordSmith and Quickword when it comes to embedding formatted text in your documents.

The bottom line here is this: because all office suites have a free trial period, we recommend installing all of them and seeing which one you like best.

CAUTION *Many word processors on the Palm don't support some advanced formatting features and they're stripped away when you synchronize documents. When we tested these programs, Documents to Go did best with wacky stuff like text with Track Changes. Quickoffice and TinyWriter made a real mess out of the text. Documents to Go keeps the desktop version of the document intact even when it has truly unusual formatting elements (like images) that don't display on the Palm.*

14

Better Software for Bigger Screens

If you feel constrained by the anemic width of the Palm screen, you're not alone. That's why many new Palm devices (especially models from Sony and HandEra) offer dramatically higher resolutions. When you try out office suites, be sure to look for software that takes advantage of the higher resolution in your new handheld. Right now, we found WordSmith and Quickoffice took advantage of higher-resolution Palm screens. And, because these applications also support a variety of fonts and font sizes, you can pack a lot more data on the screen—provided you have strong enough eyesight to see all those little letters.

Charts and Graphs on the Palm

Spreadsheets are often reported as the most popular PC-based application in the history of computers (we're not sure who they talked to—personally, we'd vote for games). And like milk and cereal, or guitars and rock 'n roll, nothing goes with spreadsheets quite like charts and graphs. It makes sense, then, that you might want to view your spreadsheet data visually in the form of charts and graphs, even on your Palm. You're in luck: both Iambic Office and Quickoffice come with their own spreadsheet graphing tools. As you can see in the following illustration, you can make some attractive graphs using these programs.

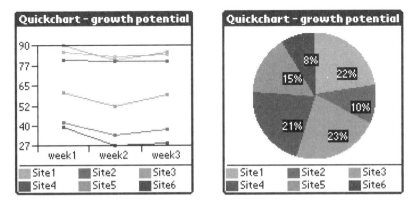

Neither of these programs is particularly intuitive, though, because they run from within their parent spreadsheet app. You won't get anywhere by tapping on TinyChart or Quickchart directly. Nonetheless, getting started with these graphing apps is easy. If you use Imabic Office, open TinySheet, select a range of cells to graph, and choose Cell | Chart from the menu. If you want to embed a chart within the spreadsheet, tap on an empty cell and choose Cell | Insert Chart instead. Then select a range of cells and draw the Enter gesture with Graffiti. Double-tap the inserted chart to view it in TinyChart.

In Quickoffice, open a spreadsheet in QuickSheet and tap on an empty cell. Then choose Chart(Range) from the list of functions. Select a range of cells for your chart and tap in another cell or use the Enter gesture. Your chart is created. To see the finished chart, double-tap the cell that now says *CHART*. QuickChart launches, and you can modify the chart and see it in all its grayscale glory.

Adobe Acrobat on the Palm

In most offices, Word and Excel pop up pretty often—but Adobe Acrobat files, also known by their file extension as PDF files, are incredibly popular as well. That's because PDFs are self-contained, fancy-looking text-and-graphic documents that display exactly the same, no matter what kind of computer you view them on. They also can't be edited, so you can distribute a PDF secure in the knowledge that some clown in room 234 won't make changes to your handiwork.

That's great but, until recently, you couldn't view them on the Palm. Today, several ways exist to display Adobe Acrobat files on your PDA. Here are two of the better ones:

■ **Documents to Go Professional** has its own PDF viewer. On the downside, this viewer strips out graphics, so it's only useful for text-based documents.

■ **Adobe Acrobat Reader for Palm** is a free program from Adobe that enables you to download PDF files to your Palm. This program lets you choose to include or strip out graphics, so you can save memory on your PDA by leaving out nonessential graphics or by leaving them in if they're needed to understand the document.

You can find other programs to do this as well—including Microbat reader, Ansyr Primer PDF Viewer, RichReader, and PDF2Doc.

PowerPoint on Your Palm

The last piece of the puzzle is PowerPoint. If you lug your laptop around so you can deliver slideshows on the road, well, we have some good news for you. Your Palm is capable of pumping slides directly to a projector—in their entire $1,024 \times 768$, full-color glory.

Depending on your needs and which PDA model you own, you have a few choices:

■ **Documents to Go Professional**   This program just won't go away! It seems like we've mentioned it a dozen times in this chapter alone. The professional version of DTG includes a PowerPoint viewer. You can't broadcast these slides on a projector or even edit them once they're on your device, but you can use this viewer to view the slides in both a text-only and graphic mode.

■ **Margi Presenter-to-Go**   If you want to plug your Palm into a projector, get Presenter-to-Go. This product is available in three versions: for the Handspring Visor (pictured in the following), as a CompactFlash card for the HandEra 330, and for the Palm m-series (which uses the Palm's standard SD memory slot). You can fit hundreds of slides in memory. They project in high-res and full-color, and you can avoid all the hassles that go with setting up, booting, carrying, and managing a laptop.

14

Printing from Your Palm

The ultimate handheld PC would probably look a lot like the Palm, but with one important difference: it would have a paper-thin printer embedded inside, enabling you to print anything you see on the screen. While that's mere science fiction for the time being, this doesn't mean you can't print stuff from a Palm. Quite the contrary: armed with a print driver, you can send a wide variety of documents from your Palm to a desktop printer or to a portable, pocket-sized printer.

To print anything from your Palm, you need to add a print driver. Several are available and selecting one isn't as easy as it sounds. You need to consider three ingredients:

■ Your operating system. Some print drivers require at least OS 4.0.

■ What you want to print. Some print drivers only print data from the Palm's four core apps, while others can print documents from certain office suites.

■ What kind of printer you want to print to. If you have your eye on a compact, battery-operated portable printer, you'll need to find a print driver that works with that printer.

This chart outlines some key data for the most common Palm print drivers:

	Printers	Software
InStep Print	Prints to almost all portable and desktop printers	The broadest range of document types, including Documents to Go, Quickoffice, WordSmith, and the Palm's own built-in applications.
IrPrint	Prints to almost all portable and desktop printers	Supports Documents to Go, WordSmith, and other apps. Has some problems printing from Handspring Visors, though.
PalmPrint	Supports most portable and desktop printers	Prints from the Palm's core apps, as well as a few third-party programs, including Quickword.
PrintBoy	Only prints 8.5 × 11-inch pages, which means it doesn't work with extremely compact printers like the Sipix Pocket Printer	Largely prints only from the Palm's core applications.

As you can see, getting a good match with your Palm device, the software you want to print, and the printer you want to use can be tricky. Be sure to visit the web site of each of these print-driver vendors to check their latest list of compatible programs and printers.

Infrared Printers for Your Palm

The easiest way to print from your Palm to a nearby printer is via infrared. Your Palm's IR port (the same one you can use to beam apps and data to other PDAs) can communicate directly with

Palms Speak "Laptop"

Technically, IrDA stands for the Infrared Data Association, which is only a bunch of companies that make IR-enabled products. More important, though, *IrDA* represents the industry-standard infrared port you can find on most laptops, handheld PCs, and printers with IR ports. If you find a printer with an IrDA port, chances are excellent it'll work with one of the Palm's print drivers.

compatible printers. A small handful of lightweight portable and IR-enabled printers are around. If you like the idea of printing wirelessly from your Palm or if you travel frequently and want to print from wherever you happen to be, look into one of these:

Manufacturer	Printer	Comments
Canon	BJC-50	Lightweight mobile printer
	BJC-80	Lightweight mobile printer
Citizen	PN-60i	Point-of-sale printer
Datamax	E-3202	Desktop thermal printer
Hewlett-Packard	LaserJet 6P	Desktop laser printer
	LaserJet 6MP	Desktop laser printer
	LaserJet 2100	Desktop laser printer
Monarch	6015	Handheld printer that fits around the Palm III
Pentax	PocketJet 200	Lightweight mobile printer, compatible with IrDA adapter
Sipix	Pocket Printer A6	Handheld portable printer

14

Bluetooth Printing

If you have a Bluetooth adapter for your Palm (or you have a model with Bluetooth built in), you can print wirelessly to a Bluetooth-enabled printer. As we wrote this chapter, our Bluetooth options in the printing world were quite limited, but we expect that will slowly start to change over the next few months.

The best example of an honest-to-goodness, working Bluetooth printer is Epson's C80 inkjet printer. It's Bluetooth-compatible and, by adding the Epson Bluetooth Adapter (a small gadget that plugs into the back of the printer), you can send print jobs to the printer from up to about 30 feet away.

Printers for Your Pocket

If you expect to do a lot of printing and want to have easy access to a portable printer, you have a few excellent choices. Forget about having to track down a desktop printer when you're on the road—just carry your printer in your pocket. We highly recommend the following three models:

- The Sipix Pocket Printer A6. This is a lightweight printer that measures only 6 × 4 × 1 inches. It's literally small enough to fit in your hand. It uses a thermal process to print on a roll of paper at about 400dpi. The Pocket Printer runs on four AA batteries and has both a serial interface and an IrDA port, which means you can print wirelessly.

- The Pentax PocketJet is a bit longer—it's 10 × 2 × 1 inches and uses thermal imaging to print 300dpi on either sheets or rolls of paper. The Pentax might be bigger, but it lets you print real letter-sized documents. It, too, uses serial and IrDA, and it uses AC power or internal rechargeable batteries for power.

- The Monarch 6015 is a clever thermal printer that wraps around the Palm III, giving you a complete Palm and printing solution in one handheld package. It runs on four AA batteries and prints at 200dpi on 2-inch-wide rolls, much like a restaurant receipt.

Printing to a Parallel or Serial Printer

What if you don't have access to an infrared printer? That's when things can get dicey. If you own a serial port printer (such as any Apple ImageWriter), then plug the Palm's HotSync cradle into the printer and, with the Palm docked, send jobs to the printer.

Most Windows users don't have serial printers, though. They use parallel printers. In that case, you need a special serial-to-parallel converter (available from Stevens Creek, the manufacturer of PalmPrint).

You have another option as well. The *PrintBoy InfraReady Adapter* from Bachmann Software is a small plug that fits into the parallel port of any printer. A small IR port turns the printer into an IR-ready device that you can use with your Palm. It's small and light, so you can carry it with you when you travel.

NOTE   *It doesn't make any difference if you print via the PC or via your Palm—the print quality is identical and everything prints out fine on standard 8.5 × 11–inch paper. If it's more convenient to print via your Palm, go for it!*

Where to Find It

Web Site	Address	What's There
Stevens Creek	**www.stevenscreek.com**	PalmPrint
DataViz	**www.dataviz.com**	Documents To Go
Blue Nomad	**www.bluenomad.com**	WordSmith
Cutting Edge Software	**www.cesinc.com**	Quickoffice
Iambic Software	**www.iambic.com**	Iambic Office
IS/Complete	**www.iscomplete.com**	IRPrint and other print drivers
InStep Print	**www.instepgroup.com**	InStep Print
Bachmann Software	**www.bachmannsoftware.com**	PrintBoy and the InfraReady Adapter

14

Chapter 15

Hacks and Other Utilities

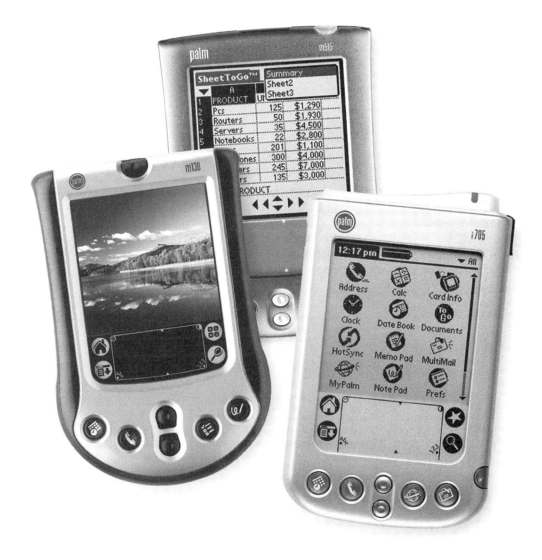

How to…

- Install and use Hacks
- Make capital letters the easy way
- Automatically correct spelling errors
- Drag and drop text
- Use the Palm buttons to load multiple applications
- Automatically remove duplicate entries from your databases
- Access "hidden" Palm memory
- Manage and beam applications
- Choose a launcher
- Protect yourself from Palm OS viruses
- Expand the Palm's clipboard
- Create your own Palm OS software
- Speed up your handheld

When you hear the word "utilities," you probably think of your monthly electric bill or those two worthless Monopoly properties (hey, $15 isn't gonna break anybody's bank). In the world of computers and Palm devices, however, utilities are software programs that add capabilities and fix problems. They're power tools, though not necessarily limited to power users.

In this chapter, we tell you about some cool and worthwhile Palm utilities. When we're done, you'll find yourself with a reliable backup that can overcome any data-loss disaster, a way to drag-and-drop text, a time-saving way to write capital letters, and lots more. Utilities may sound boring and technical, but they're actually fun, easy to use, and extremely practical.

X-Master

The mother of all Palm utilities, *X-Master* is what separates the men from the boys, the women from the girls. It's a tool Tim Allen would love, as it allows Palm devices to reach beyond their limits, to achieve "more power!" And, it's a tool many users come to find indispensable.

CAUTION   *As you learned in Chapter 10, Hacks won't work in Palm Powered handhelds equipped with OS 5. Software developers will no doubt introduce new versions of their products that support the new OS, but make sure to investigate compatibility before you install a Hack on your handheld. An unsupported bit of code could wreak serious havoc.*

What X-Master Does

Technically speaking, X-Master is an "operating system extension manager." By itself, it serves no function. But it enables the use of *Hacks*—little programs that extend the capabilities of your Palm device. Forget the negative connotations usually associated with "hacking"—these programs are here to help, not harm.

If you want to run them, you must first download and install X-Master. See Chapter 4 for information on installing programs like this—it's applicable to the Hacks you'll be downloading as well.

CAUTION   *Because Hacks tinker directly with the Palm OS, they can create the occasional glitch. The more Hacks you have installed and running, the greater the likelihood of some sort of problem. The most common is your Palm device crashing, which is usually more of an annoyance than anything else. But we encourage anyone who's working with X-Master to perform regular backups, preferably with a utility like BackupBuddy (discussed later in this chapter). This way, if the unthinkable happens (such as a total loss of data), you're protected.*

As you venture out into the world of Palm software, you may discover other Hack managers. For instance, there's *HackMaster,* the granddaddy that started this whole crazy Hack business. There's also *TealMaster,* the most robust and feature-rich of all the Hack managers. But we're partial to X-Master because we've used it extensively and it has just the features we need. Plus, it's freeware—unlike TealMaster, which costs $9.95 (still a great deal).

How to Use It

Launching X-Master is no different from launching any other program—you just tap its icon. But, as previously noted, the software is useless without any Hacks loaded. Therefore, to help you learn to use this utility, we're going to walk you through the installation of one of our favorite Hacks.

It's called *MiddleCaps,* and it saves you from having to write the Graffiti upstroke every time you want to create an uppercase letter. Instead, you simply write the letter so it crosses the invisible line between the letter and number sides of the Graffiti area. We find this enables us to write much more quickly and naturally.

MiddleCaps is freeware, as many Hacks are, so you can download and use it free of charge. (A note of appreciation e-mailed to the author is always nice.) You can find MiddleCaps at PalmGear H.Q., among other sites. Let's get it running on your Palm device.

15

1. Download MiddleCaps and install it on your Palm. You won't find an icon for it in the Applications screen. The only real evidence of Hacks appears in X-Master.

2. Tap the X-Master icon to load the utility and you'll see MiddleCaps listed.

```
X-Master
☐ MiddleCapsHack
☑ ScreenShot
☐ TealEcho 2.41
☐ AfterBurner Hack




( Details... )   ( Info )   ( Configure )
```

3. Notice the empty box to the left of the name. Tap it with your stylus and you'll see a checkmark appear. That means the Hack is now enabled. If you want to disable it, just tap the box again. (For purposes of our tutorial, please leave it enabled.)

4. Notice the Configure button at the bottom of the screen. Tap it to set up MiddleCaps (a one-time procedure).

5. You're now in the MiddleCaps Preferences screen, where you can tweak a few of the program's settings. For now, check the box marked "Caps on crossing." This means a capital letter will appear whenever you write a character that crosses between the letter and number sides of the Graffiti area. You can test it by tapping to place your cursor on the line near the bottom of the screen, and then doing some sample writing.

```
MiddleCaps Preferences  ⓘ
☑ Caps on crossing      ( OK )
☐ Bypass AutoShift
☐ Disable Keyboard      ( Cancel )
Use the arrows below to set left
and right uppercase zones in the
Graffiti area. Test your settings
using the edit field.

I..........................................................

◀▶ I          I◀▶              ↑
```

Tap OK to return to the main X-Master screen. That's it! MiddleCaps is now enabled and will work in all Palm applications—even third-party ones.

How to ... **Beam Hacks to Other Users**

X-Master has the enviable capability to beam Hacks directly to other users (see Chapter 4 for more information on beaming). But before you start, make sure the recipient has X-Master (or HackMaster or another Hack manager). If they don't, you'll need to beam a copy of X-Master before you beam any Hacks. However, X-Master doesn't include the option of beaming itself. For that, you must return to the Apps screen and tap Menu | App | Beam. Choose X-Master from the list, and then tap the Beam button. Now you can return to X-Master and beam some Hacks. Highlight the one you want to share, and then tap Menu | Extensions | Beam.

What about those other two buttons at the bottom of the X-Master screen? You can tap Details to get version information and other notes about the Hack or tap Info to get the Hack's "splash screen."

Important Notes About X-Master

You need to abide by a few rules of thumb when using X-Master on your Palm device, all of them intended to keep things running smoothly:

- ■ If you ever decide to delete a Hack from your Palm, make sure you disable it first! If you try to delete a Hack while it's still running, it could cause errors, crashes, or even data loss.

- ■ If you install two or three Hacks on your Palm, don't enable them all simultaneously. Instead, enable one at a time, making sure it works properly before enabling the next one.

- ■ If you have to reset your Palm device for any reason, a message pops up asking if you want to "reinstall your formerly active collection of system Hacks." Tap Reinstall (the equivalent of "yes") only if you're sure it wasn't a Hack that forced you to have to reset in the first place. Otherwise, tap Cancel. Then you can go back into X-Master and manually enable your Hacks again.

World's Greatest Hacks

If you were impressed by what MiddleCaps did for your Palm, wait till you get a load of some of our other favorites. Rather than list them by name, which doesn't always express what they do, we're going to list them by function. You can find all these Hacks at PalmGear H.Q.

Automatically Correct Spelling Errors

Giving Graffiti a helping hand, *CorrectHack* works like the AutoCorrect feature in Microsoft Word, automatically correcting words you frequently misspell. Alas, it doesn't have a database of its own;

15

you have to supply both the words and their correct spellings. But as you compile your list over time, you'll wind up with far fewer mistakes. And you can also use CorrectHack as shorthand for commonly used words. For instance, you write your initials, and the software automatically plugs in your full name.

Fonts…Lots and Lots of Fonts

The Palm OS comes with a whopping three fonts: regular, bold, and large. That's not nearly enough for those of us who grew up with Arial, Century Gothic, Times New Roman, and other font faves. You can have access to a boatload of typefaces if you install *FontHack 123,* which lets you replace the system fonts with fonts of your choosing. FontHack comes with just one— you'll find 20 more in the Alpha Font Collection 1.71. Both products are freeware. Beat that!

Drag and Drop Text

While you can select snippets of text by tapping and dragging your stylus, you can't drag that text to another spot and drop it in (as you can with any word processor). *TextEditHack* adds that capability to text-oriented applications like Memo Pad and even makes it easier to select text. You can double-tap to select a single word, triple-tap to select a sentence, and quadruple-tap to select all the text on the screen. Very handy.

Launch More than Four Programs with the Application Buttons

The more software you have loaded on your Palm device, the harder it becomes to hunt for the desired program icon. Enter *AppHack,* which uses two sequential presses of the application buttons to launch up to 24 programs. You needn't remember the combinations you set up—AppHack displays a cheat-sheet when you press the first button, so you can see which program will load when you press the second one. This Hack is a little confusing to work with, especially because no instructions are provided, but it sure can save time.

Enhance the Find Feature

FindHack turbocharges the Palm's Find function, remembering the last six searches you performed and letting you define up to four default searches. What's more, you can choose whether to search all installed applications, just the core apps, or only the currently loaded program. It even supports the use of wildcards—searching for "book*" would return "book," "bookmark," "bookstore," and so forth.

Look Up a Contact Without Switching Programs

While the Palm makes it easy to switch back and forth between programs, it can be a hassle to have to quit what you're doing just to look up, say, a phone number or address. *PopUp Names* pulls up your address book "on top" of the program that's currently running—and with a handy two-paned window. Thus, it's not only a timesaver, it's also a more practical way of accessing your contact list.

Improve Your Graffiti Accuracy

One of our all-time favorite hacks is *TealEcho,* which lets you see your Graffiti strokes as you write them. This "visual feedback" helps you improve your writing speed and accuracy, as it lets you see how your characters really look, as opposed to the way they're supposed to look. TealEcho (**www.tealpoint.com**) costs $11.95, but we think it's well worth the money.

Change Your Handheld's Backlight

If your handheld has a monochrome screen, you may not be wild about its method for backlighting. In Palm's early days, the entire screen would glow, with only the letters darkened. Now it's the other way around: the letters glow, but the rest of the screen stays dark. This makes the screen difficult to read unless there's little or no ambient lighting. And that's where GreenLightHack comes in. It reverses the polarity of the screen for that "old style" backlighting effect. Another freeware gem.

Liven Up Those Sound Effects

Getting tired of your handheld's boring old beeps? *TechSounds* comes with a handful of nifty audio snippets you can assign to various system functions, and enables you to download even more sound effects (**www.ecamm.com**). It also supports startup and shutdown screens, if you're into that sort of thing.

Other Utilities

X-Master works minor miracles, but it isn't the only tool you should consider owning. No Hacks can create reliable backups of your data, or give you greater flexibility in beaming software to

Protect Yourself from Too Many Hacks

If you find yourself relying on a lot of Hacks, you may want to check out a utility called *TrapWeaver* (**www.twilightedge.com**). Its sole purpose is to prevent your Palm device from crashing due to "overlapping" Hacks. In theory, it should enable you to run more Hacks simultaneously without the risk of your handheld taking a nosedive.

other users, or remove duplicate entries from your databases. And there's certainly no Hack that digs up 800K of extra memory for you to use. So read on to learn about some of the other highlights of the Palm OS utility world.

NOTE *Most of the utilities listed here can be purchased and downloaded from Handango or PalmGear H.Q.*

Backup Utilities

One of the really cool things about the Palm OS is the way it keeps a complete copy of your data on your PC. Every time you HotSync, it's like you're making a backup of your important info. If something terrible befalls your handheld—it gets lost, stolen, run over, sat on, or inexplicably wiped clean—at least you know your data lives on your PC.

That said, consider working with one or more backup utilities. Some of them are designed to improve the HotSync-backup process, while others enable you to back up key data files using "hidden" memory right inside your handheld. Of course, if your model has an expansion slot, you can make bulletproof backups using memory cards (see Chapter 13).

BackupBuddy

BackupBuddy creates a backup of every bit of data on your Palm, programs and preferences included, every time you HotSync. Doesn't the Palm OS do that? Well, yes and no. While the Palm OS does back up most of your programs and data, it doesn't necessarily catch everything. Technical details aside, if you want a 100-percent backup, BackupBuddy does the job. And if your handheld ever gets completely wiped, a regular old HotSync is all it takes to restore everything.

Version 1.5 of the program includes support for Virtual File System (VFS) media, meaning it can back up software and data stored on memory cards. (It also supports Visor Springboard modules.) On the other hand, if you're using memory media anyway, you can use it to back up your entire handheld (see Chapter 12), making BackupBuddy somewhat superfluous.

BackupPro and JBBackup

As you're about to learn in our description of FlashPro in the next section, many Palm Powered handhelds have "hidden" internal memory that can be tapped for various uses—including making backups. The benefit to this approach is major: if you're traveling and your handheld gets totally wiped (it's been known to happen), you can restore your most important data—without having to HotSync and without the need for a memory card. Call it a failsafe measure, an emergency plan, a life preserver.

Whatever you call it, it won't cost you much. For $9.95, you can purchase Handera's BackupPro or HandFort Solutions' JBBackup, both of which enable you to make backups of selected data files using your handheld's available Flash memory (again, see the FlashPro write-up for a detailed description). Of the two, we like JBBackup better because it has a few more features and supports the latest handheld models. Either way, ten bucks is a small price to pay for total peace of mind.

15

The Problem with Prequels

Palm, schmalm . . . let's talk about the really important stuff—namely, treasured sci-fi franchises that have been ruined by prequels.

Rick: First there was the colossal disappointment of *Enterprise,* the blandest, most uninteresting *Star Trek* series ever. Now, George Lucas continues to make a mockery of the *Star Wars* trilogy by serving up pabulum like *Attack of the Clones.* Maybe I'm too old, maybe I'm jaded, maybe I just expect fresh writing and decent acting, but these prequels have left me colder than a polar bear in January. They're just not *fun.* The magic is gone. And I think this is a problem inherent to the prequel formula—when you know the outcome, there's no suspense. I *know* Anakin will turn into Darth Vader in *Episode III.* For me there's no excitement in watching it happen. And don't get me started on all the ways *Enterprise* has violated *Star Trek* canon. . . . .

Dave: You, my friend, have been abducted by mind-controlling body snatchers. First, *Enterprise*: it's fresh, fun, and engaging. I enjoy the show immensely, though I'm sometimes disappointed that the stories are too "*Next Generation*-ish." It's always with the time travel, and there's often not enough "gee whiz, Batman! We're in outer space!" As for Lucas's *Episode II,* you're just off your rocker. Are you too cool to like stuff anymore? All the million-dollar book royalties gone to your head? What do you expect? To be knocked off your feet like you were watching *Star Wars* when you were 12? Not going to happen—that film is a classic, and you were lucky enough to see it for the first time at the perfect age. *Episode II* is a good film in its own right, though, and it may eventually be judged as the second best of the lot . . . unless *Episode III* really knocks our socks off, that is. Check back in the fourth edition to see what we thought of *that* movie.

"Free" Extra Memory with FlashPro

Psst! Don't let this get around, but your Palm device has been holding out on you. It has extra, hidden RAM that's just sitting around doing nothing. You see, in addition to its 2–16MB of main memory, it has a couple megabytes of Flash memory (aka the Flash ROM) where the operating system (OS) is stored. But the OS occupies only some of that space, leaving idle upwards of 1.6MB (the actual amount varies depending on your model—see the HandEra web site for a chart listing models and their available Flash memory). HandEra's *FlashPro* lets you tap into that memory, using it to store programs, data, even backups of your primary databases.

NOTE | *A few Palm devices either don't have Flash memory or don't have enough free to make FlashPro worthwhile. Among them: the Palm IIIe, Palm VII series, m100 series, and Handspring Visor series.*

Given that it ventures deep into the guts of your Palm device, FlashPro is admirably easy to use. By tapping onscreen buttons, you can see a list of the contents of main RAM and Flash memory. To move a program or database from one to the other, you simply tap to highlight it, and then tap the Move button.

FlashPro	▼ All

Name	Size
1 ATool	14.6K
2 FlashPro	41.2K
3 FPSUtil3	34.5K
4 Giraffe	19.5K
5 HackMaster	9.5K
6 HardBall	18.1K
7 JFile	58.4K
8 MineHunt	9.3K
9 Reptoids	34.7K

1743K	780K	0.0K

RAM Flash   (Move)(Delete)

NOTE   *We'd be remiss if we didn't mention Brayder Technologies' JackBack (**www.brayder.com**), a competing product that offers similar functionality. Like FlashPro, it costs $19.95.*

Extend the Clipboard with Clipper

Like most computers, Palm devices make use of a "clipboard" for copying-and-pasting text. And, like most computers, Palms can hold only one selection of text at a time in that clipboard. Clipper turns it into a repository for multiple selections, thereby expanding your copying-and-pasting capabilities. Everything you copy is retained in *Clipper* (where you can even go in and edit the text). When you want to paste something, you simply make a special Graffiti stroke to bring up the Clipper window, and then choose which snippet of text to paste.

This can come in extremely handy if you frequently write the same lengthy words or phrases. Doctors could use Clipper to create a little database of diagnoses, lawyers to maintain a selection of legal terms, and so on. Sure, you could use the Palm's own ShortCuts feature (see Chapter 14) to do much the same thing, but you'd still have to remember the shortcut keys.

How to ... # Beam Software to Another Palm User

15

Suppose you're enjoying a game of Vexed (one of our favorites), and a fellow Palm user says, "Hey, I'd like to try that!" Generous sort that you are, you agree to beam a copy of the game (which is perfectly legal because Vexed is freeware). To do so, return to the Applications screen, and then choose Menu | App | Beam. Find Vexed in the software list, tap to highlight it, then tap the Beam button. Point your Palm device at the other person's Palm device, and then wait a few seconds for the transfer to complete. Presto! You've just shared some great software—wirelessly!

Remove Duplicate Entries with UnDupe

If you routinely work with ACT!, Outlook, or some other third-party contact manager on your computer, it's not uncommon to wind up with duplicate entries on your Palm device. This can also happen if you import additional databases into Palm Desktop. Whatever the cause, the last thing you want to have to do is manually delete these duplicates from your records. *UnDupe* does it automatically, ferreting out duplicate entries in Address List, Date Book, Memo Pad, and To Do List, and then eliminating them in one fell swoop.

Manage (and Beam!) Your Files with Filez

The more you work with software, the more you need a good file manager. *Filez* lets you view, edit, copy, move, delete, and beam virtually any file on your handheld. It's not the most user-friendly program of its kind, but it does have one feature that makes up for it: it's free.

Filez	7.6M / 7.7M	▼ RAM Card 1
Filename	▶	**Creator**
PPP NetIF	✿ 🐛	ppp_
PPP NetIF_enUS	✿	ppp_
Preferences	✿ 🐛	pref
Preferences_enUS	✿	pref
psysLaunchDB	🐛 🖪	psys
Saved Preferences	🖪	psys
Security	✿ 🐛	secr
Security_enUS	✿	secr
SerialLib	✿	swrp
Setup	✿ 🐛	setp

[Details...] [Filter...]   ☐ Hide ROM

Beaming is one of Filez's most admirable capabilities. As you may recall from Chapter 4, beaming programs and data to other Palm users isn't only practical, it's just plain fun. But the Palm OS is a bit limited in terms of what it can beam. Specifically, it can't beam Hacks or e-books or certain kinds of databases. That's where Filez comes in—it can beam just about anything.

The Wonderful World of Launchers

As you know from poring over Chapter 2 (you did pore, didn't you?), the Palm OS enables you to assign applications to different categories—the idea being to help keep your icons organized and more easily accessible. However, a variety of third-party programs take this idea to a much higher level and with much better results. In this section, we introduce you to a few of our favorite launchers—programs that organize your apps, simplify certain features, and, in some cases, slap on a much prettier interface.

What should you look for when choosing a launcher? Here are a couple key features to consider:

 Support for memory cards   If your handheld has an expansion slot (as most do nowadays), your launcher should have direct support for memory cards. That means you can install applications on a card, but still organize them as you see fit from within the launcher.

- ■ **Support for color and/or high-res screens** A good launcher should take full advantage of your screen's capabilities, meaning it should offer a colorful visage and let you tweak the colors to your liking. If you have a Sony CLIÉ with a higher-resolution screen, choose a launcher that supports it directly. You'll be able to fit more icons on the screen at a time (if you desire to) and enjoy a nicer-looking interface.

- ■ **Support for themes** Part of the fun of using a launcher is customizing your handheld's interface. Some launchers let you install themes (or "skins," to use MP3 parlance) that dramatically alter their appearance (while maintaining the same basic layout and functionality). The standard Palm OS interface looks downright stark in comparison to these nifty themes, which are usually free to download (though the launchers themselves cost a few bucks).

- ■ **Support for jog dials** If you have a Kyocera QCP 6035, Sony CLIÉ, or another model with a jog dial, make sure to choose a launcher that supports it. That way, you can still enjoy the benefits of one-handed operation.

A Few of Our Favorite Launchers

We've tried most of the launchers out there, including the one that attempts to re-create the—horrors—Windows desktop on your handheld's screen. Rest assured, that one isn't among our favorites (but if the idea intrigues you, by all means check it out—it's called GoBar). These are:

As with most Palm software, you can try demo versions of these launchers before plunking down your hard-earned cash. We recommend you use each one for at least a week so you can really get to know it.

- ■ **Launch 'Em** It's not the most stylish-looking launcher we've seen, but *Launch 'Em* does have simplicity and flexibility in its corner. The software uses a tabbed interface to organize your icons, so you can switch categories with a single tap of the stylus. It costs $14.95.

15

■ **MegaLauncher**   When Rick made the move to a Sony CLIÉ N760C, this is the launcher he chose to go with it. In addition to its crackerjack support for memory media and high-resolution color screens, *MegaLauncher* offers a wealth of advanced features (including one-tap beaming, deleting, and copying) and comes with a handful of attractive themes. It costs $19.95.

■ **SilverScreen**   Dave's launcher of choice, *SilverScreen* offers the most glamorous interface of any launcher and a growing library of way-cool themes. It's also the only launcher to replace the core-app icons with icons of its own, thus creating an even more customized look. In short, if you're big on bells and whistles, this is the launcher for you. However, we should point out that SilverScreen is a bit on the slow side—the unfortunate by-product of its graphics-laden interface.

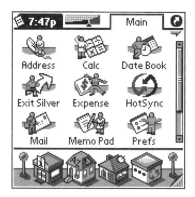

Palm Antivirus Utilities

Unless you've been living under a rock, you know that computer viruses can wreak havoc on a PC and even propagate from one system to another without users' knowledge. Viruses are an unfortunate

Did you know?

Solutions to a Problem That Doesn't Exist

Although no fewer than five companies (including heavyweights like McAfee and Symantec) have released virus-protection software for the Palm OS, at press time, there's no known record of a virus ever harming a Palm device or data. If you want our humble opinion on the subject, these companies have acted irresponsibly, creating fear to create sales and effectively challenging programmers to design Palm OS viruses.

fact of computer life. They aren't, however, a part of Palm life, at least not at press time. While a few Palm viruses are known to be floating around out there and several companies have introduced virus-protection software, do yourself a favor and don't bother wasting any money or energy on them.

Create Your Own Palm Programs

Ever wonder why there's so much third-party software available for Palm devices? Maybe because it's so easy to write programs for the platform. While the more sophisticated applications do require programming experience and professional development tools, utilities are available that enable you to design basic Palm software with ease. Indeed, if you're willing to tackle a short learning curve, you can create customized applications for your personal or business use.

NOTE   *If you're looking for software to create databases, see Chapter 14.*

Here's a quick rundown of some of the tools available to budding Palm software developers:

- **AppForge**   A powerful development tool (available in Standard and Professional editions), *AppForge* lets you write for the Palm OS, using Microsoft Visual Basic 6.0.

- **CodeWarrior**   Reputed to be the most popular Palm OS-development package, *CodeWarrior* (available for both Windows and Macintosh) requires extensive programming knowledge. It's based on the C and C++ programming languages.

- **NSBasic/Palm**   Remember that BASIC programming class you were forced to take in high school or college? Now you can put the knowledge to practical use. *NSBasic/Palm* (see Figure 15-1) lets you create Palm OS apps with everyone's favorite programming language. Okay, show of hands: who remembers what BASIC stands for?

- **PDA Toolbox**   Formerly known as PalmFactory, *PDA Toolbox* doesn't require much in the way of programming knowledge. Rather, the software employs a graphical interface and makes software design as easy as dragging-and-dropping elements on to a simulated Palm screen. You can even create your own icons for your programs.

15

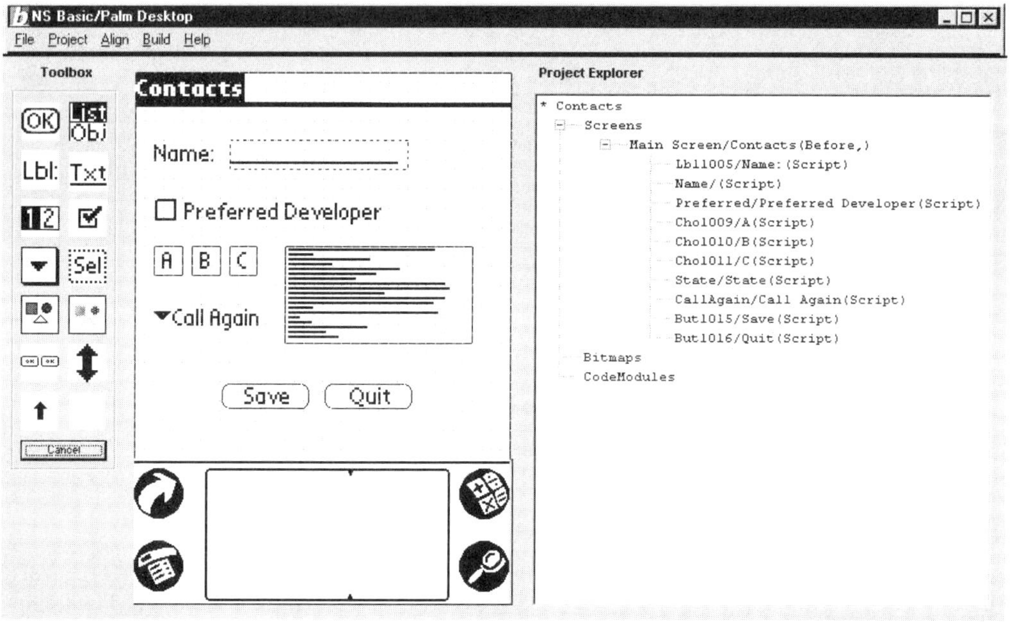

FIGURE 15-1 If you can remember your BASIC training, you can program for the Palm with NSBasic/Palm.

- **Satellite Forms Enterprise Edition** Suppose you have an idea for a Palm program and want to create a prototype before hiring a programmer. Or, you want to design a special order form for your outside-sales team, one that links to your company's inventory database. Puma Technology's *Satellite Forms* can handle all this and more. It's a robust software-development package that can create sophisticated Palm programs. Although it uses a graphical environment—not unlike PDA Toolbox's—some database and programming knowledge is necessary.

- **SuperWaba** Okay, we don't pretend to understand Java but, if you do, *SuperWaba* is a "Java Virtual Machine" that runs on the Palm OS (among other platforms).

Make Your Palm Device Run Faster

Like any computer, a Palm device runs only as quickly as its microprocessor allows. If you're working with a particularly large database or spreadsheet, or if you're running a search and have a large number of records, you may find your Palm device a bit more sluggish than you prefer. Oh, well, not much you can do about it, right?

Wrong. Thanks to so-called "overclocking" software, it's possible to turbocharge your device. A popular pastime among speed-hungry computer users, *overclocking* is the technique of forcing a processor to run at faster-than-rated speeds. Assuming all goes well, the result can be a significant speed boost.

CAUTION   *Overclocking is a try-at-your-own risk technique, one that can result in crashed Palms, lost data, possibly even a fried processor. One guaranteed side effect is shortened battery life. Overclocking is recommended neither by Palm, Inc., nor the authors of this book.*

Given the possible disasters associated with overclocking, why bother with it? Shaving a few seconds off certain operations is certainly a plus, but the more likely answer is some users like to tinker, to push the envelope. If you're one of them, check out Daniel Wee's Afterburner 3.10.

TIP   *If you're going to run the risk of overclocking, at least do it sensibly. Don't jack up the clock speed to maximum—increase it gradually, starting with a small increment. Then use your handheld for a few days to see if any adverse effects result.*

One final note: If you really want better performance, buy a Sony CLIÉ NR70/NR70V or T665C. These models have 66 MHz processors—quite a step up from the 16 MHz chips found in the earliest Palm handhelds and the 33 MHz chips in most other models. In-the-wings handhelds that run Palm OS 5 (see Chapter 10) will run faster still, so if you're concerned about performance, consider upgrading to a newer, speedier model.

Where to Find It

Web Site	Address	What's There
PalmGear H.Q.	**www.palmgear.com**	Afterburner, Clipper, SuperWaba, and virtually every other Hack and utility under the sun
Linkesoft	**www.linkesoft.com**	X-Master
Blue Nomad Software	**www.bluenomad.com**	BackupBuddy
HandEra	**www.handera.com**	BackupPro, FlashPro
AppForge, Inc.	**www.appforge.com**	AppForge
PDA Toolbox	**www.pdatoolbox.com**	PDA Toolbox
Puma Technology	**www.pumatech.com**	Satellite Forms
NS Basic Corp.	**www.nsbasic.com**	NSBasic/Palm
Metrowerks	**www.metrowerks.com**	CodeWarrior

15

Chapter 16

Time and Money Management

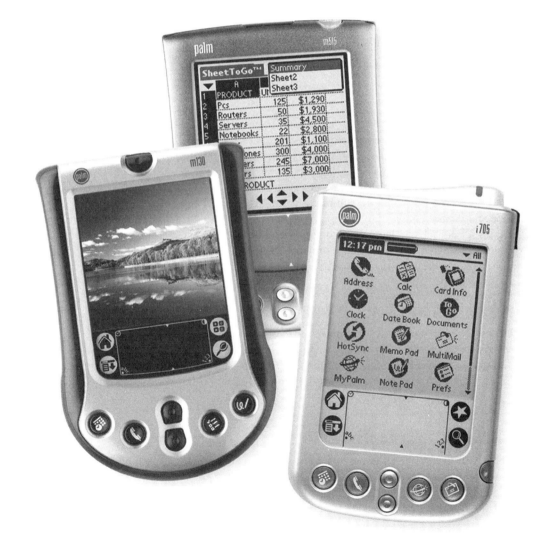

How to...

- Track your finances with the Palm
- Keep up with Quicken data entry on your Palm
- Calculate loans using your Palm
- Calculate restaurant tips and divide dining bills with the Palm
- Track your investments on the Palm
- Get stock price updates via the Internet
- Get wireless stock quotes with your Palm
- Manage projects and clients with the Palm
- Keep up with time zones
- Calculate the time between any two dates

There's a saying where Dave grew up: you can never have enough time or enough money. Actually, we're pretty sure this expression is common to most places, but Dave tends to ramble on and on about New Jersey on occasion. And, because there's no reasonable way to discuss authentic New York pizza in this book, we've covering this topic instead.

No device in the world—at least not yet—is going to give you more time or money just as a happy consequence of owning it. But many programs for the Palm are designed to maximize what time and money you have by helping you manage it better. Project management systems help you track your jobs and clients, financial programs manage your checkbook, and portfolio systems let you stay on top of your investments. In this chapter, we round up a few of the best of each.

Manage Your Money with the Palm

"Money," the Swedish rock band Abba once said. "Money, money," they continued. In all, they said it three times, as in, "money, money, money." We couldn't agree more. Your Palm is an ideal pocket-sized tool for keeping track of your money. You can use it as an extension of your desktop financial management program or as a stock tracker—and a lot of little applications in between.

Rock Bands to Live By

We need to make a strong caveat at this point: neither Dave nor Rick is particularly fond of the recently-mentioned Abba (any more—Rick boogied to "Fernando" every night through his formative years). But since you're relying on this book for advice anyway, we humbly give you our top choices for music to listen to as you troubleshoot your PC or surf the Web with your Palm:

Dave: The dual art forms of Electric Blues and 60s Rock really constitute the height of Western culture. For the most part, it's all been downhill since then, made painfully obvious by whatever that stuff is that Rick forces me to listen to when I visit his office or ride in his car. No, I say, stop the madness. Listen to The Beatles, Pink Floyd, Velvet Underground, Kristin Hersh, Throwing Muses, and The Call, and you're pretty well set. If you have a few dollars left over, pick up some Peter Himmelman, B. B. King, Dire Straits, and Eric Clapton. You won't be disappointed. And, whatever you do, don't buy anything Rick is about to recommend.

    Rick: Not unless you have good taste and want to *enjoy* what you're listening to. With the exception of The Beatles, Dave feels all music should be weird or depressing—or both, ideally. Give me Billy Joel, Green Day, Smash Mouth, Simon and Garfunkel, Alanis Morrissette, or Big Bad Voodoo Daddy. Yes, that's right, I don't listen to artists or bands just because they're unpopular or unknown. That's Dave's job. Oh, and for the record, Dave doesn't even like jazz—proof positive that he's a few sandwiches short of a picnic.

    Dave: There Rick goes again, making me look bad. Of course, he'd throw in a few good selections because he knows you're all reading this. Just wait till you're not paying attention and check out what he listens to.

Keep Up to Date with Quicken

You know who you are. No sooner do you get home from dinner and a movie, than you rush to the PC and enter your receipts in Quicken. It's a habit, it's an addiction. Well, your Palm, together with the right software, can now save you the agony of waiting until you get home: relax and enjoy the movie, because *Pocket Quicken* lets you enter your expenses into your Palm as they happen.

    Pocket Quicken isn't a Palm-based replacement for the entire Quicken application on your desktop. Instead, it's a handheld companion that lets you store payments, deposits, and account transfers in your Palm and synchronize the transactions with Quicken on the desktop at your next HotSync. You can also review your account balances and analyze old transactions. If you're a Quicken user and you methodically enter all your receipts into the program, then this is a program you should try.

    Before you begin using Pocket Quicken, you should perform a HotSync. This transfers your accounts and categories from the desktop version of Quicken to your Palm. Be sure to do this before you take your Palm on the road expecting to enter any transactions!

    Once you have a chance to synchronize the apps and get Pocket Quicken configured with your desktop settings, look at the Pocket Quicken interface. Pocket Quicken has two views: the display toggles between the Accounts view (which lists your accounts and current balance) and the Register view, where you enter and review transactions (both seen in Figure 16-1).

    When you want to enter a new transaction, tap the New button at the bottom of the screen and choose whether you're creating a payment, a deposit, or a cash transfer. Then fill out the resulting dialog box as appropriate. Pocket Quicken includes Quicken's AutoFill tool (which completes the transaction for you when it recognizes what you're entering). You can also choose to use a "memorized" transaction from a pick list to speed your entry.

16

Accounts		
Name	**Type**	**Balance**
Savings	Bank	14,492.15
Balance Total:		**14,492.15**
(Edit...) (Register)		

Register	▼ All	
Date ▼ Ref & Payee		**Amount**
12/19 Rick		-130.00
12/19 DEP Cbrt		1000.00
12/19 DEP Tap		258.00
12/19 Kris		-15.00
12/19 DEP Zd		250.00
▼ New Transactions		14,492.15
(New...) (Accounts)		

FIGURE 16-1   Pocket Quicken's two major views

You can lock prying eyes out of your records with a four-digit PIN. To protect your Quicken data, start Pocket Quicken, and choose Options | Security from the menu. Then create your PIN.

If you use your Palm frequently to store transactions, the data can add up. It's easy to keep it in check, though, and preserve your Palm's memory. To trim your transactions to a manageable size, choose Actions | Trim History. Then delete old transactions based on date or by the oldest set of entries. Remember, though, don't delete any entries that haven't yet been HotSynced.

Accounts		
Name	**Type**	**Balance**
Savings	Bank	14,492.15

Remove from History ⓘ

Remove transactions from:

▼ All accounts

and | Before | **12/19/99**
| Oldest | ▼ 10 items

(Remove) (Cancel)

Use Other Cash Management Tools

If you aren't a Quicken user or you don't want the capability to synchronize your Palm with a desktop finance program, some other applications are still out there you might want to try. Specifically, look at some of these:

■ **PocketMoney**   An outstanding alternative to Pocket Quicken, *PocketMoney* is a comprehensive personal finance program that interfaces with a handful of other Palm apps and a number of desktop financial programs (including Quicken and Microsoft Money).

■ **BankBook**   Another great personal finance program, the interface is simple enough to let you enter transactions on-the-fly, as they happen. You can later synchronize with your desktop finance program.

■ **Personal Money Tracker**   This is a popular finance package for your Palm that's ideal for non-Quicken users. It has a conduit that synchronizes the Palm data with a standard CSV file on the desktop. You can then import that data into a spreadsheet or personal finance software.

■ **Ultrasoft Money**   Considered by many to be the best money management application for the Palm, *Money* synchronizes with Microsoft Money on the desktop to deliver complete financial management on the PDA. If you want Money's features but don't use a desktop finance program, *Ultrasoft Checkbook* is the non-sync alternative.

■ **Accounts and Loans**   This program lets you track your bank account balances and loan information in one application. The program is easy to use and lets you export your financial data to the Memo Pad.

Streamline Your Day with Other Financial Tools

What is the Palm if not convenient? That's why we love to load up the Palm with tools that make it easier to do mundane tasks like pay bills and calculate loans. Real estate and loan professionals use the Palm to calculate amortizations, and you can too. In truth, there are dozens of these kinds of programs floating around, and you can try them all quickly and easily from PalmGear.com. *Financial Consultant,* for instance, turns any Palm-powered PDA into a business calculator that includes many of the most useful features of Hewlett-Packard and Texas Instruments calculators. The program comes with 90 pre-programmed functions, including loan payments, interest rate conversions, and onscreen amortization schedules. *Loan Pro,* from Infinity Software, is a similar loan-analysis calculator that can be used by professionals or consumers for any kind of amortized purchase—like houses, cars, and boats (if you can afford a boat, by the way, give Dave or Rick a call. We have some

16

business ideas we'd like to run past you). *Triloan* takes a different approach to the problem of real estate calculations by displaying up to four loans at once on the same screen, letting you visually compare several different financial profiles side-by-side. There's also *LoanUtil,* a small application that tells you monthly payments, total amount of loan, or interest rate, depending on what data you enter. Tap the icon marked three at the bottom of the screen and you're taken to a Compare screen that lets you directly compare two different loan offers based on the same principal.

```
┌─────────────────────────────────┐
│ LoanUtil - Primary Loan      ⓘ  │
│ First Pay Date:   ( 12-1999 )   │
│ Last Pay Date:    ( 11-2003 )   │
│ # of Payments:        48.00     │
│ Amount Borrowed:   $ 12943.00   │
│ Interest Rate:     19.000 %     │
│ Monthly Payments:               │
│                                 │
│ [1|2|3]  (Calculate) [        ] │
└─────────────────────────────────┘
```

Have we whetted your appetite for handy financial tools? Here are a few other kinds of programs you might want to try:

- **Shopping Assistant**   At the top of this little heap is a program called *HandyShopper,* designed, quite simply, to help you shop more efficiently and to save money in the process. It lets you maintain lists of products you want to buy and you can even tell HandyShopper in which store (and what aisle) you found it. Then, you can later go back and track down the products more easily. For us, one of the most interesting features is its capability to compare the actual price of two similar products. Suppose you're buying tissue paper that costs $4.99 for 10 ounces, and another brand sells 12 ounces for $5.49. Which is the better deal? Find out by choosing Record Best Buy from the menu, and then enter the price and quantity in the Best Buy dialog box. For the record, you should buy the second item because it's cheaper by about 4 cents per ounce.

```
┌─────────────────────────────────┐
│ Untitled ▾            ▾ All ⓘ   │
│ ▾ All Stores          Q (  $  ) │
│ ┌─────────────────────────────┐ │
│ │         Best Buy            │ │
│ │         Product            │ │
│ │          A       B         │ │
│ │ Price:  12.99   14.49      │ │
│ │ Quantity: 10     12        │ │
│ │                  ( Go! )   │ │
│ │ ( Done )                   │ │
│ └─────────────────────────────┘ │
└─────────────────────────────────┘
```

■ **Tip Calculator**   Let's be honest—no one needs a program to help them calculate a restaurant tip or to help them divide a bill among a few people. And to add insult to injury, there must be a hundred tip calculators floating around PalmGear.com. But if you want to try one, give EZTip a spin. *EZTip* enables you to enter the total amount of a bill, add a tip, and then evenly divide the total among a number of diners.

■ **Currency Conversion**   Traveling? You might want to know what $50 is worth in yen, euros, or rubles. A few programs can retrieve current exchange rates when you HotSync and other programs can pull the rates down in real time via a wireless connection. We suggest you check out Travel Pal or, if you have a wireless-enabled Palm that can use PQAs, try the L3 Currency Converter from **Palm.net**.

■ **Car Maintenance Tracking**   If you want to stay on top of your car's routine maintenance, try TotalCar (on the left) or VehicleLog (on the right). These programs also track your gas mileage—or if that's all you care about, try a program called MPG.

Track Your Investment Portfolio

One of the Internet's biggest killer apps, it turns out, seems to be investment Web sites. Then the Internet crashed, we all lost our money, and no one wanted to know what our investments looked like anymore. If you're one of those few people who still have a few stocks with a non-zero balance, then you might want to track your portfolio on the go.

That's where your Palm comes in. You can use any one of a number of portfolio management packages to watch your investments. Most investment programs for the Palm let you check your portfolio's health from anywhere, anytime. Suppose you don't get a chance to check the paper's business pages until you get on the subway in the morning. You can update your portfolio right from your seat on the train and instantly know your new positions.

If you like the idea of using your Palm for portfolio management, give either one of these programs a shot:

■ **Stock Manager**   One of the most complete portfolio managers for the Palm, *Stock Manager* is a color app that works both wirelessly and whenever you HotSync. It retrieves your current stock prices, as well as the day's high, low, change, and volume.

16

Stock Manager also lets you set alerts on all your stocks based on current price, profit, and profit percentage. The program enables you to categorize your stocks into different portfolios and a conduit lets you export your portfolio to an Excel-compatible CSV file.

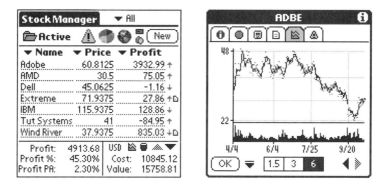

■ **StockPilot** Do you love to see your holdings in lots of different ways? Then you'll love StockPilot. While we prefer Stock Manager, this is a good alternative, and it's a little cheaper ($19 instead of $25). *StockPilot* tracks a lot of details about your holdings, including dividends, profits, fee as a percentage of stock value, and total value. StockPilot lets you "watch" a stock, even if you don't own it. The elegant display shows your portfolio in three columns, each of which is customizable to show different details, like stock symbol, shares, profit, and more.

Streamline Your Day with Time Management Tools

Time management isn't only about getting that spreadsheet to your client on time or tracking how many hours you were on the road delivering two tons of fertilizer to a nearby town. Time

Get Stock Quotes Wirelessly

You needn't be satisfied with getting stock prices via HotSync sessions. That's so, well, late '90s. If you have a Palm VII, Palm i705, Kyocera QCP 6035, Samsung I300, or wireless modem/phone for your handheld, then options are available for getting stock updates wirelessly and immediately. Check out these Palm Query Apps:

■ **BigCharts** Provides quotes, charts, and news on your stocks.

■ **Bloomberg** Quotes and news on your stocks. Bloomberg also lets you track a personal portfolio and track its progress.

■ **E*Trade** Get summaries, quotes, Index summaries, charts, news, and track stocks with your own watch lists.

management can be little things—like knowing how many days are between two project milestones. Here's a small collection of utilities we think you might appreciate having on your Palm:

- **Time Traveler**   This program is a fairly comprehensive time-zone manager that lets you find the time difference between your current location and major cities around the world. One of its most interesting features is in the Time Travel screen, where you can specify your flight itinerary (including your departure location and time, followed by your arrival location and time). *Time Traveler* calculates the actual travel time, taking time zone changes into account. This way, you know how many magazines to buy for your upcoming plane flight.

- **BigClock**   We mentioned this program elsewhere in the book, but it's a winner and deserves mention here as well. Use *BigClock* to display the time (if your Palm recharges in the HotSync cradle and you set it to stay on while in the cradle, it can be a desktop clock), play up to four different sets of alarms, and serve as a counter or countdown timer.

- **BlueMoon**   When was the last time you changed the filter in the furnace, checked the oil in your car, or called your mom? These are tasks that don't always lend themselves to regular To Do List or Date Book entries, largely because they happen infrequently and not always on a predictable schedule. But *BlueMoon* is designed to accommodate just those kinds of recurring tasks.

- **Timeout**   Do you take enough breaks during the day? If not, you might be heading down the road to stress and heart failure, like our friend Rick. *Timeout* is a simple program that pops a reminder on the Palm screen randomly throughout the day to tell you to take a short break and relax.

- **Date Wheel**   This clever program lets you calculate the number of weeks, days, or business days between any two dates. You can also specify a duration, like ten business days, and find the necessary start or end date. *Date Wheel* is essential for any manager

16

who needs to assign deadlines or determine if enough time exists between two dates to get a job accomplished.

Where to Find It

Web Site	Address	What's There
PalmGear	**www.palmgear.com**	Applications, including all the apps discussed in this chapter
Palm.Net	**www.palm.net**	Palm Query Apps
AvantGo	**www.avantgo.com**	Wireless financial channels, including Bloomberg

Chapter 17 Playing Games

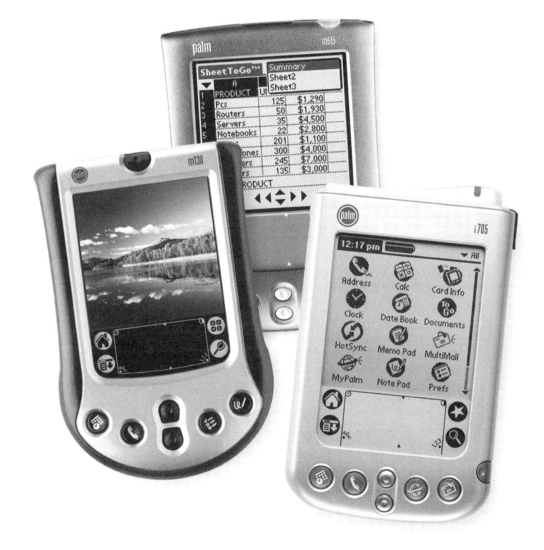

How to...

- ■ Configure the volume on your Palm for gaming
- ■ Enable IR games
- ■ Install new games
- ■ Control games on your Palm
- ■ Get a real joystick for your Palm
- ■ Install and play the bundled Palm games
- ■ Play interactive fiction games
- ■ Use the Palm as a substitute for dice
- ■ Find color games for your color Palm
- ■ Find great games for your Palm
- ■ Turn your Palm into a Game Boy

Of course, spreadsheets, databases, document readers, and memos are all well and good. If that's all you ever plan to do with your Palm, that's fine—you're just unlikely to ever get invited to one of Dave's or Rick's parties.

Your Palm is a miniature general-purpose computer and, as a result, it can do almost anything your desktop PC can do, including playing games. Sure, there are major limitations. The display is pretty small and the processor isn't nearly as fast, which can limit the kinds of games you play; but the fact remains your Palm is a great game machine for passing the time in an airport, on a train, in a meeting (while you look like you're taking notes), or any other place where you're bored with doing productive activities. In this chapter, we discuss what you should know to get the most out of your Palm as a gaming machine and we recommend some of the best games for you to try.

Turning Your Palm into a Game Machine

No, playing games isn't exactly rocket science, but before you get started with them, you should learn a few things that'll come in handy. You should know, for instance, how to control your Palm's volume, install applications, and control beaming. After all, games out there let you multiplay using the IR port.

Control the Palm's Game Volume

At the top of the list is the Palm's sound system. The Palm has a control for how loud to play game sounds. Logic dictates you'll want to set this loud enough to hear what's going on in your game, but this might not always be the case. As much as we like to play games, we don't always want others to know that's what we're doing. Fortunately, setting the game sound level low or even off completely is possible. This means you'll play your games without sound but, if you're at work, we think you'll agree that's a wise decision.

To tweak game sounds, do this:

1. Tap the Prefs icon to open your Preferences application.

2. Switch to the General category by tapping the Category menu at the top-right corner and choosing General.

3. Find the Game Sound entry and choose the volume level you're interested in.

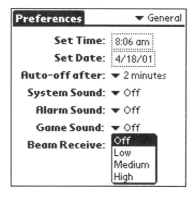

TIP   *If you play a game that squeaks and squawks even if the sound is off, the game must have its own sound preferences. Check the game's menu for a preferences control to set the sound volume.*

Enable Beaming

If you know other Palm users, you might want to try your hand at some head-to-head games via the Palm's IR port. It's fun and addictive, and very nearly sociable. For two games on different Palms to find each other, though, you need to set your Palm to receive beams automatically from other handhelds. The control for this option is in the same place as game sounds. Do this:

1. Tap the Prefs icon to open your Preferences application.

2. Switch to the General category by tapping the Category menu at the top-right corner and choosing General.

3. Look for the entry called Beam Receive and make sure it's set to On.

Install Games

Installing games is a snap. We discussed how to install applications on your Palm in Chapter 4, and working with games is no different. After all, a game is only another kind of Palm app.

17

If you're new to downloading applications from the Internet, you need to know that most apps come compressed in one of two popular formats:

■ **Zip**   This is the standard way of managing files in Windows. To install a Zipped file, you need a program capable of unzipping it first. Typically, this means using an app like WinZip.

■ **Sit**   Macintosh files are compressed in the SIT format, which can be uncompressed with a program like Aladdin Stuffit Expander.

Once expanded, you'll probably have a folder with several files in it. Installation instructions typically come in one or more file formats:

■ Plain text files, which are usually called something clever like readme.txt or install.txt.

■ Web pages. Double-click them to see the directions in your Web browser.

■ Adobe Acrobat files, which end with the PDF file extension. You need Adobe Acrobat to read these files, though it's probably already installed on your computer. If not, visit **adobe.com** to get this popular document reader.

■ Finally, one or more files with PRC and PDB extensions should exist. These are Palm apps that need to be installed on the Palm to play the game. Open the Install tool and use the Add button to set these files for installation at the next HotSync.

SHORTCUT   *If you use WinZip, a faster way to install apps in the Install tool is simply to drag the PRC and PDB files from the WinZip window into the Install Tool dialog box (they'll dynamically expand as you drag them, meaning you needn't unzip the files into a folder on your hard disk at all) or simply double-click them.*

TIP   *Need to pause a game? Turn off your Palm or switch to another application. The game remains frozen until you turn it back on again.*

How to ...   Control the Games

Now you're all set to start playing some Palm games, but where's the joystick? There isn't one, silly. Most action games use the buttons on the Palm case to control the action. While the game is running, the Date Book, Address Book, Memo Pad, and To Do List buttons are typically diverted to game controls and won't switch you to the usual apps. To find out which buttons do what in a given game, you can experiment (our favorite way, actually) or check the game documentation. In most games, you can find basic instructions by checking the game's Help option on the menu.

CAUTION *If you reset your Palm while a game is paused, the game session you were playing will be lost and you'll need to start over.*

Game Controller Peripherals

As you see later in this chapter, lots and lots of cool games are available for the Palm—more than we could ever fit in this book, in fact. Some are so addictive, you might miss a meeting trying to get the high score. But they all have the same basic limitation—you need to use a stylus or the six buttons on the Palm's case to control the action.

Depending on which Palm model you own, there could be a better way. Add-on game controllers let you get a more authentic arcade experience, complete with joystick or gamepad, instead of mashing down on the Palm's buttons. Here are some options:

- **Micro Innovations Game Controller**   This *Game Controller* is a clip-on gadget for the Palm m100 and m105. It communicates with the Palm through the HotSync port and duplicates the look and feel of a Game Boy. The Game Controller has a D-pad (like a joystick you mash with your thumb) and four control buttons. You can map the six Palm buttons to these controls, so you can operate almost any Palm game using the Game Controller. The main advantage of the Game Controller—aside from more authentic arcade gaming—is you're not wearing out the Palm's buttons by playing games. It's available in many retail stores and online.

- **GamePad**   The *GamePad,* from WorldWideWidgetWorks, is a clip-on game controller for Palm III-series models. It looks and works much the same as the Game Controller from Micro Innovations, but it's obviously designed for different Palm models.

17

- **GameFace**   This add-on for the Handspring Visor is a little different: instead of something that replaces the buttons on the case, this peripheral covers them. When you push the buttons or yank on the joystick on the *GameFace,* those controls directly push down on the Visor's buttons. The GameFace makes some games, especially games that benefit from a joystick, more fun. Unfortunately, it doesn't save on wear and tear, and playing too many games could eventually affect the responsiveness of the Visor's buttons.

■ **SnapNPlay**   Unlike Handspring's GameFace, the *SnapNPlay* from TT-Tec communicates with the Visor through the serial port; it doesn't just line up with the Visor's buttons and press down on them for you. This makes it work a lot like the two controllers for the Palm we already mentioned. SnapNPlay delivers an eight-way D-pad, two fire buttons, and a suite of nongaming controls—buttons for power, the menu, and the Application screen. You also get vibration feedback, just like in a Nintendo game controller. SnapNPlay triggers vibration when a game plays sound, though. This means, in many games, the controller vibrates continuously, like some sort of wrist massager, unless you turn off that feature.

Looking Professional

Dave: I know some people who worry about the proliferation of games for their Palm device. And their concern might be justified. Remember the Commodore Amiga? It was a great home computer that had its heyday back in the late 1980s. The Commodore Amiga could have been a contender—it was that good but, because the system's 4,000-color display and stereo sound was so well matched for game playing, the business world ignored the Amiga, derisively calling it a "game machine." No one took it seriously and the Amiga slowly died away as the IBM PC gained an overwhelming foothold in the business market. We might see this happen all over again with the Palm, especially if Microsoft's Pocket PC manages to establish itself in the business world and depicts the Palm as a lightweight, business-hostile, handheld PC.

Rick: Nah. The corporate world knows Palm handhelds are for business first. Games are just a perk, like e-books. And, thankfully, Palm is a little smarter about marketing than Commodore was. (As I recall, the company's motto was, "Advertising? Who needs advertising?") And Palm is already a household name, whereas the mention of Amiga usually drew blank stares. The Pocket PC will never truly threaten the Palm juggernaut until Microsoft fixes the operating system, which is unlikely to happen because Microsoft doesn't have a clue.

Installing the Bundled Games

Depending on which model you purchase, you might find that several games come with the Palm. To see if your Palm has any games, open the Install Tool application on the Desktop and click the Add button. The Open dialog box opens automatically in the Add-on folder, which will contain any bundled games that haven't already been installed. Select one or more, and then HotSync.

About Color

If you have a Palm-powered PDA with a color display, you have a delicious gaming experience in the palm of your hands (no pun intended). Color games look every bit as good and, in fact, quite a bit better—than what you see on your kid's Game Boy. Our favorite hunting ground for games, **palmgear.com**, makes it easy to tell whether a game (or any application, for that matter) is color: the site places a colorful paintbrush icon next to any application that supports color. On the PalmGear home page, the new software list identifies color apps in this way:

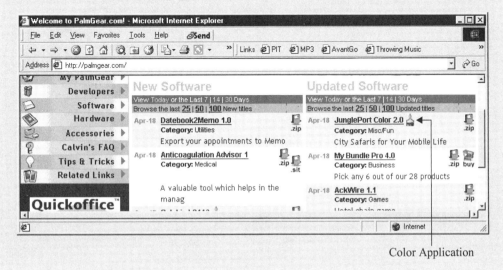

Color Application

17

If you're looking at the detailed application description, the color icon is always shown next to the product's name, like this:

Color Application

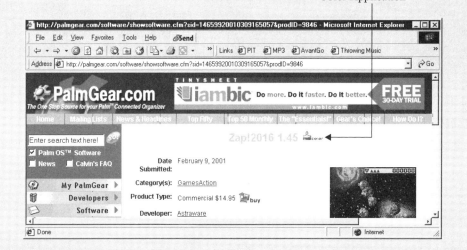

Finally, the easiest way to find color applications at PalmGear is to search the archives. Choose Software | Search the Archives from the Navigation menu on the left side of the PalmGear screen. On the Software Archives page, enter a software category to search for and be sure to click the Search for Color Applications check box, as you can see in the following. Your search results will only include color apps.

Color Application

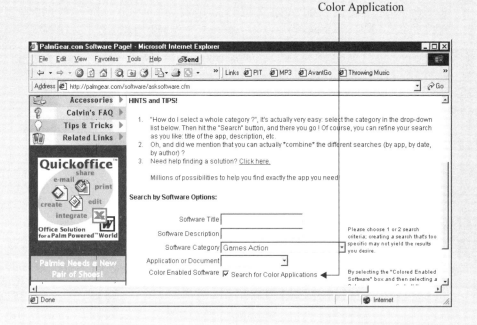

Playing IR Games

As we already mentioned, infrared-capable games are a cool way to pass the time when you're traveling with another Palm-equipped person. A variety of IR games is available in a variety of genres, action and board games being the most popular. To connect two Palms, start the game on both handhelds and tap the Connect or Start button. You need to follow ordinary beaming rules, that is, you must be close enough to receive the beam, but not too close.

If your opponent doesn't have a copy of the game you want to play, beam it. Many IR games can be beamed, even if they're commercial products. If they're commercial, then the beamed copy will often work in conjunction with the one from which it was beamed or it'll work for a short period of time—like two weeks.

A number of IR games are on the Web. You can download games like Rapid Racer (a 1982-style arcade racing game), Codefinder (a Mastermind-like 2-player puzzle), or 3D Bingo (yes, it's bingo on the Palm). Perhaps the best examples of infrared gaming, though, are IR Battleship and IR Pong. These games, pictured in the following, are definitely worth keeping on your PDA for head-to-head gaming opportunities. Or try Scrabble, which lets you play the old game of word creation against as many as three other people at once using infrared.

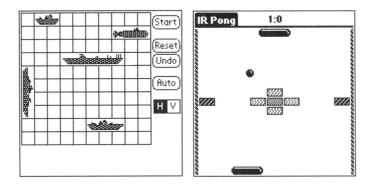

NOTE   *All these games are available from **www.palmgear.com**.*

Playing Text Adventures

Remember Zork? How about Douglas Adams's *Hitchhikers Guide to the Galaxy* text adventure? What about Trinity? These were all games that were popular 15 years ago, at the dawn of the modern personal computer age. Text adventures put you in a text-based world, with flowing narratives and extensive text-based descriptions of your surroundings. When it was time to make your hero do something, you typed instructions into your PC at a text prompt. The computer then moved you along through the story based on your decisions. These games were often fiendishly clever, composed largely of logic puzzles and intellectual challenges.

So, why are we telling you all this? Text adventures are long-lost icons for the museum, right?

Not quite. Text adventures have made something of a comeback in the last few years, largely because handheld PCs like the Palm are an ideal format for playing them. And, though their name has changed with the times—they're now often called *interactive fiction* instead of text adventures—they're still a lot of fun to play. No Palm gamer would consider his Palm complete without one or two interactive fiction games installed for a rainy day at the airport (see Figure 17-1).

Unlocking Interactive Fiction Files

You can find hundreds of interactive fiction titles on the Internet. But these files aren't playable all by themselves. They usually come encoded in something called Z-Code. Like a spreadsheet or document file, a *Z-Code* file is useless without the appropriate reader app. In this case, you need a program called Pilot-Frotz (or Frotz, for short). Install Frotz, and you can play any interactive fiction games you find and transfer to your Palm.

Frotz essentially gives you the same experience as if you had played these text adventures 15 years ago. It displays the game's text on the screen and provides you with a text prompt in which to enter your next move. When you start the game, you see the Frotz list view, along with any games you have currently installed. To play a game, tap its name, and then tap the Play button.

From there, you're taken to the game view, where you play the game. Unlike those early text adventures, Frotz gives you a few graphical tools that make these games easier to play. Here's how to use Frotz:

- If the game displays a long text description, you might see the word "MORE" to indicate more text occurs after this pause. Tap the screen to continue.

- To enter your text command, write it in the Graffiti area.

FIGURE 17-1 Interactive fiction combines good old-fashioned storytelling with a bit of brain-teasing puzzle-solving.

■ You can display a list of common verbs and nouns (seen on the right in Figure 17-2) by tapping the right half of the Palm screen in any spot where no text exists. Instead of writing Look, for instance, tap the menu and tap the word "Look."

■ You can tap any word in the story and that word appears on the text prompt line. Thus, you can assemble your command from the menu and words already onscreen, instead of writing it all from scratch with Graffiti.

■ If you want your character to move, tap any blank space on the left half of the Palm screen. You'll see a map window, like the one on the left side of Figure 17-2. Tap the desired compass direction. Other icons help you Enter, Exit, and go up or down stairs.

> **TIP** *You can add custom words and phrases to the word list. Enter the desired word or phrase at the text prompt and select it with your stylus. Then choose List | Add from the menu. To see custom words, open the list menu, and then tap on the first entry, USER LIST.*

Your position is automatically saved when you leave the game to do something else with your Palm. If you want to switch to another title, choose File | Force Quit to go back to the List view to choose another game. If you do that, though, your position in the current game is lost.

Finding Interactive Fiction Titles

Interactive fiction is scattered around the Web. Try both of these sites:

■ **www.refalo.com/palm/interactive.htm**

■ **www.csd.uwo.ca/~pete/Infocom**

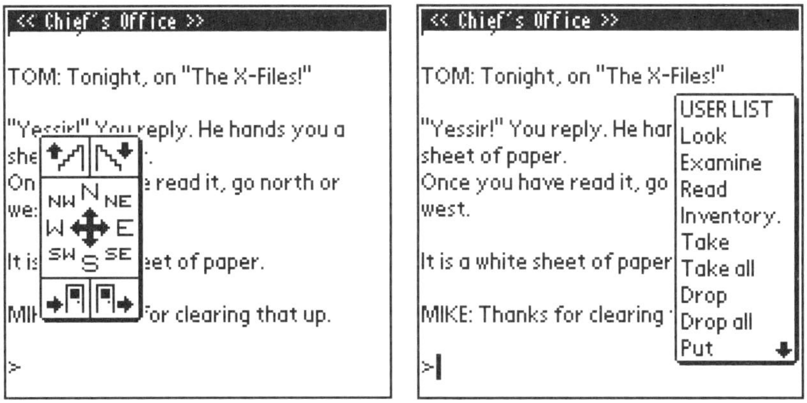

FIGURE 17-2   Frotz helps you play interactive fiction titles by displaying common commands and mapping tools.

Getting Started with Text Adventures

So, you want to try your hand at interactive fiction, but that text prompt is a little intimidating? Fear not, because entering commands in a text adventure isn't too hard. You can enter only a verb—like **Look**—or a complete sentence, such as **Pick up the compass**. Each game has something called a *parser* that's designed to decrypt your input. Here's a primer to get you started:

Directions

Compass points are frequently used: **north, south, east, west,** or any combination, like **northeast** or **southwest**. You can also use one- and two-letter abbreviations, like **n** and **se**. Also: **up, down, in, out, enter,** and **exit**.

Looking Around

The old-reliable command is simply **Look**. You can combine Look with anything that makes sense: **look up**, **look down**, or **look inside**.

Action Verbs

Anything: Push, pull, open, close, take, pick up, pump, give, swim, turn, screw, burn. When you deal with more than one object, you can use the word **All**, as in **Take All the coins**.

Make Sentences

You have to combine nouns and verbs into complete sentences to accomplish much in these games. Manipulating objects is the name of the game and the way to solve the puzzles, as in **Take the money**, **Pick up the compass**, **Read the book**, or **Close the gate with the red key**.

Using the Palm as Dice

If you like to play board games in the real world, you might be interested in using your Palm as a virtual pair of dice. After all, the Palm is harder to lose (we always misplace the dice that go with our board games). Several apps are available, but many of them have the disadvantage of requiring run-time modules of programming languages like Forth or C to run properly on the Palm. We don't care for that approach because it's just extra stuff you have to install.

Some dice simulators you might want to try include Gamers Die Roller, DicePro, and Roll Em, all available from **PalmGear.com**.

The Universe of Palm Games

The best part about the Palm is it's so easy to try out new software. Most programs are only a download away and they're easy to uninstall later if you get tired of them. Even if you download a commercial application, you can probably still try it out for a short time. The vast majority of

Game Discs

Occasionally, you might find game compilation discs in the store or online. They promise to deliver hundreds of unbeatable Palm games for only $15–$25. Should you invest in one of these discs?

Our opinion: probably not. The collection might sound promising, but anyone with a halfway decent Internet connection can get all the games they like from a site like **Palmgear.com** or **palmgamingworld.com** just as easily, without spending a dime. Remember: Palm games are tiny compared to games for the PC, and they download in seconds.

Also, remember you won't get the full, registered version of shareware games, even though the disc itself cost you cash. Instead, these discs are sort of like samplers for folks who want a guided tour of someone else's idea of the "best" games for the Palm. If you like a game you found on the disc, you'll still have to pay to keep playing it, just as if you downloaded it from the Internet.

commercial software has a trial period or simply annoys you with reminders to register. If you like it, buy it. If not, delete the game to make room for something you do want.

Card and Board Games

Games based on paper and cardboard—like board games, card games, and games of chance—transition well to the Palm because they're games you can relax with, take your time with, and return to after the dentist calls your name. Versions of nearly every game you can think of are available—Blackjack, Hearts, Poker, Ma Jong, Yahtc, Scrabble, chess, and more.

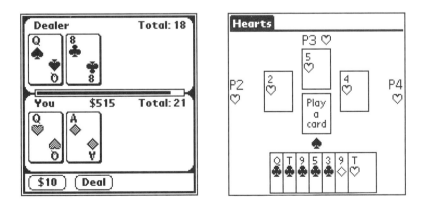

Puzzle Games

We love puzzles. Many puzzle games for the Palm come from the PC and other traditional gaming sources. You'll recognize Tetris, for instance. But other games have been invented just for the small PDA screen. Bejeweled, shown in the following illustration, is an insanely addictive title that should, without a doubt, be on your PDA. Other puzzles, like Vexed, Bounce Out, Collapse, and Alien Attack, are worth checking out as well.

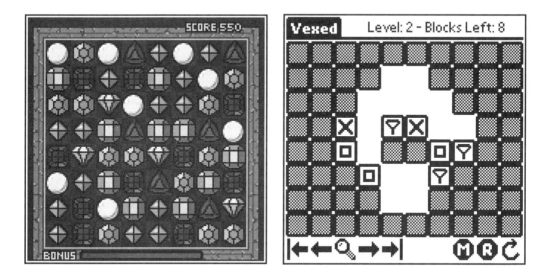

Arcade-Style Games

Did you pump an untold number of quarters into arcade machines in the '80s? Rick and Dave sure did. Games like Tank Pilot (pictured left), Pac Man (pictured right), Galax, Zap! 2000, and Graviton will test your dexterity and remind you of the good old days, when arcade games were high-tech.

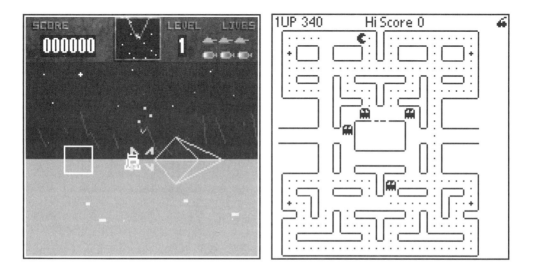

Action-Strategy Games

For those folks who want a compromise between the frenetic pace of arcade games and the cerebral thrill of interactive fiction, there's role playing and action-strategy. These games let you don some armor and go fight for gold, glory, or the king's honor. One of the most popular games in this genre is Kyle's Quest, a title for which you can download dozens of add-on adventures. If that doesn't excite you, check out Galactic Realms (on the right), a space-based strategy and domination game. If you're nostalgic for Dungeons and Dragons, there's Dragon Bane (pictured on the left), a classic dungeon, puzzle, and combat title.

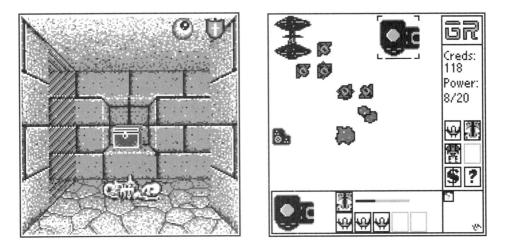

Turn Your Palm into a Game Boy

Your Palm is already about the same size as a Game Boy, right? Well, a few emulation programs now make it possible to play Game Boy games on your Palm. To prove we're not pulling your leg, here's a screen shot of a Palm running a real Game Boy title:

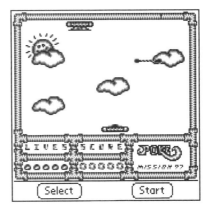

17

SimPalm

Don't forget to try SimCity. More or less the same game as the original 1980s' city-builder, *SimCity* lets you build a town from scratch, complete with roads, buildings, utilities, and recreation facilities. It's just like the original SimCity, except this one fits on your Palm.

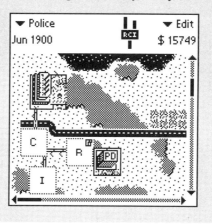

Here's how it works: you install a Game Boy emulator on your Palm, and then download and install Game Boy game ROM files. The ROM file is a duplicate of the game program, which someone copied from the Game Boy cartridge and converted to a format for the PC. You then install the ROM file on your Palm (though you typically must convert it to a Palm file first, using a conversion program that comes with the Game Boy emulator software).

If you already own a slew of Game Boy titles, this might be something you want to check out. For everyone else, a few caveats exist.

- First and foremost, it's illegal to download and install Game Boy games you don't already own copies of. The Game Boy ROMs (the game code, essentially) are copyrighted—making illegal copies is against the law. So, if you don't own a Game Boy game, you're not supposed to download a copy of it from the Internet for your Palm.

- Game Boy emulators are potentially dangerous. Emulating a Game Boy on the Palm takes programmers to the bleeding edge of Palm software design and using these programs—while generally safe—could conceivably lead to a loss of data. If you try one of these emulators, you need to realize you're experimenting and you should back up your Palm's data regularly.

- The sad truth is Game Boy games aren't that good. It's fun to try them out as a novelty, but most Palm games are much, much better.

That said, two popular Game Boy emulators are available for the Palm right now: PalmBoy and Liberty. Both of these programs are easy to install and play a wide variety of Game Boy titles. You can download Palm-ready Game Boy titles from the PalmBoy and Liberty Web sites, and also from an assortment of other gaming Web sites. If you don't mind long URLs, you can find titles at these sites:

- **kojote.emuunlim.com**
- **http://www.gambitstudios.com/freesoftware.asp**

Where to Find It

Web Site	Address	What's There
WinZip	**www.winzip.com**	WinZip file compression tool for Windows
Aladdin Systems	**www.aladdinsys.com**	Stuffit Expander file compression tool for the Mac
Micro Innovations	**www.mic-innovations.com**	Game Controller
PalmGear	**www.palmgear.com**	Games for the Palm (get Frotz here)
PalmGamingWorld	**www.palmgamingworld.com**	One-stop surfing for all sorts of games for the Palm
TT-Tec	**www.tt-tec.com**	SnapNPlay game controller for Visor

17

Chapter 18

Graffiti Enhancements and Alternatives

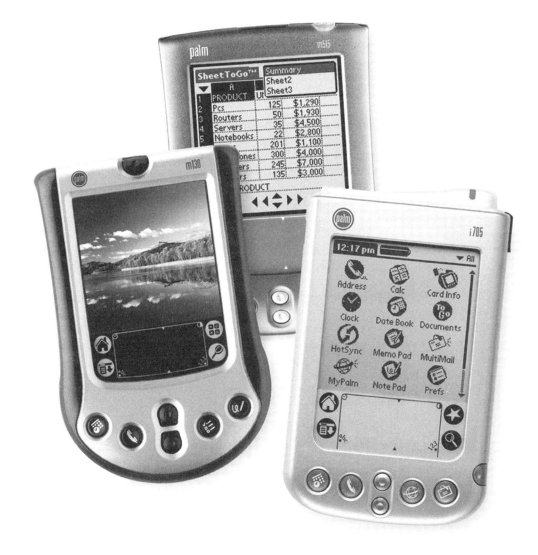

How to…

- Enter data using your thumbs
- Turn the Graffiti area into a keyboard
- Make the Graffiti area more functional
- Replace Graffiti with a different handwriting recognition engine
- Replace the built-in keyboard with other keyboards
- Write anywhere on the Palm's screen
- Take advantage of "digital ink"
- Write faster with word-completion software
- Tweak Graffiti so it's more responsive to your handwriting
- Improve Graffiti recognition without third-party software

Many of us have a love/hate relationship with Graffiti, the handwriting-recognition software used by all Palm OS devices. Some users take to it right away, finding it a speedy and convenient method for entering data. Others just plain don't like it or can't get the knack. For those folks (who have absolutely nothing to be ashamed of, really), we present this chapter on Graffiti enhancements and alternatives.

Suppose you don't mind Graffiti, but find it too slow to keep up with your thought processes— or too inflexible to recognize your particular style of handwriting. The answer could lie in one of many available "Graffiti assistants," which can not only speed data entry, but also make your handwriting more recognizable.

Maybe you've been using the onscreen keyboard as an alternative to Graffiti, but find it too small or cumbersome. There are keyboard alternatives as well, some of them quite radical. And maybe you're just ready to give Graffiti the old heave-ho and try some other means of data entry. Full-blown replacements are out there, and they let you say goodbye to Graffiti forever.

We divided all these products into four categories: overlays, which actually cover the Graffiti area; assistants, which give Graffiti a helping hand; keyboards, which substitute for the stock onscreen keyboard; and replacements, which send Graffiti packing.

NOTE   *In this chapter's discussion of keyboards, we're talking about software options. We look at actual keyboards in Chapter 20.*

Overlays: Wallpaper for the Graffiti Area

One of our favorite tips for Palm users is to apply a piece of Scotch 811 Magic Tape to the Graffiti area. This not only protects the area from scratches, it also adds a tackier writing surface that many people find preferable to the slippery screen. A new breed of plastic overlays takes this idea several steps further, redefining the Graffiti area's functionality and protecting it at the same time.

How Overlays Work

The entire Graffiti area—buttons and all—is sensitive to pressure. That's why when you tap a button or write something with your stylus, your Palm responds. The overlays simply take advantage of this fact, using special software to reprogram the Palm's responses to your taps and strokes. The products take different approaches to this, as you see in our overview of each one.

Introduction to FitalyStamp

Before we unveil Textware Solutions' FitalyStamp, we have to tell you about Textware Solutions' Fitaly Keyboard—a replacement for the built-in Palm keyboard discussed later in this chapter. It's a fairly unusual product, but with practice it can increase your data-entry speed.

The problem with pop-up keyboards like Fitaly (and the standard keyboard, for that matter) is they occupy a major chunk of the viewable area of the Palm's screen. FitalyStamp offers a solution: an overlay that moves the keyboard from the screen to the Graffiti area.

As you can see from the previous photo, the key layout is quite unusual. The idea is to minimize the distance your stylus needs to travel (more on that later in this chapter, when we look at the Fitaly Keyboard). But FitalyStamp also provides cursor-control buttons, numbers, symbols—even the Palm's ShortCut and Command functions. Thus, while there's a learning curve involved with the keyboard itself, there's also a lot of convenience. And FitalyStamp is a colorful, attractive addition to your Palm device—an important consideration for those who prize aesthetics.

Put Your Thumbs to Work

ThumbType is a Japanese import that not only does away with Graffiti, but also does away with your stylus. This original and inventive overlay uses a Braille-like keyboard that responds to thumb-presses, effectively enabling you to type with your digits. It also makes for a very different Palm computing experience.

ThumbType uses a QWERTY-style layout. Each letter has a little raised nub that you press lightly with a finger (thumbs aren't mandatory—if you place your Palm device on a flat surface, you may prefer to use your index fingers). As with a traditional keyboard, pressing SHIFT activates each key's secondary function (usually a number or symbol). Pressing SHIFT a second time lets you produce a capital letter, and pressing it a third time activates the CAPS-LOCK.

You'll notice that ThumbType has no Applications, Menu, Calc, or Find buttons, despite the fact that it covers them. Indeed, what if you need access to the Graffiti area to enter a ShortCut or a copy/paste command? Must you pull off the overlay and disable the software driver? Nope. ThumbType has a smarter solution. When you tap the little *g* next to the space bar, a "virtual" Graffiti area appears on the screen:

Now you can access the Applications screen, Calculator, and so forth or even write with Graffiti strokes like you normally would. Clever!

It's normal to be dubious about ThumbType, which looks too small and awkward to actually work. But it does, and not at all badly. We found we could type a bit faster with ThumbType than with the built-in keyboard—but we were a bit faster still with Graffiti. Nevertheless, this is an innovative and practical alternative, one Graffiti detractors may find preferable.

If you decide to try ThumbType, make sure to order the right one. There are two different versions: one for the Palm V series, the other for most other Palm OS devices.

The Virtual Graffiti Area

Two Palm Powered handhelds—the HandEra 330 and Sony CLIÉ NR70 series—take a unique (and very cool) approach to Graffiti. Like the ThumbType keyboard, these models employ a virtual Graffiti area, one that appears in the bottom portion of the screen. The difference is that the HandEra and Sony have no physical Graffiti area at all—just a larger screen than other Palm devices. Thus, Graffiti pops up when you need it, but disappears to give you more reading area when you don't. Ingenious! (The Sony's color screen also makes possible the use of "skins" for the Graffiti area, which are just about the coolest thing ever.)

Have Your Keyboard and Graffiti, Too

If you're often hopping between Graffiti and the built-in keyboard, and wishing you had an easier way to do so, Softava's Silkyboard is the answer. This overlay covers the Graffiti area with a large, easy-to-read QWERTY keyboard that enables full-time tap-typing, but also lets you use Graffiti without having to change modes.

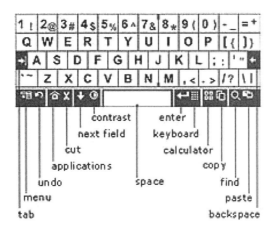

Silkyboard's key advantage is it provides access to a keyboard without sacrificing any screen estate. Its secondary advantage is protection of the Graffiti area. Working with the overlay is as simple as tapping on the letter or number you want to enter, and holding down your stylus for a "long tap" when you want a capital letter or punctuation mark. Indeed, Silkyboard's learning curve is slight. And, if you get mixed up, you can go back to using Graffiti just by drawing the strokes on top of the letters. (The overlay even has the two little arrows that divide the letter and number areas.)

Given that different Palm devices have slightly different Graffiti areas, Silkyboard is available in several varieties. Make sure you order the right one for your model. A simple

18

calibration routine is all that's required to set up the driver software, and a handy applicator strip is provided to make sure the overlay is applied without any air bubbles.

If you prefer to write with a keyboard but don't want to give up Graffiti entirely, Silkyboard is a great best-of-both-worlds solution.

Make Graffiti Smarter

One of the most ingenious overlays is TapPad, which doesn't try to replace or revamp Graffiti, but merely gives it a boost.

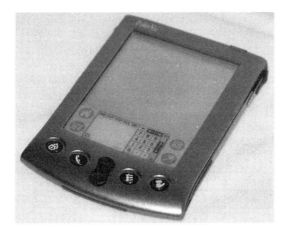

TapPad's benefits can be summed up thusly:

- Protection of the Graffiti area and a tackier surface that makes handwriting more comfortable.

- The addition of a keypad in the numeric half, thus enabling you to enter addresses and phone numbers much more quickly (and more easily, in our opinion).

- One-tap buttons for six commonly used commands: undo, cut, copy, paste, delete, and backspace. (Interestingly, Graffiti doesn't even have a delete stroke, which erases characters to the right of the cursor. It offers only backspace, which erases characters to the left.) The Undo button alone is worth the price of admission.

- Left-right and up-down scroll buttons for easier cursor movement and document navigation. If you ever tried to place your cursor in between two letters or at the beginning of a line, you know what a struggle it can be. The left-right buttons move your cursor one space at a time, greatly simplifying its placement. And the up-down scroll buttons are a major improvement over the Palm's skinny scroll bars and tiny arrows.

- A host of shortcut and pop-up tools designed to simplify data entry. Space doesn't permit us to list them all, but we think they're outstanding.

Our Favorite Graffiti Aids

Rick: While I never travel without my Stowaway Keyboard, most of the time I prefer to use plain old Graffiti. But my accuracy could always use improvement, which is why I've become a big fan of TealEcho. It reproduces my Graffiti strokes in digital ink as I make them, so I can see what my characters look like (and make sure they're drawn correctly). Best $11.95 you can spend on your Palm, if you ask me.

Dave: Personally, I don't use any Graffiti enhancements (my Jedi Master won't allow me to take the easy way out of any situation, lest it weaken my mind and allow the Dark Side to gain a foothold). I use my Graffiti zone just the way God intended it, but I always have a keyboard with me on trips so I can write long documents on airplanes and in my hotel room. I mainly use the Stowaway keyboard, though I've also been experimenting with Logitech's KeyCase, which is a flexible, cloth-based keyboard.

If you want superb protection for the handwriting area along with some Graffiti-related perks, you're likely to love TapPad.

Graffiti Replacements: A Software Solution

Love the idea of Graffiti, but don't like Graffiti itself? We understand—some of those special characters are just plain tough (Dave can't make a *j* to save his life, and who can remember the stroke for the percent sign?). CIC's Jot, born for Windows CE devices but eventually ported to the Palm OS, replaces Graffiti with a more natural—and familiar—character set.

And that's only one of Jot's advantages. It also frees you from the Graffiti area, enabling you to write anywhere on your Palm device's screen. Even better, it leaves a trail of "digital ink" beneath your stylus tip, so you can see what you're writing as you write, as with a pen and paper. Finally, Jot recognizes a variety of cursive characters (see Figure 18-1), handy for those who mix script with print. Tricky Graffiti letters like *q*, *v*, and *y* are much easier to make with Jot.

Our problem with Jot is the way it handles punctuation. Like Graffiti, it has an "extended mode" that you access by drawing a vertical line. Then you write the desired symbol (such as a period or an exclamation point), and another vertical line to return to Letter mode. This is a rather slow and awkward method, especially for frequently used punctuation like the period. In Graffiti, all it takes is a double-tap.

Still, Jot's more traditional character set makes writing easier, particularly for new Palm users who don't have to unlearn all of Graffiti's special strokes. Not sure this is the Graffiti alternative for you? Try before you buy. As with most Palm software, you can download a demo for a test drive.

If you own a Handspring Treo that has a keyboard instead of the traditional Graffiti area, you can add handwriting-recognition capabilities by installing Jot.

18

Now write like you normally do and not be confined to special characters. Jot recognizes all these forms.

FIGURE 18-1   Jot can recognize five versions of the letter *A* alone, meaning it's more accommodating to your style of writing.

Keys, Please

Like to tap-type? Many users prefer the built-in keyboard to Graffiti, if only because it has no real learning curve. Of course, some software developers think they can do the keyboard one better, as evidenced by Textware Solutions' Fitaly Keyboard and a few interesting Hacks.

QWERTY, Meet Fitaly

The Fitaly Keyboard (so named for the layout of its keys, like QWERTY) proceeds from the assumption that the Palm's own built-in keyboard requires too much hand movement. Because it's so wide, you have to move your stylus quite a bit, leading to slow and often inaccurate data entry. The Fitaly Keyboard arranges letters in a tightly knit group designed to minimize stylus travel. Hence, you should be able to tap-type much more quickly.

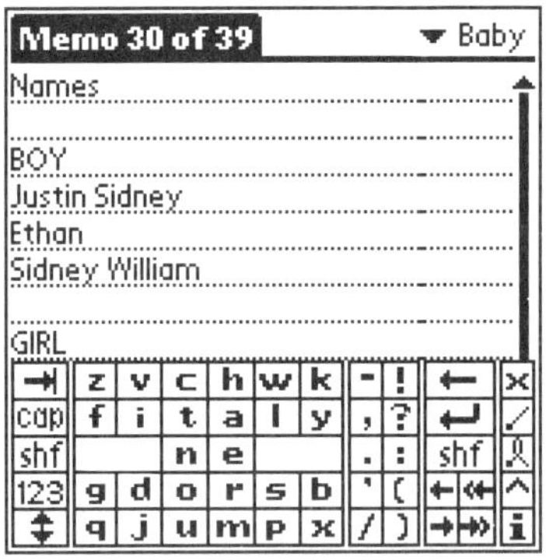

Clearly, Fitaly represents a radical departure from the standard QWERTY keyboard, and therefore has a high learning curve. Make that practice curve: it could take you several days to master the layout, and even then you might decide you don't like it. The moderate speed gain may not offset the difficulty in learning an entirely new keyboard.

On the other hand, Fitaly is much more practical than the stock built-in keyboard, in part because it makes most common punctuation marks readily available, without the need to shift modes (or even tap the SHIFT key). And when you do access the Numeric mode (done by tapping the 123 button, as with the standard keyboard), you gain access to a number of extended characters (including fractions, the Euro symbol, and more).

If you like the idea of Fitaly but hate sacrificing a big chunk of the screen, check out FitalyStamp—a plastic overlay that moves the keyboard right on top of the Graffiti area. It's covered earlier in this chapter.

Hacks

In Chapter 15, you learned all about X-Master and the little OS enhancements (*Hacks*) that work with it. Let's talk about two that are expressly related to the Palm's onscreen keyboard.

Keyboard Hack

If you've spent any time with the Palm's standard onscreen keyboard, you've probably been frustrated at having to switch modes to access numbers and punctuation. Horace Ho's Keyboard Hack solves the problem by replacing the standard keyboard with a slightly modified one. His keyboard sports 69 keys, including a numeric keypad and a row of punctuation keys. It also has left/right keys for moving your cursor a space at a time.

> **NOTE** *The latter feature, the cursor-control keys, was suggested by a Keyboard Hack user. The author of the program incorporated it into the next version. This is part of what makes the Palm community so great: so many software developers are just regular folks who are happy to hear from regular users. You can have a voice in the evolution of Palm software!*

Graffiti&Keyboard

Some Palm device owners like to use the onscreen keyboard most of the time, and occasionally bop back to Graffiti to write numbers or enter ShortCuts. Problem is, for Palm devices that run an

18

What About a Real Keyboard?

Thumbs, overlays, styluses—whatever you use to enter data on your Palm device, it won't be as fast as an actual keyboard. Fortunately, actual keyboards do exist for Palms—lots of them. To find out all about them, see Chapter 20.

OS older than 4.0, when the keyboard is active, the Graffiti area is not. *Graffiti&Keyboard* overcomes that limitation, allowing the keyboard and Graffiti area to operate simultaneously. Yes, there's a Hack for just about everything.

Give Graffiti a Helping Hand

Here's a novel idea: Rather than trying to build a better Graffiti than Graffiti, why not simply cut down on the number of letters necessary to write a word? Or make it so you can write anywhere on the screen, instead of just in the Graffiti area? How about tweaking the recognition engine so it's more accommodating to your handwriting? These are among the goals of Graffiti assistants— software tools that just make life with Graffiti a little easier.

How to ... Improve Graffiti Recognition

For all its quirks, Graffiti is actually an excellent handwriting-recognition tool. If you plan to stick with it, you can use these tips to improve accuracy.

- Write big. If your characters fill up the bulk of the Graffiti area, they're more likely to be accurately recognized.

- Don't write on an angle. Many of us do just that when writing with pen and paper, but that's poison to Graffiti. Keep your strokes straight.

- Take advantage of the built-in Graffiti Help application, which provides a graphical cheat sheet for all Graffiti strokes. Go to Prefs | Buttons | Pen, then choose Graffiti Help from the list of available options. Now, whenever you draw a line from the Graffiti area to the top of the Palm's screen, the Help applet appears.

- Having trouble with the letter *V*? Draw it backwards, starting from the right side and ending with the left. You needn't add the little tail (as with the standard Graffiti *V*) and the letter will come out perfectly every time.

■ Having trouble with the letter *B*? Forget trying to draw it Graffiti's way—write the number 3 instead. Similarly, writing the number 6 gives you a good *G* every time, while the number 8 creates the perfect *Y*. Naturally, you should still make these characters on the letter (that is, left) side of the Graffiti area.

■ Start your *R* at the bottom of the letter instead of the top. That initial downstroke often produces the ShortCut symbol instead of an *R*.

Was This the Word You Were Looking For?

Remember the old game show "*Name That Tune*"? The host would describe a song, and the contestant would say, "I can name that tune in three notes." Imagine if Graffiti could adopt that precept, guessing the word or phrase you're writing as you write it. By the time you entered, say, the *e* in "competition," the software would have figured out the rest of the word, thereby saving you six additional pen-strokes.

That's the appeal of CIC's WordComplete, a Palm utility that helps you write faster by helping you write less. As you enter characters, a box containing possible word matches appears. If you spy the word you're after, just tap it. The more letters you enter, the closer you get to the correct word (if it's in the software's database).

Obviously, for little words like "the" and "to," the program won't help much. But for longer words, it can indeed save you some scribbling. And WordComplete lets you add your own words and/or short phrases to its database, which can definitely save you time in the long run. Let's look at its features and operation.

WordComplete

Once you install WordComplete on your Palm device (it's compatible with all models), run the program and tap the Enable WordComplete check box. You see a number of options appear:

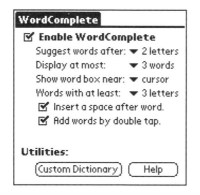

■ **Suggest words after**   After how many letters should the software start suggesting words? The default is two, but you can make it anywhere between one and four.

■ **Display at most**   How many matches should the software display at a time? You have to experiment to decide your preference. Obviously, more matches means a greater likelihood of your desired word appearing, but it takes a bit longer to glance through a longer list.

■ **Show word box near**   Where should the suggestion box pop up—next to the cursor or near the bottom of the screen? We think the former is the most practical, as it cuts down on stylus travel.

■ **Words with at least**   What's the minimum word length WordComplete should attempt to guess? Three letters? Four? You can make your selection here.

■ **Insert a space after word**   Leave this box checked if you want the software to automatically add a space after you tap a word. Most of the time this is quite helpful, except when you're about to end a sentence with a punctuation mark. Then you have to draw a backspace stroke.

■ **Add words by double tap**   WordComplete supports the use of a custom dictionary to which you can add your own words. With this option checked, it's as simple as double-tapping a word with your stylus, then tapping the Add option from the little box that appears. (You hear a beep confirming the word has successfully been added.)

■ **Custom Dictionary**   Tap this button to manually add words to the software's dictionary. Although the aforementioned double-tap method limits you to adding one word at a time, here you can add multiple words (such as proper names) or even short phrases.

NOTE   *If you do add proper names to the dictionary, take note that they're case-sensitive. This means if you add "Rick Broida," you have to use a capital* R *if you want WordComplete to show the name while you're writing.*

Goodbye, Graffiti Area!

Ever notice the Graffiti area is kind of, well, small? Most of us aren't used to writing in such a confined space, and that alone can be a source of Graffiti contention. Fortunately, there's a utility that can liberate your stylus from that tiny box, effectively turning the entire Palm screen into one big Graffiti area.

CIC's RecoEcho enables you to write—using Graffiti characters—anywhere on the screen. What's more, it leaves a trail of "digital ink" beneath your stylus tip, which goes a long way toward helping you produce more accurate characters. You see what you write as you write it, just as you would with a pen on paper.

RecoEcho

After you launch the program, you simply tap a check box to enable it. Then you set three simple options:

■ **Write in full screen**   If, for some reason, you don't want to write on the screen itself (but only in the Graffiti area), uncheck this box. You still see your pen strokes as you write, provided the next option is still checked.

- ■ **Show ink**   If you prefer not to see the trail of "ink" as you write, uncheck this box.
- ■ **Ink width**   Choose 1 for a thin trail of ink, 2 for a thicker trail. This is simply a matter of personal preference.

When RecoEcho is activated, you see a large arrow at the top of the screen. This designates an invisible line separating the letter and number sides, just like in the standard Graffiti area. Now, write on the screen as you normally would, and presto: you're free to write as large as you like.

The Best Little Graffiti Tweak in Town

Part of the challenge in learning and mastering Graffiti is that you can't see your characters as you write them. (Actually, if you have HandEra's 330 or Sony's CLIÉ NR70, you can—their virtual Graffiti areas leave a trail of digital ink beneath your stylus. Very cool.)

That's where TealEcho comes in. This simple utility displays your pen strokes on the main screen as you make them in the Graffiti area. As a result, you can gauge just how accurate (or inaccurate) your characters are. Sounds like no big deal, but trust us when we say TealEcho goes a long way toward improving Graffiti accuracy.

Graffiti, Your Way

Finally, we come to the one product that really manhandles Graffiti, that says, "Look, can't you just learn to understand *my* writing?" It is TealPoint Software's TealScript, a utility that lets you tweak Graffiti so it's more responsive to your style, or replace it altogether with a customized character set.

If you're willing to battle one of the steepest learning curves we've encountered in a piece of Palm software, the benefits are truly worthwhile. TealScript works its wizardry through the use of custom profiles, which contain the Graffiti character set as you define it. In other words, you teach TealScript how you like to write, and it teaches Graffiti to accommodate your penmanship.

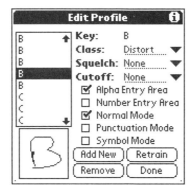

The letter *v* is a good example of how this works. Your profile can include the standard character—the one with the little tail we always forget to add—and a regular *v* you added yourself. Similarly, instead of always having to write capitalized versions of letters like *R* and *B*, you can add lowercase versions.

As confusing as TealScript can be to work with, it's not totally out of the question for novice users. That's because it comes with an already-built profile that helps you overcome the most commonly miswritten Graffiti characters. So, right out of the box it's useful. And while TealScript may not be the friendliest program around, it's by far the best way to make Graffiti an ally instead of an obstacle.

Where to Find It

Web Site	Address	What's There
Textware Solutions	**www.fitaly.com**	Fitaly Keyboard, FitalyStamp
Link Evolution Corp.	**www.thumbtype.net**	ThumbType
Softava	**www.silkyboard.com**	Silkyboard
TapPad	**www.tappad.com**	TapPad
Communications Intelligence Corp.	**www.cic.com**	Jot, RecoEcho, WordComplete
Horace Ho	**www.horaceho.net**	Keyboard Hack
Konstantin Klyatskin	**www.palmgear.com**	Graffiti&Keyboard
TealPoint Software	**www.tealpoint.com**	TealScript, TealEcho

Chapter 19

The Great Handheld Multimedia Machine

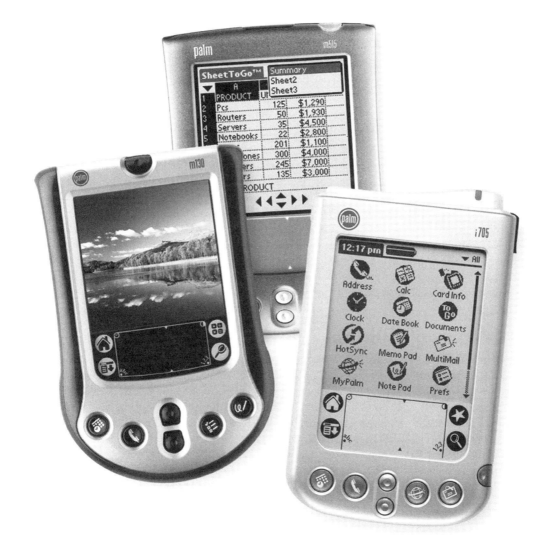

How to…

- Find electronic books (aka e-books)
- Choose a Doc viewer
- Read e-books on your Palm device
- Convert text files to the Doc format
- View photos and other images on your Palm device
- Watch movies on your Palm device
- Paint images on the Palm
- Share and collaborate on sketches with two Palms
- Use an outliner to organize your ideas
- Capture Palm screenshots
- Use the Palm for music
- Manage your MP3 collection using a Palm

You know the future has arrived when a device the size of a Pop Tart can hold an entire Stephen King novel, the full contents of a photo album, a few of your favorite musical tunes, and can help you sketch, paint, and compose music. Now that you've seen some of the minor miracles Palm devices can perform, it should come as little surprise to learn they're great for all sorts of multimedia tricks as well.

Indeed, many users find the ability to read electronic books (aka e-books) and carry digital images around in their pocket a major perk of Palm devices. You can pay nothing at all and read hundreds of literary classics or pay discounted prices for mainstream titles. In this chapter, you learn everything you need to know about using your Palm as a multimedia powerhouse.

Build a Library of E-Books

Before Palm devices came along, a growing collection of electronic books—mostly public-domain classic literature, like Voltaire's *Candide* and Sir Arthur Conan Doyle's *Sherlock Holmes* stories—existed on the Internet. Because these works had already been converted to computer-readable text, why not copy them to Palm devices for reading anytime, anywhere?

In theory, you can simply paste the text into a memo. But there's a snag: documents are limited to about 500 words, so even short stories are out of the question. Hence, the emergence of one of the first third-party applications: *Doc,* a simple text viewer that had no length limitation (other than the amount of RAM in the Palm itself). Doc rapidly became a de facto standard, not only for e-books, but also for documents created in desktop word processors and converted for Palm handhelds.

NOTE   *In this chapter, we mostly discuss the e-book aspect of Doc files. If you want to learn more about creating and editing text files in a Palm word processor, see Chapter 14.*

Did you know?

Doc Files Don't Discriminate

The Doc format works with both Palm OS devices and the Pocket PC. So sharing Doc files (like e-books) with Pocket PC users is often as simple as giving them a copy of the file. If they have a Doc reader on their handheld, they can read the text without any sort of conversion process.

Choose a Doc Viewer

Many people make this mistake: they download a bunch of nifty e-books from MemoWare (or wherever), load them on to their Palms, then spend lots of time trying to figure out why they can't "see" their e-books. (When you install software, there's usually an icon for it.) The reason, of course, is they don't have a Doc viewer installed. Without one, there's no way to view Doc files.

Fortunately, plenty of Doc viewers are out there—all free or quite inexpensive. The best place to start is with Palm's own program, Palm Reader, available at **www.Palm.com**. Here's a rundown of some other choices:

Doc Viewer	Noteworthy Features
CSpotRun	Free. Supports auto-scrolling.
Isilo	Supports HTML and .txt files, as well as Doc files—also uses the Sony CLIÉ's HiRes+ resolution, a great feature if you have an NR70.
WordSmith, Quickword, FastWriter	These programs, discussed in Chapter 14, can all double as word processors.
TealDoc	Supports images and links between documents. Advanced search options.

All these programs are available from PalmGear H.Q.

Here's what Palm Reader, CSpotRun, and TealDoc look like, side by side:

He looked apologetically at me. "There's no eavesdropping of course, but we don't want to upset our very excellent service with any rumours of ghosts in the place. There's too much shadow and oak panelling to trifle with that. And this, you know, wasn't a regular ghost. I don't think it will come again--ever."

"You mean to say you didn't keep it?"

"What sort of physique?" said Sanderson.

"Lean. You know that sort of young man's neck that has two great flutings down the back, here and here--so! And a little, meanish head with scrubby hair--And rather bad ears. Shoulders bad, narrower than the hips; turn-down collar, ready-made short jacket, trousers baggy and a little frayed at

▼ BM

A ◀▮▶ ▬▮▬ ▮▐▶ ▼ 17% ▼ Doc

say it," he said, "in all kindliness, but that is the plain truth of the case. Even at the first glance he struck me as weak."

He punctuated with the help of his cigar.

"I came upon him, you know, in the long passage. His back was towards me and I saw him first. Right off I knew him for a ghost. He was transparent and whitish; clean through his chest I could see the

Ⓧ ◀ (15%) ◀▮ 🔍 ▮▶ (AAₐ) ↻ ⬇ 🗑

19

An E-Book Love Affair

Several years ago, Rick found himself on a train with nothing to do for several hours. Then he remembered he'd loaded an e-book on his Palm just before leaving. He started reading, found the novel totally engrossing, and passed the time as happy as a clam. From that day forward, Rick vowed never to travel anywhere without an e-book. And when people ask him to explain what that little gadget is he's holding, he says it's a handheld PC—and a portable library.

NOTE   *Not all readers can read all documents. Most of these programs handle the Doc format just fine, but some documents are stored in proprietary formats that only some of these readers can access. Isilo, for instance, has a special format that supports hypertext and fancy formatting. PalmReader and TealDoc can't read Isilo documents.*

Make Room for the Books

Before we delve into the details of finding, buying, and viewing e-books, you should know that e-books can be extremely large documents—another reason to consider buying a Palm device with lots of memory. Jules Verne's *The Mysterious Island,* for instance, takes a whopping 622K, while the infamous biography *Monica's Story* nabs 500K. If your Palm device has only 2MB of RAM, you could wind up sacrificing a major chunk of its memory for only one e-book.

Fortunately, not all titles are quite so gargantuan. Most short stories are under 50K and, even Stephen King's novel, *The Girl Who Loved Tom Gordon,* is a reasonable 226K. If you're particularly strapped for space, you can always try freeing some: delete infrequently used games and other applications, remove unwanted AvantGo channels, and clear out other e-books you've already read (no sense keeping them loaded).

Free E-Books and E-Books for Sale

There are dozens of online sources for e-books, both free and commercial. The former are works considered public domain: either their copyrights have expired (as in the case of classic literature) or they've been written and released by authors not seeking compensation. Literally thousands of titles are available in the public domain, many of them already converted to the Doc format.

Commercial titles aren't unlike what you'd buy in a bookstore: they've simply been converted to an electronic format and authorized for sale online. Notice we didn't mention Doc: most commercial e-books are created using a proprietary format, meaning a special viewer is required. This is primarily to prevent unauthorized distribution—unlike actual books, commercial e-books aren't meant to be loaned out or given to others. When you buy one, you're effectively buying a license to read it on your Palm device and only your Palm device.

Find Free Stuff

If one site is synonymous with Palm Doc files, it's MemoWare (**www.memoware.com**, Figure 19-1). Here, you can find thousands of texts divided into categories such as business, history, travel,

Our Favorite E-Books

Rick: I have turned into an e-book zealot in recent months, recommending MemoWare and Peanutpress.com to friends, family, and any strangers who will sit still for five seconds. Among the great titles I've read on my Palm are *Angela's Ashes, Battlefield Earth, Kick the Can,* and *'Tis.* I also enjoyed rereading *The Most Dangerous Game,* a story I remembered fondly from high school. I got that one free from MemoWare.

Dave: I have to commend Rick on the progress he's made. When I met him a scant five years ago, he hadn't yet learned to master the written word. Since then, I've seen him get his equivalency diploma, start on "chapter books," and even sign his name in ink instead of crayon. Bravo, Rick! Well done! As for me, I find the best for the buck is the magazine *Fantasy & Science Fiction*—Peanut Press has a good assortment of them going back to 1997. I'm rarely disappointed by any of those tales and a month's worth of bedtime reading is in each collection.

biography, sci-fi, and Shakespeare. Whether you're looking for a collection of Mexican recipes, a Zane Grey western, a sappy love poem, or a classic work by Dickens, this is the place to start.

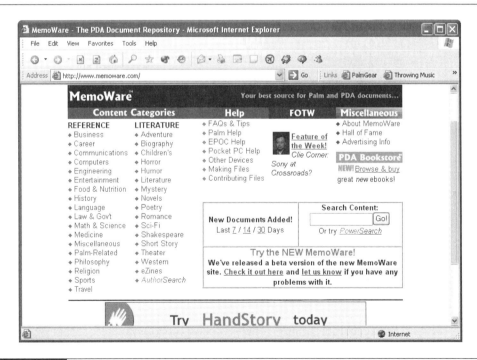

FIGURE 19-1   MemoWare is a good source for electronic books.

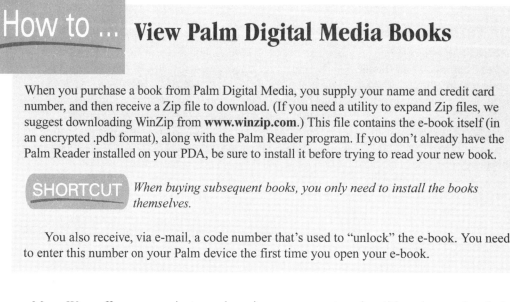

How to ... **View Palm Digital Media Books**

When you purchase a book from Palm Digital Media, you supply your name and credit card number, and then receive a Zip file to download. (If you need a utility to expand Zip files, we suggest downloading WinZip from **www.winzip.com**.) This file contains the e-book itself (in an encrypted .pdb format), along with the Palm Reader program. If you don't already have the Palm Reader installed on your PDA, be sure to install it before trying to read your new book.

SHORTCUT *When buying subsequent books, you only need to install the books themselves.*

You also receive, via e-mail, a code number that's used to "unlock" the e-book. You need to enter this number on your Palm device the first time you open your e-book.

MemoWare offers a convenient search engine, so you can type in a title or keyword to find what you're looking for quickly. It also has links to other e-book sites, although none is as comprehensive. Finally, MemoWare provides numerous links to software programs (most for Windows, a few for Mac) that turn computer documents into Doc files.

Find Commercial Stuff

The thing about public domain e-books is that most of them are, well, old. Somerset Maugham and Jack London are all well and good for catching up on the classics you promised yourself you'd read one day but, sometimes, you just want a little Stephen King. Or Mary Higgins Clark. Or Captain Kirk. Fortunately, you can have them all on your Palm, provided you're willing to pay for them.

The top place to go for contemporary, mainstream fiction, and nonfiction is, without a doubt, Palm's own online bookstore, Palm Digital Media (at **www.peanutpress.com**). The site offers hundreds of books from many well-known authors.

Other Sources for Contemporary E-Books

Palm Digital Media might be the largest source for commercial e-books, but other Web sites also offer contemporary works. You might also want to check out:

- **Electron Press**   A couple dozen original fiction and nonfiction titles, all priced at $5 or less.

- **Fictionwise**   A growing collection of novels and short stories—most in the sci-fi and fantasy genres—from some prominent fiction authors. Reader ratings can help you decide which stories to buy.

Make Your Own E-Books

Become a published author! Well, not published in the Stephen King sense. More in the "kooky old uncle who staples his warnings about how mailboxes are alien mind-control devices to telephone poles" sense. Nonetheless, if you have your own documents, short stories, novellas, or doctoral thesis you'd like to covert to a format that's readable on the Palm, you have a lot of options, including these most common ones:

- Word and text (.txt) format documents are fine if your audience is using a Palm word processor like WordSmith, FastWriter, Documents to Go, and so on. But you can't read a Word file in an e-book app like Palm Reader, so this isn't the most common solution.

- Palm eBook Studio is a $30 program available on the Palm Web site that lets you easily convert text and images to a format that's compatible with both Palms and Pocket PCs.

- MakeDoc (for Windows users) and MakeDocDD (an equivalent program for Mac users) are free, no-frills, doc converters.

Build an Electronic Photo Album

Factoring in inflation, cost-of-living increases, and so forth, a picture is now worth 1,256 words—a rather significant jump in value. All the more reason you should store your photos on your Palm device. As a personal benefit, you'll never be without a picture of your spouse, kids, cats, and other loved ones. As a practical benefit—well, the possibilities are endless. Real estate agents can carry snapshots of available properties. Sales teams can show product photos to prospective buyers. Travelers can look at street maps of unfamiliar cities.

With the right software, you can create cool photo albums on your Palm device. The process is quite simple: electronic images on your desktop PC (whether scanned, transferred from a digital camera, or downloaded from the Web) are converted to a Palm-readable format, and then installed when you HotSync. Then you load up your viewer and, well, view 'em.

If you're lucky enough to have a Palm-powered device with a color screen, this section is definitely for you. While grayscale models can certainly take advantage of photo-album software, the screens leave much to be desired—namely, color.

Read in Bed Without Disturbing Your Spouse

Since the dawn of time, one seemingly insurmountable problem has plagued the human race: how to read in bed without disturbing one's spouse. Torches didn't work. They crackled too loudly and tended to set the bed on fire. Battery-operated book lights didn't work either. They made books too heavy, leading to carpel reader syndrome. But, finally there's an answer: the Palm handheld. Just load up a novel and turn on the backlight. You'll have no trouble seeing the screen in the dark and your spouse won't even know it's on. PDA or marriage saver? You be the judge.

19

Understanding Electronic Images

As you might know, electronic images stored on your computer are usually in one of many different file formats. Photos downloaded from digital cameras and the Internet are often JPEGs, for instance, while scanned photos often wind up as BMPs or TIFs. The differences between these formats aren't important—what's important is you can't simply transfer them directly to your Palm device. Instead, you must use utility software (usually included with the viewer) to convert them to a Palm-compatible format.

NOTE *Not all these utilities support all kinds of graphics formats. The one bundled with Album To Go, for instance, supports only BMP, GIF, and JPEG. If you work with other formats, like TIFF, you'll need a standard image-editing program to convert those images to a more standard format.*

Choosing a Photo-Viewing Software

Many programs enable you to view images on your Palm device, many of them quite similar in their form and function. Here are some of the most common programs for viewing images on your Palm:

■ **Album To Go** This excellent program is a companion to the photo-sharing site, **ClubPhoto.com**. The software is designed to work like a handheld photo album and includes a Windows desktop utility for converting your pictures for the Palm. You can also select images directly from the ClubPhoto Web site for transfer to the Palm.

■ **HandStory Suite** This multifaceted program displays e-book doc files, Web clips, memos, and digital images. The desktop transfer process is elegant. Right-click an image on the desktop, and then choose Save to Palm from the menu.

- **SplashPhoto**   Like Album To Go, SplashPhoto lets you view slideshows of images on your Palm. Its excellent desktop utility is available for both Windows and Macintosh, and it can tweak your photos before transferring them to the handheld.

- **Photogather**   This program has a nice "browse" mode for scrolling though thumbnails of images stored on your Palm. It also supports high-res Sony CLIÉ PDAs. Beware, though: Photogather sends full-resolution images to the Palm, instead of shrinking them to fit on the screen.

Viewing JPEGs Without Conversion

All those programs convert your digital images to a small, compressed, and uniquely Palm format expressly for viewing on your PDA. That's usually a good thing because it saves space on your PDA and makes the images display faster. Think of it this way—do you really want to transfer huge 2 megapixel images to your Palm when a tiny 30KB file will look just as good on the small screen?

That's one side of the argument. But, what if you have digital images from your digital camera on a Memory Stick or SD card that you want to insert directly into your CLIÉ or Palm? Or, what if you simply want to drag-and-drop images from your PC into your Palm without messing with a converter first? This can be done—you need a special program that can interpret JPEG images. One of the better ones is AcidImage, from Red Mercury. *AcidImage* is a good

19

image viewer that can handle a wide variety of file formats, including JPG, BMP, and GIF. Sony CLIÉ owners will appreciate that it's also compatible with the NR70's HiRes+ resolution mode. Another alternative is called JpegWatch. Like AcidImage, *JpegWatch* can read JPEG images from your Palm's memory card and convert it to a viewable format on-the-fly.

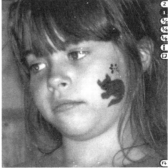

CAUTION   *Large digital images take up a lot of room on your memory card and can take a while to display on your Palm. This sort of application is best reserved for PDAs with lots of memory and faster processors.*

Other Image Viewers

Fond as we are of the album-based programs you just read about, a slew of other image viewers are out there. Here are some other cool ones:

- **FireViewer**   The most powerful image viewer available for the Palm OS, FirePad's *FireViewer* has a wealth of features not found elsewhere. It can be used with wireless Palm devices to download images, maps, and even live video feeds. FireViewer itself is free, but the utility needed to convert images and movies to FireViewer format will set you back $20. It's available for Windows and Macintosh.

- **PixScreen Palm**   *PixAround* is a computer program that lets you stitch together digital photos to create 360-degree panoramas, which you can scroll around to create a kind of virtual-reality experience. *PixScreen Palm* lets you view PixAround-created scenes on your handheld. The software supports color and grayscale Palms, and it lets you beam scenes to other Palm users. Very cool.

Mapmaker, Mapmaker, Make Me a Map

Wouldn't it be cool if you could have street-level maps handy when you visit unfamiliar cities? You can, and they won't cost you a dime. Point your Web browser to Yahoo! Maps or one of the many other online cartography sources, generate the map you need, and then save it to your hard drive. Now, run it through your image viewer's conversion software and load it on to your Palm device. If you want something a little more sophisticated (and precise), check out XMaps Handheld Street Atlas USA Edition from Delorme (**www.delorme.com**). It's designed specifically to display maps on your handheld.

Watch Movies on Your Palm Device (Sort of)

Why would anyone want to watch a jerky, low-resolution movie on a screen not much larger than a matchbook? This question has been a source of much debate between Dave and Rick, who have chosen to leave you with this simple explanation: if you want to do it, you can. Third-party programs like FireViewer, MGI PhotoSuite Mobile Edition, and TealMovie all make it possible.

NOTE   *Most Sony CLIÉ models come with* gMedia, *which can play video clips.*

When we talk about watching movies on your Palm device, we don't mean feature films like *The Matrix*. We mean video clips or animated shorts that can range from seconds to hours, depending on how much memory you have available. Remember, even short clips—especially those in color—can take up a lot of memory, but a 128MB memory card can easily hold two hours of video.

Paint on the Palm

You're probably wondering why you might want to paint on a handheld computer so small it fits in your pocket. Well, in the world of computers, the answer is often "because you can." Programmers have never let something as silly as a technical limitation get in the way of doing something, so when the Palm came out, programmers literally seemed to scramble to become the first to create a paint program for their favorite handheld PC.

But, aside from that admittedly flippant answer, the capability to sketch things out on your Palm is a handy feature. You can draw a map to sketch the way to lunch, outline a process, or design a flowchart. You can also doodle—use the Palm as a high-tech Etch-a-Sketch for those boring times when you're waiting for the train or pretending to take notes in a meeting.

Painting on your Palm is fun and productive, but you need to remember these limitations:

■ Depending on the paint program you choose, you might be limited to shades of gray, a 256-color palette, or thousands of colors. If you have a color Palm, you're obviously best off with a full-color paint program. But, if you have a grayscale Palm, choose a program

19

that supports the number of colors your Palm can handle. Some old Palm devices can't show 16 shades of gray. The bottom line is your images will look kind of like this:

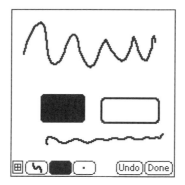

■ Most Palm models have a resolution of 160 × 160 pixels, though newer HandEra and Sony CLIÉ PDAs break that barrier with resolutions like 320 × 320 and even 320 × 480. The more pixels you have, the better, but even the highest resolution devices don't give you a lot of room in which to draw. After your images are transferred to a PC, you'll find they're very, very small. So, drawing something on the Palm you later plan to export to, say, a PowerPoint presentation, generally isn't feasible.

■ Not many Palm paint programs support printing directly from the Palm, which means, in some cases, what you draw on the screen pretty much stays on the screen. If you *can* print your work of art, it'll print as rough and jagged on paper as it looked onscreen. If you want to achieve high-resolution paper output, you should, instead, try a drawing program (discussed in the upcoming bulleted point "Diddle").

The Great Color Debate

Dave: Well, I guess I should get this off my chest right away. Sure, I think the Palm is a great device for showing off your wallet-sized pictures. And I've used it for paint and drawing applications on occasion. With the advent of color models like the Palm IIIc, m505, and Visor Prism, though, I've had something of an epiphany. It's this: grayscale stinks. Don't get me wrong: shades of gray are fine for text entry, number crunching, and looking up the pizza joint's phone number. But, if you want to do any sort of graphics on a Palm, you need to get a color model.

Rick: Well, of course, painting pretty pictures is best done with a color palette. And if you artists out there are content to work on a canvas that's about five square inches, then have at it. But I wouldn't buy a color model for this reason alone. In fact, I didn't become a convert to color until Sony unveiled the high-resolution CLIÉ N760C. It has four times the resolution of the Palm IIIc, m505/515, Visor Prism, Treo 90, and so forth and, therefore, makes maps, photos, and even e-books look markedly better. I still think color is superfluous for many users, but if you do want a color screen, opt for one with a higher resolution. You won't be sorry.

As we mentioned, a plethora of painting tools exist for the Palm—so many, in fact, we decided to narrow the crop for you to only a pair of programs you should evaluate. We assembled the best of the litter for you to evaluate.

■ **TealPaint**   Perhaps the most full-featured paint program for the Palm, TealPaint seems to do it all. *TealPaint* has a complete set of painting tools, including lines, shapes, fill tools, an eraser, and a variety of brushes. The program starts you in the following screen, which displays thumbnail images of your pictures and lets you view, edit, or animate them. Using TealPaint, you can copy-and-paste selections of your image, not only within the same picture, but in any picture in your database. TealPaint is also an animation tool. You can even use TealPaint to create animations by playing all the images in a particular database in sequence. To make a simple bouncing ball, for instance, make a series of images in which the ball moves a bit in each successive image. Next, tap the Anim button, and then tap the first picture in your series.

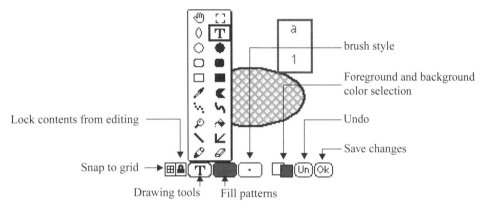

■ **Diddle**   *Diddle* is a free, neat little drawing program that enables you to sketch with a minimum of clutter to get in the way of your drawing. The interface is composed of a set of graphical menus at the top of the screen—you can choose from among various drawing styles, line thickness, and text. For the most part, the program is easy to explore on your own—just start drawing.

NOTE   *TealPaint comes with a PC-side utility for viewing and saving images within Windows. A MacPac is also available for using TealPaint files on the Macintosh.*

Collaborate on a Sketch

Drawing on a Palm is usually a solo affair, but what if you're in a meeting trying to lay out office furniture with your business partner? What then, huh? Okay, some better examples might be out there, but work with us for a moment.

Okay, we have a better example! Suppose you're in a long, boring meeting. If you have the right drawing software, you can doodle on your Palm and have it immediately show up on a partner's Palm, who can then add to your drawing and beam it back to you. All the while, your boss is none the wiser.

19

Anyway, if your buddy, business partner, or intern owns a Palm, the two of you can sketch your ideas on your Palms. The results can appear simultaneously in both devices more or less in real time. That's totally cool, if you ask us.

Most collaborative sketch programs do their magic via the Palm's IR port. Here are some popular apps you can try:

■ **Beamer**   This simple program has a few buttons, and it's free. With *Beamer,* you can write short notes in a screen that resembles the Note Pad or draw free-form images in a blank sketchpad. When you're ready, tap the beam button—it looks like a tilde (~) sign—to beam it to another nearby Palm. The recipient can add to your drawing and beam it back.

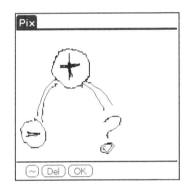

■ **Zapster**   Similar to Beamer, *Zapster* has a slightly more elegant interface. On the downside, it's shareware and costs $10. Like Beamer, you use it to draw, and then beam your work to another Palm, where it can be edited and returned.

The newest craze in the PDA world is Bluetooth (all the kids are trying it). *Bluetooth,* as you probably learned in Chapter 13, is a short-range wireless networking technology you can use for a whole slew of applications, including connecting your Palm to the Internet using a cell phone as a modem. If your Palm has Bluetooth capabilities (such as via the Palm Bluetooth Card), you can use Palm's BlueBoard application to share an onscreen sketch board with up to three other Palm users at once.

Experiment with Fractals

If you're somewhat new to computing, you might have missed the fractal craze of the '80s. That was when everyone and their cousin seemed to be writing a graphics program for the PC, Amiga, Atari, and TI/99 that generated fractal images.

What's a fractal, you ask? A *fractal* is a class of mathematics invented in the 1970s by a mathematician named Benoit Mandelbrot. This is more interesting than it might sound—it's concerned with reproducing infinitely repeating structures, both mathematically and visually.

Consider a mountain, for instance—you can zoom in on the structure and, no matter how far you zoom, the structure remains essentially the same, all the way down to the rocks that make up the mountain. Another example: think of a fiord. On the surface, calculating the total perimeter of the shoreline seems easy but, as you enlarge the fiord, you find there's a virtually infinite amount of structure to the shore, as it weaves back and forth in tiny jagged edges. All this has practical applications, though, because fractal equations do a darned good job of drawing computer-rendered natural objects like trees, mountains, snowflakes, and flowers. When done well, the perceived reality can be stunning.

All this is great, but what about the Palm? Well, you can use your Palm to draw fractal sets that are beautiful in their own right, and you can experiment with them by zooming in and letting the Palm render the new scene. No matter where you zoom, you get an interesting picture and you can always zoom in further.

A few fractal programs are available for the Palm. You won't get stunning, full-color results like you can on a Mac or PC, but you can have fun, nonetheless. Try Fractal Maker, Fractal Maker Color, or P.Fract—all available at **www.palmgear.com**.

One word of warning: The Palm's processor is no supercomputer. As a result, the time it takes your Palm to draw a fractal onscreen might well remind you of drawing fractals on 486's and Amigas in the '80s. It can take quite some time to render each image.

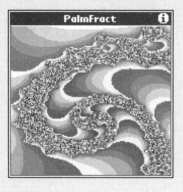

Outline Your Ideas

Outliners are an interesting class of software. Not quite a Memo Pad or a To Do List, and not quite a drawing program, *outliners* help you organize your thoughts into a logical and manageable order.

Typically, outliners use a hierarchical approach to data management. This might sound imposing, but the basic idea is that your ideas are generally related to each other. So, start with a single note, and then nest subnotes within it, as if you had a data tree with branches that grew off the main topic. By grouping related ideas together, it's easier to stay organized and arrange your data in a format that works for you.

The Palm has several excellent idea organizers with which you can experiment:

■ **BrainForest**   This program is, perhaps, the most complete organizer for the Palm and serves as an action item tracker, checklist manager, outliner, idea keeper, and project planner. *BrainForest* uses Tree, Branch, and Leaf metaphors to enable you to nest notes within each other, thus grouping items in a logical manner. Items are numbered using traditional outlining notation (like 1.2.3, for the third leaf in the second branch of the first tree of data). You can also export specific items to the Palm's To Do List and Memo Pad. BrainForest also enables you to prioritize, sort, and rearrange items by dragging-and-dropping.

■ **Idea Pad**   *Idea Pad* is a diagram editor that lets you create flow charts, text outlines, and other graphical representations of the strange little thoughts in your head. Diagrams can be exported to the desktop, where you can insert them in your favorite graphics program. Text outlines can be exported to word processors.

■ **MindManager Mobile**   *Mind maps* are nonlinear outlines that show the relationship between related topics. They often look like cascading groups of thought bubbles, with spider-like connections holding them together. They let you take notes or brainstorming in a free-form way, without being restricted to a rigid format. The leading mind-mapping software for the Palm is MindManager 2002 Mobile Edition. *MindManager* lets you create original mind maps on the Palm or synchronize with the desktop version of MindManager. Either way, you start with a central hub concept and branch out from there, adding ideas, tasks, and data in radiating branches. Branches can be nested, long-form notes can be attached, and the program makes use of graphic icons and color to highlight certain areas of a map. Although the program can stand on its own, its real power comes when you synchronize a map made on the Palm and feed it back to the desktop for inclusion in PowerPoint presentations, e-mails, or Web pages.

```
┌──────────────────────────────┐
│ MindManager  ⌂ ✳ ☰           │
│                               │
│                ┌─⏰talk to t...│
│                ├─⌐grand caym...│
│ 3 cathy chu...─┐├─⌐disc rates?│
│                               │
│  ╭─────────────────────────╮ │
│  │ underwater photo course  │ │
│  ╰─────────────────────────╯ │
│                               │
│ sunset hou...  ┌─⌐digital or fi...│
│ group trav...─┘               │
│                               │
│ ┌─┐┌─┐                        │
│ │+││✎│                        │
│ └─┘└─┘                        │
└──────────────────────────────┘
```

Capture Screenshots of the Palm Display

Perhaps you've thumbed through this book, some Palm web sites, or a magazine like *Handheld Computing* and wondered what it would be like to have lunch with Dave and Rick. (Answer: like keeping a pair of six-year-olds entertained in line at McDonald's.) You might also have wondered how everyone seems to be able to capture screenshots of the Palm display and publish them in ordinary desktop software. As it turns out, capturing Palm screens isn't that hard to do because several tools are available to automate (at least partially) the process for you.

The easiest way to capture a screen from your Palm—and our favorite, by far—is by using *ScreenShot Hack,* one of the many Palm OS extensions that work with X-Master and HackMaster (see Chapter 15). ScreenShot Hack is a great general-purpose tool because you needn't do anything special to activate it. There are no countdowns until the screen is captured (unless you specifically set a capture delay), no menu funky selections. Just display the screen you want to capture and draw the screen capture gesture in the Graffiti area (there's even a way to capture screens on devices like the Handspring Treo that don't have Graffiti areas).

```
┌──────────────────────────────┐
│ ScreenShot          ⓘ        │
│                               │
│ Trigger Stroke               │
│  ▼ Numeric                    │
│ Trigger Delayed 3   sec      │
│  ▼ From Graffiti  ▼ To Calc  │
│ ☑ Beep                       │
│ Screenshots: 11 (2124 KB)    │
│ (View) (Remove last) (Remove all)│
│ Registered to                │
│ Dave                         │
│  ( OK )                       │
└──────────────────────────────┘
```

Most importantly, the program converts the images to a usable file format for you—many other screenshot utilities don't. You have two choices for how to get images to the PC:

- **The ScreenShot Conduit**   This is a separate program you need to download and install. The conduit grabs the captured screens from the Palm and puts them in BMP or GIF format in a folder of your choice.

- **The ScreenShot Converter**   If you don't want to use the conduit, the images are transferred to the PC anyway (as long as you set the System conduit to Handheld Overwrites Desktop). Then you need to use the ScreenShot Converter utility (again, a separate program you need to download and install) to transform the images into Windows bitmap files.

You can use either method, though we prefer the conduit—it's a bit more automated. Once you have the images on your PC, you can convert them to any format you like. In this book, for instance, Dave uses Jasc's Image Robot to convert all the BMP screenshots automatically into TIF format, Osborne's file format of choice. Because the whole process is automated, no one has to sit around saving files over and over again to get them into the right format.

Make Music on the Palm

Believe it or not, you can use the Palm for a number of music applications. The Palm has a built-in speaker for creating (admittedly, very basic) sounds and the display is perfectly suited for music notation in a small space. If you're a musician, be sure to check out some of these applications.

Metronome and Drumming Software

It doesn't take a rocket scientist to figure out the Palm's sound capabilities aren't exactly symphonic in nature. So, one obvious application for your Palm is to keep time, either as a drum machine or a metronome. In fact, this would have come in handy a long time ago—Dave used to carry a guitar around wherever he went and having a metronome or a minidrum machine in a box as small as the Palm would have been really cool.

- **Meep**   This is your standard metronome. *Meep* has a slider for choosing any tempo from 40 to 280 beats per minute and you can select up to 8 beats per measure, as well. You can work from onscreen counts or add an audible beep to each beat.

- **Responsive Metronome**   Another simple metronome tool, *Responsive Metronome* enables you to choose any tempo from 35 to 300 beats per minute, and both see (via a pulsing quarter note) and hear the beat. This program is quite simple. In fact, there's no on/off switch for the beat—you have to disable both the audio and video filters to shut it off.

- **Pocket Beat**   This app simulates a drum kit right on your Palm. It can remember two distinct tempos and you can switch between them easily by using onscreen controls or the Scroll button. *Pocket Beat* can also play straight or shuffle beats, and it can vary between 40 and 196 beats per minute. The best part, though, is you can tap out your own meter on the Palm screen—Pocket Beat memorizes the tempo and plays it accordingly.

Here you can see images from Meep, Responsive Metronome, and PocketBeat:

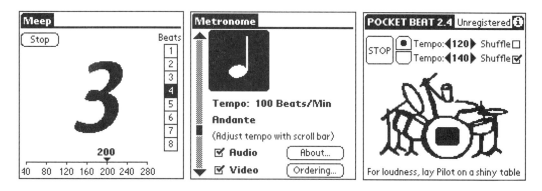

Portable Music Lessons

Budding musicians can carry around the following applications with them to bone up on notes, keyboard positions, and fingering:

- ■ **MusicTeacher**   This program can be used as an aid to learning to sing *prima vista*—that is, by reading sheet music by sight. Several tunes are stored in the *MusicTeacher* database and you can also enter your own using the onscreen keyboard.

NOTE   *This program is interesting because it's written in Java and uses a Java interpreter on the Palm to run. Because it's only a Java app, the MusicTeacher program can also be found on the Web and runs from within a web browser window. You can find it at* **mathsrv.ku-eichstaett.de/MGF/homes/grothmann/java/waba**.

- ■ **GTrainer**   If you're learning to play guitar and you don't want to be forever tied to "tab" sheet music, try *GTrainer*. This app displays a note onscreen and you need to tap the correct place on the guitar fretboard. It isn't enough to choose the right note—you have to tap the correct octave, as well.

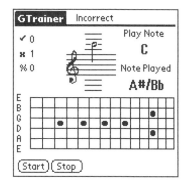

- **McChords**   If you're learning piano, *McChords* is an essential portable tool for working through chord fingerings. It shows you which keys to press to form the majority of chords you need to master basic piano playing.

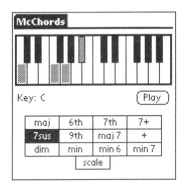

- **PChord**   This program, shown in the following, is indispensable for anyone trying to get the hang of the guitar. In fact, PChord also supports mandolin, banjo, violin, and other stringed instruments. Choose a chord and PChord displays a variety of ways to finger it. PChord includes every chord we could think of, including obscure (minor 9th and stacked fourths) chords you might play only once in a great while. As such, it's a good memory jogger even for experienced players. Similar programs to try include Guitar Power and FretTrainer, and CDB FretBoard Trainer.

Tools for Musicians

Several programs are around to help you tune your instruments. We're not sure we'd rely on the Palm for instrument tuning, but you can certainly try these apps and see if they do the job for you.

- **Guitar Tuner Lt**   *Guitar Tuner Lt* is great for tuning a guitar. Dave has used it himself on several occasions. It comes with standard and alternative tunings. Tap the appropriate onscreen string and the tone plays for several seconds. Or, tap the Auto button to hear each string's tone in turn.

■ **Musician Tools**   This application is easily one of the best all-around utilities for all the Palm-wielding musicians out there. *Musician Tools* combines three utilities into a single interface and does them all well. You'll find a metronome that carries in temp from 40 to 210 beats per minute and one to eight beats per measure. The output is both audible and visual. (Other metronome tools are described in the previous section "Metronome and Drumming Software.") An excellent tuning fork also emits a tone for various notes and a number of base frequencies. Finally, the program includes a circle of fifths.

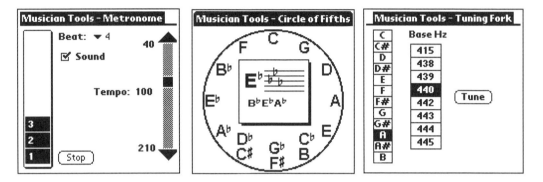

Music Annotation and Recording

You might have experimented with (or frequently use) applications on the Mac or PC that enable you to compose and play music. Those programs generally let you drag notes on to musical staffs or play an onscreen keyboard to construct musical compositions. Well, you can do the same thing on the Palm—the screen is a bit smaller and you don't have multiple voices to hear your multitimbral creations. Here are a few applications you can try:

■ **TS Noter**   This unusually named program is an online favorite because it's so good at helping you create music. *TS Noter* features a staff and a set of tools for placing notes and rests. When you create your song, you can save it, play it, or even export it as an alarm for the Palm's Date Book. A desktop companion program lets you play the music you create on your Palm from a PC using a MIDI instrument.

■ **miniPiano**   This program enables you to play an onscreen keyboard while the notes you strike get added on a staff. You can then play back your creation. miniPiano has a *Free Play* mode in which the keys are duration-sensitive—the longer you hold the stylus on the key, the longer it plays.

■ **Palm Piano**   This simple program records the notes you tap out on a four-octave keyboard and it can play back the results. *Palm Piano* has some simple editing tools built in, but it doesn't have rests and there's no way to select note lengths—they all play back at the same timing.

■ **PocketSynth**   Like Palm Piano, this program enables you to create music by tapping on an onscreen keyboard. *PocketSynth* enables you to select note lengths and rests, though, which gives you more composing flexibility. Unfortunately, you must select the length of the note, and then tap it on the keyboard, which makes the composition process less than entirely fluid.

Play MP3s

If you have a Handspring Visor, you might know it has the capability to play MP3 music files using the MiniJam Springboard module. Snap in the module and you can listen to music at near-CD audio quality through a pair of headphones. Likewise, most Sony CLIÉ models have a built-in MP3 player and can access songs stored on a Memory Stick. Some Palm models, like the Palm V, m100, and m105, can play MP3s through the *PyroPro* (from **PocketPyro.com**), which is a sled-style peripheral that snaps on to the bottom of the PDA and turns it into an MP3 player. PocketPyro claims that a version for m-series Palms (which have the universal connector and SD card slot) is coming soon, so you might want to keep your eyes open for that as well.

But whether or not you can play MP3s from your Palm, you can at least use your Palm to organize and listen to digital music while you're at your desktop PC. If you're adventurous, check out *MP3Remote*, which lets you control the popular WinAmp desktop MP3 player via the Palm's IR port. This makes your Palm a fully cordless MP3 remote control, but it also requires you to use WinAmp on a computer (most likely a laptop) that has an IrDA port.

Important MP3 Sites

Here are some web sites you can visit to download music files, check out new artists, and get up-to-speed on digital music.

- **www.mp3.com**
- **www.emusic.com**
- **www.ubl.com**
- **www.rollingstone.com**
- **www.cductive.com**

19

Manage MP3s

If you've been around the Palm block a few times, you no doubt know a million Palm-sized databases are out there that track everything from your stocks to your favorite books to your CD collection. MP3s are no different. Half a dozen apps are out there that promise to make your life a nirvanaesque dream through MP3 management. Actually, a few of them are pretty good. Here are our favorites:

■ **Playster** Now this program is pretty darned cool. *Playster* searches your hard disk for MP3s and synchronizes the track data—like title, artist, genre, year, and comments—with a database on your Palm. If you're, um, "extremely diligent" (yeah, that's the expression we were trying to think of) about entering all the data for all your tracks, you can do it at your leisure on your Palm and the changes get HotSync'd back to the PC. You can even build custom play lists stored on your PC as M3U files for your favorite MP3 player to play for you. Because Dave is an, um, "extremely diligent" person, he loves this app.

Playster 1.0	580 Songs
▼ Song	▼ Artist
☐ take	Throwing Mu...
☐ santa claus	Throwing Mu...
☐ Mexican Wo...	Throwing Mu...
☐ The River	Throwing Mu...
☐ Juno	Throwing Mu...
☐ Marriage Tree	Throwing Mu...
☐ Run Letter	Throwing Mu...
☐ Saving Grace	Throwing Mu...
☐ Drive	Throwing Mu...
☐ Downtown	Throwing Mu...

(Playlist) (Find)

■ **Nappy** If you visit Kazaa, Morpheus, or some other MP3 download site on a frequent basis, you might want to try *Nappy,* a program originally named after the now largely defunct Napster service. You can use Nappy to make a note of songs you'll download later, when you're at home and sitting in front of your own Internet connection.

Use the Palm as a MIDI Controller

The Palm—a little personal organizer that stores phone numbers—can act as a MIDI controller? Bah, you say. It's true, though. After all, you've seen that many developers have created music applications for the Palm and it does, in fact, have a serial port. That's the same port the Mac and PC typically use to communicate with MIDI instruments. So it's possible—and many people use their Palm for this very, if somewhat unusual, purpose.

You can build your own MIDI interface for your Palm and connect it to a keyboard. You can find instructions for such a device at **fargo.itp.tsoa.nyu.edu/~gsmith/Pilot/PilotMidi.htm**.

What Is MIDI?

MIDI stands for Musical Instrument Digital Interface, and it's been used for well over a decade as a common language for electronic instruments to communicate with each other. Many keyboards are MIDI-enabled, which means if you connect a PC to the keyboard, it can control the music and play complex patterns without human intervention. Likewise, you can even connect a MIDI interface to an electric guitar and use the guitar to record music directly to a PC. You could also use the guitar to control a MIDI keyboard, thus giving the guitar a range of voices and sounds impossible to get any other way. MIDI cables are available that connect a PC's serial port to MIDI devices like keyboards.

Here are a pair of interesting MIDI applications for the Palm:

- **Palm MIDI Desktop** The sound files that constitute the alarms on your Palm are written in the MIDI language. This means they're easily edited. Using the Palm MIDI Desktop program, you can change the alarms on the PC and save them back to your Palm.

- **Theremini** Familiar with the sound of a Theremin? A *Theremin* is how Jimmy Page got that distinctive sound on so many classic Led Zeppelin albums. Well, you don't have to bring a small science lab on stage with you anymore because now you can use Theremini. Connect your PC to a synthesizer and reproduce Theremin-like sounds. The Palm's Theremin interface is clever—simply move the stylus around the screen: one way for amplitude and the other way for frequency. The control lends itself to improvisation. If you don't have a MIDI interface, you can play the Theremin sounds through the Palm speaker.

Where to Find It

Web Site	Address	What's There
Club Photo	**www.clubphoto.com**	Album To Go
Electron Press	**www.electronpress.com**	Small collection of e-books for sale
FictionWise	**www.fictionwise.com**	Palm-formatted short stories for sale
Firepad	**www.firepad.com**	FireViewer
MemoWare	**www.memoware.com**	Thousands of books and articles, all formatted for the Palm
MIDI for the Palm	**fargo.itp.tsoa.nyu.edu/~gsmith/Pilot/ PilotMidi.htm**	MIDI information, including how to create an interface for the Palm
Palm Digital Media	**www.peanutpress.com**	Commercial e-books for sale

Web Site	Address	What's There
PalmGear	**www.palmgear.com**	Virtually all the applications found in this chapter
PixAround.com	**www.pixaround.com**	PixScreen Palm
TealPoint Software	**www.tealpoint.com**	Home of TealPaint and other Teal products
SplashData	**www.splashdata.com**	SplashPhoto

Chapter 20

Accessories and Upgrades

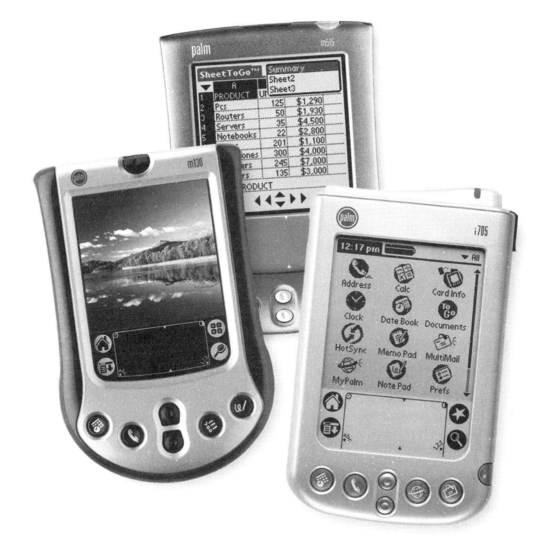

How to...

- ■ Choose a case
- ■ Choose a stylus
- ■ Choose a keyboard
- ■ Protect your screen from dust and scratches
- ■ Add more memory
- ■ Navigate the world with a GPS receiver
- ■ Connect your serial HotSync cradle to a USB port
- ■ Recharge your Palm's battery while on the road
- ■ Extend your Palm's battery life
- ■ Mount your Palm device in your car (or golf cart)
- ■ Turn your Palm device into an MP3 player
- ■ Help a lost Palm find its way home

There's more to Palm devices than just software. We're talking gadgets, gear, accessories—the stuff that makes your handheld your own and extends its capabilities beyond what mere software can accomplish. Take the Targus USB Charge and Sync Cable, an invaluable travel companion that lets you synchronize—and recharge—your handheld by plugging it into any USB port. Or the PyroPro, a clip-on MP3 player for Palm models. In this chapter, we look at these and other accessories and upgrades. For starters, let's tackle cases—a subjective category if ever there was one.

> **NOTE** *Most of the items we spotlight in this chapter are for Palm-branded handhelds, but some are compatible with other models. If you own, say, a Handspring or Sony device, check the manufacturers' Web sites for leads to product-specific accessories and upgrades.*

Pick a Case, Any Case

As a new Palm owner, one of the first things you need to determine is how you plan to convey the device. In your pocket? Briefcase? Purse? Clipped to your belt? Backpack? Dashboard? Your answer will help determine the kind of case you should buy.

There are cases for every Palm model and every occasion, and picking one can be a tough call indeed. Do you opt for practical or stylish? (The two are often mutually exclusive.) Do you look for lots of extras like card slots and pen holders, or try to keep it as slim as possible? Do you shell out big bucks for a titanium shell that can withstand being run over by a car? (This happens quite a bit, believe it or not.)

> **NOTE** *A few Palm devices, like the Palm m100 and Visor Edge, have "built-in" screen covers that negate the need for a protective case (though you may still want one to hold a pen, paper, business cards, and so forth).*

Because there are so many varieties out there, and because everyone's case needs are different, we're going to start by steering you to the case manufacturers themselves, then offer a few general tips and suggestions.

> **NOTE**   *Although most of the products in this chart are indeed cases, a few are better described as holders. These include the CM220 Universal Car Mount, which needs no description, and the Bond Latch, which allows you to wear your Palm device around your neck (no, we're not making this up).*

Company	Phone	URL	Cases Offered
Arkon Resources	(626) 358-1133	**www.arkon.com**	Car Mounts
Case Techworks	(877) 342-2273	**www.casetechworks.com**	Various for Palm, Handspring. and Sony models
Dooney & Bourke	(877) 366-6399	**www.dooney.com**	Various
E&B Company	(800) 896-2273	**www.ebcases.com**	Slipper
Force Technology	(800) 944-7090	**www.force.com**	Bond Latch
Franklin Covey	(800) 819-1812	**www.franklincovey.com**	Various
InnoPocket	N/A	**www.innopocket.com**	Metal cases for Palm and Handspring models
MarWare	(954) 927-6031	**www.marware.com**	Leather and neoprene cases
Palm, Inc.	(800) 881-7256	**www.palm.com**	Various
Parallel Design	N/A	**www.paralleldesign.com**	Personality Pack screen covers
RhinoSkin	(307) 734-8833	**www.rhinoskin.com**	Various metal, aluminum, and leather cases

Here are some things to keep in mind as you shop for a case:

- **Style**   If you're an executive-minded person, you may have purchased a Palm m515 and want a case to match. That means leather. If you're planning to tote the Palm in a suit pocket, look for something that doesn't add much bulk, like E&B's Slipper or Palm's Slim Leather Case (see Figure 20-1).

- **Portability**   In the summer, when the tight clothes come out and the jackets get stowed, pockets are hard to come by. That's when something like Palm's Leather Belt Clip Case can come in mighty handy.

- **Screen protection**   When your Palm is bouncing around in a pocket, purse, or briefcase, the last thing you want is for some piece of flotsam to gouge or scratch the screen. That's one of the main reasons behind getting a case in the first place. For Palm V, m505, and m515 owners, we highly recommend the Parallel Designs Personality Pack (see Figure 20-2), a colorful hard-plastic screen shield. Very cool.

FIGURE 20-1   The Palm Slim Leather Case secures the Palm m515 (and similar models) by sliding into the left-hand stylus silo.

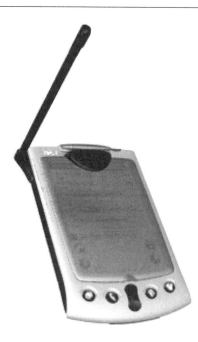

FIGURE 20-2   The Personality Pack provides ultracool screen protection.

■ **Drop protection**   Gravity—it strikes without warning (especially if you're a klutz like Rick), and it can fatally wound a Palm device in a matter of milliseconds. A case made of neoprene or metal, like MarWare's SportSuit or InnoPocket's Metal Deluxe, can save the day if your Palm gets knocked or dropped to the floor.

■ **Moron protection**   We've heard more than a few stories of people driving over their Palm devices. Why they're being left in the driveway in the first place is beyond us, but there's one case that's better suited to handle such punishment than any other: RhinoSkin's Titanium Hardcase. Made of durable titanium, this thing could survive a missile strike.

■ **Velcro**   Some cases rely on Velcro to keep your Palm device secured. While we look upon this as a necessary evil (who wants a big square of the stuff stuck to the back of their Palm?), we do try to avoid such cases when possible.

The Stylus Decision

Many Palm users are perfectly happy with the stylus that came with their Palm device—until they get a look at some of the alternatives. Indeed, while those bundled pens do get the job done, they're not as comfortable or versatile as they could be. For instance, wouldn't a thicker or heavier writing implement feel better in your hand? And wouldn't it be nice if it doubled as an ink pen? These are just some of the options available to the discriminating Palm user.

As with cases, we wouldn't presume to pick a stylus for you. That's a matter of personal preference. So, here's a look at some of the stylus makers and their offerings.

Product	Phone	URL	Comments
Cross DigitalWriter	(800) 722-1719	**www.cross.com**	Various executive-minded sizes and styles, many with multifunction designs
LandWare Floating Point	(800) 526-3977	**www.landware.com**	Unique flexible tip lends the feel of writing on paper
PDA Panache	(800) 270-7196	**www.pdapanache.com**	Wide assortment of sizes and styles
Pentopia Chameleon	(800) 637-0004	**www.pentopia.com**	Multifunction replacement styluses

There are basically two kinds of styluses: those that are too large to fit in a Palm's stylus holder, and those that aren't. The former we'd classify as "executive" styluses: they seem right at home in a suit pocket or briefcase. The Cross DigitalWriter falls into this category—it's big, comfy, and has that classy business look.

Replacement styluses, on the other hand, supplant the stock Palm pen. These include the LandWare Floating Point and Pentopia Chameleon. Both fit snugly in your Palm's stylus silo, and the latter doubles as a ballpoint pen.

20

TIP *If your Palm should happen to crash, the last thing you want is to have to hunt down a toothpick or paper clip in order to press its Reset button. Thus, look for a stylus that hides a reset pin. Most of them do; it's usually accessible simply by unscrewing one end of the barrel.*

Keyboards

If you typically enter a lot of data into your Palm device—memos, e-mail messages, business documents, novels—you've probably longed to replace your stylus with a keyboard. After all, most of us can type a lot faster than we can write by hand. Fortunately, there are a multitude of keyboards available for Palm devices, all of them priced under $100.

Okay, but what kind? Handheld keyboards fall into three broad categories: full-size models that allow for touch typing, palm-size models that give your thumbs a workout, and "inventive" models designed to fit a niche. In the sections that come, we give you the skinny on a few of our favorite keyboards from the first two categories. You're sure to find one—or maybe more than one—that meets your needs.

NOTE *There's an easy argument to be made in favor of owning two or three keyboards for your handheld PC. You could keep a full-size model on hand for boardroom note-taking and carry a thumb board for when you're out and about. That's what we do—and we're professionals!*

Full-Size Keyboards

We don't blame you if the notion of carrying around a standard computer keyboard for use with your tiny little handheld PC is making you chuckle. That would be pretty silly, wouldn't it? Still, what better way to do some serious writing than a full-size set of keys? Of the handful of options now available (including models from Belkin and LandWare), there's simply no better solution than the Palm Portable Keyboard (which also sells under the name Stowaway, depending on which brand of handheld you own—see **www.thinkoutside.com** for details).

As you can see in Figure 20-3, this amazing keyboard folds up to the size of a small diary, and unfolds to produce a set of keys comparable to a notebook PC's. It's a bit pricey at $99 (we've found better prices on eBay, especially for the versions that are compatible with older Palm models), but you won't regret the investment.

The Palm Portable Keyboard/Stowaway does have one disadvantage: limited compatibility. That is, you have to buy the version that's designed to work with your particular handheld model, and if you decide to upgrade someday, the keyboard probably won't be compatible with your new handheld. This is a problem that plagues just about all portable keyboards—but there's a solution.

It's called the Pocketop Portable Keyboard, and instead of requiring a direct connection to your handheld, it works wirelessly via infrared ports. That means it's compatible with virtually

FIGURE 20-3 The Palm Portable Keyboard, aka Stowaway, puts a comfy set of keys beneath your fingers, then folds up and fits in a pocket.

any model (including handhelds that use Microsoft's Pocket PC operating system), so it should be able to "stay with you" for the duration.

The Pocketop's keys are smaller and less comfortable than those of the Stowaway, but it also becomes even more compact when folded. It's a truly ingenious product, one that's well worth investigating.

Thumb-Style Keyboards

If you've ever seen one of those BlackBerry pagers or taken a gander at one of Handspring's Treo handhelds, you may have noticed that in place of a Graffiti area, they have tiny built-in keyboards.

For anyone who's now thinking, "Say, I wish *my* handheld had one of them thar keyboards!" we'd like to remind you that "them thar" is not proper grammar, no matter how many times you hear Dave use it. Fortunately, you can buy a clip-on "thumb board" for just about any handheld, usually for less than $50.

The one we like best is Seiko's aptly named ThumBoard, which is available for the Palm V, m500, and Visor series. The ThumBoard connects to the bottom of the device, enveloping roughly the bottom third of it (including the buttons and Graffiti area). It includes power, application, and function buttons, plus separate number and arrow keys. Most Palm OS operations are available as secondary-key functions. The only downside? You can't beam anything when the keyboard is attached.

Protect Your Screen

Keeping your screen pristine is the first rule of Palm ownership. Why? One word: scratches. A scratch in the Graffiti area can result in inaccurate handwriting recognition. A scratch on the main screen can impair its visibility. Fortunately, it's relatively simple to forestall such disasters.

What causes scratches? If your Palm device is flopping around unprotected in a purse or briefcase, any loose item—keys, paper clips, a pen, or pencil—can create a scratch. That's why we highly recommend a case (see the first section of this chapter). More commonly, however, little specks of grit and other airborne flotsam accumulate on your screen, and when you run your stylus over one of them—scratch city.

> **CAUTION** *Dave is a big fan of tapping on his screen with his big grubby fingers. They leave behind oil and smudges, which are more likely to trap dust and grit. Rick, who is much daintier, says that if you must use a finger, at least use your fingernail.*

We recommend you buy a lens-cleaning cloth, the kind used to wipe dust from eyeglasses and camera lenses. Every day, just give your screen a little buff and polish to keep it free of dust and grit. Or, consider one of the following products.

WriteRight

If you want serious screen protection, you'll need something like Fellowes' WriteRight. These plastic overlays cover your screen from top to bottom, thus ensuring that your stylus causes no damage. They also provide a tacky surface that makes for easier handwriting, and they cut down on glare. The only drawback? WriteRights cut down on contrast, too, making the screen a little tougher to read. If you consider that a small price to pay for total screen protection, these plastic sheets are the way to go.

PDA Screen Protectors

We're not sure this deal will still be around by the time you read this, but it's worth checking out. At a Web site called **FreeScreenProtectors.com**, you can order an entire box of CompanionLink PDA Screen Protectors (which are similar to WriteRights but don't affect contrast) and pay only for shipping. That's right—just enter the coupon code "FREESP" when placing your order, and the sheets are free. Sounds too good to be true, but we placed an order and received our box within about three days. Shipping cost about six bucks. Woo-hoo—free stuff!

Add More Memory

Like money, you can never have too much memory. If you run out, you'll have no room for new stuff unless you delete applications or data (that you may still need). One solution is HandEra's FlashPro (see Chapter 15), a software utility that lets you access several hundred kilobytes of extra RAM. If that's not enough, or you've filled that space and now need more, you'll have to consider memory-expansion hardware.

How to ... Protect with Scotch Tape

The Graffiti area is where most stylus contact occurs, and therefore it's where scratches are most likely to result. You could cut a WriteRight sheet to fit just the Graffiti area—or you could buy yourself a roll of 3M's Scotch Magic Tape 811. It's exactly the right width for most Graffiti areas (exceptions include the m100 series and Kyocera QCP 6035), and one roll will last you a lifetime. Plus, its slightly rough surface makes for less-slippery handwriting—always a plus. Just cut a piece to cover the input area and replace it every month or so. You'll never see a single scratch.

Specifically, there are third-party services that can upgrade your handheld's memory or provide you with a do-it-yourself kit. Let's look at some of these services:

Service	URL	Upgrade
Gethightech, Inc.	**www.gethightech.com**	DIY kits for PalmPilot and Palm III series
STNE Corp.	**www.stnecorp.com**	In-house upgrades for most Palm, Visor, and CLIÉ models
Tony Rudenko	**www.palmpilotupgrade.com**	In-house upgrades for most Palm, Visor, and CLIÉ models

Unless you're extremely handy with a soldering iron, consider one of the services that perform in-house upgrades. That means you'll have to part with your handheld for at least a few days: you send it to the company, they perform the upgrade and then send it back to you.

CAUTION *Whether you do it yourself or farm it out, any memory upgrade performed on any handheld will automatically void the warranty. That's because it involves removing and replacing memory chips on the main circuit board.*

We should note here that when your handheld is returned to you, its memory will be wiped clean. When you HotSync, your programs and data will be restored—but you might want to consider running a utility like BackupBuddy (see Chapter 15) before sending away your handheld.

While there are some definite caveats to consider, in-house upgrades are usually successful and inexpensive. STNE Corp., for instance, can upgrade a Palm m100 from 2MB to 8MB for just $55.95, and a Sony CLIÉ N760C from 8MB to 16MB for $109.95. Prices fluctuate, so it may cost even less by the time you're ready to upgrade!

Navigate the World with a GPS Receiver

Dave is a huge fan of the Global Positioning System, the network of orbiting satellites used to pinpoint one's exact position on the planet. That's because he tends to get lost in his own driveway. Still, GPS is undeniably valuable if you're driving on unfamiliar roads or trying to find your way to, say, a new client's office. And many Palm devices can take full advantage of GPS, thanks to products from Delorme, Rand McNally, and Thales Navigation.

Delorme's Earthmate is a pocket-sized GPS receiver that uses a special cable to connect to virtually any Palm device (including the CLIÉ and Visor). XMap is a Palm OS map viewer that lets you download and display street maps created on Delorme's Web site or with their Street Atlas U.S.A. software. Thales Navigation's Magellan GPS Companion takes a slightly different approach—it's a clip-on module available for the Palm V series and m500 series. Rand McNally's Navman works similarly.

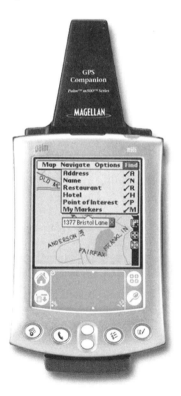

You can learn more about using GPS with your Palm device in Chapter 11.

NOTE *Visor users can take advantage of special GPS modules that plug into their handhelds' Springboard slots. These include the Nexian HandyGPS and Magellan GPS Companion. See the Handspring Web site for details.*

Connect Your Serial HotSync Cradle to a USB Port

For many Windows and Macintosh users alike, serial ports are at a premium. If your system simply doesn't have room for another serial device, where are you going to connect your HotSync cradle? Too bad you can't just plug it into one of those USB ports—they're just sitting around doing nothing.

Sounds like you're a candidate for a USB-to-serial adapter. True to its name, it allows you to plug a serial device—in this case your HotSync cradle—into a USB port. Several companies make these adapters, but there are two we consider ideally suited for Palm use. Both are a snap to install (just load a software driver, then plug 'em in), and both come with drivers for Windows *and* Macintosh. They are:

 PalmConnect USB Kit

 Keyspan USB PDA Adapter

Recharge Your Palm's Batteries While on the Road

A Palm handheld with a rechargeable battery is a mixed blessing. Sure, you don't have keep a pocketful of fresh Duracells on hand, but what happens if you're on the road and the Palm runs out of juice? You could buy one of Palm's Travel Kits, but they cost $50 and require you to find an electrical outlet. There are a couple other solutions we prefer.

Tech Center Labs' Emergency Chargers are clever little contrivances that use ordinary alkaline batteries to power and/or recharge your Palm or Visor. The company offers a variety of other charging products, including one that plugs into your car's cigarette lighter.

iBIZ offers products similar to Tech Center Labs', including a 9-volt-battery charger for the Palm V series and car chargers for most Palm Powered handhelds. The company also offers USB HotSync cable/chargers, which we think are very cool for travelers.

Another excellent option is the Instant Power Charger from a company called Electric Fuel. Instead of charging your batteries from a wall outlet, Instant Power tops off your PDA with a

Our Favorite Accessories

Rick: It's not really an accessory, but I wouldn't be caught dead without my 128MB Memory Stick, which has a permanent home in my Sony CLIÉ and holds a boatload of games, e-books, and MP3 files. But the real star is my Stowaway keyboard, a marvel of modern engineering that lets me write while traveling without having to schlep a notebook. They'll have to pry it out of my cold, dead fingers when I shuffle off this mortal coil.

Dave: I'm in a state of transition, like when the African Swallow sheds its winter skin, leaves the safety of the pond, and learns to fly. If you had asked me a month ago, I would have said that my Minstrel wireless modem and Stowaway keyboards were essential gear for my Handspring Visor. But now that I've switched to a Sony NR70V, the only gadget I really need is a pair of Memory Sticks: a 128MB stick for storing pictures, songs, and e-books, plus a Bluetooth Memory Stick for accessing the Internet via my Bluetooth phone. That, and whatever I can pry out of Rick's cold, dead fingers.

disposable power source. The charger is actually a sort of fuel cell that combines a safe embedded fuel with oxygen drawn from the air. Stored in its aluminum pouch, the charger has a shelf life of about two years. Once you open the pouch, it's good for about three months. That means you can put one in your travel bag and have the peace of mind that you'll have power anytime you need it.

To get started with Instant Power, you need to buy an Instant Power Charger kit that includes a single disposable power cartridge and a connection cable for whatever model handheld you own. There are versions for just about every Palm OS-powered PDA, as well as wireless modems, digital cameras, Pocket PCs, and even camcorders. Since the power cartridges are interchangeable, you can charge up your entire mobile arsenal without worrying about carrying three different kinds of batteries or chargers.

You should be able to charge your PDA about three times with a single Instant Power cartridge. After you deplete it, just toss it in the trash, but keep the cable—you need to replace only the interchangeable cartridges.

Make Your Palm or Visor Rechargeable

If you like the idea of using rechargeable batteries, but don't want to deal with external chargers and frequent swapping, you may want to investigate the eXtend FullCharge. Available for the Palm III series, Palm VII series and battery-using Visor models, FullCharge puts a pair of rechargeable NiMH batteries inside your handheld—and lets you leave them there. A replacement battery-compartment cover has two holes where you plug in the included AC adapter (or optional car charger). Presto—now your handheld is rechargeable, just like a Palm m505 or Visor Edge.

Mount Your Palm Device in Your Car (or Golf Cart)

Is your car your castle? Your office? Your home away from home? If so, your Palm device deserves a place of honor—and a place where you can access it while keeping at least one hand on the wheel.

CAUTION *In all seriousness, you should never, ever try to use your Palm while driving. If you must look something up or write something down, wait until you're stopped at a light. Or, ask a passenger to do it for you.*

Two similar products—Arkon Resources' CM220 Universal Car Mount (see Figure 20-4) and Revolve Design's UniMount—put your Palm device at arm's reach. The CM220 can hold virtually any model, and comes with hardware for attaching to your car's windshield or dashboard. The UniMount is available in different styles for different models; there's even a Power UniMount that works like the aforementioned eXtend FullCharge to recharge your Palm while it's in the cradle.

Fore!

There are several nifty golf scorecard programs available for the Palm—any serious golfer would do well to consider one. (We're partial to IntelliGolf, which you can find at **www.intelligolf.com**.) Of course, you'll need a place to store your Palm while you're on the links. Revolve Design offers pull-cart and electric-cart adapters for the UniMount, so you can have easy access to your electronic scorecard.

FIGURE 20-4 The Arkon CM220 Universal Car Mount uses suction cups to attach to your windshield, but also comes with dashboard mounting hardware.

Recovering Lost Handhelds

No one ever means to lose anything, but it happens. The only thing worse than losing your PDA would be realizing that whoever found it probably wouldn't know how to go about returning it to you. Sure, an address label pasted to the back might do the trick, but we have a better solution: StuffBak.com.

For as little as $1.95, you can buy a specially coded StuffBak label to paste on the back of your handheld. The finder need only call a toll-free number or visit the StuffBak Web site to arrange for its return, which requires little effort and includes a reward. You pay a $14.95 transaction fee, plus shipping charges and any cash reward you care to offer. (StuffBak's own reward is a pack of its labels, valued at $20.) If you believe people are generally honest, this is an inexpensive and potentially painless way to help a lost handheld find its way home.

Where to Find It

Web Site	Address	What's There
Fellowes	www.fellowes.com	WriteRight and other accessories
Tech Center Labs	www.talestuff.com	Emergency chargers
IBIZ	www.ibiz.com	Pocket Charger
Magellan	www.magellangps.com	Magellan GPS Companion
Delorme	www.delorme.com	Earthmate, Solus Pro
Rand McNally	www.randmcnally.com	Navman GPS
Keyspan	www.keyspan.com	USB PDA Adapter
Extend Computer & Instrument	www.extendcomputer.com	FullCharge
Arkon Resources	www.arkon.com	CM220 Universal Car Mount
Revolve Design	www.revolvedesign.com	UniMount
StuffBak.com	www.stuffbak.com	StuffBak labels
Pocketop	www.pocketop.net	Pocketop Portable Keyboard
Seiko	www.seiko-austin.com	ThumBoard
Think Outside	www.thinkoutside.com	Palm Portable Keyboard/Stowaway

20

Chapter 21

Problems and Solutions

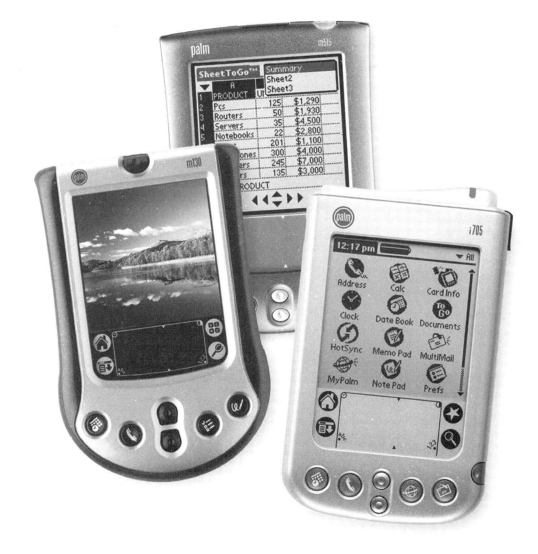

How to...

- Reset your Palm device
- Avoid battery-related problems
- Prevent and fix scratched screens
- Fix a screen that no longer responds properly
- Free some extra memory
- Resolve Hack conflicts
- Fix alarms that don't "wake up" your Palm
- Deal with a handheld that suddenly won't HotSync
- Fix a clock that doesn't advance the date
- Obtain warranty repairs
- Obtain nonwarranty or accident-related repairs
- Back up your Palm's data
- Solve COM port issues
- Troubleshoot HotSync glitches
- Manage two Palms on one PC
- HotSync one Palm on two PCs
- Find answers to problems on the Web
- Upgrade from an old Palm device to a new one
- Upgrade the Palm OS

No computer is perfect. Windows is about as far from the mark as you can get, Macs have problems of their own, and even Palm devices suffer the occasional meltdown. Usually it's minor: an alarm that fails to "wake up" the unit or a wayward Hack that causes the occasional crash. But sometimes something downright scary happens, like a sudden and inexplicable lockup that wipes the Palm's entire memory. In this chapter we help you troubleshoot some of the most common Palm maladies and, hopefully, prevent the worst of them.

NOTE   *Many common problems are addressed on Palm's Web site (and the sites of other Palm device manufacturers). We're not going to rehash them here, but we are going to suggest you check out those sites if you've got a problem we haven't addressed. Chances are good you'll find a solution.*

We also look at some upgrade options, including moving from an old Palm device to a new one, and upgrading the Palm OS.

Cure Palm Problems with a Reset

Just as rebooting a computer will often resolve a glitch or lockup, resetting your Palm device is the solution to many a problem. And it's usually the first thing you need to do if your Palm crashes—or just acts a little strangely.

Just What Is a "Crash," Anyway?

When a computer crashes, that generally means it has plowed into a brick wall and can no longer function. Fortunately, whereas a car in the same situation would need weeks of bump-and-paint work, a computer can usually return to normal by being rebooted. In the case of Palm devices, a "reset" is the same as a "reboot."

When a Palm device crashes, one common error message is "Fatal Exception." Don't be alarmed; this isn't nearly as terminal as it sounds. It simply means that the Palm has encountered a glitch that proved fatal to its operation. Very often an onscreen Reset button will appear with this error, a tap of which performs a "soft reset" (as we describe in the next section). Sometimes, however, the crash is so fierce that even this button doesn't work. (You know because you tap it and nothing happens.) In a case like that, you have to perform a manual reset.

Different Ways to Reset a Palm Device

On the back of every Palm device, there's a little hole labeled RESET. Hidden inside it is a button that effectively reboots the unit. When that happens, you see the Palm startup screen, followed a few seconds later by the Prefs screen. That's how a successful reset goes. About 98 percent of the time, everything will be as you left it—your data, your applications, everything.

Technically speaking, there are three kinds of resets: soft, warm, and hard. (Mind out of the gutter, please.) The details:

- **Soft**   Only in rare instances do you need to perform anything other than a soft reset, which is akin to pressing CTRL-ALT-DELETE to reboot your computer. You simply press the Reset button, then wait a few seconds while your Palm resets itself. No data is lost.

- **Warm**   This action, performed by holding the scroll-up button while pressing the Reset button, goes an extra step by bypassing any system patches or Hacks you may have installed. Use this only if your Palm fails to respond to a soft reset, meaning it's still locked up, crashing, or stuck in a "boot loop" (the Palm logo is flashing or the screen is displaying garbage). No data is lost, but you have to manually re-enable any system patches or Hacks.

- **Hard**   With any luck, you'll never have to do this. A hard reset wipes everything out of your Palm's memory, essentially returning it to factory condition. In the exceedingly rare case that your Palm is seriously hosed (meaning it won't reset or even turn off), this should at least get you back to square one. If it doesn't, your handheld is toast and will need to be replaced (more on repair/replacement options later in this chapter). The good news is this: even after a hard reset, all it takes is a HotSync to restore all your data. Some third-party applications may have to be reinstalled manually, but most will just reappear on your handheld. It's like magic!

How to ... Perform Warm and Hard Resets

There's a bit of a trick to doing a warm or hard reset successfully. With your Palm device on or off (it doesn't matter), hold down the scroll-up button (for a warm reset) or the power button (for a hard reset), then press and release the Reset button on the back of the unit. Now, here's the trick: *wait until the Palm logo appears onscreen* before releasing the scroll or power button. If you release both buttons simultaneously, before the logo appears, all you get is a soft reset.

The Toothpick Story

A couple years ago, Rick was having lunch with a couple of his buddies when he pulled out his PalmPilot Personal to jot a few notes. To his horror, it wouldn't turn on (a problem he later attributed to the extremely cold weather, which can indeed numb a pair of batteries). A press of the Reset button was in order, but Rick didn't have the right tool—namely, a paper clip. So he asked the waitress to bring him a toothpick—the other common item that's small enough to fit in the reset hole. Presto: the Palm sprang back to life.

The moral of the story is, be prepared. If your Palm crashes and you need to reset it, the last thing you want is a desperate hunt for a paper clip or toothpick. Fortunately, many styluses have "reset tips" hidden inside them. And now, a tip about tips.

TIP *If your handheld has a metal stylus, it may surprise you to learn that it's stowing a reset tip. Where's it hiding? Unscrew the top (or, in some cases, the bottom) from the barrel to find out. If your handheld came with a plastic stylus and uses AAA batteries, you can break a toothpick in half and stow it in the battery compartment, resting between the two cells. Now you'll always have a reset tip handy.*

Avoid Battery Problems

Batteries are the lifeblood of any Palm device. When they die, they take your data with them, effectively returning your Palm to factory condition. That's why it's vital to keep a close eye on the battery gauge shown at the top of the Applications screen (see Figure 21-1), and to take heed when the Palm notifies you that your batteries are low.

Of course, if you HotSync regularly, a wiped Palm isn't the end of the world. Once you've replaced (or recharged) the batteries, a HotSync is all it takes to restore virtually everything. Still, there's no reason to let things reach that point. Following are some tips to help you avoid most battery-related incidents.

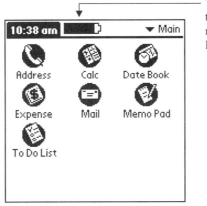

The battery gauge tells you how much juice your Palm has left.

| **FIGURE 21-1** | All Palm devices equipped with Palm OS 3.0 and later have this handy—and fairly accurate—battery gauge at the top of the screen |

Keep 'Em Fresh

Suppose you head off to Bermuda for a two-week getaway (you lucky vacationer, you), leaving your work—and your Palm—behind. When you return, don't be surprised to find the Palm dead as a doornail. That's because it draws a trace amount of power from the batteries, even when off, to keep the memory alive. If the batteries were fairly low to begin with, the long period of inactivity might just polish them off.

The obvious solution is to keep your Palm with you as much as possible. (It's great for games, e-books, and other leisure activities, remember?) Alternately, if you know you're going to be away from it for a while, put in a pair of new batteries before you leave (or just leave it in the cradle if it's a rechargeable model).

TIP *You can use rechargeable batteries in place of alkalines, but be aware that the battery meter won't accurately display their charge status. NiMH rechargeables work best—we recommend avoiding rechargeable NiCad and alkaline cells.*

Swap 'Em Quick

The documentation for nonrechargeable Palm devices says that when replacing batteries, you shouldn't leave them out for more than 60 seconds (lest data loss occur). This is true, to a point. Near-dead batteries aren't supplying much power to the memory, so when you remove them, the memory can indeed fade fast. On the other hand, if you're replacing batteries that are still reasonably healthy, it can be half an hour or more before the memory gets wiped.

Of course, it can be difficult to gauge the batteries' precise remaining strength, so follow this rule of thumb: swap them fast. Pop the old ones out, pop the fresh ones in, and you're done. It's exceedingly rare to lose data when you adhere to this method—but you should always do a HotSync first anyway, just to be safe.

Emergency Rescue for Rechargeable Palms

You've been on the road for weeks, your handheld has warned you repeatedly that the battery is low, and there's not a charging cradle in sight. That's the Catch-22 of the rechargeable battery: no Duracells to buy, but no easy way to recharge on the road. That is, unless you have one of the many portable charging accessories now available. See Chapter 20 for more details.

Fix Scratched Screens

Scratches happen. They happen most often when your stylus hits a piece of dust or grit. That's why it's important to keep your screen as clean as possible (we recommend a daily wipe with a lint-free, antistatic cloth). Better still, take a few preventative steps:

- **Tape** A piece of Scotch Magic Tape 811 placed over the Graffiti input area (where most scratches occur) not only makes existing scratches less tangible while you're writing, but also prevents future scratches and provides a tackier writing surface.

- **WriteRight sheets** As discussed in Chapter 20, Fellowes' WriteRight sheets are plastic overlays that protect the entire screen. They won't remove scratches, but they will prevent them and, like the tape, make them less pronounced.

- **Screen Clean** Creator Tim Warner says that this bottle of goo—which closely resembles car wax—removes 99 percent of all screen scratches. Basically, you wipe it onto the screen, wait five minutes, then buff it off. Make no mistake: Screen Clean won't fix a really deep scratch, but it does work as advertised on light ones. And it leaves your screen as bright and shiny as the day you unpacked it.

Fix a Screen That No Longer Responds Properly

As noted in Chapter 2's discussion of the Digitizer option, it's not uncommon to experience some "drift" in the screen's response to your stylus taps. An example: you have to tap just a bit to the left or right of your desired target for the tap to be recognized. This occurs over time, when the accuracy of the digitizer (the hardware that makes the screen respond to your input) degrades.

Unless the digitizer has gotten so off-kilter that you can no longer operate your Palm device, the solution is to hit the Prefs icon, then choose Digitizer from the right-corner menu. Here you can reset the digitizer, effectively making your Palm good as new. If you can't even manage to tap Prefs, you can do a soft reset (as described earlier in this chapter). That gets you to the Prefs screen, where you should at least be able to select the Digitizer option.

How to ... Cure "Mad Digitizer Syndrome"

What happens when the digitizer gets so out of whack that your Palm device essentially becomes inoperable? This problem, which some have dubbed "Mad Digitizer Syndrome," tends to plague older models, though it can strike even if your handheld is only a year or two old. One very effective way to cure MDS is with a utility called AutoDigi, which automatically recalibrates the digitizer after a reset. You can buy the $15 program at PalmGear (**www.palmgear.com**). If your screen is really giving you trouble, check out OnDigi, a Hack that automatically recalibrates the digitizer each time you turn on your handheld.

Reclaim Memory for Software and Data

A common problem among Palm users—especially those who discover games and e-books—is running out of memory. As we discussed in Chapters 15 and 20, there are ways (both software and hardware) to increase the available RAM in your Palm device. Of course, those are long-term solutions. If you suddenly find yourself in a memory crunch and need space for something important (say, a work-related spreadsheet), you need to do a little housekeeping and clear a little space.

Solving Memory-Related HotSync Failure

If you try to install a new program or database and your Palm device doesn't have enough memory, the HotSync will fail—and fail again every time thereafter. Assuming you can't free up enough space on your handheld to accommodate the new item(s), you have to venture onto your hard drive. Specifically, locate the *c:\palm\yourusername\install* or *c:\program files\palm\ yourusername\install* folder (the "holding tank" for software waiting to be installed during HotSync), and delete everything that's in there. Now you should be able to HotSync successfully.

NOTE   *Deleting programs and data from the Install folder doesn't permanently delete them from your hard drive. When you choose items to be installed on your Palm device, copies are placed in the Install folder. The original files remain.*

How to Delete

To delete software from your Palm device, tap the Applications button, then choose Menu |
App | Delete…

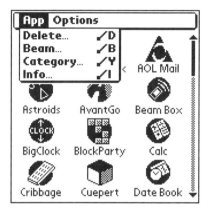

In a few seconds, you see a list of all the applications, utilities, games, etc. installed on your
Palm. What you won't find here are e-books, Doc files, image files, individual spreadsheets, and
other kinds of data. For items like those, you need to use their respective applications to delete
them. Say you imported some documents into WordSmith or some photos into Album To
Go—the only way to delete those documents or photos is from within the two programs.

As you can see, the Delete screen tells you the size of each item, so you know just how
much space you free up with each deletion. To remove something, just tap it to highlight it, then
tap Delete…

What to Delete

Don't bother culling through your contact list or appointment calendar. Though they may be large, deleting a handful of entries will have a negligible impact on the Palm's total memory. Programs, on the other hand, can add up quickly. Here's a list of items to consider ditching:

- **Games**   Although many of them are relatively small, some, like SimCity, can eat up a pretty large chunk of memory. If you don't play it anymore, or can live without it for a while, ditch it.

- **E-books**   No sense keeping books you've already read, especially if they occupy several hundred kilobytes of RAM.

- **Data files**   Spreadsheets, photos, movies, Doc files, and databases can be quite large. Eliminate the ones you no longer need.

Resolve Hack Conflicts

It bears repeating (see Chapter 15 for the first time we said it) that as marvelous as Hacks are, they can wreak havoc on Palm devices. This is especially true if you run more than two or three simultaneously, as these little bits of code can conflict with one another. If you find that your Palm is crashing on a regular basis, you may have to investigate your Hacks. Here's what you should do:

1. Start X-Master, then uncheck the box next to each Hack to disable it.

2. Go back to using your Palm device. If you find that the crashes no longer occur, a Hack is the likely culprit. To help pin down which one, go on to Step 3.

3. Launch X-Master again, then enable just one Hack. Use your Palm device normally, and see if the crashes return. If not, enable a second Hack. Through this process of elimination, you should be able to figure out which one is causing the problem. When you do, stop using it.

Fix a Palm that Won't "Wake Up" for Alarms

It's easy to fall out of love with your Palm device when an alarm you set fails to go off (meaning the Palm doesn't "wake up" and beep). There are several reasons this can happen, from low batteries to a corrupted alarm database to a conflict with third-party software. The first is easy to resolve by making sure your Palm has fresh batteries (or is adequately charged). For the other two problems, try a soft reset, which very often does the trick.

If you use a third-party program that has anything to do with alarms (such as ToDo Plus, DiddleBug, and so forth), it's very possible this is causing the snafu. To troubleshoot it, try doing a warm reset (hold the scroll-up button while pressing the Reset button). This will disable any Hacks or third-party applications that tie into the operating system. Set an alarm in Date Book and see if it works. If so, then another program is very likely to blame. A process of elimination should help you determine which one. In any case, you may to have discontinue using that program if it keeps fouling up your alarms.

If none of these options work, it's possible your Palm device is damaged. Contact the manufacturer for service.

Beaming Problems

Having trouble beaming? Chances are good the problem is caused by one of three factors. First, make sure the two handhelds aren't too close together. People often make the mistake of holding their Palm devices right next to each other, which can give the infrared transceivers trouble. Keep the units at least a foot or two apart (their range is about five feet).

Second, make sure the Beam Receive option is checked in the Prefs | General screen. While you may not have unchecked it yourself, sometimes it just seems to happen.

If neither of these suggestions solves the problem, try moving to a darker area. Beaming doesn't always work if you're in a brightly lit room or outdoors on a sunny day.

If all else fails, you might want to perform a soft reset on both Palms; that might clear up a problem that was keeping your devices from chatting with each other.

The Date Won't Advance

This is a known issue that afflicts mostly the Palm IIIx and Palm V. According to Palm, it's caused by low batteries, meaning the problem should abate if you replace or recharge yours. At the same time, try a soft reset.

If this doesn't do the trick, third-party software or a hardware defect may be to blame. The only real effective way to find out for sure is to do a hard reset, which will wipe all third-party software and restore the Palm to its factory settings, then set the clock to 11:59 P.M. and note the date. Wait a minute, then turn the unit on and see if the date has advanced. If so, it's probably a software glitch. If not, a repair may be in order.

It's no mean feat to pin down a software conflict. It could be a Hack or an application that has some link to the calendar. If you're able to figure out which program is the culprit, contact the developer to see if there's a fix (or at least some acknowledgement of the problem).

The Last Chapter

Dave: Well, this is the last chapter… and it's almost complete. It was a blast to write this book, but I have to admit that I'm a kind of burnt out on all this tech writing stuff. I think I'll take my half of the advance (a cool half-million or so) and move to Bermuda. There, I'll build a cottage on the beach and let my army of trained monkey butlers bring me cool drinks all day long. I'll pass the time staring at the waves as they gently break onto the sandy, white beach, and occasionally dabble at writing a best-selling novel on my Palm with a Stowaway keyboard. My MP3 player will be loaded up with Kristin Hersh music and my cats will be napping in my lap. Yep, that's what I'm going to do…

Rick: Always with the monkey butlers. As for me, now that the yoke of another book has been lifted, I'll be returning to the soup kitchen where I volunteer three times a week, though not before I finish the urban-beautification program I spearheaded and the fundraiser for Greenpeace. Just have to decide which charities will be getting my royalty checks this year—always a tough choice. Honestly, there's no better reward for months of hard work than good old philanthropy. Oh, but, uh, your plan sounds really good too…

Deal with a Handheld that Will No Longer HotSync

It worked fine yesterday, but today your handheld just refuses to HotSync. We hear your pain—this drives us up the wall, too. We wish we could blame Windows, because it's just the kind of nonsense we've come to expect from it, but this is usually due to a Palm software, hardware, or cradle problem.

Best bet? Start with a soft reset. Use the end of a paper clip (or unscrew the barrel of your metal stylus to find a hidden tip) to press the Reset button on the back of your handheld. In many cases, this will solve the problem outright, and you can get back to playing Bejeweled. If it doesn't, consider reinstalling Palm Desktop. This action won't affect your data, but it will provide a "fresh" version of HotSync Manager—which often solves HotSync problems. If you're not comfortable with that step or it doesn't work, consult your manufacturer's Web site for other remedies.

The Mysterious m500/m505 Cradle Crisis

Has your Palm m500 or m505 suddenly stopped synchronizing? The culprit may be electrostatic discharge (ESD), which has fried more handhelds over the years than Palm would like to admit. In this case, it's fried cradle. Palm *has* admitted that some m500 and m505 cradles are more susceptible to ESD than others, and will replace yours if it has the problem. Visit Palm's Web site (**www.palm.com/support**) for information on the exchange program. At press time, it was scheduled to end on September 30, 2002. Unless Palm decides to extend it, you may have to shell out your own hard-earned cash to get a replacement cradle.

Resolve COM Port Issues

Ah, the wonders of the PC's COM ports. COM ports are communication ports usually associated with the serial ports on your PC. If you are connecting your Palm to a Windows-based PC and your HotSync cradle uses an old-fashioned serial port, you'll need to know just a teeny-tiny bit about COM ports——unless something goes awry, in which case you'll need to know more. If you have a Mac or a USB-powered HotSync cradle, you can sit this one out.

Know Your COM Ports

For starters, your Palm's HotSync cradle needs to be plugged into a serial port, and the COM port associated with that port can't be shared with anything else.

Ninety-nine percent of the time, the Palm Desktop installation software figures out what COM port to use all by itself. If you later move things around, though, you may need to do some detective work. Use this table to figure out what COM port you're using:

If...	Then...
There's only one serial port on my PC	It's COM1
The cradle is plugged into a small 9-pin port	It's COM1
The cradle is plugged into the big 25-pin port	It's COM2
The cradle is plugged into a serial port that is part of an expansion card.	It's a little hard to say from here. Experiment!

NOTE *These port descriptions apply to older PCs and may not match yours. Consult your system documentation for specific COM port identifications.*

TIP *If you only have one of those big, 25-pin ports available on the back of your PC, it's probably COM1, and you can use the 9-pin to 25-pin adapter that came with your Palm to make the connection.*

Troublesome USB Ports

Most Palm models now feature a USB connector that lets you connect without fiddling with all the bizarre serial port issues that can crop up. But if you have USB, you're not out of the woods yet. Keep these things in mind:

■ On the PC, USB is only guaranteed to work with Windows 98 or higher. If you still have Windows 95, get with the program—upgrade if you expect to reliably use USB devices like the Palm's HotSync cradle.

■ If your HotSync cradle sometimes fails to work, you might have too many USB devices connected to a single USB port. Move the cradle to another USB port.

■ You might need a powered USB hub—there may not be enough juice in the port to supply power to all the devices you have connected, and that may cause the HotSync cradle to cut out.

■ Check the Handspring, Palm, and Microsoft Windows Web sites for more USB troubleshooting information.

Troubleshoot HotSync Glitches

If you can't get your Palm to talk to your PC, there are a number of likely causes. Consider the following list a checklist for resolving the issue.

- Start by making sure the HotSync cradle is plugged securely into a serial or USB port.

- Verify that the correct COM/USB port is configured in the HotSync Manager (see Chapter 3 for details on this). If you're in doubt, try the other COM port choices available in the HotSync Manager to double-check.

- Shut off any applications that might be trying to take control of the COM port, like fax programs or remote-control applications.

- Try a lower HotSync speed. This is especially important on older laptops or early Pentium/ 486-based PCs.

- Close the HotSync Manager and restart it. Also, as noted earlier, try a soft reset on the Palm itself.

- Upgrade to the newest Palm Desktop software, which you can download from Palm's Web site. It may include a slightly updated version of HotSync Manager that addresses common problems.

- If none of those things work, your Palm or the HotSync cradle may be defective. If possible, test the system on another PC.

Avoid the Timeout Problem

Some older PCs communicate poorly with the HotSync cradle, especially the very first time that you try to HotSync. If you keep getting an error message that says the Palm has "timed out," you need to use a trick that'll keep the Palm's data port open indefinitely, allowing the PC to successfully HotSync. To do that, follow these steps:

1. Tap on the HotSync icon on your Palm.

2. Press the scroll button in the up direction and simultaneously tap and hold the stylus on the upper-right corner of the screen. You should immediately see a dialog box that says **DLServer Wait Forever is ON**.

3. HotSync. The Palm should now successfully connect without any timeout errors. After the HotSync, the Palm will revert to its ordinary mode (wait forever will be off) and you probably won't experience this problem anymore.

Solve the Most Common HotSync Problems

The checklist we provided earlier in the chapter can get you through all kinds of HotSync issues. But the fact remains that there are just a few pesky problems that account for about 90 percent of all the HotSync issues we've ever encountered——and they're all pretty easy to diagnose and solve.

The Palm Reports a COM Port Conflict

A device or application is probably just hogging the port. Communication software like fax programs and remote-control software are designed to grab and hold a COM port, so they might interfere with the HotSync Manager. Disable those programs before HotSyncing.

NOTE *The HotSync Manager hogs the COM port as well. If you disconnect the HotSync cradle and plug something else in—like a modem—the new device won't work unless you shut off the HotSync Manager.*

The Palm Aborts a HotSync Immediately

If you press the HotSync button on the cradle and the Palm immediately insists that the COM port is in use—so fast that it doesn't seem possible for the Palm to have even checked—the solution is to perform a soft reset on your Palm. After it resets, the HotSync should work fine.

When HotSyncing, the Palm Displays the HotSync Screen but Absolutely Nothing Else Happens

Frequently, this problem is just a result of the HotSync Manager not running on the PC, or one of the HotSync dialog boxes is open. If you open the Custom dialog box to change conduit settings, for instance, the HotSync will not run and you won't get an error message—so look on the desktop for an open dialog box.

The HotSync Conspiracy

That may sound ominous, but we just wanted to get your attention. If you have a Palm that uses alkaline batteries, don't leave it lying in the HotSync cradle for an extended period of time. That's because the HotSync cradle drains the batteries. At least, that was the case with older models like the Palm III. If you have a Palm device that has rechargeable batteries, you needn't worry about that, because the cradle actually recharges the batteries.

When HotSyncing, This Message Appears: "An application failed to respond to a HotSync"

This one is easy to fix. When you started the HotSync, an Address Book or Date Book entry was probably left open in Palm Desktop. Your Palm can't successfully HotSync with one of those entries open for editing, so you should close the entry and try again.

Outlook HotSync Problems

As you learned in Chapter 3, most Palm devices come with a special conduit for synchronizing with Microsoft Outlook. It's called PocketMirror, and we could fill a separate book with information on using and troubleshooting it. Fortunately, you can get lots of helpful assistance from Chapura, the company that makes it (**www.chapura.com**).

Work with Windows 2000

If you're a Windows 2000 user, you'll be glad to know the OS gets along with Palm Desktop just fine. However, at press time there were a few known issues you should consider:

- Windows 2000's "hot undock" feature, usually found on notebook systems, may not work with HotSync Manager running. Solution: shut down HotSync Manager before performing the undock.
- Infrared HotSyncs won't work. Solution: download the HotSync 3.1.1 updater from Palm.

Work with Windows NT 4.0

Just one item to be aware of here: Windows NT 4.0 doesn't support USB, so you can't use a handheld that has a USB cradle. It may be possible to purchase a serial cradle for any given model—check with the manufacturer.

Work with Windows XP

As with every new version of Windows, XP brought with it a raft of synchronization and other problems. Many Palm, Handspring, and Sony users reported they couldn't HotSync with the new OS, while others encountered problems with XP's multiple user profiles. You may need a patch, a new version of Palm Desktop, or some other solution entirely. Visit your handheld maker's

Web site for more details. In the meantime, consider this: If you upgrade your PC to Windows XP or buy a new one that has it already installed, you need to make sure you use Palm Desktop 4.0.1 or later. If you have an earlier version, you can download the latest one from Palm's Web site.

NOTE   *Palm Desktop doesn't support Windows XP's "switch user" option, which allows multiple users to log onto their PCs at the same time. If you have multiple user profiles set up, each person needs to log out at the end of their session, while the next person logs in.*

Manage Multiple Palms or PCs

The Palm OS allows you to HotSync the same Palm to more than one PC, or to HotSync several Palms to the same PC. Surprisingly, most Palm owners are reluctant to try this out ("I was always kind of afraid to HotSync two Palms to my PC," Rick once told Dave in a particularly confessional moment).

Two Palms on a Single PC

If you have two Palms and only one computer, you're not alone. In fact, it's a pretty common scenario: many married couples have their own Palms and want to HotSync to the household computer.

Here's what you need to do:

1. Be absolutely sure that both Palms have different user names. Check this by tapping on the HotSync icon on each Palm and looking at the name in the upper-right corner. Identically named Palms, HotSynced to the same PC, will irretrievably thrash the data on the PC and both Palms.

2. Put the Palm in the HotSync cradle and go. The first time the second Palm is inserted, your PC will ask if you want to create a new account for the other Palm. Click Yes.

CAUTION   *If both Palms have the same user name for some reason, do not attempt to HotSync them to the same PC! In fact, change their names before you HotSync at all, to prevent accidentally HotSyncing the Palms in the wrong PC.*

TIP   *As long as you're using two Palms in the same family—like a pair of m500s—you can use one HotSync cradle for both handhelds. However, you can't always mix and match. A Palm V, for instance, won't work with an i705 cradle, and vice versa. However, it is possible to have multiple cradles connected to the same PC. You could have one plugged into a serial port and another into a USB port, for instance, or plug two cradles into two USB ports.*

Two PCs for a Single Palm

The Palm can keep two different PCs straight just as easily as one PC can keep a pair of Palms straight. When you HotSync, the Palm updates the second PC with whatever data it previously got from the first PC, and vice versa. This is a great way to keep your office PC and home computer in synch, or a PC and a Mac—the Palm can serve as a nonpartisan conduit for keeping all the data in agreement.

TIP *While not essential, we recommend making sure that you have the same version of the Palm Desktop on both PCs. If you're using a PC and a Mac, you can't do that, but you should keep up with the latest release of the Mac Palm Desktop.*

Of course, the most efficient way to use a dual-PC system is to acquire a second HotSync cradle. You can buy an additional one for about $30, or you can get a HotSync cable instead, which is a little more streamlined for traveling.

Obtain Service and Repairs

Palm problems, while relatively infrequent, come in all shapes and sizes. Yours may be as simple as an alarm that won't go off or as dire as a device that won't turn on. Fortunately, technical support and repair services are available from the respective manufacturers. Below we've compiled a table of their phone numbers and Web addresses:

Company	Tech Support	Customer Service	Web Site
Palm	(847) 262-7256	(888) 956-7256	www.palm.com
Handspring	(716) 871-6448	(716) 871-6442	www.handspring.com
HandEra	(515) 252-7522	(515) 252-7522	www.handera.com
Sony	(877) 760-7669	(877) 760-7669	www.sony.com

Obtain Nonwarranty or Accident-Related Repairs

Right up there with the awful sound of your car crunching into another is the sound of your Palm device hitting the pavement. A cracked case, a broken screen, a dead unit—these are among the painful results. And unfortunately, if you drop, step on, sit on, or get caught in a rainstorm with your Palm device, your warranty is pretty much out the window.

All is not lost, however. If your Palm is damaged, or develops a problem after the warranty has expired, you may still have options. For a fee (usually $100–125), Palm and Handspring, for instance, will usually replace a broken or out-of-warranty unit with a refurbished one. It's not cheap, but it's probably cheaper than buying a brand new Palm. Other manufacturers may handle such situations differently. The bottom line is, if something terrible happens to your device, it's worth a phone call to the company to see what options are available. You may be able to pay for repairs or buy a refurbished one for less than the cost of a new unit.

Extended Warranty Plans

If you have at least 90 days remaining on your original one-year warranty, you can purchase an extended warranty directly from Palm (for Palm-branded products only, and available only to U.S. residents). Alternately, you can purchase a one-time screen-replacement plan within the first

30 days of your purchase date. (The screen is the most likely casualty in a Palm mishap, and the standard warranty doesn't cover it.)

Plan prices vary a bit depending on your model. See Palm's Web site for details.

Other Sources for Help

As we've noted many times already, you can find oodles of help on handheld manufacturers' Web sites. In addition, there are several independent sites that offer tips, tricks, hints, and technical solutions. If you're looking for answers that aren't in this book or on the Palm/Handspring/Sony Web site, try some of these.

Site	Description
www.palmgear.com	Look for both the Tips/Tricks section and Calvin's FAQ.
www.pdabuzz.com	This site has a message board area in which you can post questions and read answers to common questions. It also contains Palm-related product news and reviews.
alt.comp.sys.palmtops.pilot **comp.sys.palmtops.pilot**	These newsgroups are available to anyone with a newsreader like Outlook Express. They are threaded message boards that contain questions and answers about Palm issues. You can post your own questions, respond to what's already there, or just read the existing posts.

Upgrades

If you're like Dave, you're probably a little obsessed with having the latest and greatest of everything. Gotta have the latest Palm, the latest version of the OS, and the fanciest wetsuit. This section helps you manage two key maneuvers—upgrading to a new Palm device, and upgrading to OS 3.5.

NOTE   *If you're seeking information on adding more memory to a Palm device, see Chapter 20.*

Upgrade from an Old Palm Device to a New One

To those of you still living with a Pilot 5000, we salute you. But when you finally decide you're ready for a nicer screen, more memory, and a bunch of cool accessories that won't work with your old model, we'll be here for you. Specifically, we're here to help you make the move from an older Palm to a new one—an increasingly common task these days, now that the devices have been around for over five years.

Unlike upgrading to a new PC (which requires an obnoxious amount of effort), upgrading to a new Palm device is shockingly easy. Here's the process in a nutshell:

1.   Do one last HotSync of your old Palm device.

2. Turn off your PC, unplug the old HotSync cradle, and plug in the new one. (Chances are good the new handheld won't be able to use the old cradle. C'est la vie.) If your new cradle has a USB connector, install the new version of Palm Desktop *before* doing the cradle swap.

3. Turn on your PC and install the Palm Desktop software that came with your new handheld. Go ahead and place it in the same C:\Palm directory (or whatever's appropriate) where the previous version was installed. Don't worry—all your data will be preserved!

4. HotSync your new handheld. When you do, a box appears listing your user name from your old model. Click it, then choose OK. This will restore all your data.

NOTE *Whether or not all your third-party software is restored during the first HotSync depends in part on the age of your old Palm device and which OS is installed on it. We highly recommended purchasing and using Blue Nomad's BackupBuddy (see Chapter 15) prior to switching handhelds. On the other hand, if you don't have much third-party software installed, it's not a difficult task to manually reinstall it.*

Upgrade the OS

If you have a Palm III, IIIc, IIIx, IIIxe, V, or Vx, you can upgrade it to Palm OS 4.1. It has a bevy of nifty new features, including the Note Pad application found in the "m" series, enhanced security options, integrated Internet support, and more. All this can be yours for just $29.95. Is it worth it? That's up to you to decide, but we should point out that there's third-party software available that duplicates near all of OS 4.1's enhancements.

What about OS 5 (see Chapter 10)? Alas, you can't upgrade any existing handheld to that version, as it requires a different processor. If you want OS 5, you'll have to buy new hardware. Hey, time marches on, stands still for no man, and all that. Sometimes you just need to loosen the purse strings.

Where to Find It

Web Site	Address	What's There
PalmGear H.Q.	**www.palmgear.com**	PalmVHack, StayOffHack, NoStreak, X-Master
Blue Nomad	**www.bluenomad.com**	BackupBuddy
Tech Center Labs	**www.talestuff.com**	Palm V Emergency Charger
PalmLife	**www.palmlife.com**	Screen Clean
Fellowes	**www.fellowes.com**	WriteRight
Palm, Inc.	**www.palm.com**	Extended warranty programs, OS 4.1 upgrade

Index